Random House Writer's Reference

Revised and Updated

Joseph W. Sora, editor

RANDOM HOUSE REFERENCE
NEW YORK   TORONTO   LONDON   SYDNEY
AUCKLAND

Random House Writer's Reference, Revised Edition

Copyright © 1999, 2003 Random House, Inc.

All rights reserved under International and Pan-American Copyright Conventions. No part of this book may be reproduced in any form or by any means, electronic or mechanical, including photocopying, without the written permission of the publisher. All inquiries should be addressed to Random House Reference, Random House, Inc., New York, NY. Published in the United States by Random House, Inc., New York and simultaneously in Canada by Random House of Canada Limited.

Random House is a registered trademark of Random House, Inc.

This book is an update of the *Random House Webster's English Language Desk Reference, Second Edition*, published in 1999.

This book is available for special purchases in bulk by organizations and institutions, not for resale, at special discounts. Please direct your inquiries to Random House Premium Sales, fax 212-572-4961.

Please address inquiries about electronic licensing of reference products, for use on a network or in software or on CD-ROM, to the Subsidiary Rights Department, Random House Reference, fax 212-572-6003.

Visit the Random House Reference Web site: www.randomwords.com

Typeset and printed in the United States of America.

Library of Congress Cataloging-in-Publication data is available upon request.

0 9 8 7 6 5 4 3 2 1

ISBN 0-375-72009-X

Contents

How to Use This Book · vii

Part I.
Guide for Writers · 1

1. Mastering Grammar · 3
Parts of Speech · 3
  Nouns · 4
  Pronouns · 8
  Verbs · 19
  Adjectives · 36
  Adverbs · 40
  Prepositions · 45
  Conjunctions · 45
  Interjections · 49
Phrases, Clauses, and Sentences · 50
  Phrases · 50
  Clauses · 51
  Sentences · 54

2. Usage Basics · 69
Style · 69
  Shifts in Tone and Style · 69
  Parallel Structure · 70
Using Verbs · 73
  Shifts in Mood · 73
  Shifts in Tense · 74
  Voice—Active and Passive · 77
  Shifts in Voice · 79
Using Nouns and Pronouns · 79
  Shifts in Person · 79
  Shifts in Perspective · 81
  Shifts in Number · 81
  Person and Number with Collective Nouns · 82
  It, They, and You · 83
Usage Glossary · 83

3. Spelling — 103
Spelling Rules — 103
Rules of Word Division — 105
Words Most Often Misspelled — 105
   Using a Spell Checker — 112
Words Often Confused — 112

4. Punctuation and Capitalization — 127
Punctuation — 127
Types of Punctuation Marks — 128
   Apostrophe — 128
   Brackets — 128
   Colon — 130
   Comma — 132
   Dash — 137
   Ellipsis — 138
   Exclamation Point — 139
   Forward Slash — 140
   Hyphen — 140
   Italics/Underlining — 142
   Period — 143
   Parentheses — 144
   Question Mark — 146
   Quotation Marks — 146
   Semicolon — 149
Capitalization — 151
   Geography — 152

Part II.
Enhancing Vocabulary — 155

5. Building Blocks of English — 157
Introduction — 157
Prefixes — 157
   Common Prefixes — 157
   List of Prefixes — 159
Suffixes — 169
   Common Suffixes — 169
   List of Suffixes — 171
Roots — 184
   Common Greek and Latin Roots — 185
   List of Roots — 186

6. Word Histories — 209

7. Borrowed Words — 241
French — 241
German — 244
Greek — 246
Italian — 247
Japanese — 249
Latin — 250
Spanish — 252
Yiddish — 253

8. Specialized Vocabularies — 255
Business — 255
Computers and Technology — 259
Entertainment — 265
Fashion — 266
Food — 270
Law — 271
Politics — 274
Publishing — 276
Religion — 277
Science — 280
Sports — 284

9. Short Forms: Abbreviations and Acronyms — 287
Formation and Use — 289

Part III.
Academic and Business Writing — 291

10. The Stages of Writing — 293

11. Academic Writing — 297
Sample Research Paper (APA and MLA) — 297
Reference Lists — 309
Preparing and Marking Up a Manuscript — 312
    Proofreader's Marks — 313

12. Business Writing — 317
Sample Executive Summary — 317
Sample Cover Letter — 319
Sample Business Memo — 321

Contents

Online Resources for Writers — 323
Research Aids — 323

Ready-Reference Guide — 324
The World — 324
  Nations of the World — 324
  Continents — 329
  Great Oceans and Seas of the World — 329
  Notable Mountain Peaks — 330
  World Time Differences — 332
  U.S. Time Differences — 333
Facts About the United States — 334
  Major U.S. Cities — 335
  Distances Between U.S. Cities — 338
  Major American Holidays — 338
  Presidents of the United States — 339
Space — 340
  Planets of the Solar System — 340
  First-Magnitude Stars — 340
Forms of Address — 341
  Government (U.S.) — 341
  Religious Leaders — 342
  Miscellaneous — 344
Alphabetical List of the Elements — 344
Weights and Measures — 345
  Metric System — 347
Signs and Symbols — 349
  Astrology — 349
  Astronomy — 349
  Biology — 350
  Business — 350
  Monetary — 350
  Miscellaneous — 351

Index — 352

How to Use This Book

The *Random House Writer's Reference* is both a reference and a complete guide to clear, effective writing. While it is certainly not meant to replace a dictionary or thesaurus, this book can be used to look up the correct spellings, histories, and meanings of particular words; the correct format for MLA and APA bibliographical citations; the meanings of proofreader's marks; or any of the useful facts and figures contained in the Ready-Reference section. Not only a handy reference work, the *Random House Writer's Reference* also meets the needs of beginning and intermediate writers by providing full lessons on some of the most important aspects of student and professional writing, including straightforward explanations of the rules of grammar, usage, and punctuation; clarification of points of style; and sound advice on writing term papers and business letters.

If you are looking to gain a better grasp of grammar, or if you are trying to refresh the skills you have, consult the first section—Mastering Grammar—and Chapter 1, Parts of Speech, which covers the rules of grammar as they apply to each of the basic units of a sentence, including all the parts of speech, phrases, and clauses. Not only are the functions of the individual parts of speech clearly conveyed within Parts of Speech, but the relationships between words used in phrases, clauses, and sentences are also discussed in great detail. This section culminates in the sentence, detailing the nature of a grammatically correct sentence and ways to avoid the most common sentence errors, including fragments and run-ons.

Building on the rules of grammar discussed in Mastering Grammar, the next chapter—Usage Basics—focuses on the application of those rules. Here, the most common style issues faced by writers as they strive to forge clear, effective prose are discussed in chapters detailing parallel sentence structure and shifts in tone, mood, perspective, and tense. The Usage Glossary that concludes this chapter contains those words that are often used incorrectly. If, for example, you are not sure if a particular word or phrase can be used in formal writing or speech, look up the word in the Usage Glossary and you will most likely find your answer.

Rather than try to memorize the correct spelling of all the words in the English language (a somewhat impossible task), you might consult the Spelling Rules that begin the Spelling chapter. Understanding these rules and knowing when to apply them is a sure way of alleviating many spelling problems. The spelling chapter also contains the correct spelling of those words that are most often misspelled—a very handy list that should be consulted when a word doesn't appear "quite right." A word processor's spellchecker is certainly useful, but it will not catch words that are spelled correctly and resemble the correct word you wish to use ("to" and "too," for example). To answer the shortcomings of a word processor, the Words Often Confused glossary, listing pairs of similar words and their proper use, has been included. Like the Usage Glossary, the Words Often Confused glossary can also be consulted when you are not sure if a word is being used correctly.

The Punctuation and Capitalization chapter describes when and how to use the various punctuation marks, detailing the function of each mark and providing numerous examples that demonstrate correct and incorrect usages of those marks. The marks are listed in alphabetical order, so you might also use this section as a glossary if you are unsure about the particular use of a punctuation mark. The rules of capitalization follow the discussion on punctuation marks.

The first section of this book focuses largely on grammar and mechanics, the next section—Enhancing Vocabulary—concentrates on the meanings and histories of words and offers numerous possibilities for adding to the "flavor" of your writing. Enhancing Vocabulary begins with Chapter 5, Building Blocks of English, which defines the building blocks of many English words. Gaining a better understanding of these prefixes, suffixes, and roots can be an effective way to improve your overall vocabulary, particularly if you are preparing for a standardized test such as the SAT. Chapter 6, Word Histories, is a glossary of words with interesting histories. As modern English is derived from a variety of languages, Chapter 7, Borrowed Words, groups words according to the language from which they were borrowed and provides a glimpse into their meaning and history. Chapter 8, Specialized Vocabularies, provides definitions for terms and jargon that are specific to particular professions, disciplines and interests, including business, computers and technology, law, and sports. Chapter 9, Short Forms, discusses the differences between acronyms, abbreviations, and symbols and, through useful examples, describes how each is formed.

The final section—Academic and Business Writing—includes three chapters: Chapter 10, The Stages of Writing; Chapter 11, Academic Writing, with a sample research paper in APA and MLA format; and Chapter 12, Business Writing, which provides a sample of business writing, including a sample executive summary and business memo.

Use the appendix to seek additional writing guidance and advice from any of the listed Web sites in the Online Resources for Writers section. To supplement your writing with facts and figures, use the Ready-Reference section that follows. Many of the most useful facts (city and country populations, distances, measurements, etc.) can be found here. In addition, those figures that change over time (populations, for example) have been updated to reflect the most recent census figures.

As you can see, the *Random House Writer's Reference* is a variety of writing and reference books combined into one. Some sections can be accessed as specialized glossaries and lists while others can be read straight through. Consult sections to improve the clarity and style of your writing and keep this book near your writing area.

PART ONE

Guide for Writers

Mastering Grammar

To play a sport well, one must first learn the rules of that sport. In this sense, writing is much like a sport. The ability to write and speak well requires a basic understanding of grammar. The rules of grammar tell writers how and when words are to be used if they are to express ideas as clearly as possible. This chapter discusses the rules of grammar as they apply to words, phrases and clauses, and sentences.

Parts of Speech

In order for a sentence to express an idea clearly, words must work together, which implies that individual words have different jobs or functions when they are arranged in a sentence. For example, a word that refers to a person, place, or thing is classified under the part of speech known as a noun. Those words that refer to an action are called verbs. As you will see in this chapter, there are rules of grammar for each of the parts of speech. There are eight general functions words can have, thus there are eight parts of speech: nouns, pronouns, verbs, adjectives, adverbs, prepositions, conjunctions, and interjections. Generally speaking, *pronouns* take the place of nouns; *adjectives* are used to describe nouns; *adverbs* describes verbs and adjectives; *prepositions* relate nouns to other words; *conjunctions* connect groups of words; and *interjections* express strong emotions. The functions of each of the parts of speech are discussed at greater length in this chapter.

It is important to note that the same words can have more than one function. Therefore, the same word can be multiple parts of speech. For example, the word **help** can function as both a noun and a verb.

Help as a Noun
   *The offer of **help** was greatly appreciated.*
   Here **help** refers to a thing, being the type of "offer".

Help as a Verb
   *They **help** the community by volunteering their time to tutor illiterate adults.*
   Here **help** expresses an action.
   In the examples below, **early** functions as both an adverb and an adjective.

Early as an Adverb
   *I think you ought to go to bed **early** tonight.*
   Here **early** describes when "you ought to go to bed".

Early as an Adjective
   *I had an **early** appointment this morning.*
   Here **early** describes the type of "appointment".

Since the same word can be many parts of speech, you must determine how the word is functioning within a sentence before you can label it a specific part of speech. You cannot assume that any word will always be the same part of speech and fulfill the same grammatical function.

Nouns

The function of a noun is to name a person, place, thing, idea, state, or quality.

People	Places	Things
Mary	library	flowers
physicist	Ontario	mutiny
American	coastline	computer
cousin	Paris	house
Mr. Jones	city	rabbit

Ideas	States	Qualities
democracy	hunger	integrity
equality	poverty	courage
Hinduism	happiness	sincerity
justice	rage	decency
evil	joy	bravery

Types of Nouns
Proper Nouns
Proper nouns name particular people, places, and things. Proper nouns include people's names, political and geographical places (regions, countries, states, cities, towns, etc.), building names, languages, nationalities, and religions. The first letter of a proper noun is always capitalized.

People	Places	Things
Mary	*Ontario*	*Ford Mustang*
Uncle Ed	*Paris*	*the Bible*
American	*Olympus*	*the Big Dipper*
Roman Catholic	*the Empire State Building*	*December*

For more information on **capitalizing proper nouns**, see page 151.

Collective Nouns
Collective nouns name groups of people or things. Common collective nouns include:

team	*clan*	*flock*
tribe	*pack*	*committee*
assembly	*couple*	*minority*
association	*crowd*	*number*
audience	*family*	*pair*
board	*flock*	*part*
class	*group*	*percent*
commission	*half*	*press*
committee	*herd*	*public*
company	*jury*	*series*
corporation	*legion*	*staff*
council	*majority*	

Collective Nouns and Agreement
Like indefinite pronouns collective nouns may be either singular or plural, depending on their meaning in the sentence. This means that knowing when to use the singular or plural form of the verb with a collective noun can be a challenging endeavor.

Determine agreement for each collective noun on a sentence-by-sentence basis. If the sentence implies that the group named by the collective noun acts as a single unit, use a singular verb. If the sentence implies that the group named by the collective noun acts individually, use a plural verb.

*The budget committee **is** voting on a new accountant this week.*
*The budget committee **are** in complete disagreement about the choice of a new accountant.*

The phrases "the number" and "the total" are usually singular, but the phrases "a number" and "a total" are usually plural:

***The number** of new members **is** astonishing.*
***A number** of new members **were** at the meeting.*

When the collective nouns "couple" and "pair" refer to people, they are usually treated as plurals:

***The pair are** hosting a New Year's open house.*
***The couple have** bought a large apartment with a view of the river.*

The third person plural, **are,** agrees with **the pair;** the third person plural **have** agrees with **the couple.**

For more information on: **agreement between nouns and verbs**, see page 55; **singular and plural verb forms**, see page 55.

Mass Nouns
Mass nouns name qualities or things that cannot be counted and do not have plural forms:

laughter	sand	valor
exhaustion	anger	wheat

Compound Nouns
Compound nouns are made up of two or more words. The words may be separate, hyphenated, or combined:

boarding pass	mother-in-law	housework
high school	off-ramp	schoolroom

For more information on using **hyphens**, see page 140.

Possessives (Possessive Case)
When a noun is used to show possession or ownership, the noun is said to take the possessive case, as in the following examples:

***Bill's** joy*

*Susan and **Frank's** house*

To form the possessive case add an apostrophe and an "s" to singular nouns (**Bill's, Frank's**). If a singular noun ends in an "s," and adding an "s" to the noun makes it difficult to pronounce, simply add an apostrophe to the s (Dickens' novels).

To form the possessive case of plural nouns, simply add an apostrophe to the ending "s" (bosses' rules, drivers' road).

A good test for knowing if the possessive is called for is to see if the phrase can be rewritten using "of". Since the above examples above could be rephrased **the joy of Bill** and **the house of Susan and Frank,** the possessive case can be used.

For more information on the **possessive case**, see page 14.

Plurals
The plural form of most nouns is created by simply adding an "s" to the noun, as in the following examples:

Singular	*Plural*
toad	toads
car	cars
song	songs

Nouns that end in "s", "x", "z", "sh", and "ch" are made plural by adding "es".

Singular	*Plural*
box	boxes
boss	bosses
sash	sashes
hero	heroes

Usually nouns that end in "o" preceded by a consonant are made plural by adding "es", e.g., hero, heroes.

Nouns, however, that end in "o" and reflect Italian musical terms are made plural by adding just an "s", e.g. soprano, sopranos

Nouns that end in "y" preceded by a consonant are made plural by changing the "y" to "i" and adding "es", e.g. fly, flies

Nouns that end in y preceded by a vowel are made plural by adding only "s", e.g. valley, valleys.

Lastly, there are some nouns that have irregular plural forms. Many of them are listed below. They are grouped according to the particular manner by which they are made plural.

Singular	Plural
calf	calves
half	halves
knife	knives
thief	thieves
wife	wives
sheep	sheep
deer	deer
fish	fish
species	species
foot	feet
tooth	teeth
mouse	mice
man	men
goose	geese
ox	oxen
child	children
alumna (fem.)	alumnae
nebula	nebulae
vertebra	vertebrae
alumnus (masc.)	alumni
radius	radii
stimulus	stimuli
memoradum	memoranda
medium	media
datum	data
basis	bases
oasis	oases
thesis	theses
criterion	criteria
phenomenon	phenomena

Pronouns

Generally speaking, the function of a pronoun is to take the place of a noun, phrase, clause, or sentence, as in the following example:

Ellen *has been working on the* ***project*** *for a long time.* ***She*** *spends eight hours a day on* ***it.***

In this example, the pronoun **she** replaces the proper noun **Ellen;** the pronoun **it** replaces the noun **project.** The words replaced by pronouns—**Ellen** and **project**—are called the *antecedents* (see below).

In the above example, personal pronouns are being used. Other types of pronouns discussed in this chapter include: *compound personal pronouns, interrogative pronouns, relative pronouns, demonstrative pronouns, and indefinite pronouns.*

Antecedents

An antecedent is the noun, phrase, clause or sentence to which a pronoun sometimes refers. Pronouns must agree with their antecedents in number and, often, gender. This means a singular pronoun is used to refer to a singular antecedent. Similarly, a plural pronoun is used to refer to a plural antecedent. A masculine pronoun refers to a masculine antecedent; a feminine pronoun refers to a feminine antecedent. In the above example (under Pronouns), singular pronouns (*she* and *it*) refer to singular antecedents. In addition, *she* refers to **Ellen,** a feminine antecedent.

Ambiguous References to Antecedents

Make sure that the reference is clear when two pronouns could logically refer to either of two antecedents. If the reference to an antecedent is not specific, confusion can arise. The following example demonstrates how ambiguities can occur.

Unclear

The manager *told* **Mrs. Greenberger** *that she will have to train* **her** *new people by June.*

As the sentence is written, it is unclear whose new people have to be trained as we do not know whether the possessive pronoun **her** refers to **the manager** or **Mrs. Greenberger.**

An unclear pronoun reference can usually be clarified by rearranging the sentence or by using the noun rather than the pronoun, as in the following examples:

Revised
> **Mrs. Greenberger's manager** told **her** to train **her** new people by June.

Unclear
> When you have finished with the **stamp** and bound the **report**, please return **it** to the storeroom.

Here, it is not clear whether **it** refers to **stamp** or **report**.

Revised
> When you have finished with the **stamp** and bound the **report**, please return **the stamp** to the storeroom.

For more information on **agreement between nouns and pronouns**, see **shifts in number** on page 81.

Types of Pronouns
Personal Pronouns

Personal pronouns that refer to the speaker are known as first-person pronouns. Those that refer to the one spoken to are known as second-person pronouns; those that refer to the person, place, or thing spoken about are known as third-person pronouns.

Personal pronouns can also refer to the gender of their antecedent and the number (singular or plural) of their antecedent. Study the chart below to determine the type of antecedent to each personal pronoun refers.

	First person	*Second person*	*Third person*
Singular			
Nominative	I	you	he, she, it
Possessive	my, mine	your, yours	his, her, hers, its
Objective	me	you	him, her, it
Plural			
Nominative	we	you	they
Possessive	our, ours	your, yours	their, theirs
Objective	us	you	them

From the chart we see that the personal pronoun **she** is a third-person, singular pronoun. As noted, personal pronouns must agree with their antecedent, therefore **she** can only refer to a feminine, single person or thing (such as a female animal or a ship).

As you can no doubt tell from the chart, there are quite a lot of personal pronouns. Using pronouns correctly can be challenging, however, the task is made easier by understanding the functions each pronoun has in a sentence, which is discussed in the following section.

Case

Personal pronouns can also be understood in terms of case. The English language has three cases: nominative, objective, and possessive, which are listed on the left side of the above chart. As the chart above indicates, pronouns often assume different forms for different cases. In the possessive case, the first-person plural pronoun **we** becomes **our** or **ours** depending upon its place in the sentence. A pronoun's case also depends upon how the pronoun is used and how it relates to other words in a sentence.

In general, pronouns take the nominative case when they function as the subject of a sentence or clause and the objective case when they function as the object of a verb or a preposition. Pronouns and nouns take the possessive case to indicate ownership.

As noted in the preceding section, nouns change form only in the possessive case. This change usually takes the form of adding an "s" to the noun. Nouns do not change form in the nominative and objective cases. As the chart above indicates, pronouns, in contrast, often change form in the nominative, objective, and possessive cases.

Nominative Case

The nominative case is sometimes called the "subjective case" because it is used when pronouns function as the subject of a sentence. Subjects are discussed at greater length in the Sentences section of this chapter. For now, we need only know that the subject is the person, place, or thing which the sentence is about.

The following examples illustrate how personal pronouns are used in the nominative case.

*Neither she nor **I** will be attending.*
***We** understand the lesson.*

> In these examples, the first-person singular pronoun **I** and the first-person plural pronoun **we** refer to the subject of the sentence.

*It is **me**.*
*The fastest runners are Lenore and **her**.*

What is wrong with these sentences? In both examples, the objective form of the pronouns (**me** and **her**) are being used when the nominative is called for. While "it is me" can be used in informal speech, in formal speech and writing, the nominative forms must be used.

Note how well the sentences read when the correct cases are used:

*It is **I**.*
*The fastest runners are Lenore and **she**.*

As the above examples illustrate, the nominative form of a pronoun is commonly used in a phrase that complements or gives more information about the subject. When a personal pronoun complements a subject, it is called a predicate nominative or subject complement. Since **it** and **the fastest runners** are the subjects of the sentences, and therefore in the nominative case, the complementing pronouns **I** and **she**, or the predicate nominatives, must also be in the nominative case.

Since the predicate nominative can sound overly formal, revising the sentence can often produce a less artificial sound, as in the following examples:

Overly formal
The delegates who represented the community at last evening's town board meeting were **he and I**.

Revised
He and I were the delegates who represented the community at last evening's town board meeting.

For more information on **complements**, see page 58.

Objective Case
The objective case is used when a personal pronoun is a direct object, indirect object, or object of a preposition. Objects are a type of complement that provide additional information about other

words in a sentence. Objects are discussed at greater length in the sentences section of this chapter. For now, we need only understand that direct objects describe who or what receives the action of a verb. Indirect objects describe to whom or for whom a verb is dedicated. The object of a preposition is the word a preposition links to other words in a sentence. Note the following example:

Pronoun as direct object
   Bob's jokes **embarrassed me.**

   Me, as the direct object of **embarrassed,** describes who was embarrassed.

Pronoun as indirect object
   The glaring sun **gave** my friends and **me** a headache.

   Me, as the indirect object of **gave,** describes to whom a headache was given.

Object of a preposition
   The cat leaped onto the bed and curled up **beside me.**

   Beside, a preposition with **me** as its object, links **me** to **the cat.**

For more information on: **complements and objects**, see page 59; using the objective and nominative case after "than or as," see page 13.

Nominative and Objective after "Than" or "As"
Note the following examples:

She had more fun with him than **I.**
She had more fun with him than **me.**

If the missing text is inserted, the sentence read as follows:

She had more fun with him than **I** *(had with him).*
She had more fun with him than *(she had with)* **me.**

Depending on the case of the pronoun used after **than,** the sentence has very different meanings. In the first example, the missing text would logically follow the pronoun. Thus, the first-person nominative is used, as **I** would be the subject and the phrase in parentheses. In the second example, the missing text would logically precede the pronoun, therefore, the objective **me** (which also functions as the object of the missing phrase) is used.

Figuring out where you would most likely insert the missing text (i.e., before or after the pronoun following "than" or "as") is a good basis for determining the correct case of the pronoun. If the text would precede the pronoun, use the objective case; if the text would follow, use the nominative case.

Possessive Case
As with nouns, the possessive case of a pronoun is used to show ownership. The possessive pronouns my, her, your, our, and their are used before a noun.

> This idea was **my idea,** not **your idea.**
>
> The pronouns **my** and **your** are used to express ownership of the noun **idea.**
>
> The possessive pronouns *mine, hers, yours, ours,* and *theirs* are used after a noun or when the pronoun is meant to take the place of a noun: This idea was **mine,** not **yours.**
>
> The pronouns **mine** and **yours** occur after the noun and are being used to replace **my idea** and **your idea.**
>
> **His** can be used either before or after a noun.
>
> Although he says that it is **his** idea, we know it is not really **his.**

Note: Never use an apostrophe with, or add an "s" to, a possessive pronoun. The following personal pronouns are already possessive and have no need for an apostrophe: my, mine, your, yours, her, hers, its, our, ours, their, and theirs. Do not confuse the contraction it's (for it is) with the possessive pronoun its.

Gerunds and the Possessive Case
A gerund is the -ing form of the verb (swimming, snoring) used as a noun.

Possessive pronouns and nouns often precede gerunds, as in the following examples:

The landlord objected to **my** having guests late at night.

Using **me** instead of **my** in the above sentence would be incorrect.

The possessive form of a pronoun is not used before a gerund when it would create a clumsy sentence.

Awkward
The neighbors spread the news about **his wanting** to organize a block party.

Revised
We heard from the neighbors that **he wants** to organize a block party.

For more information on **gerunds**, see page 35.

Compound Personal Pronouns

Possessive and objective forms of personal pronouns combined with "self" or "selves" are compound personal pronouns. The chart below lists the various compound personal pronouns.

Singular	*Plural*
myself	ourselves
yourself	yourselves
himself	themselves
herself	
itself	

Compound personal pronouns can be used to intensify or add emphasis to a noun or pronoun:

I myself have never given much thought to the matter.
Mary and **Bob** hung the striped wallpaper **themselves.**

In both examples, the intensive use of the compound personal pronoun **myself** emphasizes the subjects **I** and **Mary and Bob.**

Compound personal pronouns can also be used reflexively or to show that the subject of the sentence also receives the action of the verb:

I treated **myself** to a new pair of shoes.
Michael kept telling **himself** that it was not his fault.

In these examples, the reflexive use of the compound personal pronoun shows that the action of the verbs "treated" and "telling" is directed toward the subjects **I** and **Michael**.

Compound personal pronouns should not be used when the regular personal pronoun will suffice. Note the following examples:

Awkward
Sarah and **myself** went out to dinner.

Revised
Sarah and **I** went out to dinner.

Relative Pronouns

Which, that, who, whom, and *whose* are relative pronouns. *Whom* is the objective case form of *who*. *Whose* is the possessive case form of *who*. As these pronouns require an antecedent they are considered definite relative pronouns.

When *which, who, whom,* and *whose* are used interrogatively or to ask a question they do not require an antecedent, as is discussed below under Interrogative Pronouns.

Relative pronouns are used to tie together or relate groups of words. Relative pronouns begin subordinate clauses or relative clauses. Clauses are a group of words that contain a subject and a verb. In the examples below, the relative clauses indicated in italics depend upon other words in the sentence to which the relative pronouns function as a link.

Debbie enrolled in the **class** *that her employer* recommended.
Charles has a **friend** *who lives* in Toronto.

In the first example, the relative clause **that her employer** describes **class** and is linked to **class** by the relative pronoun

that. In the second example, the relative clause **who lives** describes **friend** and is linked to it by the relative pronoun **who**. In both examples, the relative pronouns are definite because they have antecedents (**class** and **friend**).

Indefinite Relative Pronouns

Unlike definite relative pronouns, indefinite relative pronouns do not require an antecedent. Indefinite relative pronouns may or may not have an antecedent, depending upon their use in a sentence. Following is a list of some common indefinite pronouns.

all	*everything*	*none*
another	*few*	*nothing*
any	*little*	*one*
anybody	*many*	*other*
anyone	*more*	*others*
anything	*most*	*several*
both	*much*	*some*
each	*neither*	*somebody*
either	*no one*	*someone*
everybody	*nobody*	*something*

In the examples below, the indefinite relative pronouns **much** and **everyone** are used without an antecedent:

Someone arrived at the party early, **much** *to the embarrassment of the unprepared host and hostess.*
Everyone *stayed late, too.*

Note, however, that indefinite relative pronouns can be used with an antecedent, as in the following examples:

The **casserole** *was so delicious that* **none** *was left by the end of the meal.*
A few of the relatives usually lend a hand when my **husband** *undertakes one of* **his** *home repair projects.*

Agreement and Indefinite Pronouns

As discussed on page 55, subjects must agree with their verbs. When the subject, however, is an indefinite pronoun, agreement becomes a much trickier task because, as noted, indefinite pronouns can refer to singular or plural subjects.

Traditionally, certain indefinite pronouns were treated as singular, some were always considered plural, and some could be both singular and plural. As language changes, however, many of these rules have changed. For example, **none** was traditionally treated as a singular pronoun, however, when the sense is "not any persons or things," the plural is more commonly used, as in the following example:

*The rescue party searched for survivors, but **none were** found.*

When **none** is clearly intended to mean "not one" or "not any," it is followed by a singular verb:

*Of all my court cases, **none has** been more stressful than yours.*
***None** of us **is** going to the concert.*

The following lists are presented as general guidelines, not hard-and-fast rules. In general, use singular verbs with indefinite pronouns.

Indefinite Pronouns That Are Most Often Considered Singular

anybody	everybody	nothing
anyone	everyone	one
anything	everything	somebody
each	many	someone
either	neither	everybody
nobody		

Indefinite Pronouns That Are Always Considered Plural

both	others
few	several
many	

Indefinite Pronouns That Can Be Considered Singular or Plural

all	most
any	none
more	some

Interrogative Pronouns

Which, what, who, whom, and *whose* are interrogative pronouns that are used to ask questions. As noted above, and as in the examples below, interrogative pronouns do not require a specific antecedent.

What did you call me for in the first place?
Whom have you called about this matter?
Whose is that?

Demonstrative Pronouns
This, that, these, and *those* are demonstrative pronouns that are used to point out nouns, phrases, or clauses. Demonstrative pronouns can be placed before or after their antecedents.

> **This** is the **book** I told you about last week.

> In this example, **this** points to the noun **book**.

> Demonstrative pronouns, however, do not require an antecedent, as in the following example:

> I will take two of **these.**

> Note the agreement—a plural demonstrative pronoun is used to point out an assumed plural noun, being the things **I will take two of.**

Using Pronouns
For further information on when to use particular pronouns (e.g., *who* vs. *whom*; *that* vs. *which*) look up the particular pronoun in the Usage section that begins on page 83.

Verbs

The function of a verb is to express an action, an occurrence, or a state of being.

Action	Occurrence	State of being
jump	become	be
swim	happen	seem

Types of Verbs
There are three types of verbs: action verbs, linking verbs, and auxiliary verbs.

Action verbs can describe mental as well as physical actions. The verb *think*, for example, describes a mental action, one that cannot be seen. *Welcome, enjoy, relish, ponder, consider,* and *deliberate* are also examples of action verbs that describe unseen mental actions.

Transitive Action Verbs

Action verbs are divided into two groups, transitive and intransitive, depending on how they function within a sentence. A transitive verb is a verb that requires a direct object to complete its meaning. The direct object receives the action of the verb:

> My son **eats** a piece of **cake** every afternoon.
> My sister **took** the **book** off the shelf.

> In these examples, the action verbs **eats** and **took** require the direct objects **cake** and **book** to complete their meaning, i.e., to describe what has been eaten and taken.

Intransitive Action Verbs

An intransitive verb is a verb that does not require a direct object to complete its meaning:

> My friends **laughed**.
> Even the baby **giggled**.

> Neither **laughed** nor **giggled** require a direct object to complete the actions they represent.

Many verbs can be either transitive or intransitive.

Transitive
> Carlos eats **breakfast** at 7:30, **lunch** at 12:30, and **dinner** at 6:30.
> Carlos eats at regular times.

> In the first example, the direct objects **breakfast, lunch,** and **dinner** answer the question: What does Carlos eat? In the second example, **eats** is being used without a direct object and is therefore intransitive.

Ergatives

Some verbs that can be both transitive and intransitive are ergatives. An ergative is a verb in which the subject of the intransitive form is also the object of the transitive form:

>The boat **capsized**.
>They **capsized** the **boat**.

>In the first example, **boat** is the subject (not the direct object) of the intransitive verb **capsized**. In the second example, **boat** is the object of **capsized** as a transitive verb.

Linking Verbs

Linking verbs describe an occurrence or a state of being. They connect parts of a sentence, often a noun or pronoun to a predicate adjective or adverb. The most common linking verb is the verb *to be*.

>He **is** happy.
>He **plays** happily.

>In these examples, the linking verbs **is** and **plays** link the predicate adjective **happy** and the adverb **happily** with the noun **He**.

For more information on **predicate adjectives** and other types of **complements**, see page 58.

Linking Verbs and Action Verbs

The following verbs can function as both linking and action verbs.

appear	look	smell
become	prove	sound
feel	remain	stay
grow	seem	taste

To determine whether the word is functioning as a linking verb or as an action verb, examine its role in the sentence.

>The **child grew** tired by the end of the evening.
>My mother **grows** the best **tomatoes** I have ever eaten.

In the first example, the verb **grew** (the past tense of to grow) links **tired** with **child** and is therefore a linking verb. In the second example, **grows** has the direct object **tomatoes** and is therefore a transitive action verb.

Auxiliary Verbs

An auxiliary verb, or helping verb, is used with a main verb to form a verb phrase. Only specific forms of certain verbs can function as auxiliary verbs. They are listed below:

do	can	am	have
does	could	are	has
did	shall	is	had
may	should	was	
might	will	were	
must would			

To form a grammatically correct verb phrase, the above verb forms must be combined with other verb forms in specific ways, which are described below.

The verb forms in the first two columns can be combined only with the present infinitive of the main verb as in the examples below:

Frank **should place** the book on the shelf.
I **could eat** the pie.
He **might run** to the store.

The verb forms in the third column can be used with the present and past participles of the main verb:

Frank **is placing** the book on the shelf.
He **was running** to the store.
The rock **has fallen.**

The verb forms in the fourth column can be used with the past participle of the main verb:

Frank **has placed** the book on the shelf.
I **have eaten** the pie.
He **has run** to the store.

The Principal Parts of Verbs: Regular and Irregular Verbs

The principal part of verbs refers to the basic forms that verbs can take in fulfilling a variety of functions. In English, all regular verbs have four principal parts or forms: the present infinitive; the past tense; the present participle; and the past participle.

Present infinitive	Past tense	Past participle	Present participle
Play	played	played	playing
Walk	walked	walked	walking
Bake	baked	baked	baking

Play, walk, and *bake,* like the majority of English verbs, are regular and change their form by adding -ing, -ed, or -d to the infinitive. However, many verbs do not follow this pattern. As you can see from the list below, these irregular verbs form their past tense and past participle in a number of different ways: some change an internal vowel and add -n to the past participle; some retain the same spelling in all three forms or in the past tense and past participle; some follow no discernible pattern.

Irregular verbs, however, follow the rules of regular verbs in forming the present participle (add -ing to the present infinitive).

The following list includes the most common irregular verbs. For information about verbs not included below, consult a dictionary. If a verb is regular, the dictionary will usually give only the infinitive. If the verb is irregular, the dictionary will include the past tense and past participle along with the infinitive; if only two forms are given, the past tense and the past participle are identical.

Common Irregular Verbs

Present Tense	Past Tense	Past Participle
arise	arose	arisen
bear	bore	borne, born
beat	beat	beaten
become	became	become
begin	began	begun
bend	bent	bent
bet	bet, betted	bet
bid	bid, bade	bid, bidden
bind	bound	bound
bite	bit	bitten

Present Tense	Past Tense	Past Participle
blow	blew	blown
break	broke	broken
bring	brought	brought
burn	burned, burnt	burned, burnt
burst	burst	burst
buy	bought	bought
catch	caught	caught
choose	chose	chosen
cling	clung	clung
come	came	come
creep	crept	crept
cut	cut	cut
deal	dealt	dealt
dig	dug	dug
dive	dived, dove	dived
do	did	done
draw	drew	drawn
dream	dreamed, dreamt	dreamed, dreamt
drink	drank	drunk
drive	drove	driven
eat	ate	eaten
fall	fell	fallen
fight	fought	fought
find	found	found
flee	fled	fled
fling	flung	flung
fly	flew	flown
forbid	forbade, forbad	forbidden, forbid
forget	forgot	forgotten, forgot
forgive	forgave	forgiven
freeze	froze	frozen
get	got	got, gotten
give	gave	given
go	went	gone
grow	grew	grown
hang (suspend)	hung	hung
hang (execute someone)	hanged	hanged
hear	heard	heard
hide	hid	hidden
hold	held	held
keep	kept	kept
kneel	knelt	knelt
know	knew	known

Present Tense	Past Tense	Past Participle
lay (put down)	laid	laid
lead	led	led
lie (rest; recline)	lay	lay
lose	lost	lost
mistake	mistook	mistaken
pay	paid	paid
ride	rode	ridden
ring	rang	rung
rise	rose	risen
run	ran	run
see	saw	seen
set	set	set
sew	sewed	sewed, sewn
shake	shook	shaken
shrink	shrank	shrunk
sing	sang, sung	sung
sit	sat	sat
slay	slew	slain
speak	spoke	spoken
spend	spent	spent
spring	sprang	sprung
stand	stood	stood
steal	stole	stolen
strike	struck	struck
swear	swore	sworn
sweep	swept	swept
swim	swam	swum
take	took	taken
teach	taught	taught
tear	tore	torn
throw	threw	thrown
wake	woke, waked	woken, waked
wear	wore	worn
weep	wept	wept
win	won	won
wind	wound	wound
wring	wrung	wrung
write	wrote	written

Tense

Tense refers to the form of a verb that indicates the time of the action, occurrence, or state of being expressed by the verb. Tense is different from time. The present tense, for instance, shows present time, but it can also indicate future time or a generally accepted belief.

English has two groups of tenses: the simple tenses (present, past, and future) and the perfect tenses (present perfect, past perfect, and future perfect). In addition, there are progressive forms of each of the simple and perfect tenses.

The Simple Tenses

The simple tenses generally show that an action or state of being is taking place now, in the future, or in the past relative to the speaker or writer, i.e., before the speaker has made the statement. The simple tenses indicate a finished, momentary, or habitual action or condition.

	Regular verb	*Irregular verb*
Present:	smile (smiles)	go (goes)
Past:	smiled	went
Future:	will (shall) smile	will (shall) go

The verbs in parentheses refer to the third-person singular (he, she, it) form of the verb. The present tense is created with the addition of -s or -es when the third-person singular is used. When the first- and second-person singular and plural are used (I, we, you, they) the present infinitive form of the verb is to be used.

Note: "Shall" is rarely used except in very formal speaking and writing, to express determination, and in laws and directives.

The Present Tense

Except when the subjects are singular nouns or third-person singular pronouns, the form used for the present tense is the same as the present infinitive form of the verb (I walk, you skip, we jump, they catch). With singular nouns or third-person singular pronouns, -s or -es is added to the infinitive (Robert walks, she skips, it jumps, he catches).

For more information on **agreement between pronouns and verbs**, see page 17.

The verb "be" is an exception because it changes form to reflect both person (first, second, or third) and the number of people (singular or plural).

Mastering Grammar

	Singular	Plural
First person	I am	we are
Second person	you are	you are
Third person	he, she, it is	they are

The present tense is used:

To state present action
Nick **prepares** the walls for painting.

To show present condition
The secretary **is efficient.**

To show that an action occurs regularly
Louise **prepares** a report for her supervisor **every week.**

To show a condition that occurs regularly
The traffic **is** usually backed up at the bridge in the evening.

To indicate future time, as an alternative to the future tense when a specific time (e.g. tomorrow) is indicated
The income tax refund **arrives tomorrow.**

To state a generally held belief
Haste makes waste.

To state a scientific truth
A body in motion **tends** to stay in motion.

To discuss literary works, films, etc.
In Hamlet, Claudius **poisons** his brother, **marries** his former sister-in-law, and **seizes** the throne.

To narrate historical events as if they were happening in the present time (the "historical present")
In 1781 Cornwallis **surrenders** to Washington at Yorktown.

The Past Tense

The past tense of regular verbs is formed by adding -d or -ed to the infinitive. The past tense of irregular verbs is formed in a variety of ways. Consult the table on pages 23 for past tense forms of irregular verbs.

As in the present tense, the verb "be" changes form in the past tense to reflect speaker and number.

	Singular	Plural
First person	I was	we were
Second person	you were	you were
Third person	he, she, it was	they were

The past tense is used:

To show actions and conditions that began and ended in the past, or were true at a particular time in the past
Johnny **walked** the dog **last night.**
Joan **was** very **happy.**

To show recurring past actions that do not extend to the present
During World War II, Eric **saw** the fighting through the lens of a camera.

The Future Tense

The future tense is formed by using the auxilliary verbs "will" or "shall" plus the present infinitive form of the verb.

Unlike the past and present tenses, the verb "be" (when it is not being used as an auxiliary verb) takes only one form in the future tense—"be".

The future tense is used:

To show a future action
Tomorrow the sun **will set** at 6:45 p.m.

To show a future condition
They **will be** excited **when they see the presents.**

To indicate intention
The Board of Education has announced that it **will begin** repairs on the town pool as soon as possible.

To show probability
The decrease in land values in the Northeast **will most likely continue** into next year.

The Perfect Tenses

The present and past perfect tenses are formed when the present and past participles of the auxiliary verb "have" are combined with the past participle of another verb (which could also be "have"). The future perfect is formed when the auxiliary verb "will" (or "shall") is combined with the past participle of another verb.

	Regular verb	*Irregular verb*
Present:	have (has) smiled	have (has) gone
Past:	had smiled	had gone
Future:	will have smiled	will (shall) go

The Present Perfect Tense
The present perfect is formed with the present tense of the auxiliary verb "have" plus the past participle of the main verb.

The present perfect tense is used:

To show completed action
  Martin **has finished talking** to his clients.

To show past action or condition continuing into the present
  We **have been waiting** for a week.

To show action that occurred at an unspecified past time
  I **have reviewed** all the new procedures.

The Past Perfect Tense
The past perfect tense is formed by using the past tense of the auxiliary verb "have" plus the past participle of the main verb.

The past perfect tense is used:

To show one action or condition completed before another
  By the time her employer returned, Linda **had completed** all her assigned tasks.

To show an action that occurred before a specific past time
  By 1930, insulin **had been** isolated, refined, and distributed.

To show that something that was assumed or expected did not in fact happen
  We had hoped to have the new cabin ready by the first of June.

The Future Perfect Tense
The future perfect tense is formed by using the auxiliary verbs "will" and "have" plus the past participle of the main verb.

The future perfect tense is used:

To show a future action or condition that will be completed before another
  By the time you read this letter, Bill **will have left** California for Mexico.

To show that an action will be completed by a specific future time
  By tomorrow, the bonds **will have lost** over fifty percent of their face value.

For more information on **using tenses**, see page 25.

Progressive Forms

Progressive forms are verb phrases that show continuing action or action that is in progress at the time the statement is written. The progressive forms are created by using the present participle of the main verb with past, present, and future forms of the verbs "to be" and "to have."

The present progressive is used to show continuing action or condition. It is made with the present form of the verb "to be" plus the present participle.

> I **am finishing** the painting while the children are at camp.
> Medicine **is becoming** increasingly specialized.

The past progressive is used to show an action or condition continuing in the past and to show two past actions occurring simultaneously. It is formed with the past form of the verb "to be" plus the present participle:

> She **was becoming** disenchanted with the radical diet.
> Mike fell off his bike while he **was watching** a cat climb a tree.

The future progressive is used to show continuing future action and to show continuing action at a specific future time. It is formed with "will" plus "be" plus the present participle:

> She **will be studying** all night.
> **Will** you **be traveling** to Japan again in the spring?

The present perfect progressive is used to show that an action or condition is continuing from the past into the present and/or the future. It is formed with the present form of the verb "to have" plus "been" plus the present participle:

> The amount of pollution **has been increasing** dramatically.
> I **have been waiting** for a train for fifteen minutes.

The past perfect progressive is used to show that a continuing past action has been interrupted by another. It is formed with "had" plus "been" plus the present participle:

Alice **had been taking** a detour through town until the new bridge was finished.
The workers **had been planning** a strike when the management made a new offer.

The future perfect progressive is used to show that an action or condition will continue until a specific time in the future. It is formed with "will" plus "have" plus "been" plus the present participle.

By Monday, I **will have been working** on that project for a month.
Next September, they **will have been traveling** for nearly a year.

Mood

The mood of a verb shows how the writer or speaker regards what he or she is saying. The form of the verb changes to indicate the mood of the verb. In English, there are three moods: the indicative, the imperative, and the subjunctive.

Indicative Mood

By far, verbs are most often used in the indicative mood. The indicative mood is used to state a fact or to ask a question:

Henry James **wrote** "The Turn of the Screw."
We **hold** soccer games only on Saturdays.
Did T.S. Eliot **have** a great impact on twentieth-century literature?
Do you **hold** soccer games only on Saturdays?

Imperative Mood

The imperative mood is used to make requests, give directions, or express commands. Frequently, the subject (usually "you") is understood rather than stated.

Get up!
Turn left at the convenience store.

While you could begin either of the above sentences with "you," it is not necessary for the meaning of the sentence to be conveyed.

"Let's" or "let us" can also be used before the basic form of the verb in a command:

Let's go to Mario's for dinner.

Subjunctive Mood

The subjunctive mood has traditionally been used to state wishes or desires, requirements, suggestions, or conditions that are contrary to fact. In these instances, the subjunctive is most often reflected in the use of the verb form **were,** as in the following examples:

*He acted as if he **were** the owner.*
*I wish I **were** more organized.*

In both of examples, an idea contrary to fact is expressed. In the first example, **he** is clearly not the owner; in the second example, I am clearly not "organized".

The subjunctive is also required in clauses expressing desire, demand, resolution, recommendation, or motion. In the present tense, these uses of the subjunctive require the bare infinitive form of the verb.

*I move that the minutes **be** (not are) accepted.*
*He recommended that she **hire** (not hires) an attorney.*
*They demanded that he **come** (not comes) immediately.*

Often the present subjunctive is used in idioms and set phrases:

*Far **be** it from me . . .*
*If need **be** . . .*
***Be** that as it may.*
*The people **be** damned.*
***Come** rain or **come** shine.*
*As it **were** . . .*
***Suffice** it to say . . .*
***Come** what may . . .*

In these idioms, the present subjunctive is reflected in the use of the verb form "be" and the bare infinitive of other verb forms. For more information on using **moods**, see page 31.

Phrasal Verbs

A phrasal verb is a combination of a verb and one or more adverbs or prepositions. The meaning of the phrase is often idiomatic and is not predictable from the individual parts of the phrasal verb. Examples of phrasal verbs are: *call off, catch on, get along with, put up with, send for, show up, stand up to, take off,* and *throw away.*

> It won't take you long to **catch on** to the new routine.
> She has trouble **getting along with** her coworkers.
> What time did they finally **show up?**
> You ought to **stand up** to him.
> Did your flight **take off** on time?
> She has **thrown away** several opportunities.

Verbals

A verbal looks like a noun, but functions as an adjective, adverb, or noun. All verbals can be modified by adverbs and adverbial phrases. They can also take objects and complements. Since they are not verbs, however, they cannot function as the only verb form in a sentence. Taken together, the verbal and the words related to the verbal constitute the verbal phrase.

> *Signs* **hung on this wall** *will be removed.*
>
> **Hung on this wall** is a type of verbal phrase called a participial phrase. It is functioning as an adjective by modifying "signs." In order to avoid being an incomplete sentence, the clause **will be removed** must be included.
>
> **Eating a low-fat diet** *reduces the risk of many diseases.*
>
> **Eating a low-fat diet** is a gerund phrase functioning as a noun. It is the subject of the verb "reduces."
>
> *She likes* **to read science fiction** *novels.*
>
> **To read science fiction novels** is an infinitive phrase functioning as a noun. It is the object of the verb "likes."

Infinitives

The infinitive is the basic form of a verb:

to grin
to talk
to snore
to walk
to drop

Note: dictionaries list words in the present infinitive which is the infinitive form without "to," i.e., "grin," "talk," "snore," etc.

Present Infinitive

The present infinitive ("to" + the verb) is the most common use of the infinitive. It refers to the same time as the main verb.

> *I love* **to go** *to Paris in June.*

> In this example the present infinitive **to go** is a noun functioning as the direct object of the verb "love".

The present infinitive can also function as a noun subject, beginning a clause that acts as the subject of the main verb.

Noun subject
   To go *to Paris would be nice.*

Present infinitive as adjective
   My grandmother's house is the **place to go** *for great pancakes.*

Adverb
   This plane **is to go** *to Paris.*

> In the first example, the infinitive **to go** modifies the noun **place**. In the second example, **to go** modifies the verb **is**.

Perfect Infinitives

The infinitive can also be perfect. The perfect infinitive ("to have" + the past participle) reflects time before the action expressed in the main verb:

> *He is said* **to have eaten** *everything in the freezer.*

The perfect infinitive can also be used to express a wish or desire for something that might happen or will not happen.

> *We hope* **to have moved** *into our new house before Christmas.*
> *She would like* **to have won** *that award.*

Split Infinitives
There is a longstanding convention that prohibits placing a word, usually an adverb, between "to" and the verb. This convention is based on an analogy with Latin, in which an infinitive is only one word and therefore cannot be divided. Criticism of the split infinitive was especially strong in the nineteenth century when the modeling of English on Latin was popular.

The fact of the matter is that split infinitives can both create confusion and less awkward sentences.

> We had **to** carefully **drive** through the snowstorm.
> We **drove** carefully through the snowstorm.
> Many American companies expect **to increase** their overseas investments by more than double in the next decade.
> Many American companies expect **to** more than **double** their overseas investments in the next decade.

> In the first set of examples, the split infinitive creates a confusing sentence. In the second set of examples, inserting the split infinitive makes for a clearer sentence, meaning the writer must ascertain whether the sentence is made clearer or less clear with the split infinitive.

Participles
As noted, the participle form of a verb can be in the past (laughed) or the present (laughing). When either past or present participles are used with an auxiliary verb (has laughed, is laughing) the perfect tenses are formed, which are discussed on page 22.

When past and present participles are used without an auxiliary verb they are simply participles and function as adjectives:

> Where is the **finished product?**
> I refuse to stay in a cabin that does not have **running water.**

> In the first example, **finished** describes **product.** In the second example, **running** describes **water.**

For more information on **using participles**, see page 33.

Gerunds
Gerunds are the form of the verb that are created by adding -ing to the present infinitive. While gerunds look exactly like present par-

ticiples, they are not used as a verb but rather nouns as in the following examples:

> *I try to avoid **falling** when I go **skiing**.*

In this example, **falling** and **skiing** are gerunds of the verbs fall and ski. Both are being used as nouns.

Adjectives

The function of an adjective is to modify or describe a noun or a pronoun, as in the following examples:

> *The illness has affected **twelve** people in the apartment complex.*
>
> *The **eerie** noise seems to come from the basement.*

In the above examples **twelve** and **eerie** tell us something more about the nouns **people** and **noise**. Since **twelve** tells us how many people it is called a limiting adjective. Since **eerie** describes what kind of **noise** it is called a descriptive adjective.

Nouns as Adjectives

Nearly any noun can function as a descriptive adjective.

> *The **produce** stand is open all night.*
> *He has always enjoyed **piano** concertos.*

Since the nouns **produce** and **piano** describe the kind of **stand** and **concerto,** they are descriptive adjectives.

Pronouns as Adjectives

While nouns generally function as descriptive adjectives, pronouns generally function as limiting adjectives. The demonstrative pronouns *this, that, these,* and *those;* the interrogative pronouns *which* and *what;* and the indefinite pronouns *some, another, both, few, many, most, more,* etc., can all function as adjectives.

> ***This** bus is rarely on time in the winter.*
> ***Which** chores do you dislike the least?*
> ***Some** people have managed to get tickets for the concert.*

In the above examples, **this, which,** and **some** quantify or limit the nouns **bus, chores,** and **people** by defining the group or subset of buses, chores, and people, to which the writer could be referring.

Proper Adjectives

An adjective derived from a proper noun is called a proper adjective. Many of these adjectives are forms of people's names, as in Emersonian, from the nineteenth-century writer Ralph Waldo Emerson.

Shavian wit (Shaw)
Italian food
Chinese silk
March wind

For more information on **capitalizing proper adjectives**, see page 151.

Compound Adjectives

An adjective made up of two or more words is called a compound adjective. The words in a compound adjective may be combined or hyphenated.

nearsighted
soft-shelled
open-and-shut
hardworking
close-by

A compound adjective that is not hyphenated when it is another part of speech becomes hyphenated when it acts as an adjective, as in the following examples:

*Is there a grocery store **close by**?*
*Yes, Sam's Market is a **close-by** grocery store.*

Consult a dictionary to find out whether or not a particular compound adjective is to be combined or hyphenated.

Appositives

Like adjectives, appositives are also used to describe a noun. An appositive is a word or a phrase that appears next to a noun or pronoun and explains or identifies it.

Both physicists, **Marie Curie and he,** worked on isolating radium.
Mr. Brown, **our English teacher,** went on the class trip with us.
Marie Curie and he tells us who "both physicists" are; **our English teacher** tells us who "Mr. Brown" is.

While the appositives in the above examples are set off by commas, appositives can also be marked by em dashes or a colon. Use an em dash when the appositive is very long or separate from the word it is describing.

The car parked in the garage—**a shiny red sports model that had just been purchased**—attracted Sarah's attention.

Use colons when the appositive appears at the end of the sentence.

My grocery list included: **peas, carrots, hot-dogs, chicken, and orange juice.**

When an appositive is very simple or clearly belongs to the word it is describing, no punctuation is used.

My boss **Sam** is often late for work.

Sam, describing who "my boss" is, does not need to be set off by commas.

For more information on using colons, commas, and dashes, see page 128.

Determiners

A determiner, sometimes also called a noun marker, is a word that determines the use of a noun without actually modifying or describing it. Determiners are placed before nouns or noun phrases.

Examples of determiners are the articles *a, an,* and *the;* the demonstrative pronouns *this, that, these,* and *those;* the possessive pronouns *my, your, her, his, our, their;* and indefinite pronouns such as *some* and *each.*

The form of the determiner must agree with the noun to which it is pointing, as in the following example:

These *toys must be given to the child.*

As "toys" is plural, a plural determiner (**these**) is used.

Indefinite and Definite Articles
The article determiners *a* and *an* are called indefinite articles because they do not determine or point to a specific noun. *The* is a definite article because it points to a specific noun.

*I went to **a** country.*
*I bought **an** animal.*
*I went to **the** country nearest to my own.*
*I bought **the** animal no one else wanted.*

For more information on using **a/an**, see page 84.

Adjectives and Comparison
Many descriptive adjectives can be used to express degrees of a quality or trait, as in the following example:

Positive
 *The dog is **small.***

Comparative
 *This dog is **smaller.***

Superlative:
 *That dog is **smallest.***

As the examples illustrate, the three degrees in which a noun or pronoun can be described are called positive, comparative, and superlative. In addition to adding the endings -er to form the comparative degree and -est to form the superlative degree, adjectives can also express comparison with the words *more/most, less/least*.

Avoid using double comparatives or double superlatives.

*Amanda gets a bigger allowance because she is **more older** than I am.*
*She is the **most nicest** girl in the class.*

Both of these sentences sound awkward and wordy because **more** and **most** are unnecessary. Eliminating **more** and **most** would dramatically improve the sentences.

Irregular Adjectives

Some adjectives, however, change form to express comparative and superlative comparisons.

Positive	Comparative	Superlative
good	better	best
bad	worse	worst
little	littler, less, lesser	littlest, least
many, some, much	more	most

-er and -est are not to be used with the above words

Comparative vs. Superlative

In general, use the comparative form to compare two things; use the superlative form to compare three or more things, as in the following examples:

Wiskers was the **smarter of the two** hamsters.
Trixie was the **best of all** the dogs at the show.

Adverbs

While an adjective is used to describe a noun or pronoun, the function of an adverb is to modify or describe a verb, an adjective, or another adverb. Adverbs add description and detail to writing by more closely focusing the meaning of a verb, an adjective, or another adverb. They describe by telling where, when, how, or to what extent.

Where:
He nearly ran **over** the edge.

When:
Yesterday it snowed; **today** it all melted.

How:
I **quickly** changed the topic.

To what extent:
The child has **fully** recovered from her illness.

Asking whether or not a word determines where, when, how, or to what extent is a good way to figure out if a word is an adverb. In the above examples, **nearly** tell us where "he . . . ran";

yesterday and **today** tell us when "it snowed" and when "it all melted"; **quickly** tells how "I . . . changed the topic"; and **fully** tells us to what extent "the child has . . . recovered".

Forms of Adverbs

Many adverbs are formed by adding -ly to an adjective.

Adjective	Adverb
slow	slowly
usual	usually
late	lately
forceful	forcefully

For more information on when to use the adverb or adjective form of a word, look the word up in the **Usage Glossary** that begins on page 83.

As discussed below, the presence of -ly is never a sure way of determining whether or not a verb is an adverb, particularly since many adverbs have two forms—with -ly and without -ly.

Adverbs with two forms
high/highly
sharp/sharply
late/lately
loud/loudly
near/nearly
wrong/wrongly
slow/slowly

Knowing when to use which form is often a question of formality. Use the -ly form in more formal writing, do not use it in less formal writing.

Informal
   You speak **loud.**

Formal
   You speak **loudly.**

In some instances, the choice of form depends on the idiomatic or common use of the word. *Nearly,* for example, is used to mean "almost," while *near* is used to mean "close in time." *Slow* is used in spoken commands with short verbs that express motion, such as "drive" and "run" (Drive slow) and combined with present participles to form adjectives (a slow-moving vehicle). *Slowly* is commonly found in writing, and is used in both speech and writing before a verb (He slowly swam across the cove) as well as after a verb (He swam slowly through the waves).

Adverbs vs. Adjectives

If the verb's direct object is followed by a word that describes the verb, the word must be an adverb.

> He muttered the words **angrily**.
>
> Since **angrily** modifies the verb "muttered," we know it is an adverb.
>
> If the direct object is followed by a word that describes that object, the word must be an adjective.
>
> The red pepper made the soup **spicy**.
>
> The adjective **spicy** modifies the noun **soup**.
>
> Deciding whether to use a word as an adjective or an adverb depends upon the meaning you wish to convey. Compare the following pairs of sentences:
>
> His mother called him **quiet**.
>
> His mother called him **quietly**.

In the first sentence the adjective **quiet** modifies the pronoun "him," suggesting that "his mother" described him as being **quiet**. In the second example, the adverb **quietly** modifies the verb "called" and therefore describes the manner, or how, in which his mother called him.

Adverbs and Comparison

Like adjectives, adverbs also take different forms when they are used to make comparisons. The three forms are the positive degree, the comparative degree, and the superlative degree.

Positive Degree

The positive degree is the basic form of the adjective or the adverb, the form listed in the dictionary. Since the positive degree does not indicate any comparison, the adjective or adverb does not change form.

Comparative Degree
The comparative form indicates a greater degree by comparing two things. In the comparative form, adjectives and adverbs generally add -er or more.

Superlative Degree
The superlative form indicates the greatest degree of difference or similarity by comparing three or more things. In this form, adjectives and adverbs generally add -est or most.

Using Less/Least/More/Most or -Er/-Est
Most adjectives and adverbs of three or more syllables and nearly all adverbs ending in -ly use more/less and most/least to form the comparative and superlative degrees:

Positive	Comparative	Superlative
customary	more/less customary	most/least customary
regular	more/less regular	most/least regular
admiring	more/less admiring	most/least admiring
slowly	more/less slowly	most/least slowly
harshly	more/less harshly	most/least harshly
rudely	more/less rudely	most/least rudely

Irregular Adverbs
Some adverbs are irregular in the comparative and superlative degrees, as shown in the table below:

Positive	Comparative	Superlative
well	better	best
badly	worse	worst

Distinguishing Adverbs from Adjectives
Many adverbs end in -ly, but this is not a reliable way to distinguish adverbs from adjectives. Not all adverbs end in -ly (far, fast, little). There are some adjectives that end in -ly (curly, surly, lovely). Some words function as both adjectives and adverbs (early, well). As noted, the part of speech is determined by the word's function in the sentence, not by its ending.

For more information on using particular adjectives or adverbs (good vs. well, for example), look up the word in the **Usage Glossary** that begins on page 83.

Prepositions

The function of a preposition is to connect and relate a noun or pronoun to some other word in the sentence.

Common Prepositions

about	by	outside
above	concerning	over
across	despite	past
after	down	regarding
against	during	round
along	except	since
amid	excepting	through
among	for	throughout
around	from	till
as of	in	to
at	inside	toward
before	into	under
behind	like	underneath
below	near	until
beneath	of	up
beside	off	upon
besides	on	with
between	onto	within
beyond	opposite	without
but	out	

Compound Prepositions (Two or More Words)

according to	by reason of	in spite of
along with	by way of	instead of
apart from	except for	on account of
as for	in addition to	out of
as of	in case of	up to
as regards	in front of	with reference to
aside from	in lieu of	with regard to
because of	in place of	with respect to
by means of	in regard to	with the exception of

Prepositional Phrases

Since a preposition links words to a noun or pronoun, it always has an object, being the noun or pronoun it is linking to other words in the sentence. The preposition with its object and any modifiers is called a prepositional phrase.

*She walks **toward the mountain**.*
*He was fired **on account of his gross negligence**.*

In these examples, **toward the mountain** and **on account of his gross negligence** are the prepositional phrases that the prepositions **toward** and **on** are linking to **walks** and **fired**.

In both of the above examples, the prepositional phrases are functioning as adjectives because they are modifying verbs. Prepositional phrases can also function as adjectives, as in the following examples:

*Melinda is the girl **with the missing front tooth**.*
*The reporter **in the red dress** asked the first question.*

Prepositions and Adverbs

To distinguish between prepositions and adverbs, remember that prepositions, unlike adverbs, can never function alone within a sentence. A preposition must always have an object.

*They went **in**.*
*They went **in** the house.*

In the first sentence, **in**, lacking an object, functions as an adverb. In the second sentence **in,** connecting "the house" to "went," functions as a preposition.

Conjunctions

The function of a conjunction is to connect words, phrases, or clauses. The three kinds of conjunctions are coordinating, correlative, and subordinating.

Coordinating Conjunctions

A coordinating conjunction connects sentence parts (individual words, phrases, or clauses) of equal rank. Following are the most common coordinating conjunctions:

and	*or*
but	*so*
for	*yet*
nor	

As the examples below illustrate, each of the conjunctions are used to express difference relationships between the parts of a sentence the conjunction is being used to connect.

The children cleaned up quickly **and** quietly.

In this example, **and** shows a connection between the adverbs "quickly" and "quietly."

The living room was extremely elegant **but** surprisingly comfortable.
My supervisor will never give us half days on Friday, **nor** will she agree to our other demands.
She took good care of the houseplant, **yet** it wilted and lost its leaves.

In these examples, **but, nor,** and **yet** show a contrast between two parts of the sentence.

All the restaurants were closed, **so** we ended up eating peanut butter and jelly sandwiches.

In this example, **so** shows the result of the fact that "the stores were closed" was "we ended up eating peanut butter and jelly sandwiches."

Laura stayed in the office late all week, **for** she had to finish the project by Friday.

Here, **for** shows causality, i.e., that "Laura stayed in the office late because she had to finish the project by Friday."

Correlative Conjunctions

When some of the above coordinating conjunctions are used with *both, either, neither, not only, not,* and *whether,* they become correlative conjunctions. Correlative conjunctions are also used to link sentence parts of equal grammatical rank and always work in pairs to connect words, phrases, or clauses.

both . . . and
either . . . or
neither . . . nor
not only . . . but also

not . . . but
whether . . . or

Both the bank **and** the post office are closed on national holidays.

In this example, the two elements "bank" and "post office" are connected by the correlative conjunctions **both** and **and**.

When using correlative conjunctions, it is important to write or speak in **parallel structure**, which is discussed at greater length on page 70.

Subordinating Conjunctions
A subordinating conjunction is a word that connects two thoughts by making one subordinate to, or dependent on, the other.

To "subordinate" suggests making one statement less important than the other:

Although some people tried to repair the tennis courts, they were unable to gain sufficient public backing.

The main idea, "they were unable to gain sufficient public backing," is an independent clause (complete sentence); the subordinate idea, "**Although** some people tried to repair the tennis courts," is a dependent clause that functions here as an adverb. Either clause may come first in the sentence.

Common Subordinating Conjunctions

after	even though	though
although	if	till
as	if only	unless
as of	in order that	until
as long as	now that	when
as soon as	once	whenever
as though	rather than	where
because	since	whereas
before	so that	wherever
even if	than	while
that		

For more information: on **independent clauses**, see page 51; on **subordinate, or dependent, clauses**, see page 51.

Subordinating Conjunctions vs. Prepositions

A word such as *until, before, since, till,* or *after* can function as either a preposition or a subordinating conjunction. Remember that subordinating conjunctions, unlike prepositions, connect two complete ideas.

After you finish reading that book, *may I borrow it?*
After lunch *I am going shopping for a new pair of shoes.*

In the first example, *after* connects the subordinate clause *you finish reading that book* with the independent clause *may I borrow it* and is therefore a subordinating conjunction. In the second example, *after* relates lunch to when *I am going shopping for a new pair of shoes* and is therefore a preposition.

Conjunctive Adverbs

A conjunctive adverb is an adverb that functions as a conjunction by connecting two clauses or sentences and describing their relationship to each other.

Common Conjunctive Adverbs

also	however	next
anyway	incidentally	nonetheless
besides	indeed	otherwise
consequently	instead	still
finally	likewise	then
furthermore	meanwhile	therefore
hence	moreover	thus
nevertheless		

Transitional Phrases

Expressions that are used to link complete ideas are called transitional phrases. Common transitional phrases, include:

after all	for example
as a result	in addition
at any rate	in fact
at the same time	in other words
by the way	on the contrary
even so	on the other hand

The school building is in great disrepair; **for example,** *the roof is leaking, the paint is peeling, and the heating system works erratically.*

As the above example illustrates, a semicolon is used before a conjunctive adverb (**for example**) or a transitional phrase that is placed between main clauses. The adverb or phrase that follows is set off by a comma.

For more information on **punctuating conjunctive adverbs**, see page 133.

Interjections

An interjection is a word used to express strong emotion. It functions independently within a sentence. In Latin, the word *interjection* means "something thrown in." In a sense, interjections are "thrown in" to add strong feeling.

For maximum effect, interjections should be used sparingly in your writing. Since they are independent from the rest of the sentence, they are set off by commas or followed by an exclamation point.

Common Interjections

ah	darn	ouch
alas	hey	shh
bah	nonsense	well
bravo	oh	wow

Darn! The cat got out again.
Oh, I didn't expect you so early.
Hey! Do you know what you're doing?

Phrases, Clauses, and Sentences

As noted, the rules of grammar need to also be understood as they relate to words when they are made to work together. Words work together on three levels: as phrases, clauses, and sentences. A phrase is a group of words that act as a particular part of speech or part of a speech but does not have a related verb and subject. A clause, one level up from a phrase, can also act as a part of speech but has a subject and a verb. A sentence, the highest and most complete level in which words work together, is a complete thought and contains a subject and a predicate, which is a verb with any complements or other describing words.

Phrases

A phrase is a group of related words that does not contain both a subject and a verb. Because they often function as parts of speech, phrases are logically classified as verb phrases, noun phrases, prepositional phrases, and verbal phrases. Verbal phrases are discussed on page 50. The other types of phrases are discussed below.

The most common types of phrase are prepositional phrases. A prepositional phrase is a group of words that opens with a preposition and ends with a noun or pronoun. Prepositional phrases can function as adjectives, as adverbs, or, occasionally, as nouns.

As adjectives
   The **price of the dinner** was exorbitant.

   Of the dinner, by telling us to what the price pertains, describes **price.**

As adverbs
   The joggers ran with determination.

   By telling us how *the joggers ran,* **with determination** is functioning as an adverb.

As nouns
   Beyond the oak tree is out of bounds.

   Beyond the oak tree describes a place and is therefore functioning as a noun.

Verb Phrases

A verb phrase contains a main verb and an auxiliary verb.

   The cat **has eaten** the carnations.
   Let's go to the movies.
   Can you **read** his handwriting?

Noun Phrases

A noun phrase contains a noun and one or more modifiers.

   The **brilliant sunshine** only made the **old house** look more dilapidated.

*I have heard that she is a **very interesting speaker.***
*A **tall, blue heron** stood motionless on the shore.*

For information on phrases as **fragments** or incomplete sentences, see page 64.

Clauses

When a group of words contain both a subject and a verb, they become a clause. There are two types of clauses: independent (main) and dependent (subordinate).

Independent Clauses

An independent (main) clause can stand alone as a complete sentence.

Although he woke up early, **he missed his train.**
After Marcia graduates from college, **she plans to open a catering business.**

Both **he missed his train** and **she plans to open a catering business** can stand alone as complete sentences and are therefore independent clauses.

Dependent Clauses

A dependent (subordinate) clause functions as a part of speech that relates to an element in the main clause.

In the examples under independent clauses above, **Although he woke up early** and **after Marcia graduates** are dependent clauses that cannot stand alone as complete sentences.

As the above examples suggest, dependent clauses function as parts of speech—as adjectives, adverbs, and nouns.

Adjective Clauses

An adjective clause is a subordinate clause that modifies a noun or pronoun. It usually begins with a relative pronoun: *which, what, whatever, who, whose, whom, whoever, whomever,* or *that.*

It may also begin with words such as *when, where, before, since,* or *why*. An adjective clause almost always follows the word it modifies, as in the following examples:

> We hired the candidates **who came with the strongest recommendations.**
>
> The child **whom you saw in the magazine is my niece.**

For more information: on **relative pronouns**, see page 16; on grammatically incorrect adjective clauses, see **Dangling Modifiers** on page 67.

Adverb Clauses

An adverb clause is a subordinate clause that modifies a verb, an adjective, an adverb, or a verbal. Adverb clauses usually begin with subordinating conjunctions. Unlike adjective clauses, adverb clauses can be separated from the word they modify and can be placed anywhere in the sentence. If the clause is placed at the beginning or in the middle of a sentence, if is often set off by commas.

> **Since the guests were so convivial, I soon forgot my troubles.**
>
> **Since the guests were so convivial** explains why **I soon forgot my troubles** and therefore functions as an adverb.

For more information: on **subordinate conjunctions**, see page 47; gramatically incorrect adjective clauses, see **Dangling Modifiers** on page 67.

Noun Clauses

A noun clause is a subordinate clause that acts as a noun. Noun clauses can function as subjects, objects, and predicate nouns within sentences. They begin either with a relative pronoun or with a word such as *how, why, where, when, if,* or *whether*.

Noun clauses can be difficult to identify. Since so many different words can be used to begin a noun clause, the opening word itself cannot be used as a determinant. You must discover the function of the clause within the sentence to identify it as a noun clause.

As subject
> **Whoever washes the dishes** *will be allowed to choose which program to watch.*

As direct object
> *Do you know where they went* **on vacation?**

As object of a preposition
> *They talked about whether they could take* **the time off from work.**

As predicate nominative
> *That is* **what I meant.**

Elliptical Clauses

An elliptical clause is a subordinate clause that is grammatically incomplete but nonetheless clear because the missing element can be understood from the rest of the sentence.

> The word elliptical comes from ellipsis, which means "omission." The verb from the second part of the comparison may be missing, or the relative pronouns that, which, and whom may be omitted from adjectival clauses. Often, elliptical clauses begin with as or than, although any subordinating conjunction that makes logical sense can be used. In the following examples, the omitted words are supplied in parentheses:

> *Chad's younger cousin is as tall as he (is).*
> *Aruba is among the islands (that) they visited on their recent cruise.*
> *When (he was) only a child, Barry was taken on a tour around the world.*
> *Although (they were) common fifty years ago, passenger pigeons are extinct today.*

For information on dependent clauses as **fragments** or incomplete sentences, see page 64.

Sentences

A sentence is the expression of a complete thought. In order for a sentence to be a complete sentence, it must have both a subject and a predicate, being the two basic parts of every sentence.

The simple subject is the noun or pronoun that identifies the person, place, or thing the sentence is about. The complete subject is the simple subject and all the words that describe or modify it. The predicate contains the verb and explains what the subject is doing. The simple predicate contains only the verb; the complete predicate contains the verb and any complements and modifiers.

Subject	Predicate
The motorcycle	*veered away from the boulder.*
Calico cats	*are always female.*

In order for a sentence to be complete sentence, it must contain both a subject and predicate, both of which are discussed below.

Subjects

As noted, the subject is the noun or pronoun that is doing the action. Often, it will be located at the beginning of the sentence, as in the following example:

I recommend that company highly.

Here, the subject *I* is doing the action *"recommend."*

Sometimes the subject will follow the verb, as in questions and in sentences beginning with here and there.

*There are two **roads** you can take.*

In the above example, the verb "are" comes before the subject **roads** but nonetheless agrees with it.

The same is true of the placement of the subject and verb in the following question, as the verb "is" comes before the subject "briefcase":

*Where is your **briefcase?***

Hard-to-Locate Subjects
In some instances, the subject can be difficult to locate. In commands or directions, for instance, the subject is often not stated because it is understood to be you.

> Subject: Predicate:
> (you)   *Please unload the dishwasher and tidy the kitchen.*
> (you)   *Just tell me what happened that evening.*

In questions, too, subjects can be difficult to locate because they often follow the verb rather than come before it. Rewriting the question as a statement will make it easier to find the subject.

Question
> *Are **you** planning to go to Oregon this weekend or next?*

Rewritten as a statement
> ***You** are planning to go to Oregon this weekend or next.*

> If you are having trouble locating the subject of a sentence beginning with there or here, try rephrasing the sentence:

> *There is your **wallet** on the table.*
> *Here are the **peaches** from the farm market.*

Rewritten
> *Your **wallet** is there on the table.*
> *The **peaches** from the farm market are here.*

Agreement
A subject must agree with its verb in number. A singular subject takes a singular verb. A plural subject takes a plural verb.

To determine whether or not to use the singular or plural form of the verb, after you have located the subject, decide whether that subject is singular or plural.

> If the subject is plural, it takes the plural form of the verb:

> *The **bicycles** are red.*
> ***Frank, Sarah, and Jay** eat lunch together everyday.*

> There are a number of plural nouns that are regarded as singular in meaning, as well as other nouns that can be both singular and plural, depending on the context of the

sentence. Acoustics, athletics, economics, gymnastics, mathematics, physics, politics, and statistics, for example, are often treated as singular nouns.

Acoustics is the branch of physics that deals with sound.
The **acoustics** in the new hall **are** excellent.
Statistics is the science that deals with the collection and analysis of numerical data.
The **statistics show** that the town's population has increased by 22 percent in the past decade.

Often, a phrase or clause will intervene between a subject and a verb. These intervening words do not affect subject–verb agreement, as illustrated in the following example:

The **supervisor** of the department, together with her sales force, **is** taking the 8:30 shuttle to Washington.

Even though **sales force** is plural, the third-person singular **is** is used because **supervisor** is the subject of that verb.

Singular subjects connected by *or, nor, either . . . or,* and *neither . . . nor* take a singular verb if both subjects are singular, a plural verb if both subjects are plural.

Either your supervisor or your colleague has to take responsibility for the error.
Neither boots nor shoes are included in the one-day sale.

If a subject consists of both singular and plural nouns or pronouns connected by *or* or *nor,* the verb usually agrees with the nearer noun or pronoun.

In the following sentence, the plural verb **want** is closest to the plural noun **students** and, therefore agrees with it:

Neither the teacher nor the students want to be here.

Notice that the verb becomes singular when **teacher** and **students** are reversed:

Neither the students nor the teacher wants to be here.

Practice in this matter varies, however, and often the presence of one plural subject, no matter what its position, results in the use of a plural verb. Sometimes writers place the plural subject closer to the verb to avoid awkwardness:

Awkward
Neither we nor she has distributed the memo yet.

Revised
Neither she nor we have distributed the memo yet.

> Two or more subjects, phrases, or clauses connected by **and** take a plural verb because whether the individual subjects are singular or plural, together they form a compound subject, which is always plural:
>
> **The president and her advisers were** behind schedule.
> **The faculty and staff have** planned a joint professional retreat.

However, when the subjects joined by *and* refer to the same object or person or stand for a single idea, the entire subject is treated as a unit. Most often, the personal pronoun or article before the parts of the compound subject indicates whether the subject is indeed seen as a unit.

> As with other matters of agreement, this varies widely in actual use:

Singular
Ham and Swiss is my favorite sandwich.

> In this example, **Ham and Swiss** is treated as a singular type of sandwich
>
> My **mentor and friend guides** me through difficult career decisions.
>
> **Mentor and friend** are the same person and therefore the third-person singular form **guides** is used.

Plural
Ham and Swiss make a great sandwich.

> Here, each ingredient is treated as separate.

My mentor and my friend guide *me through difficult career decisions.*

Mentor and friend are two different people in this example.

Mixed units
Ham and eggs was *once considered a nutritious and healthful breakfast; now,* ***cereal and fresh fruit are*** *considered preferable.*

Nouns that refer to weight, extent, time, fractions, portions, or amount considered as one unit usually take a singular verb; those that indicate separate units usually take a plural verb.

In the first example below, the subject is considered as a single unit and therefore takes a singular verb. In the last example, the subjects are considered as individual items and therefore take a plural verb.

Seventy-five cents is *more than enough to buy what you want at the penny carnival.*
Fifty pounds of homegrown tomatoes are *being divided among the eager shoppers.*

Inverted Sentences
Inverted sentences place the subject after the verb for emphasis.

High on the cliff above the ocean ***stood the diver.***

On a rack behind the door ***hung a dripping raincoat.***
Even more significant ***was the lack of a firm objective.***

In these examples, the ending subjects **diver, raincoat,** and **the lack of a firm objective** become the focus of the sentences as they are placed at the end of their sentences.

Predicates and Complements

In addition to a verb, complete predicates often contain a complement. A complement is a word or word group that completes the meaning of the verb. There are four primary kinds of sentence complements: direct objects, indirect objects, object complements, and predicate nominatives (nouns, pronouns, and adjectives). Predicate nominatives are also called subject complements.

Direct Objects

A direct object is the noun, pronoun, or word acting as a noun that completes the meaning of a transitive verb by receiving the action. (Intransitive verbs do not have direct objects.)

> To help decide if a word is a direct object, ask What? or Whom? after an action verb:
>
> Martha won **the stuffed dog.**
>
> What did she win? **The stuffed dog** which is the direct object of the sentence.

For more information on **transitive and intransitive** verbs, see page 20.

Indirect Objects

An indirect object is a noun or pronoun that names the person or thing that something is done to or given to.

> Indirect objects are located after the verb and before the direct object and are therefore found only in sentences that have direct objects. Indirect objects answer the questions "To whom?" "For whom?" "To what?" or "For what?"
>
> My aunt lent **me** her motorcycle.
>
> To whom did my aunt lend her motorcycle? To **me,** the indirect object of the sentence.

Object Complements

An object complement is a noun or adjective immediately following a direct object. It either renames or describes the direct object.

> She called him a **fool.**
> We made the platypus **our mascot.**
>
> In describing the direct objects "him" and "platypus," **fool** and **our mascot** function as direct objects.

Subject Complements or Predicate Nominatives

Subject complements, like object complements, are also found in the predicate of a sentence.

A subject complement is a noun, pronoun, or adjective that follows a linking verb and gives further information about the subject of a sentence.

> A predicate noun or pronoun follows a linking verb to identify the subject of a sentence:
>
> *The new head of the division will be* **Henry Williams.**
> *Which of those two phones is the* **newer one?**
>
> A predicate adjective follows a linking verb to describe the subject of a sentence:
>
> *The vegetable soup smells* **delicious.**
> *My daughter's stamp collection grows* **larger** *and* **more valuable** *every day.*

Sentence Forms and Forming Sentences

Now that you know the basic parts of a sentence—subject, verb, and complement(s)—you can begin to see how complete sentences are formed.

The following five sentence forms are the basic templates on which all sentences are built.

1. Subject + intransitive verb
   Bond prices fell.
2. Subject + transitive verb + direct object
   Bob hummed the song.
3. Subject + transitive verb + direct object + object complement
   The committee appointed Eric secretary.
4. Subject + linking verb + subject complement
   The gift was a silk scarf.
5. Subject + transitive verb + indirect object + direct object
   The clerk gave us the receipt.

Independent and dependent clauses can be combined in various ways to create four basic types of sentences: simple, compound, complex, and compound-complex.

Simple Sentences

A simple sentence is one independent clause, being a group of words that contain simply a subject and a predicate. This does not mean, however, that a simple sentence must be short. Both the subject and the verb may be compounded. In addition, a simple sentence may contain describing phrases. By definition, though, a simple sentence cannot have a subordinate clause or another independent clause.

Heather shopped.

Heather is the subject, **shopped** is the predicate.

Either my mother or my great-aunt bought and wrapped this lovely crystal decanter.

In this sentence **Either my mother or my great aunt** functions as the compound subject; **bought and wrapped** is the compound predicate; **this lovely crystal decanter** is the phrase functioning as a direct object.

Compound Sentences

A compound sentence is two or more independent clauses joined together. Since the clauses in a compound sentence are independent, each can be written as an individual sentence. A compound sentence does not have dependent clauses. The independent clauses can be connected by a comma and a coordinating conjunction (and, but, or, for, so, yet) or by a semicolon. If the clauses are very short, the comma before the coordinating conjunction may be omitted.

Mary went to the concert, but Bill stayed home with the baby.
Eddie typed the report in three hours; Fran spent five hours editing it.
I ate lunch and then I took a nap.

For more information on using **semicolons** and **commas**, see page 127.

Complex Sentences

A complex sentence contains one independent clause and one or more subordinate clauses. To distinguish it from the other clauses, the independent clause in a complex sentence is called the main clause. In a complex sentence, each clause has its own subject and verb. The subject in the main clause is called the subject of the sentence; the verb in the main clause is called the main verb. An independent clause can stand alone as a complete sentence; a dependent clause cannot.

> As we were looking over your sign-in sheets for May and June, **we noticed a number of minor problems.**

> In this example, **we noticed a number of minor problems,** because it could stand alone as a sentence, is the main clause. The words preceding the main clause would not form a complete sentence without the main clause and is therefore the dependent clause.

Compound-Complex Sentences

A compound-complex sentence has at least two independent clauses and at least one dependent clause. The compound-complex sentence is so named because it shares the characteristics of both compound and complex sentences. Like the compound sentence, the compound-complex has at least two main clauses. Like the complex sentence, it has at least one subordinate clause. The subordinate clause can be part of an independent clause.

> When the heat comes, **the lakes dry up,** and **farmers know that their crops will fail.**

> As you probably guessed, **the lakes dry up** and **farmers know that their crops will fail** are the main clauses; **when the heat comes** is the dependent or subordinate clause.

Sentence Functions

In addition to the form they take, sentences, like parts of speech, can also be classified according to their function. There are four main types of sentences: declarative, interrogative, imperative, and exclamatory.

Declarative Sentences
A declarative sentence makes a statement and always ends with a period:

On Thursday we are going to see a movie.
We have been waiting for two weeks for the movie to open here.

Interrogative Sentences
An interrogative sentence asks a question and always ends with a question mark:

Are we going to see the movie on Tuesday?
How long have you been waiting for the movie to open?

Imperative Sentences
An imperative sentence makes a command. In many instances, the subject of an imperative sentence is understood to be *you* and is therefore not stated. In other instances, the sentence may be phrased as a question but does not end with a question mark.

As a statement
Take this money in case you change your mind.
Clean up that mess!

As a question
Will you please reply at your earliest convenience.
Would someone please move those books to the top shelf.

Exclamatory Sentences
An exclamatory sentence conveys strong feeling and always ends with an exclamation point. Many exclamatory sentences are very strongly stated declarative sentences. Since the exclamatory sentence conveys strong emotions, they should be used sparingly in formal writing.

They still haven't called!
The dress is ruined!

Sentence Errors
Sentence errors fall into three main divisions: parts of sentences set off as though they were complete (fragments), two or more

sentences incorrectly joined (run-ons), and sentence parts misplaced or poorly connected to the rest of the sentence (misplaced, dangling, or squinting modifiers).

Fragments

A fragment is part of a sentence presented as though it were a complete sentence. The fragment may lack a subject or verb or both, or it may be a subordinate clause not connected to a complete sentence. Since fragments are not complete sentences, they do not express complete thoughts.

No subject
   Ran to catch the bus.
   Ate all the chocolate hidden in the drawer.

No main verb:
   The box sitting in the trunk.
   The man in the room.

No subject or main verb
   Feeling happy.
   Acting poorly.

No independent clause
   When I woke him up early this morning.
   If it is as pleasant as you expect today.

Correcting Fragments

Fragments are often created when phrases and subordinate clauses are punctuated as though they were complete sentences. Recall that phrases can never stand alone because they are groups of words that do not have subjects or verbs. To correct phrase fragments, add the information they need to be complete.

Phrase fragment
   a big house

Corrected
   A big house **at the end of the block burned down last night.**
   My sister recently bought a big house.
   She earned enough money to buy a big house.

In the first example, the fragment becomes the subject of the predicate that has been added. In the second example, the fragment becomes the direct object as the subject and verb have been added. In the third example, the fragment becomes the object of the preposition as a subject, verb, and direct object have been added.

Subordinate clauses, unlike phrases, contain subjects and verbs. Like phrases, however, they do not convey complete thoughts. A subordinate clause can be completed by connecting it to a main clause or by dropping the subordinating conjunction.

Subordinating clause fragment
If it is as pleasant as you expected today.

Corrected
It is as pleasant as you expected today.
If it is as pleasant as you expected today, **we will be able to go to the beach.**

In the first example, the subordinating conjunction "if" has been dropped. In the second example, an independent clause has been added.

Run-ons

A run-on is two complete ideas incorrectly joined. Run-ons are generally classified as either comma splices or fused sentences.

A comma splice incorrectly joins two independent clauses with a comma.

Mary walked into the room, she found a mouse on her desk.

A fused sentence runs two independent clauses together without an appropriate conjunction or mark of punctuation:

Many people are afraid of computers they do not realize how easy it is to learn basic tasks.

Correcting Run-on Sentences
There are four ways to correct both the comma splices and the fused sentences that are reflected in the above examples.

1. Separate the clauses into two sentences.
   Mary walked into the room. She found a mouse on her desk.
   Many people are afraid of computers. They do not realize how easy it is to learn basic tasks.
2. Insert a comma and coordinating conjunction between clauses to create a compound sentence.
   Mary walked into the room, and she found a mouse on her desk.
   Many people are afraid of computers, for they do not realize how easy it is to learn basic tasks.
3. Insert a semicolon between the clauses.
   Mary walked into the room; she found a mouse on her desk.
   Many people are afraid of computers; they do not realize how easy it is learn basic tasks.
4. Subordinate one clause to the other to create a complex sentence.
   When Mary walked into the room, she found a mouse on her desk.
   Many people are afraid of computers because they do not realize how easy it is to learn basic tasks.

For more information on **comma splices**, see page 65.

Misplaced Modifiers

A misplaced modifier occurs when the modifier appears to describe a word it was not intended to describe.

As a general rule, a modifier should be placed as close as possible to the word it modifies. When a clause, phrase, or word is placed too far from the word it modifies, the sentence may fail to convey the intended meaning and therefore produce ambiguity or amusement. When this occurs, the modifier is called "misplaced."

Words Misplaced
   I **almost drank** a whole quart of water.

Revised
   I **drank almost** a whole quart of water.

> Note the difference in meaning in the examples. In the first example, the sentence could mean that the speaker did not drink any water; in the second example the intended meaning—the speaker drank nearly a whole quart—is clearly expressed.

Phrases misplaced
   We all stared at the woman who was talking to the **governor with green spiked hair.**

Revised
   We all stared at the **woman with green spiked hair** who was talking to the governor.

   In the first example, the governor is described as having **green spiked hair.** The intended meaning of the sentence is reflected in the revised example.

Clauses misplaced
   I bought Brie **in the new shop on North Road that cost $8.00 a pound.**

   We saved the balloons for the children **that had been left on the table.**

Revised
   I bought Brie **that costs $8.00 a pound in the new shop on North Road.**
   We saved the balloons **that had been left on the table** for the children.

Dangling Modifiers

A dangling—or unattached—modifier occurs when a modifier, the phrase or clause meant to describe a noun or pronoun, does not logically or grammatically describe anything in the sentence because the noun or pronoun to which the modifier refers is either in the wrong place or missing. Like misplaced modifiers, dangling modifiers cause confusion.

Dangling modifiers
   While **reading the paper,** the birds on the railing caught my eye.
   Drinking a cup of coffee, the cat leaped on the table.

Revised:
   While **I was reading the paper,** the birds on the railing caught my eye.
   While **I was drinking a cup of coffee,** the cat leaped on the table.

Because the modifiers **reading the paper** and **drinking a cup of coffee** are not firmly attached to the subject **I** in the first examples, we might believe they are associated with the subjects of the main clauses, being **the birds** and **the cat** (neither of which can read the paper or drink a cup of coffee).

Squinting Modifiers

A "squinting" modifier can refer to either a preceding or following word and therefore cause ambiguity and confusion.

Squinting modifier
  *The case that the prosecution had **prepared quickly** forced it to declare the defendant's sister a hostile witness.*

  In this example, it is not clear if **quickly** refers to the speed at which the prosecution is to **declare the defendant's sister a hostile witness** or the rate at which **the prosecution had prepared** the case.

Revised
  *The case that the prosecution had **quickly prepared** forced it to declare the defendant's sister a hostile witness.*

  Or

  *The case that the prosecution had **prepared** forced it to **quickly** declare the defendant's sister a hostile witness.*

2

Usage Basics

In the previous section we looked at the functions of words as they are reflected in the nature of the various parts of speech. In this section, we will examine the actual use of words in sentences. A recurring theme in this section is the importance of maintaining consistency in *style, tone, structure, mood, tense, voice, perspective* and *person*. As you will see, consistency often allows ideas to be expressed more clearly and prevents reader confusion.

Style

Shifts in Tone and Style

Tone is the writer's attitude toward his or her readers and subject. As pitch and volume convey tone in speaking, so word choice and sentence structure help convey tone in writing. Tone can be formal or informal, humorous or earnest, distant or friendly, pompous or personal. Different tones are appropriate for different audiences, meaning that writers should first gain an understanding of their audience before adopting a particular tone.

Style is a writer's way of writing. Style comprises every way a writer uses language. Elements of style include tone, word choice, figurative language, grammatical structure, rhythm, and sentence length and organization. A piece of writing is more powerful and effective if consistent tone and style are maintained throughout.

Shift
   Reporters who assert that freedom of the press can be maintained without judicial intervention are out of their minds.

The style of the sentence shifts from elevated or formal to colloquial or informal. The first clause, **Reporters . . . intervention** reflects a formal use of language, while **out of their minds** is an informal phrase. If the writer is to maintain a consistency, the sentence should be rewritten to reflect a uniform style, as in the following example.

Revised
Reporters who assert that freedom of the press can be maintained without judicial intervention are greatly mistaken.

Replacing **out of their minds** with the more formal **greatly mistaken** allows the sentence to maintain a consistent style.

Note the shifts in style in the sentence below and the revised that creates a uniform style amongst the two sentences.

Shift
Their leave taking was marked by the same affability that had characterized their entire visit with us. Later, we discussed what **cool dudes** they were.

Revised
Their leave taking was marked by the same affability that had characterized their entire visit with us. Later, we discussed **their good humor, consideration, and generosity.**

Parallel Structure

Parallel structure, or parallelism, means that grammatical elements that share the same function will share the same form. Parallel structure also ensures that ideas of equal rank are expressed in similar ways and that separate word groups appear in the same grammatical forms.

Individual words, phrases, clauses, or sentences can be paralleled. For example, adjectives are paired with adjectives, and verbs correspond with matching verbs in tense, mood, voice, and number (discussed below under Using Verbs). Parallel structure helps coordinate ideas and improves the readability of sentences.

Adjectives

In the first example below **needed food,** a two-word verbal functioning as an adjective that describes "Allison", is not parallel with **hot** and **cranky,** single adjectives that also describe "Allison". Replacing **needed food** with **hungry** maintains parallelism through the consistent use of single adjectives to describe "Allison". Lacking parallelism, the first example sounds clumsy, particularly when it is compared to the second example.

Not parallel
Allison was hot, cranky, and **needed food.**

Parallel
Allison was **hot, cranky, and hungry.**

The examples below also reveal the advantages of adhering to the rules of parallelism with respect to adjectives.

Not parallel
Sam is **organized, efficient, and works hard.**

Parallel
Sam is **organized, efficient, and industrious.**

Not parallel
Cursed be the social wants that sin against the strength of youth!
Cursed be the social ties that warp us from the living truth!
Cursed be the sickly forms that err from honest nature's rule!
The gold that gilds the straighten'd forehead of the fool is also **cursed.**

Parallel
Cursed be the social wants that sin against the strength of youth!
Cursed be the social ties that warp us from the living truth!
Cursed be the sickly forms that err from honest nature's rule!
Cursed be the gold that gilds the straighten'd forehead of the fool.

Verbs

In the first example below, the verb "know" is written as both a gerund (**knowing**) and as and infinitive (**to know**). The use of the verb in the sentence is therefore not parallel. This is corrected in the second example in which **knowing** is used in both clauses.

Not parallel
> **Knowing how to** win is important, but **it is even more important to know how** to lose.

Parallel
> **Knowing how to** win is important, but **knowing how to** lose is even more important.

In the examples below, the sentences have been corrected to reflect a consistent use of verb forms, thereby maintaining parallelism.

Not parallel
> **We can go out** to eat, or **ordering** a pizza would do as well.

Parallel
> **We can go out** to eat, or **we can order** a pizza.

Not parallel
> He has **plundered** our seas, **ravaged** our coasts, and **was burning** our towns.

Parallel
> He has **plundered** our seas, **ravaged** our coasts, and **burnt** our towns.

Nouns

In the first example below, the noun **knowledge** is used in the first clause, while two nouns, **ignorant** and **thing,** are used in the second clause. The second example expresses the same ideas, while maintaining parallelism by using the same number of nouns in both clauses.

Not parallel
> The only good is **knowledge,** and evil is the only **ignorant thing.**

Parallel
> The only good is **knowledge,** and the only evil is **ignorance.**

Series

Items in a series have greater impact when arranged in parallel order. The items can be phrases, clauses, or individual words as in the example below:

Passions, prejudices, fears, and **neuroses** spring from ignorance, and take the form of **myth** and **illusions.**
—Sir Isaiah Berlin

In the opening of A Tale of Two Cities, Charles Dickens arranged paired items in a series for a powerful effect:

It was the **best of times,** it was the **worst of times,** it was the **age of wisdom,** it was the **age of foolishness, it was the** epoch of belief, it was the **epoch of incredulity,** it was the **season of Light,** it was the **season of Darkness,** it was the **spring of hope,** it was the **winter of despair . . .**

Using Verbs

Shifts in Mood

As noted on page 31, English has three moods: indicative, imperative, and subjunctive. Abruptly shifting from one mood to one another can confuse the reader, making one's writing less effective.

Confusing
   Stroke the paint on evenly, but **you should not** dab it on corners and edges.

   Confusion is caused because the first clause (**Stroke the paint**) is in the imperative and the second clause **you should not** is in the indicative. Note how much smoother the revised sentence, below, reads.

Revised
   Stroke the paint on evenly, but **don't** dab it on corners and edges.

Or
   You should stroke the paint on evenly, but **you shouldn't** dab it on corners and edges.

   In the revised sentences, the shift is avoided because all the verbs within the sentence are in the same mood. In the first example, both clauses are in the imperative. In the second example, both clauses are in the indicative.

The examples below demonstrate the pitfalls of shifting moods in a sentence and possible ways of rewriting those sentences to avoid such shifts.

Confusing
The cleaning service **asked that they get** better hours and **they want** to work fewer weekends as well.

In the examples below, the phrases shift from the subjunctive to the indicative.

Revised
The cleaning service **asked that they get** better hours and **that they work** fewer weekends as well.

Or
The cleaning service **asked to work** better hours and fewer weekends.

Or
The cleaning service **wants to work** better hours and fewer weekends.

Confusing
If the rain **stopped** and the sun **comes** out, we could have a picnic.

Revised
If the rain **stopped** and the sun **came** out, we could have a picnic.

Or
If the rain **stops** and the sun **comes** out, we can have a picnic.

For more information on **moods**, see page 31.

Shifts in Tense

A shift in tense occurs when the tenses of verbs within a sentence or paragraph do not logically match. The sequence of tenses refers to the relationship among the verbs within a sentence or in sentences that follow each other. Illogical shifts in verb tenses confuse readers and muddle meaning. For clarity and sense, all the verbs must accurately reflect changes in time. Using tenses correctly allows you to express the desired sequence of events correctly. Note the following example:

Confusing
> Throughout the eighties the junk-bond market **rose** steadily; as a result, small investors **invest** heavily from 1985 to 1989.

Revised
> Throughout the eighties the junk-bond market **rose** steadily; as a result, small investors **invested** heavily from 1985 to 1989.

> In the first example, the sequence of tenses is past (**rose** in the first clause) to present (**invest** in the second clause). The sentence is confusing because the first clause implies an event that has seemingly ended (the "junk-bond market **rose**"), while the second refers to an action that is ongoing.

> In the revised example, since both **rose** and **invested** are in the past tense, the sentence makes more sense and reads much better.

If you are using the present tense to narrate the events in a literary work, be careful not to slip into the past tense.

Simultaneous Actions

> If the actions described occur at approximately the same time, the tenses of all the verbs must be the same, as in the following examples:
> The audience **applauded** when the conductor **mounted** the podium.
> Although we **analyzed** the data, we **could not come** to a firm conclusion.
> William Carlos Williams **was** a pediatrician in Paterson, New Jersey, who **wrote** some of the most distinctive verse of the twentieth century.

> In all of these examples, the actions referred to in the first and second clauses occur at the same time. Hence, the same tense is used in both clauses.

Actions Occurring at Different Times

If the verbs within a sentence describe actions that have occurred, are occurring, or will occur at different times, the tenses of the verbs must be different to express the different time sequence.

> The conference **had been** over for an hour by the time I arrived.
> I asked if he **had consulted** his attorney last week.

In the first example, the past perfect tense (**had been**) is used to refer to an action that has ended before another (i.e. "by the time I **arrived**"). The simple past (**arrived**) is used to show an action that has simply begun and ended.

In the second example, the past perfect **had consulted** is used to signify an action that has ended before the time "I **asked,**" which is in the simple past.

Conditional Sentences

When the situation described in the main clause can only occur if a condition represented in another clause is met, a conditional clause is used. Conditional clauses usually begin with "if" or "unless".

> *We'll stay home **if it rains**.*
> *We'll go **unless it rains**.*

If it rains and **unless it rains** are conditional clauses; **we'll stay** and **we'll go** are the main clauses because the actions to which they refer (**stay** and **go**) can only occur if the actions (**rains**) referred to in the conditional clauses occur.

If the situation described in the main clause is likely to occur, use the present tense in the conditional clause and the future tense ("will" or "won't") in the main clause:

> ***If you take** the train, you **will** be in the center of the city by 3:00.*
> ***If you wear** boots, your feet **won't** get cold.*

If the situation described in the main clause is imaginary or unlikely to occur, use the past tense form in the conditional clause and "would", "might", or "could" in the main clause.

> ***If I had** her address, I **could send** her flowers.*
> ***If wishes were** horses, beggars **would ride**.*
> ***If he called** me, I **might go**.*

If you want to describe a conditional situation that actually occurred in the past, use the past perfect form in the conditional clause and "would have" in the main clause.

If they had arrived *on time, we* ***would have*** *been able to go to a movie.*

The curtains ***would not have*** *gotten wet* ***if I had remembered*** *to close the windows.*

For more information on **tenses**, see page 25.

Voice—Active and Passive

Voice shows whether the subject of a verb acts or is acted upon. There are two voices: active and passive. In the active voice, the subject of the verb does the action to which the verb refers, as in the following example:

*I **hit the ball** across the field.*

In this example, the subject, **I,** does the action, **hit.**

When the subject of the verb receives the action, the verb is in the passive voice:

*The **ball was hit** by me.*

Here, the subject, **ball,** receives the action, i.e., it **was hit.**

To convert an active verb to a passive verb, a form of verb "to be" is used with the past participle.

Active
*The **storms damaged** many homes.*
*Mary's **dog bit** Christopher.*
***Keats wrote** "The Eve of St. Agnes."*
***Sean will make** dinner.*

Passive
*Many **homes were damaged** by the storms.*
***Christopher was bitten** by Mary's dog.*
*"The Eve of St. Agnes" **was written** by Keats.*
***Dinner will be made** by Sean.*

Note: Only transitive verbs (those that take objects) can show voice. For more information on **transitive and intransitive verbs**, see page 20.

Using the Active Voice

In general, use the active voice to emphasize the performer of the action. Except for a small number of specific situations, which are described below, the active voice is usually clearer and more powerful than the passive voice.

>The ball **was passed by me.**
>**I passed** the ball.

>Both sentences express the same idea, yet the first sentence, which is in the passive voice, is much wordier and less clear than the second example, which is in the active voice.

Using the Passive Voice

>The passive voice is preferable to the active voice:

When you do not wish to mention the subject or the performer of the action
>A mistake **has been made.**
>A check **has been returned** marked "insufficient funds."

When it is necessary to avoid vagueness
>**Furniture is manufactured** in Hickory, North Carolina.

>>Writing this sentence in the active voice—**They manufacture furniture in Hickory, North Carolina**—requires using the vague **they.** To whom does **they** refer?

When the performer of the action is not known
>Plans for fifty units of low-income housing **were unveiled** at today's county meeting.
>The computer **was stolen.**

>>The passive voice is used in the first example because the writer does not know who **unveiled** the "plans"; in the second example the writer does not know who **stole** "the computer".

When the object or result of the action is more important than the person performing the action
>**The driver was arrested** for speeding.
>**The chief suspect was freed** on bail pending trial.

>>In the first example, it is more important to know that the "driver" was arrested rather than who actually made the arrest. In the second example, the freeing of the "chief

suspect" is more important than to know who actually did the freeing.

Shifts in Voice

Sentences often more clearly convey information when the same voice is maintained throughout the sentence.

Note the following examples:

Confusing
As **we finished** our coffee, the servers **were seen** clearing the adjacent tables.

Revised
As **we finished** our coffee, **we saw** the servers clearing the adjacent tables.

Maintaining the active voice in both clauses by allowing **we** to be the main performer of the action (**we finished; we saw**) creates a clearer, crisper sentence.

In the examples below, the sentence is revised to make "the cook" the consistent performer of the action or "the bread dough" the consistent recipient of the action.

Confusing
The cook **mixed the bread dough** until it was blended and then **it was set** in the warm oven to rise.

Revised
The cook **mixed the bread dough** until it was blended and then **set it** in the warm oven to rise.

Or
The **bread dough was mixed** until it was blended, and then **it was set** in the warm oven to rise.

Using Nouns and Pronouns

Shifts in Person

Person refers to the form a pronoun or verb takes to show the person or persons speaking: the first person (I, we), the second person (you), or the third person (he, she, it, they). As the pronouns indicate, the first person is the person speaking, the second person is the person spoken to, and the third person is the person, concept, or thing spoken about.

Shifts between second- and third-person pronouns cause the most confusion.

Confusing
When **one** shops for an automobile, **you** should research various models in consumer magazines and read all the advertisements as well as speak to salespeople.

In this example, the second person pronoun **you** follows **one**, a third-person pronoun, resulting in a confusing, less than clear sentence.

Revised
When **you** shop for an automobile, **you** should research various models in consumer magazines and read all the advertisements as well as speak to salespeople.

Or
When **one** shops for an automobile, **one** should research various models in consumer magazines and read all the advertisements as well as speak to salespeople.

Or
When **people** shop for an automobile, **they** should research various models in consumer magazines and read all the advertisements as well as speak to salespeople.

The following examples illustrate common shifts in person and different ways to revise such shifts.

Confusing
When **a person** applies themselves diligently, **you** can accomplish a surprising amount.

Revised
When **people** apply themselves diligently, **they** can accomplish a surprising amount.

Or
When **you** apply yourself diligently, **you** can accomplish a surprising amount.

Or
> When **a person** applies himself or herself diligently, **he or she** can accomplish a surprising amount.

For more information on **personal pronouns**, see page 10.

Shifts in Perspective

Shifts in perspective are related to shifts in person as both change the vantage point from which a story is told. As with other shifts, there will be occasions when it is desirable to shift perspective, but unnecessary shifts confuse readers.

Confusing
> The **frothy surface** of the ocean danced with bursts of light, and **the fish swam lazily through the clear water and waving plants.**

Revised
> The **frothy surface** of the ocean danced with bursts of light; **below, the fish swam lazily through the clear water and waving plants.**

In the above example, the reader's perspective shifts from above the water, where he or she could see **the frothy surface** to below the water where one would have to be to see **fish** swimming through **the clear water and waving plants.** Without a transition to signal this change a perspective, the sentence is confusing. Inserting **below** provides that transition.

Shifts in Number

Number indicates whether the noun or personal pronoun refers to one (singular) or more than one (plural). Shifts in number occur with nouns and personal pronouns because both change form to show differences in number. Confusion with number occurs especially often between a pronoun and its antecedent and between words whose meanings relate to each other. Remember to use singular pronouns to refer to singular antecedents and plural pronouns to refer to plural antecedents.

Confusing
> If **a person** does not keep up with household chores, **they** will find that things pile up with alarming speed.

They, the third-person plural pronoun, is being used to refer to a singular noun—**a person.** Note the revised below:

Revised
If **a person** does not keep up with household chores, **he or she** will find that things pile up with alarming speed.

Or
If **people** do not keep up with household chores, **they** will find that things pile up with alarming speed.

Confusing
All the repair **stations** have a good **reputation.**

In this example, a singular noun, **reputation,** is associate with a plural noun, **stations.**

Revised
All the repair **stations** have good **reputations.**

Person and Number with Collective Nouns

Maintaining consistency of person and number is especially tricky with collective nouns since many can be either singular or plural, depending on the context. Once you establish a collective noun as singular or plural within a sentence, make sure the rest of the sentence is in agreement.

Confusing
Because my **company** bases **their** bonus on amount of income generated yearly, we must all do our share to enable **it** to give a generous bonus.

Their, a plural pronoun, refers to **company. It,** a singular pronoun, also refers to **company.** Note the revised examples below in which the pronouns of the same number are used to refer to the collective noun.

Revised
Because my **company** bases **its** bonus on amount of income generated yearly, we must all do our share to enable **it** to give a generous bonus.

Or
> Because my **company** bases **their** bonus on amount of income generated yearly, we must all do our share to enable **them** to give a generous bonus.

Confusing
> The jury **is** divided on whether or not **they** should demand additional evidence.

Revised
> The jury **are** divided on whether or not **they** should demand additional evidence.

It, They, and You

Using it, they, and you incorrectly will result in a sentence that is vague or wordy. Removing the pronoun, eliminating excess words, or revising the sentence helps produce a clearer and more vigorous style.

Wordy
> In the **cookbook it says** that wooden chopping blocks should be disinfected with bleach.

Better
> The **cookbook says** that wooden chopping blocks should be disinfected with bleach.

Usage Glossary

Language and the way it is used change constantly. This glossary provides a concise guide to contemporary English usage. It will show you how certain words and phrases are used and why certain usage is unacceptable. If you are uncertain how a particular word or phrase is to be used, look it up below.

"Informal" indicates that a word or phrase is often used in everyday speech but should generally be avoided in formal discourse. "Nonstandard" means that the word or phrase is not suitable for everyday speech and writing nor formal discourse and should be avoided entirely.

To gain a fuller understanding of the explanations offered

below, you should consult the preceding Mastering Grammar section for discussions of the parts of speech and their functions.

a/an In both spoken and written English, an is used before words beginning with a vowel sound (He carried **an umbrella**. The Nobel is **an honor**.) and when the consonants f, h, l, m, n, r, s, and x are pronounced by name (The renovations created **an L-shaped** room. Miles received **an F** in physics.)

Use a before words beginning with a consonant sound (What **a fish**! I bought **a computer**) and words that start with vowels but are pronounced as consonants (**A union** can be dissolved. They live in **a one-room** apartment). Also use a with words that start with consonant letters not listed above and with the vowel u (She earned **a C** in French. He made **a U-turn**).

For words that begin with h, if the initial h is not pronounced, the word is preceded by an (It will take **an hour**). Adjectives such as historic, historical, heroic, and habitual are commonly preceded by an, especially in British English, but the use of a is common in both writing and speech (She read **a historical** novel). When the h is strongly pronounced, as in a stressed first syllable, the word is preceded by a (I bought **a history** of Long Island).

a number/the number As a subject, a number is most often plural and the number is singular (**A number** of choices **are** available; **The number** of choices **is** limited). This guideline is followed more often in formal discourse than in speech and informal writing.

above Above is most commonly a preposition (They live on the floor **above us**) but it can also be used as an adjective (The **above entry** is incomplete). When referring to an item that has been mentioned previously, it can be used as a noun (First, please read **the above**). Both uses are standard in formal writing.

ain't The term is nonstandard for "am not," "isn't," or "aren't." It is used in informal speech and writing for humorous effect or for emphasis, usually in dialogue.

all right/alright All right is always written as two words: alright is a misspelling (Betsy said that it was all right to use her car that afternoon).

almost/most Almost, an adverb, means "nearly"; most, an adjective, means "the greatest part of" something. Most is not synonymous with almost (During our vacation we shop at that store **almost every day** and buy **most of the available snack foods**).

In informal speech, most (as a shortened form of almost) is used as an adverb. It occurs before such pronouns as all, anyone, anybody, everyone, and everybody; the adjectives all, any, and every; and the adverbs anywhere and everywhere (**Most everyone** around here is related).

The use of most as an adverb is nonstandard and is uncommon in formal writing except when used to represent particular dialects of speech.

a.m., p.m./a.m., p.m. These abbreviations for time are most frequently restricted to use with figures: The ceremony begins at **10:00 a.m.** (not "ten a.m.").

Usage Basics

among/between Among is used to indicate relationships involving more than two people or things, while between is used to show relationships involving two people or things, or to compare one thing to a group to which it belongs (The three quarreled **among themselves** because she had to choose between two of them).

Between is also used to express relationships of persons or things considered individually, no matter how many (**Between holding public office, teaching, and raising a family,** she has little free time).

and/or The combination and/or is used mainly in legal and business writing. Its use should be avoided in general writing. Rather then write "He spent the day watching television **and/or** snacking," decide whether "He spent the day watching television" or "He spent the day snacking" or "He spent the day watching television *and* snacking". If you mean "either," use or; if you mean "both," use and. To make a greater distinction, revise the phrasing (He spends his weekends watching television, snacking, *or* both).

and which/and who "And" is unnecessary when "which" or "who" is used to open a relative clause. Use "and which" or "and who" only to open a second clause starting with the same relative pronoun (Elizabeth is my neighbor **who** goes shopping every morning **and who calls me every afternoon** to tell me about the sales).

anyplace Anyplace is an informal expression for "anywhere." It occurs in speech and informal writing but is best avoided in formal prose.

anyways/anyway; anywheres/anywhere Anyways is nonstandard for anyway; anywheres is nonstandard for anywhere.

as Do not use as in place of whether: We're not sure whether (not "as") you should do that. Also avoid using as as a substitute for because, since, while, whether, or who, where its use may create confusion. As may mean "while" or "because" (**As** they were driving to California they decided to see the Grand Canyon).

as/because/since While all three words can function as subordinating conjunctions, they carry slightly different shades of meaning. As establishes a time relationship and can be used interchangeably with "when" or "while": **As** (or when) we brought out the food, it began to drizzle. Because and since, in contrast, describe causes and effects: **Because** (or since) Nancy goes skiing infrequently, she prefers to rent skis.

as/like When as functions as a preposition, the distinction between as and like depends on meaning. As suggests that the subject is equivalent to the description (**He** was employed **as a teacher**). Like, in contrast, suggests similarity but not equivalence (**Speakers like her** excel in front of large groups).

at Avoid using at after "where": Where are you seeing her (not "at")? Whether used as an adverb or as a preposition, "where" contains the preposition "at" in its definition.

at this point in time Although the term at this point in time is widely used (especially in politics), many consider it wordy and stuffy. Instead, use "now" or "at this time": We are not **now** ready to discuss the new budget, rather than We are not ready to discuss the new budget at this time.

awful/awfully Avoid using awful or awfully to mean "very" in formal discourse: We had a very (not "awfully") busy time at the amusement park. Although the use of awful to mean "terrible" (rather than "inspiring awe") has permeated all levels of writing and speech, consider using in its place a word that more closely matches your intended meaning: We had an unpleasant (not "awful") time because the park was hot, noisy, and crowded.

awhile/a while Awhile is an adverb and is always spelled as one word (We visited **awhile**). A while is a noun phrase (an article and a noun) and is used after a preposition (We rested **for a while**).

backward/backwards In formal discourse, backward is preferred: This stroke is easier if you use a **backward** motion (as an adjective). Counting **backward** from 100 can be an effective way to induce sleep (as an adverb).

bad/badly Bad, an adjective, is used to describe a noun or pronoun. Badly, an adverb, is used to describe a verb, adjective, or another adverb. (She felt **bad** because her broken leg throbbed **badly**.)

because/due to the fact that/since Because or since is preferred over the wordy phrase due to the fact that: He wrote the report longhand **because** (not "due to the fact that") his computer was broken.

being as/being that Avoid both being as and being that in formal writing. Instead, use "since" or "because." (**Since** you asked, I'll be glad to help).

better/had better The verb "had" is necessary in the phrase had better and should be retained (She **had better** return the lawn mower today).

between you and I Between you and I is incorrect because I is in the nominate case and pronouns that function as objects of prepositions, such as between, are traditionally used in the objective case (Please keep this between **you** and **me**. I would appreciate it if you could keep this between **her** and **them**).

between see **among/between**

bi- Many words that refer to periods of time through the prefix bi- (bimonthly, biannually) are potentially confusing. Ambiguity is avoided by using the prefix semi-, meaning "twice each" or occurring twice during the period of time mentioned, (semiweekly, semimonthly, semiannual). Confusion can also be avoided by using the appropriate phrases (twice a week, twice each month, every two months, every two years).

borrow off/borrow from Borrow off, considered informal, is not used in formal speech and writing; borrow from is the preferred expression.

bottom line This overworked term is frequently used as a synonym for "outcome" or "the final result" (The **bottom line** is that we have to reduce inventory to maintain profits). Careful writers and speakers avoid it for less common descriptions.

bunch Use the noun bunch in formal writing only to refer to clusters of things grouped together, such as a bunch of grapes or a bunch of bananas. In formal writing, use group or crowd to refer to gatherings of people; bunch is used to refer to groups of people or items only in speech and informal writing.

burst, bursted/bust, busted Burst is a verb meaning "to come apart suddenly." Both the past tense and the past participle are burst. The word bursted is not acceptable in either speech or writing. The verb bust and the adjective busted are both informal or slang terms; as such, they should not be used in formal writing.

but however/but yet There is no reason to combine but with another conjunction: She said she was leaving, yet (not "but yet") she poured another cup of coffee.

but that/but what As with the previous example, there is no reason to add the word but to either that or what: We don't doubt that (not "but that") you will win this hand.

calculate/figure/reckon None of these words is an acceptable substitute for expect or imagine in formal writing, although they are used in speech and informal prose.

can/may Traditionally, may is used in formal writing to convey permission; can, ability or capacity. In speech, however, the terms are used interchangeably to mean permission: Can (May) I borrow your hedge clippers? Can and may are frequently but not always interchangeable when used to mean possibility: A blizzard can (or may) occur any time during February. In negative constructions, can't is more common than mayn't, the latter being rare.

cannot/can not Cannot is occasionally spelled can not. The one-word spelling is by far the more common. The contraction can't is used mainly in speech and informal writing.

can't help but Can't help but, as in: You **can't help but** like her, is a double negative. This idiom can be replaced by the informal can't help or the formal cannot but where each is appropriate (You *can't help liking* her; You *cannot* help but like her). While can't help but is common in all types of speech, avoid using it in formal writing.

cause of . . . on account of/due to The phrases on account of and due to are unnecessary with cause of. Omit the phrases or revise the entire sentence. One cause of physical and psychological problems is **due to** too much stress can be rewritten *Too much stress causes physical and psychological problems.*

center around/center on Although both phrases are often criticized for being illogical, they have been used in writing for more than a hundred years to express the notion of collecting or gathering as if around a center point. The phrase revolve around is often suggested as an alternative, and the prepositions at, in, and on are considered acceptable with center (Their problems **centered on** their lack of expertise).

chair/chairperson Chairperson is used widely in academic and governmental circles as an alternative to "chairman" or "chairwoman." While some reject the term chairperson as clumsy and unnecessary and use the term chair for any presiding officer, regardless of sex, chairperson is still standard in all types of writing and speech.

choose/chose Choose is a verb that means "to select one thing in preference to another" (Why **choose** tomatoes when they are out of season?). Chose is the past tense of "to choose (I **chose** tomatoes over cucumbers at the salad bar).

conformity to/conformity with Although the word conformity can be followed by either "to" or "with," conformity to is generally used when the idea of obedience is implied (The new commissioner issued a **demand for conformity to** health regulations). Conformity with is used to imply agreement or correspondence (This is an idea in **conformity with previous planning**).

consensus/consensus of The expression consensus of (consensus of opinion) is considered redundant, and the preferred usage is the single noun consensus, meaning "general agreement or concord" (Since the **consensus** was overwhelming, the city planners moved ahead with the proposal). The phrase general consensus is also considered redundant. Increasingly, the word consensus is widely used attributively, as in the phrase consensus politics.

Contact The word is both a verb and a noun. As a verb, it is frequently used imprecisely to mean "to communicate" when a more exact word (telephone, write to, consult) would better communicate the idea. Contact as a noun meaning "a person through whom one can obtain information" is now standard usage (He is **my contact** in the state department).

couple/couple of Both phrases are informally used to mean "two" or "several" (I need a **couple more** cans of paint. I took a **couple of** aspirins for my headache). The expression a couple of is used in standard English, especially in referring to distance, money, or time (He is **a couple of** feet away. I have **a couple of** thousand dollars in the bank). Couple may be treated as either a singular or plural noun.

criteria/criterion Criteria is the plural of criterion, meaning a standard for judgment (Of all their **criteria** for evaluating job performance, customer satisfaction was the most important **criterion**).

data/datum Data is the plural of datum, meaning facts. Although data is often used as a singular, it should still be treated as plural in formal speech and writing: The **data pertain** (not "pertains") to the first half of the experiment. To avoid awkward constructions, most writers prefer to use a more commonplace term such as "fact" or "figure" in place of datum.

decimate The word decimate comes from a Latin term that meant "to select by lot and kill one person in ten of (a rebellious military unit)." The usual use of the word in English is "to destroy a large amount or proportion of" (Disease **decimated** the population). Some people claim that decimate should be used only to mean "to destroy a tenth of," but in fact the word has never been used this way in English. There is nothing wrong with the sense "to destroy a large amount or proportion of."

differ from/differ with Differ from means "to be unlike"; differ with means "to disagree with" (The sisters **differ from each other** in appearance. We **differ with you** on this matter).

different from/different than Although different from is the preferred usage (His attitude is **different from** mine), different than is widely accepted when a clause follows, especially when the word "from" would create an awkward sentence (The stream followed a **different course than the map showed**).

don't/does not Don't is the contraction for "do not," not for does not: I **don't** care, she **doesn't** (not "don't") care.

done Using done as an adjective to mean "through, finished" is standard. Originally, done was used as a description (The pact between them was a **done thing**), but it has become more common as a complement (Are your pictures **done** yet? When we were **done with the power saw,** we removed the blade).

doubt that/doubt whether/doubt if Doubt that is used to express conviction (I **doubt** that they intended to hurt your feelings); doubt whether and doubt if are used to indicate uncertainty: I **doubt whether** (or "if") anyone really listened to the speaker.

due to In formal discourse, due to is acceptable only after a form of the verb "to be" (Her aching back **was due to** poor posture). Due to is not acceptable as a preposition meaning "because of" or "owing to": **Because of** (not "due to") the poor weather, the bus was late.

each When each is used as a pronoun, it takes a singular verb (**Each was** born in Europe), although plurals are increasingly used in formal speech and writing in an attempt to avoid using "he" or "his" for sentences that include females or do not specify sex (**Each of them had their** (rather than "his") own agenda). More and more, the same pattern of pronoun agreement is being used with the singular pronouns anyone, anybody, everyone, everybody, no one, someone, and somebody (**Somebody left their** (not "his") jacket at the gym). When the pronoun each is followed by an "of" phrase containing a plural noun or pronoun, usage guides suggest that the verb be singular, but the plural is used often even in formal writing: **Each of the children has** (or "have") had a school physical.

When each is used as an adjective and follows a plural subject, the verb agrees with the subject: The **rooms each have** (not "has") separate thermostats.

each and every Use "each" or "every" in place of the phrase each and every, generally considered wordy (**Each of us** enjoyed the concert. **Every one of us** stayed until the end of the performance).

each other/one another Each other is traditionally used to indicate two members; one another is used for three or more (The **two children** trade lunches with **each other.** The **guests** greeted **one another** fondly). In standard practice, though, these distinctions are not observed in either speech or writing.

enormity The word enormity means "outrageousness, atrociousness, monstrousness": the enormity of his crime. It is often used to mean "great size, enormousness" (The **enormity** of the task overwhelmed her). Though this use is common, many people consider it to be an error.

enthused/enthusiastic The word enthused is used informally to mean "showing enthusiasm." For formal writing and speech, use the adjective enthusiastic (**The team was enthusiastic** about the quarterback's winning play).

-ess/-or/-er The suffix -ess has often been used to denote feminine nouns.

While many such words are still in use, English is moving increasingly toward nouns that do not denote sex differences. The most widely observed guideline today is that if the sex of the performer is not relevant to the performance of the task or function, the neutral ending -or or -er should be used in place of -ess. Airlines, for example, have replaced both steward and stewardess with flight attendant. Thus, use ambassador instead of ambassadress, ancestor not ancestress, author not authoress, poet not poetess, proprietor not proprietress, and sculptor not sculptress.

et al. Et al., the Latin abbreviation for "and other people," is fully standard for use in a citation to refer to works with more than three authors: Harris **et al.**

etc. Since etc. (et cetera) is the Latin abbreviation for "and other things," it should not be used to refer to people. In general, it should be avoided in formal writing as imprecise. In its place, provide the entire list of items or use "and so on."

Since etc. means "and all the rest," and etc. is redundant; the "and" is not needed. Many prefer to use "and so forth" or "and the like" as a substitute for etc.

-ette English nouns whose -ette ending signifies a feminine role or identity are passing out of usage. Suffragette and usherette, for example, have been replaced by suffragist and usher, respectively. *See* -ess for more information.

everywheres/everywhere Everywheres is a nonstandard term for everywhere and should be avoided in speech and writing.

except for the fact that/except that Use except that in place of the verbose phrase except for the fact that: **Except that** (not "except for the fact that" the button is missing, this is a lovely skirt.

fewer/less Traditionally, fewer, a plural noun, has most often been used to refer to individual units that can be counted (There are **fewer buttons** on this shirt. No **fewer than forty** of the fifty voters supported the measure). Less, a singular noun, is used to refer to uncountable quantities (She **eats less** every day. I have **less patience** than I used to). Standard English does not always reflect these distinctions, however. When followed by "than," less is used as often as fewer to indicate plural nouns that refer to items that can be counted (There were no **less than eight million people. No less than forty** of the fifty voters supported the measure).

figuratively/literally Figuratively, meaning "involving a figure of speech," usually implies that the statement is not true. Literally, meaning "actually, without exaggeration," implies that the statement is true (The poet Robert Frost once **figuratively described** writing poetry without regular meter and rhyme **as playing tennis with the net down.** My sister **literally passed out** when she saw what had happened to her new car). Literally is commonly used as an intensifier meaning "in effect, virtually" (The state representative was **literally buried alive** in the caucus). This usage should be avoided in formal discourse.

fix The verb fix, meaning "to repair," is fully accepted in all areas of speech and writing. The noun **fix**, meaning "repair" or "adjustment," is used informally.

fixing to/intend to Use intend to in place of the informal or dialectal term fixing to: The community **intends to** (not "is fixing to") raise money to help the victims of the recent fire.

flunk/fail Use the standard term fail in speech and writing; flunk is an informal substitute.

former/latter Former is used to refer to the first of two items; latter, the second (We enjoy both **gardening** and **painting**, the **former** during the summer and the **latter** during the winter). When dealing with three or more items, use "first" and "last" rather than former and latter (We enjoy **gardening, painting**, and **skiing**, but the **last** is very costly).

fortuitous Fortuitous means "happening accidentally" (A fortuitous meeting with a former acquaintance led to a change in plans). It is also used sometimes as a synonym for "lucky" or "fortunate."

from whence Although the phrase from whence is sometimes criticized on the grounds that "from" is redundant because it is included in the meaning of "whence," the idiom is nonetheless standard in both speech and writing (She finally moved to Kansas, **from whence** she began to build a new life).

fulsome Originally, fulsome meant "abundant," but for hundreds of years the word has been used to mean "offensive, disgusting, or excessively lavish." While the word still maintains the connotations of "excessive" or "offensive," it has also come to be used in the original sense as well (Compare the severe furniture of the living room to the **fulsome decorations** in the den).

fun Fun should not be used as an adjective in formal writing. Instead, substitute a word such as "happy," "pleasant," or "entertaining" (They had a pleasant (not "fun") afternoon at the park).

gentleman Once used only to refer to men of high social rank, the term gentleman now also specifies a man of courtesy and consideration (He behaves like a **gentleman**). It is also used as a term of polite reference and address in the singular and plural (This **gentleman** is waiting to be served. Are we ready to begin, **gentlemen?**).

get The verb get is used in many slang and informal phrases as a substitute for forms of "to be": They won't **get** (or "be") accepted with that attitude. In American English, an alternative past participle is gotten, especially in the sense of "received" and "acquired": I have **gotten** (or "got") all I ever wanted. Both have and has got (meaning "must") are occasionally criticized as being redundant, but are nonetheless fully standard in all varieties of speech and writing (You **have got** to carry your driver's license at all times).

good/well Good, an adjective, should be used to describe someone or something (**Joe** is a **good student**). Well, when used as an adverb, should describe an action (She and Laura **play well** together). Well, when used as an adjective after "look," "feel," or other linking verbs, often refers to good health (You're **looking well**).

good and/very Avoid using good and as a substitute for very: I was **very** (not "good and") hungry.

graduate The passive form, once considered the only correct usage, is seldom used today: I **graduated** (or "was graduated") from the Merchant Marine Academy last May. Although some critics condemn the use of graduate as a verb meaning "to receive a degree or diploma (from)" its use is common in both speech and writing.

great The word great has been overused in informal writing and speech as a synonym for "enthusiastic," "good," or "clever".

had drank/had drunk According to some authorities, had drank is acceptable usage: I **had drank** (not "had dranken") a gallon of milk. Had drunk, though, is fully standard and the preferred usage.

had ought/ought Had ought is considered wordy; the preferred usage is ought: She **ought** (not "had ought") to heed her mother's advice.

has/have; has got/have got The word "got" is unnecessary; simply use has or have (Jessica **has** (not "has got") a mild case of chicken pox).

half/a half a/a half Use either half or a half; a half a is considered wordy: Please give me **a half** (not "a half a") piece. I'd like half that slice, please.

hanged/hung Although both words are past-tense forms of "to hang," hanged is used to refer to executions (Billy Budd was **hanged**). Hung is used for all other meanings (The stockings **were hung** by the chimney with care).

have/of Use have rather than of after helping verbs like "could," "should," "would," "may," and "might": They **should have** (not "of") let me know of their decision earlier.

he, she; he/she The pronouns he and she refer to male and female antecedents, respectively. Traditionally, when an antecedent in singular form could be either female or male, "he" was always used to refer to either sex (A **child** is often apprehensive when **he** first begins school). Today, however, various approaches have been developed to avoid the all-purpose "he." Many people find the construction he/she (or "he or she") awkward: A **child** is often apprehensive when **he/she** (or "he or she") first begins school. The blended form s/he has not been widely adopted, probably because of confusion over pronunciation. Most people now favor either rephrasing the sentence entirely to omit the pronoun or reconstructing the sentence in the third-person plural (**Children** *are* often apprehensive when *they* first begin school).

hopefully Hopefully originally meant "in a hopeful manner" (The beggar looked up **hopefully**). It is now often used to mean "it is to be hoped; I hope; let us hope" (**Hopefully,** we'll get there on time). Although this sense is common and standard, many people consider it incorrect.

how come/why How come is an informal in speech to substitute for why. It should be avoided in formal writing.

if/whether Use whether rather than if to begin a subordinate clause when the clause states a choice: I don't know **whether** (not "if") I should stay until the end **or** leave right after the opening ceremony.

impact Both the noun and verb impact are used to indicate forceful contact (I cannot overstate the **impact** of the new policy on productivity). Some speakers and writers avoid using impact as a verb to mean "to have an effect" (Our work here **impacts** on every division in the firm).

in Several phrases beginning with in are verbose and should be avoided in formal writing. Refer to the following list.

Replace the phrase	With
in this day and age	now
in spite of the fact that	although or even though
in the neighborhood of	approximately or about
in the event that	if

The following phrases can be omitted entirely: in a very real sense, in number, in nature, in reality, in terms of, and in the case of.

in/into In is used to indicate condition or location, "positioned within": (She was **in labor**. The raccoon was **in the woodpile**.) Into, in contrast, indicates movement or a change in condition "from the outside to the inside" (The raccoon went into the shed. He went into cardiac arrest). Into is also used as a slang expression for "involved with" or "interested in" (They are really into health foods).

in regards to/with regards to Both terms are considered nonstandard terms for "regarding," "in regard to," "with regard to," and "as regards:" **As regards** (not "in regards to") your request of April 1, we have traced your shipment and it will be delivered tomorrow.

inferior than Inferior to and worse than are the generally preferred to inferior than (This wine is **inferior to** (not "inferior than") the burgundy we had last night).

inside/outside; inside of/outside of When the words inside and outside are used as prepositions, the word of is not included: Stay **inside** (not inside "of") the house. Inside of is used informally to refer to time (I'll be there **inside of an hour**) but in formal speech or writing within is the preferred usage (The dump was cleaned up **within a month**).

insignia Insignia was originally the plural of the Latin word "insigne." The plural term insignias has been standard usage since the eighteenth century.

irregardless/regardless Regardless is the standard term; avoid irregardless in both speech and writing.

its/it's/its' Its is the possessive form of it (The shrub is losing **its blossoms**.) It's is the contraction for it is (**It's a nice day**). The two are often confused because possessives are most frequently formed with -'s. Its' is nonstandard usage.

It's me/It's I The traditional rule is that personal pronouns after the verb "to be" take the nominative case (I, she, he, we, they). Today, however, such usage as it's me, that's him, it must be them is almost universal in informal speech. The objective forms have also replaced the nominative forms in informal speech in such constructions as me neither and who, them? In formal discourse, however, the nominative forms are still used: it's I, that is he.

-ize/-wise Use the suffix -ize to change a noun or adjective into a verb: category becomes categorize. Use the suffix -wise to change a noun or adjective into an adverb: other becomes otherwise.

kind of/sort of/type of Avoid using either kind of, sort of, or type of as synonyms for "somewhat" in formal speech and writing. Instead, use "rather": She was **rather** (not "kind of") slender. It is acceptable to use the three terms only when the word kind, sort, or type is stressed (This **kind of** cheese is hard to digest). Do not add "a": I don't know what **kind of** (not "kind of a") cheese that is. When the word kind, sort, or type is not stressed, omit the phrase entirely: That's an unusual (not "unusual kind of") car. She's a pleasant (not "pleasant sort of a") person.

let's Let's is often used as a word in its own right rather than as the contraction of "let us." As such, it is often used in informal speech and writing with redundant or appositional pronouns: Let's (not "let's us") take in a movie. Usage guides suggest avoiding let's us in formal speech and writing, although both let's you and me and let's you and I occur in the everyday speech of educated speakers. While the former conforms to the traditional rules of grammar, the latter, nevertheless, occurs more frequently.

like/such as Use like to compare an example to the thing mentioned and such as to show that the example is representative of the thing mentioned (Judy wants to be a famous clothing designer **like John Weitz, Liz Claiborne, and Yves St. Laurent.** Judy has samples of many fine articles **such as evening dresses, suits, and jackets**).

Many writers favor not separating such and as with an intervening word: She bought samples of many fine articles such as purses and handbags (not "samples of such fine articles as").

lots/lots of Both terms are used in informal speech and writing as a substitute for "a great many," "very many," or "much."

man The use of the term man as a synonym for "human being," both by itself and in compounds (mankind), is declining. Terms such as human being(s), human race, humankind, humanity, people, and, when necessary, men and women or women and men are widely accepted in formal usage.

-man/-person The use of the term man as the last element in compound words referring to a person of either sex who performs some function (anchorman, chairman, spokesman) has declined in recent years. Now such compound words are widely used only if the word refers to a male. The sex-neutral word person is otherwise substituted for man (anchorperson, chairperson, spokesperson). In other instances, a form without a suffix (anchor, chair), or a word that does not denote gender (speaker), is used.

The compound words freshman, lowerclassmen, underclassmen are still generally used in schools, and freshman is used in the U.S. Congress to signify a newly elected representative. These terms are applied to members of both sexes. As a modifier, freshman is used with both singular and plural nouns: freshman athlete, freshman legislators. See also chair/chairperson.

me and Me and is considered nonstandard usage when part of a compound subject: Bob and I (not "Me and Bob") decided to fly to Boston.

media Media, the plural of medium, is used with a plural verb (Increasingly, the radio and television **media seem** (not "seems") to be stressing sensational news).

mighty Mighty is used informally for "very" or "extremely" (He is a **mighty** big fighter).

more important/more importantly Both phrases are acceptable in standard English: My donations of clothing were tax deductible; more **important(ly),** the clothes were given to homeless people.

Ms. (or Ms) The title Ms. is widely used in business and professional circles as an alternative to "Mrs." and "Miss," both of which reveal a woman's marital status. Some women prefer "Mrs.," where appropriate, or the traditional "Miss," which is still fully standard for an unmarried woman or a woman whose marital status is unknown. Since Ms. is not an abbreviation, some sources spell it without a period; others use a period to parallel "Mr." It is correctly used before a woman's name but not before her husband's name: Ms. Leslie Taubman or Ms. Taubman (not "Ms. Steven Taubman").

much/many Use many rather than much to modify plural nouns: They had **many** (not "much") dogs. There were too **many** (not "much") facts to absorb.

Muslim/Moslem Muslim is now the preferred form for an adherent of Islam, though Moslem, the traditional form, is still in use.

mutual One current meaning of mutual is "reciprocal" (**Employers and employees** sometimes suffer from a **mutual** misunderstanding). Mutual can also mean "held in common, shared" (**Their mutual** goal is clearly understood).

nauseous/nauseated Nauseated is generally preferred in formal writing over nauseous (The wild ride on the roller coaster made Wanda feel **nauseated**).

neither . . . nor When used as a correlative, neither is almost always followed by nor: **neither** Caitlyn **nor** her father. The subjects connected by neither . . . nor take a singular verb when both subjects are singular (**Neither Caitlyn nor her father is** going to watch the program) and a plural verb when both are plural (**Neither the rabbits nor the sheep have** been fed yet today). When a singular and a plural subject are joined by these correlatives, the verb should agree with the nearer noun or pronoun (**Neither** the mayor **nor the council members have** yielded).

no . . . nor/no . . . or Use no . . . or in compound phrases (We had **no** milk **or** eggs in the house).

no/nothing Although the use of double negatives (They **never** paid **no** dues) was standard for many years in English, today certain uses of the double negative are universally considered unacceptable: He didn't have anything (not "nothing") to do.

nohow The word nohow, nonstandard usage for "in no way" or "in any way," should be avoided in speech and writing.

none None can be treated as either singular or plural depending on its meaning in a sentence. When the sense is "not any persons or things," the plural is more common (The rescue party searched for **survivors,** but **none were** found). When none is clearly intended to mean "not one" or "not any," it is followed by a singular verb (**Of all the ailments** I have diagnosed during my career, **none has** been stranger than yours).

nothing like, nowhere near Both phrases are used in informal speech and writing, but they should be avoided in formal discourse. Instead, use "not nearly" (The congealed pudding found in the back of the refrigerator is **not nearly** as old as the stale bread on the second shelf).

nowheres/nowhere The word nowheres, nonstandard usage for nowhere, should be avoided in speech and writing.

of Using of with descriptive adjectives after the adverbs "how" or "too" is for informal speech and writing and should be avoided in formal discourse: How long (informal use "long of") a ride will it be?

off of/off Off of is redundant and awkward; just use off (The cat jumped **off** the sofa).

OK/O.K./okay All three spellings are considered acceptable, but the abbreviation is generally reserved for informal speech and writing.

on account of/because of Since it is less wordy, because of is the preferred phrase (**Because of** her headache they decided to go straight home).

on the one hand/on the other hand These two transitions should be used together: **On the one hand,** we hoped for fair weather. **On the other hand,** we knew the rain was needed for the crops). This usage, though, can be wordy. Effective substitutes include "in contrast," "but," "however," and "yet" (We hoped for fair weather, *yet* we knew the rain was needed for the crops).

only The placement of only as a modifier is more a matter of style and clarity than of grammatical rule. In strict formal usage, only should be placed as close as possible before the word it modifies. In the following sentence, for example, the placement of the word only suggests that no one but the children was examined: The doctor examined **only the children.** In the next sentence, the placement of only says that no one but the doctor did the examining: **Only the doctor** examined the children. Nonetheless, in all types of speech and writing, people often place only before the verb regardless of what it modifies. In spoken discourse, speakers may convey their intended meaning by stressing the word or construction to which only applies.

owing to the fact that "Because" is generally accepted as a less wordy substitute for owing to the fact that.

pair/pairs When modified by a number, the plural of pair is commonly pairs, especially when referring to persons (The **three pairs** of pants were quite expensive). The plural pair is used mainly in reference to inanimate objects or nonhumans: There are four **pair** (or "pairs") of shoelaces. We have two **pair** (or "pairs") of rabbits.

people/persons In formal usage, people is most often used to refer to a general group, emphasizing anonymity (We the **people** of the United States). Use persons to indicate any unnamed individuals within the group (Will the **persons** who left their folders on the table please pick them up at their earliest convenience?). Except when individuals are being emphasized, people is generally used rather than persons.

per Per, meaning "for each," occurs mainly in technical or statistical contexts (This new engine averages fifty **miles per hour**. Americans eat fifty **pounds of chicken per person per year**). It is also frequently used in sports commentary (He scored an average of **two runs per game**). A or an is often considered more suitable in nontechnical use (The silk costs **ten dollars a yard**. How many **miles an hour** can you walk?).

percent/per cent Percent comes from the English per cent., an abbreviation of the Latin per centum. It almost always follows a number (I made **12 percent** interest by investing my money in that new account). The use of the two-word form per cent is diminishing. In formal writing, use the word rather than the symbol (%).

phenomena Like words such as criteria and media, phenomena is a plural form (of "phenomenon"), meaning "an observable fact, occurrence, or circumstance": The official explained that the disturbing **phenomena seen** (not "saw") for the past three evenings were nothing more than routine aircraft maneuvers.

plenty As a noun, plenty is acceptable in standard usage (I have plenty of money). In informal speech and writing plenty is often a substitute for "very": She was traveling **plenty** ("very" for more formal use) fast down the freeway.

plus Plus is a preposition meaning "in addition to" (My salary **plus** overtime is enough to allow us a gracious lifestyle). Recently, plus has been used as a conjunctive adverb in informal speech and writing (It's safe, **plus it's** economical). Many object to this use.

practically Use practically as a synonym for "in effect," or "virtually." It is also considered correct to use it in place of "nearly" in all varieties of speech and writing.

previous to/prior to "Before" is generally preferred in place of either expression: **Before** (not "previous to" or "prior to") repairing the tire, you should check to see if there are any other leaks.

providing/provided Both forms can serve as subordinating conjunctions meaning "on the condition that": **Provided** (or **Providing**) that we get the contract in time, we will be able to begin work by the first of the month. While some critics feel that provided is more acceptable in formal discourse, both are correct.

rarely ever/rarely/hardly The term rarely ever is used informally in speech and writing. For formal discourse, use either rarely or hardly in place of rarely ever: She **rarely** calls her mother. She **hardly** calls her mother.

real/really In formal usage, real (an adjective meaning "genuine") should not be used in place of really (an adverb meaning "actually"): The platypus hardly **looked real.** How did it **really happen?**

reason is because/reason is since Although both expressions are commonly used in informal speech and writing, formal usage requires a clause beginning with "that" after "reason is": The **reason** the pool **is** empty is that (not "because" or "since") the town recently imposed a water restriction. Another alternative is to recast the sentence (The pool is empty because the town recently imposed a water restriction).

regarding/in regard to/with regard to/relating to/relative to/with respect to/respecting All the above expressions are unnecessarily wordy substitutes for "about," "concerning," or "on": Janet spoke **about** (not "relative to," etc.) the PTA's plans for the September fund drive.

relate to The phrase relate to is used informally to mean "understand" or "respond in a favorable manner" (I don't **relate to** chemistry). It is rarely used in formal writing or speech.

repeat it/repeat it again Repeat it is the expression to use to indicate that someone should say something for a second time (I did not hear your name; please **repeat it**). Repeat it again indicates the answer is to be said a third time. In the majority of instances, repeat it is the desired phrase; again is often an unnecessary addition.

says/said Use said rather than says after a verb in the past tense: At the public meeting, he stood up and **said** (not "says") "The bond issue cannot pass."

seldom ever/seldom Seldom is the preferred form in formal discourse: They **seldom** (not "seldom ever") visit the beach.

-self (myself; herself; himself; yourself) The -self pronouns are intensive or reflexive, intensifying or referring to an antecedent (**Kerri herself** said so. **Mike and I** did it **ourselves**). Questions are raised when the -self forms are used instead of personal pronouns ("I," "me," etc.) as subjects, objects, or complements. This use of the -self forms is especially common in informal speech and writing: Many came to welcome my wife and myself (formally, use the objective "me") back from China. All these forms are also used, alone or with other nouns or pronouns, after "as," "than," or "but" in all varieties of speech and writing (Letters have arrived for everyone but the counselors **and yourselves**).

Although there is ample precedent in both British and American usage for using the -self in other constructions but those described above, the -self pronouns should be used in formal speech and writing only with the nouns and pronouns to which they refer: No one except me (not "myself" which refers to I) saw the movie.

shall/will Today, shall is used for first-person questions requesting consent or opinion (**Shall** we go for a drive? **Shall** I buy this dress or that?). Shall can also be used in the first person to create an elevated tone (**I shall** call on you at six o'clock). It is sometimes used with the second or third per-

son to state a speaker's determination to get his or her point across (**You shall** obey me).
    Traditionally, will was used for the second and third persons (**Will** you attend the party? **Will** he and she go as well?). It is now widely used in speech and writing as the future-tense helping verb for all three persons (**I will** drive, **you will** drive, **they will** drive).

should/would Rules similar to those for choosing between "shall" and "will" have long been advanced for should and would. In current American usage, use of would far outweighs that of should. Should is chiefly used to state obligation (I **should** repair the faucet. You **should** get the parts we need). Would, in contrast, is used to express a hypothetical situation or a wish (I **would** like to go. **Would** you?).

since Since is an adverb meaning "from then until now" (She was appointed in May and has been supervisor ever since). It is also used as an adverb meaning "between a particular past time and the present, subsequently" (They had at first refused to cooperate, but have **since** agreed to volunteer). As a preposition, since means "continuously from" (It has been rainy **since** June). It is also used as a preposition meaning "between a past time or event and the present" (There have been many changes **since** the merger). As a conjunction, since means "in the period following the time when" (He has called **since** he changed jobs). Since is also used as a synonym for "because" (**Since** you're here early, let's begin).

situation The word situation is often added unnecessarily to a sentence (The situation is that we must get the painting done by the weekend). In such instances, consider cutting excess words (We must get the painting done by the weekend).

slow/slowly Today slow is used chiefly in spoken imperative constructions with short verbs that express motion, such as "drive slow," "walk slow," "swim slow," and "run slow." Slow is also combined with present participles to form adjectives (He was **slow-moving.** It was a **slow-burning** fire. Slowly is used in both speech and writing before a verb (He slowly walked through the hills) as well as after a verb (He walked slowly through the hills).

so Many writers object to so being used as an intensifier, noting that in such usage it is often vague (They were so happy). So followed by "that" and a clause usually eliminates the vagueness (They were **so** happy **that they had been invited to the exclusive party**).

some Some is often used in informal speech and writing as an adjective meaning "exceptional, unusual" and as an adverb meaning "somewhat." In more formal instances, use "somewhat" in place of some as an adverb or use a more precise word in place of some as an adjective: Those are unusual (not "some") shoes. My sister and brother-in-law are going to have to rush somewhat (not "some") to get here in time for dinner.

someplace/somewhere Someplace should be used only in informal writing and speech; use somewhere for formal discourse.

somewheres Somewheres is not accepted in formal writing or speech; use the standard "somewhere": She would like to go somewhere (not "somewheres") special to celebrate New Year's Eve.

suppose to/supposed to; use to/used to Both suppose to and use to are incorrect. The preferred usage is supposed to or used to: I was **supposed to** (not "suppose to") get up early this morning to go hiking in the mountains. I **used to** (not "use to") enjoy the seashore but now I prefer the mountains.

sure/surely When used as an adverb meaning surely, sure is considered inappropriate for formal discourse. A qualifier like "certainly" should be used instead of sure (My neighbors were certainly right about it). It is used, however, in speech and informal writing (They were **sure** right about that car).

sure and/sure to; try and/try to Sure to and try to are the preferred forms for formal discourse: Be **sure to** (not "sure and") come home early tonight. **Try to** (not "try and") avoid the traffic on the interstate.

that The conjunction that is occasionally omitted, especially after verbs of thinking, saying, believing, and so forth: She said ("that" is not necessary) they would come by train. The omission of the conjunction almost always occurs when the dependent clause begins with a personal pronoun or a proper name. The omission is most frequent in informal speech and writing.

that/which Traditionally, that is used to introduce a restrictive clause that is necessary for the meaning of the sentence (They should buy the cookies **that the neighbor's child is selling**). Which, in contrast, is used to introduce nonrestrictive clauses that can be omitted from the sentence without changing its meaning (The cookies, **which are covered in chocolate,** would make a nice evening snack). This distinction is maintained far more often in formal writing than in everyday speech, where voice can often distinguish restrictive from nonrestrictive clauses.

that/which/who The relative pronoun that is used to refer to animals, things, and people. It can substitute in most cases for either which or who(m): The computer that (or which) I bought last year is already outdated. The cat that (or which) appeared on our porch during the winter is now sleeping on my bed every night. The hitchhiker that (or whom) we picked up was a student at the state university. In accepted usage, who is used only to refer to people. Which is used to refer to animals and to inanimate objects (**The puppy, which** my son gave me for Christmas, now weighs forty pounds. My best **pen, which** I had left on my desk, disappeared during the meeting).

them/those Them is nonstandard when used as an adjective: I enjoyed those (not "them") apples a great deal.

they/their/them Although the they and them are traditionally third-person plural pronouns, many people now use them as singular pronouns, in place of "he" or "she" (If anyone comes to the door, tell them I'm not at home). Some people disapprove, but it is becoming very common, especially in informal use. This is partly because there is no gender-neutral pronoun in English.

this here/these here/that there/them there Each of these phrases is nonstandard: use "this" for this here, use "these" for these here, use "that" for that there, use "them there" for "those."

thusly/thus Thusly is a pointless synonym for thus. Speakers and writers often use thusly only for a deliberately humorous effect.

till/until/'til Till and until are used interchangeably in speech and writing; 'til, a shortened form of until, is rarely used.

time period The expression time period is redundant, since "period" is a period of time: The local ambulance squad reported three emergency calls in a one-week period (not "time period").

too Be careful when using too as an intensifier in speech and writing: The dog is too mean. Adding an explanation of the excessive quality makes the sentence more logical (The dog is too mean to trust alone with children).

toward/towards The two words are used interchangeably in both formal and informal speech and writing.

try and/try to While try to is the preferred form for formal speech and writing, both phrases occur in all types of speech and writing.

type/type of In written English, type of is the preferred construction (This is an unusual type of flower). In informal speech and writing, it is acceptable to use type immediately before a noun (I like this type car).

used to could/used to be able to The phrase used to could is nonstandard for used to be able to: I used to be able to (not "used to could") touch my toes.

very The adverb very is sometimes used unnecessarily, especially in modifying an absolute adjective (It was a very unique experience). An "experience" can only be one level of unique. In such instances, it clearly should be omitted. Further, very has become overworked and has lost much of its power. Use more precise modifiers such as "extremely" and "especially."

want in/want out Both phrases are informal: use "want to enter for want in," use "want to leave" for want out: The dog wants to enter (not "wants in"). The cat wants to leave (not "wants out").

way/ways Way is the preferred usage for formal speech and writing; ways is used informally: They have a little **way** (not "ways") to go before they reach the campground.

when/where Where and when are not interchangeable: Weekends are occasions **when** (not "where") we have a chance to spend time with the family.

where/that Where and that are not interchangeable: We see by the memo **that** (not "where") overtime has been discontinued.

where at/where to Both phrases are generally considered to be too informal to be acceptable in good writing and speech: Where is John? (not "Where is John at?") Where is Mike going? (not "Where is Mike going to?")

who/whoever; whom/whomever Traditionally, who/whoever is used as a subject (the nominative case) and whom/whomever as an object (the objective case). In informal speech and writing, however, since who and whom often occur at the beginning of a sentence, people usually select who, regardless of grammatical function.

with regards to/with regard to/as regards/regarding Use with regard to, regarding, or as regards in place of with regards to in formal speech and writing (**As regards** your inquiry, we have asked our shipping department to hold the merchandise until Monday).

would have Do not use the phrase "would have" in place of "had" in clauses that begin with "if" and express a state contrary to fact: If the driver had (not "would have") been wearing his seat belt, he would have escaped without injury.

would of/could of There is no such expression as would of or could of: He would have (not "would of") gone. Also, "of" is not a substitute for "'ve": She would've (not "would of") left earlier.

you was You was is nonstandard for you were: You were (not "you was") late on Thursday.

Spelling

If words are to be used correctly, they must be spelled correctly. English spellings present some difficulties because so many words are not spelled as they sound. The following rules can serve as general guidelines. Because every rule has exceptions (many of which are also described below), remember that no spelling rule should be followed blindly. In addition to understanding the rules, you should also consult the Words Most Often Misspelled and Words Often Confused sections below. Consulting a dictionary will also insure proper spelling.

Spelling Rules

1. Silent E Dropped.
    Silent e at the end of a word is usually dropped before a suffix beginning with a vowel: abide, abiding; recite, recital. **Exceptions:** Words ending in ce or ge retain the e before a suffix beginning with a or o to keep the soft sound of the consonant: notice, noticeable; courage, courageous.
2. Silent E Kept.
    A silent e following a consonant (or another e) is usually retained before a suffix beginning with a consonant: late, lateness; spite, spiteful. **Exceptions:** fledgling, acknowledgment, judgment, wholly, and a few similar words.
3. Final Consonant Doubled.
    A final consonant following a single vowel in one-syllable words, or in a syllable that will take the main accent when combined with a suffix, is doubled before a suffix beginning with a vowel: begin, beginning; occur, occurred; bat, batted. **Excep-**

tions: h and x in final position; transferable, gaseous, and a few others.

4. Final Consonant Single.

    A final consonant following another consonant, a double vowel or diphthong, or that is not in a stressed syllable, is not doubled before a suffix beginning with a vowel: part, parting; remark, remarkable. **Exceptions:** an unaccented syllable does not prevent doubling of the final consonant, especially in British usage: traveller for traveler.

5. Double Consonants Remain.

    Double consonants are usually retained before a suffix except when a final l is to be followed by ly or less. To avoid a triple lll, one l is usually dropped: full, fully. **Exceptions:** Usage is divided, with some preferring skilful over skillful, instalment over installment, etc.

6. Final Y.

    If the y follows a consonant, change y to i before all endings except ing. Do not change it before ing or if it follows a vowel: bury, buried, burying; try, tries; but attorney, attorneys. **Exceptions:** day, daily; gay, gaily; lay, laid; say, said.

7. Final IE to Y.

    Words ending in ie change to y before ing: die, dying; lie, lying

8. Double and Triple E Reduced.

    Words ending in double e (ee) drop one e before an ending beginning in e, to avoid a triple e. Words ending in silent e usually drop the e before endings beginning in e to avoid forming a syllable. Other words ending in a vowel sound commonly retain the letters indicating the sound. Free + ed = freed.

9. EI or IE.

    Words having the sound of $\bar{e}$ (a long e) are commonly spelled ie following all letters but c; with a preceding c, the common spelling is ei. Examples: believe, achieve, besiege; but conceit, ceiling, receive, conceive. When the sound is $\bar{a}$ the common spelling is ei regardless of the preceding letter. Examples: eight, weight, deign. **Exceptions:** either, neither, seize, financier; some words in which e and i are pronounced separately, such as notoriety.

10. Words Ending in C.

    Before an ending beginning with e, i, or y, words ending in c commonly add k to keep the c hard: panic, panicky.

11. Compounds.

    Some compounds written as a unit bring together unusual combinations of letters. They are seldom changed on this account:

bookkeeper, roommate. **Exceptions:** A few words are regularly clipped when compounded, such as full in awful, cupful, etc.

Rules of Word Division

It is often necessary to divide a word at the end of a line. Words must always be divided between syllables. Consult a dictionary if you are not sure where the syllable division occurs. The following rules should also be followed to avoid confusing the reader.

1. Do not divide a one-syllable word. This includes words in the past tenses like walked and dreamed, which should never be split before the -ed ending.
2. Do not divide a word so that a single letter is left at the end of a line, as in "a-bout," or so that a single letter starts the following line, as in "cit-y".
3. Hyphenated compounds should preferably be divided only after the hyphen. If the first portion of the compound is a single letter, however, as in D-day, the word should not be divided.
4. Word segments like -ceous, -scious, -sial, -tion, and -tious should not be divided.
5. The portion of a word left at the end of a line should not encourage a misleading pronunciation, as would be the case if acetate, a three-syllable word, were divided after the first e.

Words Most Often Misspelled

We have listed here some of the words that have traditionally proved difficult to spell. The list includes not only exceptions, words that defy common spelling rules, but some that pose problems even while adhering to these conventions.

aberrant	accessible	achievement
abscess	accidentally	acknowledge
absence	accommodate	acknowledgment
absorption	according	acoustics
abundance	accordion	acquaintance
accede	accumulate	acquiesce
acceptance	accustom	acquire

Spelling

acquittal	appetite	bookkeeping
across	appreciate	bouillon
address	appropriate	boundaries
adequate	approximate	braggadocio
adherent	apropos	breathe
adjourn	arctic	brief
admittance	arguing	brilliant
adolescence	argument	broccoli
adolescent	arouse	bronchial
advantageous	arrangement	brutality
advertisement	arthritis	bulletin
affidavit	article	buoy
against	artificial	buoyant
aggravate	asinine	bureau
aggression	asked	bureaucracy
aging	assassin	burglary
aisle	assess	business
alien	asthma	cafeteria
all right	athlete	caffeine
allegiance	athletic	calisthenics
almost	attorneys	camaraderie
already	author	camouflage
although	authoritative	campaign
always	auxiliary	cancel
amateur	bachelor	cancellation
analysis	balance	candidate
analytical	bankruptcy	cantaloupe
analyze	barbiturate	capacity
anesthetic	barrette	cappuccino
annual	basically	carburetor
anoint	basis	career
anonymous	beggar	careful
answer	beginning	carriage
antarctic	belief	carrying
antecedent	believable	casserole
anticipation	believe	category
antihistamine	beneficial	caterpillar
anxiety	beneficiary	cavalry
aperitif	benefit	ceiling
apocryphal	benefited	cellar
apostasy	blizzard	cemetery
apparent	bludgeon	census
appearance	bologna	certain

challenge	consummate	desperate
chandelier	continuous	destroy
changeable	control	develop
changing	controlled	development
characteristic	controversy	diabetes
chief	convalesce	diaphragm
choir	convenience	different
choose	coolly	dilemma
cinnamon	copyright	dining
circuit	cornucopia	diocese
civilized	corollary	diphtheria
clothes	corporation	disappear
codeine	correlate	disappearance
collateral	correspondence	disappoint
colloquial	correspondent	disastrous
colonel	counselor	discipline
colossal	counterfeit	disease
column	courageous	dissatisfied
coming	courteous	dissident
commemorate	crisis	dissipate
commission	criticism	distinguish
commitment	criticize	divide
committed	culinary	divine
committee	curiosity	doesn't
comparative	curriculum	dormitory
comparison	cylinder	duly
competition	debt	dumbbell
competitive	debtor	during
complaint	deceive	easier
concede	decide	easily
conceivable	decision	ecstasy
conceive	decisive	effervescent
condemn	defendant	efficacy
condescend	definite	efficiency
conferred	definitely	efficient
confidential	dependent	eighth
congratulate	de rigueur	eightieth
conscience	descend	electrician
conscientious	descendant	eligibility
conscious	description	eligible
consensus	desiccate	eliminate
consequently	desirable	ellipsis
consistent	despair	embarrass

encouraging	finally	hierarchy
endurance	financial	hindrance
energetic	fluorine	hoping
enforceable	foliage	hors d'oeuvres
enthusiasm	forcible	huge
environment	forehead	humorous
equipped	foreign	hundredth
erroneous	forfeit	hurrying
especially	formally	hydraulic
esteemed	forte	hygiene
exacerbate	fortieth	hygienist
exaggerate	fortunately	hypocrisy
exceed	forty	icicle
excel	fourth	identification
excellent	friend	idiosyncrasy
except	frieze	imaginary
exceptionally	fundamental	immediately
excessive	furniture	immense
executive	galoshes	impostor
exercise	gauge	impresario
exhibition	genealogy	inalienable
exhilarate	generally	incident
existence	gnash	incidentally
expense	government	inconvenience
experience	governor	incredible
experiment	graffiti	indelible
explanation	grammar	independent
exquisite	grateful	indestructible
extemporaneous	grievance	indictment
extraordinary	grievous	indigestible
extremely	guarantee	indispensable
facilities	guard	inevitable
fallacy	guidance	inferred
familiar	handkerchief	influential
fascinate	haphazard	initial
fascism	harass	initiative
feasible	harebrained	innocuous
February	hazard	innuendo
fictitious	height	inoculation
fiend	hemorrhage	inscrutable
fierce	hemorrhoid	installation
fiftieth	hereditary	instantaneous
finagle	heroes	intellectual

intelligence	maneuver	nuptial
intercede	manufacturer	obbligato
interest	maraschino	occasion
interfere	marital	occasionally
intermittent	marriage	occurred
intimate	marriageable	occurrence
inveigle	mathematics	offense
irrelevant	mayonnaise	official
irresistible	meant	omission
island	medicine	omit
jealous	medieval	omitted
jeopardize	memento	oneself
journal	mileage	ophthalmology
judgment	millennium	opinion
judicial	miniature	opportunity
khaki	minuet	optimism
kindergarten	miscellaneous	optimist
knowledge	mischievous	ordinarily
laboratory	misspell	origin
laid	mistletoe	original
larynx	moccasin	outrageous
leery	molasses	paean
leisure	molecule	pageant
length	monotonous	paid
liable	mortgage	pamphlet
liaison	murmur	paradise
libel	muscle	parakeet
library	mutual	parallel
license	mysterious	paralysis
lieutenant	naive	paralyze
lightning	naturally	paraphernalia
likelihood	necessarily	parimutuel
liquefy	necessary	parliament
liqueur	necessity	partial
literature	neighbor	participate
livelihood	neither	particularly
loneliness	nickel	pasteurize
losing	niece	pastime
lovable	ninetieth	pavilion
magazine	ninety	peaceable
maintenance	ninth	peasant
manageable	noticeable	peculiar
management	notoriety	penicillin

Spelling

perceive	prevalent	rendezvous
perform	primitive	repetition
performance	prior	replaceable
peril	privilege	representative
permanent	probability	requisition
permissible	probably	resistance
perpendicular	procedure	responsibility
perseverance	proceed	restaurant
persistent	professor	restaurateur
personnel	proffer	resuscitate
perspiration	pronounce	reticence
persuade	pronunciation	reveille
persuasion	propagate	rhyme
persuasive	protégé(e)	rhythm
petition	psychiatry	riddance
philosophy	psychology	ridiculous
physician	pursuant	rococo
piccolo	pursue	roommate
plaited	pursuit	sacrifice
plateau	putrefy	sacrilegious
plausible	quantity	safety
playwright	questionnaire	salary
pleasant	queue	sandwich
plebeian	rarefy	sarsaparilla
pneumonia	recede	sassafras
poinsettia	receipt	satisfaction
politician	receivable	scarcity
pomegranate	receive	scene
possess	recipe	scenery
possession	reciprocal	schedule
possibility	recognize	scheme
possible	recommend	scholarly
practically	reference	scissors
practice	referred	secede
precede	reign	secrecy
precedence	relegate	secretary
precisely	relevant	seize
predecessor	relieve	seizure
preference	religious	separate
preferred	remembrance	separately
prejudice	reminisce	sergeant
preparatory	remiss	serviceable
prescription	remittance	seventieth

Spelling 111

several	substantial	tourniquet
sheik	subtle	tragedy
shepherd	subtly	tragically
sheriff	succeed	transferred
shining	successful	transient
shoulder	succession	tries
shrapnel	successive	truly
siege	sufficient	twelfth
sieve	superintendent	twentieth
significance	supersede	typical
silhouette	supplement	tyranny
similar	suppress	unanimous
simultaneity	surprise	undoubtedly
simultaneous	surveillance	unique
sincerely	susceptible	unison
sixtieth	suspicion	unmanageable
skiing	sustenance	unnecessary
socially	syllable	until
society	symmetrical	upholsterer
solemn	sympathize	usable
soliloquy	sympathy	usage
sophomore	synchronous	using
sorority	synonym	usually
sovereign	syphilis	utilize
spaghetti	systematically	vacancy
spatial	tariff	vacuum
special	temperament	vague
specifically	temperature	valuable
specimen	temporarily	variety
speech	tendency	vegetable
sponsor	tentative	veil
spontaneous	terrestrial	vengeance
statistics	therefore	vermilion
statute	thirtieth	veterinarian
stevedore	thorough	vichyssoise
stiletto	thought	village
stopped	thousandth	villain
stopping	through	warrant
strength	till	Wednesday
strictly	titillate	weird
studying	together	wherever
stupefy	tonight	whim
submitted	tournament	wholly

whose	written	yield
wield	wrote	zealous
woolen	wrought	zucchini
wretched	xylophone	
writing	yacht	

Using a Spell Checker

A spell checker is a computer program that checks or verifies the spelling of words in an electronic document. While it can be a valuable tool for writers, it cannot be relied upon to catch all types of spelling errors. It is most useful in finding misspellings that produce "nonwords"—words with transposed, wrong, or missing letters. For example, it will reject *ther* (for *there*) and *teh* (for *the*). However, it cannot distinguish between words that sound or look alike but differ in meaning. It will accept *to* or *too* regardless of whether the context is correct, and it will accept typos such as *on* (for *of*) or *form* (for *from*). It is important, therefore, not to rely too heavily on spell checkers and to go over your writing carefully to avoid such mistakes.

Words Often Confused

Words are often confused if they have similar or identical forms or sounds. You may have the correct meaning in mind, but choosing the wrong word will not allow you to express the meaning you intend. For example, an *ingenuous* person is not the same as an *ingenious* person. Similarly, you may be using a word that is correct in a different context but does not express your intended meaning. For example, to *infer* something is not the same as to *imply* it.

Use of the wrong word is often the result of confusing words that are identical or very similar in pronunciation but different in spelling. An example of a pair of words with the same pronunciation but different meanings is *compliment* and *complement*. Confusion may arise from a small difference in spelling, as the pair *canvas* and *canvass*; or the soundalikes may be spelled quite differently, as the pairs *manor* and *manner* or *brake* and *break*. An example of a pair of words with similar but not identical pronunciation is *accept* and *except*; they are very different in usage and grammatical function. Words may also be confused if they are spelled the same way but differ in meaning or in meaning and pronunciation. Bear can function as a noun, meaning the animal, or as a verb meaning to carry or support. Similarly, row can signify a line (lined up in a row) or a fight (they had a nasty row).

The following glossary lists words that are commonly confused and discusses their meanings and spelling for the proper usage.

accept/except Accept is a verb meaning "to receive": Please accept a gift. Except is usually a preposition or a conjunction meaning "other than" or "but for": He was willing to accept an apology from everyone except me. When except is used as a verb, it means "to leave out": He was excepted from the new regulations.

accidentally/accidently The correct adverb is accidentally, from the root word accidental, not accident: Russell accidentally slipped on the icy sidewalk. Accidently is a misspelling.

adoptive/adopted Adoptive refers to the parent: He resembles his adoptive father. Adopted refers to the child: Their adopted daughter wants to adopt a child herself.

adverse/averse Both words are adjectives, and both mean "opposed" or "hostile." Averse, however, is used to describe a subject's opposition to something (The minister was averse to the new trends developing in the country), whereas adverse describes something opposed to the subject (The adverse comments affected his self-esteem).

advice/advise Advice, a noun, means "suggestion or suggestions": Here's some good advice. Advise, a verb, means "to offer ideas or suggestions": Act as we advise you.

affect/effect Most often, affect is a verb, meaning "to influence," and effect is a noun meaning "the result of an action": His speech affected my mother very deeply, but had no effect on my sister at all. Affect is also used as a noun in psychology and psychiatry to mean "emotion": We can learn much about affect from performance. In this usage, it is pronounced with the stress on the first syllable. Effect is also used as a verb meaning "to bring about": His letter effected a change in their relationship.

aggravate/annoy In informal speech and writing, aggravate can be used as a synonym for annoy. However, in formal discourse the words mean different things and should be used in this way: Her back condition was aggravated by lifting the child, but the child's crying annoyed her more than the pain did. Aggravated is used to mean "an inflamed condition"; annoy(ed) is used to mean "harassed" or "disturbed".

agree to/agree with Agree to means "to consent to, to accept" (usually a plan or idea). Agree with means "to be in accord with" (usually a person or group): I can't believe they will agree to your proposal when they don't agree with each other on anything.

aisle/isle Aisle means "a passageway between sections of seats": It was impossible to pass through the airplane aisle during the meal service.

Isle means "island": I would like to be on a desert isle on such a dreary morning.

all ready/already All ready, a pronoun and an adjective, means "entirely prepared"; already, an adverb, means "so soon" or "previously": I was all ready to leave when I noticed that it was already dinnertime.

allusion/illusion An allusion is a reference or hint: He made an allusion to the past. An illusion is a deceptive appearance: The canals on Mars are an illusion.

a lot/allot/alot A lot is always written as two words. It is used informally to mean "many": The unrelenting heat frustrated a lot of people. Allot is a verb meaning "to divide" or "to set aside": We allotted a portion of the yard for a garden. Alot is not a word.

altogether/all together Altogether means "completely" or "totally"; all together means "all at one time" or "gathered together": It is altogether proper that we recite the Pledge all together.

allude/elude Both words are verbs. Allude means "to mention briefly or accidentally": During our conversation, he alluded to his vacation plans. Elude means "to avoid or escape": The thief has successfully eluded capture for six months.

altar/alter Altar is a noun meaning "a sacred place or platform": The couple approached the altar for the wedding ceremony. Alter is a verb meaning "to make different; to change": He altered his appearance by losing fifty pounds, growing a beard, and getting a new wardrobe.

amend/emend Amend means to make improvements or corrections in: The U.S. Constitution was first amended in 1791. The verb emend has a more technical use and usually applies to the correction of a text in the process of editing; it implies improvement in the sense of greater accuracy: The original texts of his stories have been collected and emended.

amount/number Amount refers to quantity that cannot be counted: The amount of work accomplished before a major holiday is always negligible. Number, in contrast, refers to things that can be counted: He has held a number of jobs in the past five months. But some concepts, like time, can use either amount or number, depending on how the elements are identified in the specific sentence: We were surprised by the amount of time it took us to settle into our new surroundings. The number of hours it took to repair the sink pleased us.

ante-/anti- The prefix ante- means "before" (antecedent, antechamber, antediluvian); the prefix anti- means against (antigravity, antifreeze). Anti- takes a hyphen before an i or a capital letter: anti-inflationary, anti-Marxist.

anxious/eager Traditionally, anxious means "nervous" or "worried" and consequently describes negative feelings. In addition, it is usually followed by the word "about": I'm anxious about my exam. Eager means "looking forward" or "anticipating enthusiastically" and consequently describes positive feelings. It is usually followed by "to": I'm eager to get it over with. Today, however, it is standard usage for anxious to mean "eager": They are anxious to see their new home.

any more/anymore Any more means "no more"; anymore, an adverb, means "nowadays" or "any longer": We don't want any more trouble. We won't go there anymore.

anybody, any body/anyone, any one Anybody and anyone are pronouns; any body is a noun modified by "any" and any one is a pronoun or adjective modified by "any." They are used as follows: Was anybody able to find any body in the debris? Will anyone help me? I have more cleaning than any one person can ever do.

apt/likely Apt is standard in all speech and writing as a synonym for "likely" in suggesting chance without inclination: They are apt to call any moment now. Likely, meaning "probably," is frequently preceded by a qualifying word: The new school budget will very likely raise taxes. However, likely without the qualifying word is standard in all varieties of English: The new school budget will likely raise taxes.

ascent/assent Ascent is a noun that means "a move upward or a climb": Their ascent up Mount Rainier was especially dangerous because of the recent rock slides. Assent can be a noun or a verb. As a verb, assent means "to concur, to express agreement": The union representative assented to the agreement. As a noun, assent means "an agreement": The assent was not reached peacefully.

assistance/assistants Assistance is a noun that means "help, support": Please give us your assistance here for a moment. Assistants is a plural noun that means "helpers": Since the assistants were late, we found ourselves running behind schedule.

assure, ensure, insure Assure is a verb that means "to promise": The plumber assured us that the sink would not clog again. Ensure and insure are both verbs that mean "to make certain," although some writers use insure solely for legal and financial writing and ensure for more widespread usage: Since it is hard to insure yourself against mudslide, we did not buy the house on the hill. We left late to ensure that we would not get caught in traffic.

bare/bear Bare is an adjective or a verb. As an adjective, bare means "naked, unadorned": The wall looked bare without the picture. As a verb, bare means "to reveal": He bared his soul. Bear is a noun or a verb. As a noun, bear refers to the animal: The teddy bear was named after Theodore Roosevelt. As a verb, bear means to carry: He bears a heavy burden.

before/prior to Prior to is used most often in a legal sense: Prior to settling the claim, the Smiths spent a week calling the attorney general's office. Use before in almost all other cases: Before we go grocery shopping, we sort the coupons we have clipped from the newspaper.

beside/besides Although both words can function as prepositions, they have different shades of meaning: beside means "next to"; besides means "in addition to" or "except": Besides, Richard would prefer not to sit beside the dog. There is no one here besides John and me. Besides is also an adverb meaning "in addition to": Other people besides you feel the same way about the dog.

bias/prejudice Generally, a distinction is made between bias and prejudice. Although both words imply "a preconceived opinion" or a "subjective point of view" in favor of something or against it, prejudice is generally used to express unfavorable feelings.

blonde/blond A blonde indicates a woman or girl with fair hair and skin. Blond, as an adjective, refers to either sex (I have three blond children. He is a cute blond boy), but blonde, as an adjective, still applies to women: The blonde actress and her companion made the front page of the tabloid.

borrow/lend Borrow means "to take with the intention of returning": The book you borrow from the library today is due back in seven days. Lend means "to give with the intention of getting back": I will lend you the rake, but I need it back by Saturday. The two terms are not interchangeable.

brake/break The most common meaning of brake as a noun is "a device for slowing a vehicle": The car's new brakes held on the steep incline. Brake can also mean "a thicket" or "a species of fern." Break, a verb, means "to crack or make useless": Please be especially careful that you don't break that vase.

breath/breathe Breath, a noun, is the air taken in during respiration: Her breath looked like fog in the frosty morning air. Breathe, a verb, refers to the process of inhaling and exhaling air: "Please breathe deeply," the doctor said to the patient.

bring/take Bring is to carry toward the speaker: She brings it to me. Take is to carry away from the speaker: She takes it away.

buy/by Buy, a verb, means "to acquire goods at a price": We have to buy a new dresser. By can be a preposition, an adverb, or an adjective. As a preposition, by means "next to": I pass by the office building every day. As an adverb, by means "near, at hand": The office is close by. As an adjective, by means "situated to one side": They came down on a by passage.

canvas/canvass Canvas, a noun, refers to a heavy cloth: The boat's sails are made of canvas. Canvass, a verb, means "to solicit votes": The candidate's representatives canvass the neighborhood seeking support.

capital/Capitol Capital is the city or town that is the seat of government: Paris is the capital of France. Capitol refers to the building in Washington, D.C., in which the U.S. Congress meets: When I was a child, we went for a visit to the Capitol. When used with a lowercase letter, capitol is the building of a state legislature. Capital also means "a sum of money": After the sale of their home, they had a great deal of capital. As an adjective, capital means "foremost" or "first-rate": He was a capital fellow.

censor/censure Although both words are verbs, they have different meanings. To censor is to remove something from public view on moral or other grounds, and to censure is to give a formal reprimand: The committee censored the offending passages from the book and censured the librarian for placing it on the shelves.

cite/sight/site To cite means to "quote a passage": The scholar often cited passages from noted authorities to back up his opinions. Sight is a noun that means "vision": With her new glasses, her sight was once again perfect. Site is a noun that means "place or location": They picked out a beautiful site overlooking a lake for their new home.

climatic/climactic The word climatic comes from the word "climate" and refers to weather: This summer's brutal heat may indicate a climatic change. Climactic, in contrast, comes from the word "climax" and refers to a point of high drama: In the climactic last scene the hideous creature takes over the world.

clothes/cloths Clothes are garments: For his birthday, John got some handsome new clothes. Cloths are pieces of fabric: Use these cloths to clean the car.

coarse/course Coarse, an adjective, means "rough or common": The horsehair fabric was too coarse to be made into a pillow. Although he's a little coarse around the edges, he has a heart of gold. Course, a noun, means "a path" or "a prescribed number of classes": They followed the bicycle course through the woods. My courses include English, math, and science.

complement/compliment Both words can function as either a noun or a verb. The noun complement means "that which completes or makes perfect": The rich chocolate mousse was a perfect complement to the light meal. The verb complement means "to complete": The oak door complemented the new siding and windows. The noun compliment means "an expression of praise or admiration": The mayor paid the visiting officials the compliment of escorting them around town personally. The verb compliment means "to pay a compliment to": Everyone complimented her after the presentation.

complementary/complimentary Complementary is an adjective that means "forming a complement, completing": The complementary colors suited the mood of the room. Complimentary is an adjective that means "expressing a compliment": The complimentary reviews ensured the play a long run. Complimentary also means "free": We thanked them for the complimentary tickets.

compose/comprise Compose means "to make up" or "to constitute": Twelve former Soviet republics compose the Commonwealth of Independent States. "Composed of" means "made up of" or "consisting of": The Commonwealth of Independent States is composed of twelve former Soviet republics. Comprise means "to include," "to contain," or "to consist of": The Commonwealth of Independent States comprises twelve former Soviet republics. The expression comprised of, which is increasingly common, is still considered by many to be incorrect.

continual/continuous Use continual to mean "intermittent, repeated often" and continuous to mean "uninterrupted, without stopping": We suffered continual losses of electricity during the hurricane. They had continuous phone service during the hurricane. Continuous and continual are never interchangeable with regard to spatial relationships, a continuous series of passages.

corps/corpse Both words are nouns. A corps is a group of people acting together; the word is often used in a military context: The officers' corps assembled before dawn for the drill. A corpse is a dead body: The corpse was in the morgue.

counsel/council Counsel is a verb meaning "to give advice": They counsel recovering gamblers. Council is a noun meaning "a group of advisers": The trade union council meets in Ward Hall every Thursday.

credible/creditable/credulous These three adjectives are often confused. Credible means "believable": The tale is unusual, but seems credible to us. Creditable means "worthy": Sandra sang a creditable version of the song. Credulous means "gullible": The credulous Marsha believed that the movie was true.

demur/demure Demur is a verb meaning "to object": The board wanted her to be treasurer, but she demurred. Demure is an adjective meaning "modest" or "reserved": Her response to their compliments was a demure smile.

descent/dissent Descent, a noun, means "downward movement": Much to their surprise, their descent down the mountain was harder than their ascent had been. Dissent, a verb, means "to disagree": The town council strongly dissented with the proposed measure. Dissent as a noun means "difference in sentiment or opinion": Dissent over the new proposal caused a rift between colleagues.

desert/dessert Desert as a verb means "to abandon"; as a noun, "an arid region": People deserted in the desert rarely survive. Dessert, a noun, refers to the sweet served as the final course of a meal: My sister's favorite dessert is strawberry shortcake.

device/devise Device is a noun meaning "invention or contrivance": Do you think that device will really save us time? Devise is a verb meaning "to contrive or plan": Did he devise some device for repairing the ancient pump assembly?

die/dye Die, as a verb, means "to cease to live": The frog will die if released from the aquarium into the pond. Dye as a verb means "to color or stain something": I dye the drapes to cover the stains.

discreet/discrete Discreet means "tactful"; discrete, "separate." For example: Do you have a discreet way of refusing the invitation? The mosaic is made of hundreds of discrete pieces of tile.

disinterested/uninterested Disinterested is used to mean "without prejudice, impartial" (He is a disinterested judge) and uninterested to mean "bored" or "lacking interest.": They are completely uninterested in sports.)

dominant/dominate Dominant, an adjective, means "ruling, controlling": Social scientists have long argued over the dominant motives for human behavior. Dominate, a verb, means "to control": Advice columnists often preach that no one can dominate you unless you allow them to.

elicit/illicit Elicit, a verb, means "call forth"; illicit, an adjective, means "against the law": The assault elicited a protest against illicit handguns.

emigrate/immigrate Emigrate means "to leave one's own country to settle in another": She emigrated from France. Immigrate means "to enter a different country and settle there": My father immigrated to America when he was nine years old.

eminent/imminent Eminent means "distinguished": Marie Curie was an eminent scientist in the final years of her life. Imminent means "about to happen": The thundershower seemed imminent.

envelop/envelope Envelop is a verb that means "to surround": The music envelops him in a soothing atmosphere. Envelope, a noun, is a flat paper container, usually for a letter: Be sure to put a stamp on the envelope before you mail that letter.

especially/specially The two words are not interchangeable: especially means "particularly," specially means "for a specific reason." For example: I especially value my wedding ring; it was made specially for me.

ever so often/every so often Ever so often means happening very often and every so often means happening occasionally.

everybody, every body/everyone, every one Everybody and everyone are indefinite pronouns: Everybody likes William, and everyone enjoys his company. Every body is a noun modified by "every" and every one is a pronoun modified by "every": both refer to a part of a specific group and are usually followed by "of": Every body of water in our area is polluted; every one of our ponds is covered in debris.

everyday/every day Everyday is an adjective that means "used daily, typical, ordinary"; every day is made up of a noun modified by the adjective "every" and means "each day": Every day they had to deal with the everyday business of life.

exam/examination Exam should be reserved for everyday speech and examination for formal writing: The College Board examinations are scheduled for this Saturday morning at 9:00.

explicit/implicit Explicit means "stated plainly"; implicit means "understood, implied": You know we have an implicit understanding that you are not allowed to watch any television shows that contain explicit sex.

fair/fare Fair as an adjective means "free from bias," "ample," "unblemished," "of light hue," or "attractive." As an adverb, it means "favorably." It is used informally to mean "honest." Fare as a noun means "the price charged for transporting a person" or "food."

farther/further Traditionally, farther is used to indicate physical distance (Is it much farther to the hotel?) and further is used to refer to additional time, amount, or abstract ideas (Your mother does not want to talk about this any further).

flaunt/flout Flaunt means "to show off"; flout, "to ignore or treat with disdain." For example: They flouted convention when they flaunted their wealth.

flounder/founder Flounder means "to struggle with clumsy movements": We floundered in the mud. Founder means "to sink": The ship foundered.

formally/formerly Both words are adverbs. Formally means "in a formal manner": The minister addressed the king and queen formally. Formerly means "previously": Formerly, he worked as a chauffeur; now, he is employed as a guard.

forth/fourth Forth is an adverb meaning "going forward or away": From that day forth, they lived happily ever after. Fourth is most often used as an adjective that means "next after the third": Mitchell was the fourth in line.

gibe/jibe/jive The word gibe means "to taunt, deride, jeer." The word jibe means "to be in agreement with, accord, correspond": The facts of the case didn't jibe. The word jive is slang, and means "to tease, fool, kid."

healthy/healthful Healthy means "possessing health"; healthful means "bringing about health": They believed that they were healthy people because they ate healthful food.

historic/historical The word historic means "important in history": a historic speech; a historic battlefield. The word historical means "being a part of, or inspired by, history": historical records; a historical novel.

home in/hone in The expression home in means "to approach or focus on (an objective)." It comes from the language of guided missiles, where homing in refers to locking onto a target. The expression hone in is an error.

human/humane Both words are adjectives. Human means "pertaining to humanity": The subject of the documentary is the human race. Humane means "tender, compassionate, or sympathetic": Many of her patients believed that her humane care speeded their recovery.

idea/ideal Idea means "thought," while ideal means "a model of perfection" or "goal." The two words are not interchangeable. They should be used as follows: The idea behind the blood drive is that our ideals often move us to help others.

imply/infer Imply means "to suggest without stating": The message on Karen's postcard implies that her vacation has not turned out as she wished. Infer means "to reach a conclusion based on understood evidence": From her message I infer that she wishes she had stayed home. When used in this manner, the two words describe two sides of the same process.

incredible/incredulous Incredible means "cannot be believed"; incredulous means "unbelieving": The teacher was incredulous when she heard the pupil's incredible story about the fate of his term project.

individual/person/party Individual should be used to stress uniqueness or to refer to a single human being as contrasted to a group of people: The rights of the individual should not supersede the rights of a group. Person is the preferred word in other contexts. What person wouldn't want to have a chance to sail around the world? Party is used to refer to a group: Send the party of five this way, please. Party is also used to refer to an individual mentioned in a legal document.

ingenious/ingenuous Ingenious means "resourceful, clever": My sister is ingenious when it comes to turning leftovers into something delicious. Ingenuous means "frank, artless": The child's ingenuous manner is surprising considering her fame.

later/latter Later is used to refer to time; latter, the second of two items named: It is later than you think. I prefer the latter offer to the former one.

lay/lie Lay is a transitive verb that means "to put down" or "to place." It takes a direct object: Please lay the soup spoon next to the teaspoon. Lie is an intransitive verb that means "to be in a horizontal position" or "be situated." It does not take a direct object: The puppy lies down where the old dog had always lain. The hotel lies on the outskirts of town. I just want to lie down and go to sleep. The confusion arises over lay, which is the present tense of the verb lay and the past tense of the verb lie.

To lay (put down)
Present: He lays (is laying) his dice down.
Future: He will lay his dice down.
Past: He laid his dice down.
Perfect: He has (had, will have) laid his dice down.
To lie (recline)
Present: Spot lies (is lying) down.
Future: Spot will lie down.
Past: Spot lay down.
Perfect: Spot has (had, will have) lain down.

Although lie and lay tend to be used interchangeably in informal speech, the following phrases are generally considered nonstandard and are avoided in standard English: Lay down, dears. The dog laid in the sun. Abandoned cars were laying in the junkyard. The reports have laid in the mailbox for a week.

lead/led Lead as a verb means "to take or conduct on the way": I plan to lead a quiet afternoon. Led is the past tense: He led his followers through the dangerous underbrush. Lead, as a noun, means "a type of metal": Pipes are made of lead.

learn/teach Learn is to acquire knowledge: He learned fast. Teach is to impart knowledge: She taught well.

leave/let Leave and let are interchangeable only when followed by the word "alone": Leave him alone. Let him alone. In other instances, leave means "to depart" or "permit to remain in the same place": If you leave, please turn off the copier. Leave the extra paper on the shelf. Let means "to allow": Let him work with the assistant, if he wants.

lessen/lesson Lessen is a verb meaning "to decrease": To lessen the pain of a burn, apply ice to the injured area. Lesson is most often used as a noun meaning "material assigned for study": Today, the lesson will be on electricity.

lightening/lightning Lightening is a form of the verb that means "to brighten": The cheerful new drapes and bunches of flowers went a long way in lightening the room's somber mood. Lightning is a noun that means "flashes of light generated during a storm": The thunder and lightning frightened the child.

loose/lose Loose is an adjective meaning "free and unattached": The dog was loose again. Loose can also be a verb meaning "let loose": The hunters loose the dogs as soon as the ducks fall. Lose is a verb meaning "to part with unintentionally": He will lose his keys if he leaves them on the countertop.

luxuriant/luxurious Luxuriant means "abundant, lush, or profuse": luxuriant auburn hair; luxuriant vegetation. Luxurious means "characterized by or loving luxury": a luxurious hotel suite; luxurious tastes.

mad/angry Traditionally, mad has been used to mean "insane"; angry has been used to mean "full of ire." While mad can be used to mean "enraged, angry" in informal usage, you should replace mad with angry in formal discourse: The president is angry at Congress for overriding his veto.

maybe/may be Maybe, an adverb, means "perhaps": Maybe the newspapers can be recycled with the plastic and glass. May be, a verb, means "could be": It may be too difficult, however.

moral/morale As a noun, moral means "ethical lesson": Each of Aesop's fables has a clear moral. Morale means "state of mind" or "spirit": Her morale was lifted by her colleague's good wishes.

orient/orientate The two words both mean "to adjust to or familiarize with new surroundings; place in a particular position." There is no reason to prefer or reject either word, although sometimes people object to orientate.

passed/past Passed is a form of the verb meaning "to go by": Bernie passed the same buildings on his way to work each day. Past can function as a noun, adjective, adverb, or preposition. As a noun, past means "the history of a nation, person, etc.": The lessons of the past should not be forgotten. As an adjective, past means "gone by or elapsed in time": John is worried about his past deeds. As an adverb, past means "so as to pass by": The fire engine raced past the parked cars. As a preposition, past means "beyond in time": It's past noon already.

patience/patients Patience, a noun, means "endurance": Chrissy's patience makes her an ideal babysitter. Patients are people under medical treatment: The patients must remain in the hospital for another week.

peace/piece Peace is "freedom from discord": The negotiators hoped that the new treaty would bring about lasting peace. Piece is "a portion of a whole" or "a musical or literary arrangement": I would like just a small piece of cake, please. The piece in E flat is especially beautiful.

percent/percentage Percent is used with a number, percentage with a modifier. Percentage is used most often after an adjective: A high percentage of your earnings this year is tax deductible.

perquisite/prerequisite Perquisite is a noun meaning "an accidental payment, benefit, or privilege over and above regular income": Among the perquisites of the job were a generous expense account and use of a company jet. It can also mean "something due as a particular privilege": the perquisites of royalty. A prerequisite is "something required beforehand": French 101 is a prerequisite for all other French courses. Prerequisite is also an adjective meaning "required beforehand": prerequisite knowledge.

personal/personnel Personal means "private": The lock on her journal showed that it was clearly personal. Personnel refers to employees: Attention all personnel! The use of personnel as a plural has become standard in business and government: The personnel were dispatched to the Chicago office.

plain/plane Plain as an adjective means "easily understood," "undistinguished," or "unadorned": His meaning was plain to all. The plain dress suited the gravity of the occasion. As an adverb, plain means "clearly and simply": She's just plain foolish. As a noun, plain is a flat area of land: The vast plain seemed to go on forever. As a noun, plane has a number of different meanings. It most commonly refers to an airplane, but is also used in mathematics and fine arts and to refer to a tool used to shave wood.

practicable/practical Practicable means "capable of being done": My decorating plans were too difficult to be practicable. Practical means "pertaining to practice or action": It was just not practical to paint the floor white.

precede/proceed Both words are verbs, but they have different meanings. Precede means "to go before": Morning precedes afternoon. Proceed means "to move forward": Proceed to the exit in an orderly fashion.

presence/presents Presence is used chiefly to mean "attendance, close proximity": Your presence at the ceremony will be greatly appreciated. Presents are gifts. Thank you for giving us such generous presents.

principal/principle Principal can be a noun or an adjective. As a noun, principal means "chief or head official" (The principal decided to close school early on Tuesday) or "sum of capital" (Invest only the interest, never the principal). As an adjective, principal means "first or highest": The principal ingredient is sugar. Principle is a noun only, meaning "rule" or "general truth": Regardless of what others said, she stood by her principles.

quiet/quite Quiet, as an adjective, means "free from noise": When the master of ceremonies spoke, the room became quiet. Quite, an adverb, means "completely, wholly": By the late afternoon, the children were quite exhausted.

quotation/quote Quotation, a noun, means "a passage quoted from a speech or book": The speaker read a quotation of twenty-five lines to the audience. Quote, a verb, means "to repeat a passage from a speech, etc.": Marci often quotes from popular novels. Quote and quotation are often used interchangeably in speech; in formal writing, however, a distinction is still observed between the two words.

rain/reign/rein As a noun, rain means "water that falls from the atmosphere to earth." As a verb, rain means "to send down, to give abundantly": The crushed piñata rained candy on the eager children. As a noun, reign means "royal rule," as a verb, "to have supreme control": The monarch's reign was marked by social unrest. As a noun, rein means "a leather strap used to guide an animal," as a verb, "to control or guide": He used the rein to control the frisky colt.

raise/rise/raze Raise, a transitive verb, means "to elevate": How can I raise the value of my house? Rise, an intransitive verb, means "to go up, to get up": Will housing costs rise this year? Raze is a transitive verb meaning "to tear down, demolish": The wrecking crew was ready to raze the condemned building.

respectful/respective Respectful means "showing (or full of) respect": If you are respectful toward others, they will treat you with consideration as well. Respective means "in the order given": The respective remarks were made by executive board members Joshua Whittles, Kevin McCarthy, and Warren Richmond.

reverend/reverent As an adjective (usually capitalized), Reverend is an epithet of respect given to a member of the clergy: The Reverend Mr. Jones gave the sermon. As a noun, a reverend is "a member of the clergy": In our church, the reverend opens the service with a prayer. Reverent is an adjective meaning "showing deep respect": The speaker began his remarks with a reverent greeting.

right/rite/write Right as an adjective means "proper, correct" and "as opposed to left"; as a noun it means "claims or titles"; as an adverb it means "in a straight line, directly"; as a verb it means "to restore to an upright position." Rite is a noun meaning "a solemn ritual": The religious leader performed the necessary rites. Write is a verb meaning "to form characters on a surface": The child liked to write her name over and over.

sensual/sensuous Sensual carries sexual overtones: The massage was a sensual experience. Sensuous means "pertaining to the senses": The sensuous aroma of freshly baked bread wafted through the house.

set/sit Set, a transitive verb, describes something a person does to an object: She set the book down on the table. Sit, an intransitive verb, describes a person resting: Marvin sits on the straight-backed chair.

somebody/some body Somebody is an indefinite pronoun: Somebody recommended this restaurant. Some body is a noun (body) modified by an adjective (some): I have a new spray that will give my limp hair some body.

someone/some one Someone is an indefinite pronoun: Someone who ate here said the pasta was delicious. Some one is a pronoun or adjective modified by "some": Please pick some one magazine that you would like to read.

sometime/sometimes/some time Traditionally, these three words have carried different meanings. Sometime means "at an unspecified time in the future": Why not plan to visit Niagara Falls sometime? Sometimes means "occasionally": I visit my former college roommate sometimes. Some time means "a span of time": I need some time to make up my mind about what you have said.

stationary/stationery Although these two words sound alike, they have very different meanings. Stationary means "staying in one place": From this distance, the satellite appeared to be stationary. Stationery means "writing paper": A hotel often provides stationery with its name preprinted.

straight/strait Straight is most often used as an adjective meaning "unbending": The path cut straight through the woods. Strait, a noun, is "a narrow passage of water connecting two large bodies of water" or "distress, dilemma": He was in dire financial straits. Strait is also found in older literature as an adjective meaning either "strict" or "narrow": Strait is the gate.

subsequently/consequently Subsequently means "occurring later, afterward": We went to a new French restaurant for dinner; subsequently, we heard that everyone who had eaten the Caesar salad became ill. Consequently means "therefore, as a result": The temperature was above 90 degrees for a week; consequently all the tomatoes burst on the vine.

taught/taut Taught is the past tense of "to teach": My English teachers taught especially well. Taut is "tightly drawn": Pull the knot taut or it will not hold.

than/then Than, a conjunction, is used in comparisons: Robert is taller than Michael. Then, an adverb, is used to indicate time: We knew then that there was little to be gained by further discussion.

their/there/they're These three words sound alike, but they have very different meanings. Their, the possessive form of "they," means "belonging to them": Their house is new. There can point out place (There is the picture I was telling you about) or call attention to someone or something (There is a mouse behind you!). They're is a contraction for "they are": They're not at home right now.

threw/through/thru Threw, the past tense of the verb "throw," means "to hurl an object": He threw the ball at the batter. Through means "from one end to the other" or "by way of": They walked through the museum all afternoon. Through should be used in formal writing in place of thru, an informal spelling.

to/too/two These words sound alike, but they are different parts of speech and have different meanings. To is a preposition indicating direction or part of an infinitive; too is an adverb meaning "also" or "in extreme"; and two is a number: I have to go to the store to buy two items. Do you want to come too?

tortuous/torturous These two adjectives sound similar, but they have different meanings. Tortuous means "full of twists and turns" and "convoluted": a tortuous road; tortuous logic. Torturous comes from torture and means "involving or causing pain or suffering": torturous heat; torturous memories.

track/tract Track, as a noun, is a path or course: The railroad track in the Omaha station has recently been electrified. Track, as a verb, is "to follow": Sophisticated guidance control systems are used to track the space shuttles. Tract is "an expanse of land" or "a brief treatise": Jonathan Swift wrote many tracts on the political problems of his day.

unexceptional/unexceptionable Both unexceptional and unexceptionable are adjectives, but they have different meanings and are not interchangeable. Unexceptional means "commonplace, ordinary": Despite the glowing reviews the new restaurant had received, we found it offered unexceptional meals and service. Unexceptionable means "not offering any basis for exception or objection, beyond criticism": We could not dispute his argument because it was unexceptionable.

usage/use Usage is a noun that refers to the generally accepted way of doing something. The word refers especially to the conventions of language: "Most unique" is considered incorrect usage. Use can be either a noun or a verb. As a noun, use means "the act of employing or putting into service": In the adult education course, I learned the correct use of tools. Usage is often misused in place of the noun use: Effective use (not "usage") of your time results in greater personal satisfaction.

use/utilize/utilization Utilize means "to make use of": They should utilize the new profit-sharing plan to decrease taxable income. Utilization is the noun form of utilize. In most instances, however, use is preferred to either utilize or utilization as less overly formal and stilted: They should use the new profit-sharing plan to decrease taxable income.

which/witch Which is a pronoun meaning "what one": Which desk is yours? Witch is a noun meaning "a person who practices magic": The superstitious villagers accused her of being a witch.

who's/whose Who's is the contraction for "who is" or "who has": Who's the person in charge here? Who's got the money? Whose is the possessive form of "who": Whose book is this?

your/you're Your is the possessive form of "you": Your book is overdue at the library. You're is the contraction of "you are": You're just the person we need for this job.

4

Punctuation and Capitalization

Punctuation

Punctuation marks can be understood as signs or cues that help a reader by revealing information about the content of the sentence. Note the following example:

> *Yesterday morning I overslept and took my fathers car to buy milk eggs butter and cheese the store was closed and I thought to myself its likely I will have to drink my coffee black*

> Without punctuation, it's very difficult to read the sentence. Note the same sentence with punctuation marks added:

> *Yesterday morning, the day I overslept, I drove my father's car to the store to buy milk, eggs, butter, and cheese. The store was closed so I said to myself, "It's likely I will have to drink my coffee black."*

> Punctuated, the sentence is much easier to read. In the above example, periods, by signaling the ends of sentences, tell the reader to pause. Commas, by separating words in a list, tell us "milk" "eggs" "butter" and "cheese" have a relationship with one another. The commas indicate those words are related in a series. Quotation marks indicate words that have been spoken, and an apostrophe indicates possession.

These punctuation marks and a variety of others have many functions, all of which are discussed in this section.

Types of Punctuation Marks

Apostrophe

An apostrophe is most commonly used in contractions to show where letters or numerals have been omitted.

> *I'm*   *Ma'am*
> *let's*   *the class of '99*

> In these examples, apostrophes replace "a" (I am); "u" (let us); "d" (Madam); and "19" (the class of **19**99).

> Sometimes if an author is trying to reflect a dialect of speech, apostrophes will be used: "The boys are goin' drivin' today," he said.

Plural

An apostrophe s is used to make numbers and abbreviations or acronyms (signifying nouns).

> *GI's*
> *V.I.P.'s*
> *figure 8's*
> *The handwriting is very hard to read: the n's and u's look alike.*
> *The number of Ph.D.'s awarded to U.S. citizens declined in the 1980's.*

> **Exception:** The apostrophe may be omitted in dates: 1980s.

Possession

The use of apostrophes to signify nouns and pronouns that are in the possessive case is discussed on pages 6 and 7.

Brackets

While writers use ellipses to reflect words that have been omitted from a quoted passage (see below), when writers insert something within a quoted passage, the insertion should be set off with brackets. Insertions are sometimes used to supply words that explain, clarify, or correct the contents of a direct quotation, as in the following examples:

> According to the Globe critic, "This [**Man and Superman**] is one of Shaw's greatest plays."
> "Young as they are," he writes, "these students are afflicted with cynicism, world-weariness, and a total disregard for tradition and authority." [**Emphasis is mine.**]

In the first example, "[Man and Superman]" supplies the title of the play to which "This" refers. As the original quote did not include the specific title of the play, it is necessarily set off in brackets.

In the second example, "[Emphasis is mine]" lets the reader know that the writer wishes to place additional emphasis (i.e., emphasis the original author of the quote did not in fact include) on the phrase in italics. For more information on the use of italics, see below.

In a similar fashion, brackets are used to enclose comments made in a verbatim transcript.

> *Sen. Eaton: The steady rise in taxes must be halted. [Applause]*

Placing "Applause" in brackets lets the reader know that it is not part of Sen. Eaton's statement.

The publication date, inserted by the editor, of an item to which the writer refers is also enclosed in brackets.

> *Dear Sir: Your excellent article on China [April 15] brings to mind my recent experience . . .*

Parenthesis
Brackets are used to substitute for parentheses with material already enclosed in parentheses.

> *See "Rene Descartes" (M.C. Beardsley, The European Philosophers from Descartes to Nietzsche [New York, 1960]).*

Quotations
Writers can make clear that an error in the quotation has been carried over from the original by using the Latin word "sic," meaning "thus."

"George Washington lived during the seventeenth [sic] century."
"The governor of Missisipi [sic] addressed the student body."

In the first example, "[sic]" lets the reader know that while "seventeenth century" should be written as 17th century, the author of the quote did not do so and is being quoted directly. The same logic applies to the misspelling of Mississippi in the second example.

Colon

A colon, as a mark of introduction, tells the reader that the statement preceding the colon is going to be explained by the statement following the colon, as in the following example:

This I believe: All people are created equal and must enjoy equally the rights that are inalienably theirs.
Fagles's translation of the Iliad begins: "Rage-Goddess, sing the rage of Peleus' son Achilles, murderous, doomed, that cost the Achaeans countless losses, . . ."

When one independent clause is followed by another that explains or exemplifies it (as in the above examples), the second clause may or may not begin with a capital letter.

They cannot pay their monthly bills because their money is tied up in their stocks and bonds: they are paper-rich and cash-poor.
The conference addresses a basic question: How can we take the steps needed to protect the environment without stalling economic growth?

A colon is also used to introduce a series or list.

There were originally five Marx brothers: Groucho, Chico, Harpo, Zeppo, and Gummo.

If the list following the colon is the object of a verb or a preposition, the colon is generally not used:

Before coming home, please go to the store and buy milk, bread, eggs, and butter.

The list "milk, bread, eggs, and butter" is the direct object of "buy".

Do not use a colon to introduce a list after the verb "to be" or to introduce a list following a preposition:

The courses she is taking are French, medieval history, Greek, and the nineteenth-century novel.
The committee consisted of nine teachers, twelve parents, and six business leaders.

Colons have other functions beyond introducing parts of a sentence and lists, all of which are discussed below.

Citations
The parts of a citation are separated by a colon.

Genesis 3:2
Journal of Astrophysics 43:2

In a bibliographical citation, a colon may separate the place of publication from the name of the publisher.

New York: Random House, Inc.

For more information on **citing sources**, see page 308.

Letters
A colon is used to follow the salutation in a formal letter.

Dear Mr. Czerny:
Dear Valued Customer:

Subtitles
A colon is placed between the title and the subtitle of a book.

In 1988, Brooks published Gilded Twilight: The Later Years of Melville and Twain.

Time
A colon is used to separate hours from minutes in indicating time.

1:30 p.m.
12:30 a.m.

Comma

The comma is the most frequently used mark of punctuation within a sentence. Because it is used so often, knowing when and where to use a comma correctly can be a tricky task. The main use of a comma is to clarify the structure and meaning of a sentence. Guidelines on the proper (grammatically correct, that is) use of commas is organized below according to the part of speech or part of a sentence (words, phrases, and clauses) to which commas relate.

The secondary use of a comma is to indicate emphasis, pauses, and stress. It follows that a comma should be used (in general) when you need to make it is necessary to prevent misreading. The comma tells the reader to stop briefly before reading on. Words may run together in confusing ways unless you use a comma to separate them. Use a comma in such sentences even though no rule requires one.

> *Soon after, she quit the job for good.*
> *The people who can, usually contribute some money to the local holiday drive.*

> In both examples, the pause that is naturally called for is signaled by the comma.

Adding unnecessary commas or omitting necessary ones can confuse a reader and obscure the meaning of a sentence.

Addresses and Dates
> When addresses and dates are used in sentences, each part of the date or address is a comma.

> *All contributions should be sent to the recording secretary at 4232 Grand Boulevard, Silver Spring, MD 70042, as soon as possible.*
> *She was born on Tuesday, December 20, 1901, in a log cabin near Casey Creek, Kentucky.*

> When only the month and year are given, the comma is usually omitted: We took our first trip to Alaska in August 1988.

Adjectives

In a series of adjectives, commas must be used when each adjective is considered separately, not as a modifier of other adjectives.

the beautiful, expensive dress
the happy, smiling children
the hungry, meowing cat

Do not use commas to separate adjectives that are so closely related that they appear to form a single element with the noun they modify.

the big blue balloon
several dingy old Western mining towns

As the above examples illustrate, adjectives that refer to the number, age, size, color, or location of the noun can often be understood as a single entity and are therefore not separated by commas.

To determine whether or not to use the comma in these instances, insert the word *"and."* If *"and"* cannot replace the comma without creating an awkward sentence, it is safe to conclude that a comma is not necessary.

Conjunctive Adverbs

Conjunctive adverbs can be placed anywhere in a sentence depending on where you want the emphasis. They are always set off by commas.

However, *it is important to understand everyone's point of view.*
It is important, ***however,*** *to understand everyone's point of view.*
It is important to understand everyone's point of view, ***however.***

Note: When certain conjunctive adverbs are used to connect independent clauses, the conjunctive adverb is preceded by a semicolon and followed by a comma.

For more information on punctuating conjunctive adverbs and independent clauses, see **semicolons** below.

For more information on **conjunctive adverbs**, see page 48.

Compound Sentences

Compound sentences are formed when independent clauses are grouped together by using the coordinating conjunctions *and, but, yet, for, or, nor,* and *so.* In general, the first clause is followed by a comma.

We tried to reason with him, but he had already made up his mind.
Joe is finishing high school this year, and Jennifer is a junior at Harvard.

If the compound sentence is made up of two short, independent clauses, a comma is not necessary.

I ran home after I got your call.

If there is only one subject for both clauses, the comma is generally omitted.

Bill took six cooking apples and put them into a flameproof dish.

"Bill" is the subject of "took" and "put," hence the sentence does not require a comma.

For more information on **compound sentences**, see page 61.

Dates, see Addresses and Dates above.

Phrases and Clauses

Restrictive Clauses

A phrase or clause is called "restrictive" if omitting it would change the meaning of the sentence. Restrictive phrases and clauses are not set off by commas.

The only state that is in the Hawaii-Aleutian time zone is Hawaii.
The novel that she wrote in 1996 won a literary award.

In the first example, if the phrase "that is in the Hawaii-Aleutian time zone" is removed the sentence becomes "The only state is Hawaii," which is clearly not the original meaning of the sentence. Likewise, in the second example, if the phrase "that she wrote in 1996" were removed, the meaning of the sentence would be radically altered.

Nonrestrictive Clauses
As you might have guessed, nonrestrictive clauses are not essential to the meaning of the sentence. Such phrases and clauses are set off by commas.

Her most recent novel, written in 1996, won a literary award.
Hawaii, which is the fiftieth state, is in the Hawaii-Aleutian time zone.

In the first example, removing "written in 1996" would not change the substance of the example as the reader would still know which novel "won a literary award," i.e., "Her most recent novel." "Written in 1996" is therefore additional, but unnecessary, information and needs to be set-off by commas. Similarly, removing "which is the fiftieth state" would not change the basic meaning of the sentence.

In a similar vein, transitional and parenthetical expressions that occur in the middle of the sentence require two commas to set them off, if removing them from the sentence does not change the basic meaning of the sentence.

We can, I hope, agree on a budget for next year.
You may, if you insist, demand a retraction.

Nonrestrictive Appositives
Appositives are words that give additional information about the preceding or following word or expression. Many appositives, as they could be removed without changing the meaning of the sentence, are nonrestrictive and are thus set off from the rest of the sentence with commas.

March, the month of crocuses, can still bring snow and ice.
His favorite author, Stephen King, entered the auditorium.

Note: be careful not to set off restrictive appositives, which are necessary for the meaning of the sentence, as in the following example:

My friend Mary spoke at the convention.
The crowd fell silent as the author Stephen King entered the auditorium.

If we removed "Mary" from the first sentence we would not know which "friend spoke at the convention." In the second example, if we remove "Stephen King" we would know only that an "author" "entered the auditorium."

Appositives can also be set off by dashes, as explained below under Dashes.

Introductory Words, Phrases, and Clauses

In general, a comma follows a phrase or clause that precedes an independent clause, as in the following examples:

Your honor, I object.
Theoretically, she will have to get the permission of the chairman.
Thoroughly chilled, he decided to set out for home.
Since the team was in last place, it was not surprising that only fifteen hundred fans showed up for the final game of the season.

Note: When the introductory phrase can not be removed without changing the basic meaning of the sentence (often the phrase is short) the comma is typically omitted.

In this article I will demonstrate that we have chosen the wrong policy.
At the present time the number of cigarette smokers is declining.

In the first example, removing "in this article" and "at the present time" would change the context and meaning of the sentence. Thus, both phrases are followed by a comma.

Series
A comma is used to separate words, phrases, and clauses that are part of a series of three or more items, with a word like *and* or *or* usually occurring between the last two items.

The chief agricultural products of Denmark are butter, eggs, potatoes, beets, wheat, barley, and oats.
England, Scotland, and Wales share the island of Great Britain.
Cabbage is especially good with corned beef, game, or smoked meats.
Environmentally conscious businesses used recycled paper, photocopy on both sides of a sheet, and use ceramic cups.

In the third example, all of the clauses function within an overall series and are therefore set off by commas.

Note: Some writers omit the final comma when punctuating a series, and newspapers and magazines sometimes follow this practice. Book publishers and educators, however, usually follow the practice recommended above.

Dash
A dash (two hyphens "--" on a keyboard that does not have the dash) is used to show sudden changes in thought that are in some way related to the main train of thought.

He won the game—but I'm getting ahead of the story.
She told me—does she really mean it?—that she will inform us of any changes in advance.

In the first example, the sudden end of discussion of "the game" is marked by the dash. In the second example, dashes mark a dramatic change in the speaker's main concern, i.e., from what "she told me" to whether or not she was lying.

Like the exclamation point, dashes are dramatic and thus should be used sparingly in formal writing. Do not confuse the dash with the **Hyphen,** which is discussed below.

Appositives
Where commas might cause confusion, a dash may be used to set off appositives.

The premier's promise of changes—land reform and higher wages—was not easily fulfilled.
The qualities Renoir valued in his painting—rich shadows, muted colors, graceful figures—were abundant in the ballet dancers he used as subjects.

A dash may be used to add emphasis to parenthetical material or to mark an emphatic separation between that material and the rest of the sentence.

Her influence—she was a powerful figure in the community—was a deterrent to effective opposition.
The car he was driving—a gleaming red convertible—was the most impressive thing about him.

Offensive Language
A dash may replace an offensive word or part of one.

Where's that son of a b—?
"You're full of —!" he shouted.

Speech
Halting, hesitant, or interrupted speech may be indicated by a dash.

"Well—er—it's hard to explain," he faltered.
She's really—in a way—extremely good looking."
—Henry James
"Harvey, don't climb up that—." It was too late.

Ellipsis

The ellipsis mark consists of three spaced periods (. . .). Often, it is convenient to omit part of a quotation that is being used in a paper because not all of the information in the quote is pertinent to the writer's aims. When this is done, the omission must be marked with points of ellipsis, usually with spaces between them. When the omission comes in the middle of a sentence, three points are used.

Before he founded Johns Hopkins, Gilman complained that "opportunities for advanced, not professional, studies were . . . scanty" in America's colleges in the middle of the nineteenth century (8).

Note: If the author of the quote did not intend to have the two thoughts joined together that are associated by the ellipses, then the exact words should be used.

In the above example, if the ellipses were being used to replace "not," we could assume that the author did not want to associate "scanty" with "opportunities." Replacing "not" with ellipses would therefore radically change the author's original intention and reflect a very incorrect and unethical use of ellipses.

> When the omission includes the end of one or more sentences, a period is added to the ellipses, meaning four points in total are used.

Original
Lord Byron was considered both a champion of individual liberties and a great poet.

Quoted with ellipses
According to Chris Wheatley, "Lord Byron was considered . . . a champion of individual liberties. . . ."

Note: If the sentence is complete, the period is added, resulting in four spaced periods. If the sentence is incomplete, use only three dots for the ellipsis.

Speech

> Ellipsis may also be used to indicate breaks in thought in quoted speech.

"I don't know where he is. . . ."
"If only she hadn't died so soon. . . ."

> Compared with dash (discussed above), using ellipses indicates the trailing off of thoughts and statements, as in the above examples.

Exclamation Point

An exclamation point is used to end a sentence, clause, phrase, or single word that expresses strong emotion, such as surprise, command, or admiration.

Go away!
What a week this has been!

Note: Avoid overusing exclamation points in writing. They are effective only when used sparingly.

Forward Slash

Also called "Solidus" or "virgule," a forward slash is used to separate quoted lines of poetry within the text.

> William Blake's stanza on anger in "A Poison Tree" seems as appropriate today as when it was first written: "I was angry with my friend:/I told my wrath, my wrath did end./I was angry with my foe:/I told it not, my wrath did grow."

A forward slash is used in dates and fractions.

winter 1998/99
the fiscal year 1997/98
¾ + ⅔
x/y − y/x

Options and alternatives are separated by a forward slash.

I have never seen the advantage of pass/fail courses.

Hyphen

Although a hyphen and a dash may appear to be the same at first glance, they are two very different marks of punctuation. The dash is more than twice as long as the hyphen. Recall that a dash is formed by typing two successive hyphens (--) on a word processor that does not have a dash character. The hyphen is used to group words and parts of words together, while the dash is used to clarify sentence structure.

> A common use of hyphens is as a substitute for *"to"*, with the meaning "up to and including", as in the following examples:

The text of the constitution can be found on pages 679–87.
The period 1890–1914 was a particularly tranquil time in Europe.

Hyphens should not, however, be used in conjunction with *"from."*

The Civil War lasted from 1861 to 1865.

It would be an incorrect use of the hyphen to use "from 1861–1865" in the above sentence.

Other functions of hyphens such as joining compound adjectives and dividing words are discussed below.

Compound Adjectives
When two or more adjectives precede a noun and are being used to form a single thought, a hyphen is used to relate the adjectives:

seventeenth-century philosopher
well-known singer

If the adjectives do not compose a single, related thought or if they follow the noun, a hyphen is not used.

The large, green monster
The car was double parked.

Since "large" and "green" denote separate, unrelated qualities they are separated by a comma rather than a hyphen. "double parked" occurs after the noun and is therefore not hyphenated.

Note: When two or more adjectives describe a single subject, the subject is often not repeated and the hyphen is included.

This textbook covers both macro- and microeconomics.
The study included fourth-, eighth-, and twelfth-grade students.

Dividing Words
A hyphen is used at the end of a line of text when part of a word must be carried over to the next line.

. . . insta-
bility

Words must always be divided between syllables. Consult a dictionary if you are not sure where the syllable division occurs. Avoid hyphenating Internet or e-mail addresses because they often contain hyphens naturally.

Since dividing the word at the wrong place can cause serious confusion for the reader, you should learn the Rules of Word Division on page 141.

Proper Nouns and Adjectives
When the root word of a compound is a proper noun or proper adjective, a hyphen is used to separate the prefix.

anti-American
Neo-Nazi
non-European
pro-French

Note: If you are not sure whether or not to hyphenate a compound noun, look up the word in a dictionary.

Italics/Underlining
Italics are used to emphasize or set apart specific words and phrases. In papers in which the type can not be set in italics (papers that have been handwritten or types on manual typewriter), underlining indicates italics.

Emphasis
Italics are used to show that words are to be emphasized.

The boss is *very* hard to get along with today.
Joan loaned the tape to Robert, and *he* gave it to Sally.

In these examples, the writer is using italics to draw extra attention to certain words because she wishes to emphasis them within the sentence. See Emphasis under Quotation Marks below to compare the use of quotation marks and italics in emphasizing words.

Titles
The titles of newspapers, magazines, and books are italicized.
Her job requires her to read the *New York Times,* the *Wall Street Journal,* and the *Washington Post* every day.

"Song of Myself" is the first poem in Whitman's *Leaves of Grass.* Every year *Consumer Reports* runs "Best Buy Gifts" in the November issue.

Italics are used for the titles of plays and movies and for the titles of works of art and long musical works, as in the following examples:

Shakespeare's *Hamlet*
the movie *High Noon*
Leonardo da Vinci's *Last Supper*
Handel's *Messiah*
Don Giovanni by Mozart

Italics are used for the names of ships and planes

the aircraft carrier *Intrepid*
Lindbergh's *The Spirit of St. Louis*

Foreign Words and Phrases

Words and phrases from a foreign language are italicized, while accompanying translations of those words are often enclosed in quotation marks.

As a group, these artists appear to be in the avant-garde. They are not, however, to be thought of as *enfants terribles,* or "terrible children," people whose work is so outrageous as to shock or embarrass.

Note: Words of foreign origin that have become familiar in an English context should not be italicized.

Words and Letters

Italics are used for words used as words and letters used as letters.

I can never remember how to spell *broccoli.*
Be sure to pronounce the final *e* in Nike.

Period

Periods, like exclamation points and question marks, are commonly used to end sentences.

Periods are used in both declarative and mild imperative sentences, as in the following examples:

Some of us still support the mayor. (declarative sentence)
Pass me the peas that are next to your plate. (mild imperative sentence)

Periods are also used to end statements that refer to a question.

She asked what time the train leaves.

Lastly, periods end a question that is used as a statement.

It's hot today, isn't it.

Abbreviations and Acronyms

Periods are also used in abbreviations, which are shortened forms of written words, as in the following examples:

i.e.	*Ms.*	*M.D.*
e.g.	*Dr.*	*Sept.*
etc.	*Inc.*	*Pa.*
Mr.	*U.S.*	*D.C.*
Mrs.		

Note: These are just a few of the abbreviations that require periods. To find out an abbreviation for a word, look up the word in a dictionary.

Periods are not used in U.S. Postal Service state abbreviations (NY, PA); initials used in place of personal names (FDR, JFK, LBJ); or after metric abbreviations (50 cm, 100 km).

Periods are also not used in acronyms, which are the first letter or letters of words that constitute a compound term, as in the following examples:

UNICEF	IRA	FDR
UNESCO	AIDS	JFK
NASA	OPEC	LBJ
NATO	NAFTA	

Parentheses

Parentheses are used to enclose nonessential material within a sentence. This can include facts, explanations, digressions, and examples that may be helpful but are not necessary for the sentence.

Faulkner's stories (but not his novels) were required reading for the course.
The community didn't feel (and why should they?) that there was adequate police protection.

Note: A comma is never used before a parenthesis.

Parentheses are also used to enclose part of a sentence that would be confusing if enclosed by commas.

The authors he advised (none other than Hemingway, Lewis, and Cather) would have been delighted to honor him today.

An explanatory item that is not part of the statement is enclosed in parentheses.

Parentheses are used to enclose numbers or letters that designate each item in a series.

He wrote to The Paris (Illinois) News:
The project is (1) too time-consuming, (2) too expensive, and (3) poorly staffed.

Parentheses are used to indicate an abbreviation that will be used in the remainder of the paper or article.

The Federal Trade Commission (FTC) has issued regulations on the advertising of many products.

"(FTC)" tells the reader that the writer will, for the remainder of the paper or article, refer to the Federal Trade Commission by its abbreviation—FTC.

If a full sentence is enclosed within the parentheses, the period comes before the closing parenthesis.

Seven U.S. presidents were born in Virginia. (The other southern states were the birthplaces of only one or two presidents each.) Ohio also produced seven, and Massachusetts and New York, four each.

If the parenthetical element is a fragment of a sentence, the period or comma goes outside the closing parenthesis.

Two U.S. presidents were born in Vermont (Chester Alan Arthur and Calvin Coolidge), and one was born in New Hampshire (Franklin Pierce).

Question Mark

Sentences that ask a question should be followed by a question mark.

> Who invited him to the party?
> "Is something the matter?" she asked.
> What constitutional principle did John Marshall establish in Marbury vs Madison? *in* McCullough vs Maryland? *in* Fletcher vs Peck?
> You can get us in free?

> A question mark is also used to indicate doubt about information.

> Socrates was born in 470 (?) b.c.
> The codes dates back to a.d. 500 (?)

> A question mark is not used after an indirect question or after a polite command phrased as a question.

> She asked if the application had been mailed. (indirect question)
> Won't you sit down. (polite command)

Quotation Marks

The main function of quotation marks is to enclose a direct quotation. Quotation marks are always used in pairs to mark the beginning and end of the quotation.

> "They've come back!" she exclaimed.

> All of the words contained within the quote marks constitute her statement or exclamation.

> Words or groups of words that are quoted from the original are enclosed in quotation marks.

> Portia's speech on "the quality of mercy" is one of the most quoted passages from Shakespeare.
> It was Shaw who wrote: "All great truths begin as blasphemies."

Indirect and Direct Quotations

As noted, direct quotations use quotation marks to report a speaker's exact words. "I'll be the referee for today's game," Ms.

Kinsella said. Usually, direct quotations are also marked by a phrase such as she said or he remarked, which indicates the speaker.

Indirect quotations report what was said, but not necessarily in the speaker's own words:

Ms. Kinsella said that she would be the referee for today's game.

Since the remarks do not have to be reproduced exactly, indirect quotations do not use quotation marks.

Shifts

Illogical shifts between direct and indirect quotations can become wordy and confuse readers. As the following examples show, these errors can usually be eliminated by recording a speaker's remarks with logic and consistency regardless of whether direct or indirect quotations or a combination of the two are used.

Confusing
Jill asked whether we had cut down the storm-damaged tree and was there any further damage.

Revised
Jill asked, "Did you cut down the tree damaged by the storm? Was there any further damage?"

In the first example, it's difficult to tell whether or not Jill actually asked if there "was any further damage." The second example clears up this confusion.

Confusing
My son said he was very busy and would I please take the cat to the vet.

Revised
My son said he was very busy and asked if I would take the cat to the vet.

Emphasis

Like italics, discussed above, quotation marks are also used to emphasize a word or phrase that is the subject of discussion.

The words "imply" and "infer" are not synonymous.
Such Freudian terms as "ego," "superego," "id," and "libido" have now entered popular usage and are familiar to most Americans.

Quotation marks can also be used to suggest that a word or phrase is being used ironically.

The radio blasting Roy's favorite "music" is an instrument of torture to his parents
The writer of this passage is pointing out that Roy's parents do not really regard the "music" Roy plays too loudly as an example of true music.

Quotation Marks and Other Punctuation
A quotation within a quotation is enclosed in single quotation marks.

Reading Jill's letter, Pat said, "Listen to this! 'I've just received notice that I made the dean's list.' Isn't that great?"

Question marks and exclamation points precede final quotation marks when the question mark or exclamation point is associated with the quoted words.

Once more she asked, "What do you think we should do about this?"
"Be off with you!" he yelled.

When other punctuation marks refer to the sentence as a whole (i.e., not just to the quoted statement), quotation marks follow those punctuation marks.

What do you suppose Carla meant when she said, "I'm going to do something about this"?

Final quotation marks that are **not** referring to a quoted statement always follow the sentence ending punctuation.

After dinner Ed began looking up all the unfamiliar allusions in Milton's "L'Allegro"; then, shortly after midnight, he turned to "Il Penseroso."

Use a comma between the quotation and phrases such as *according to the speaker, he said,* and *she replied* that introduce or conclude a quotation, as in the following example:

According to the speaker, "Inflation is at all time low."

Note: If a quotation consists of two or more consecutive paragraphs, use quotation marks at the beginning of each paragraph, but place them at the end of the last paragraph only. Do not use quotation marks to begin a new paragraph in a single quote.

Titles
Essays, short stories, poems, chapters of books, songs, and radio and television programs are usually enclosed in quotation marks.

Our anthology contains such widely assorted pieces as Bacon's essay "Of Studies," Shelley's "Ode to the West Wind," Gilman's "The Yellow Wallpaper," and an article on criticism from the New Yorker.
My daughter watches "Sesame Street" every morning.
"Summertime" is from Porgy and Bess.

Note: The titles of newspapers, books, and magazines are not marked by quotes but rather set in italics, as discussed earlier under Italics.

Semicolon
A semicolon is used to separate parts of a sentence, such as independent clauses, items in a series, and explanations or summaries, from the main clause. It makes a stronger break in the sentence than a comma does. In choosing among the three punctuation marks that separate main clauses—the comma, the semicolon, and the colon—a writer needs to decide on the relationship between ideas.

Clauses (independent)
Separate independent clauses not joined by a coordinating conjunction are separated by a semicolon.

The house burned down; it was the last shattering blow.
We have made several attempts to reach you by telephone; not a single call has been returned.

In both examples, the clauses before and after the semicolon could stand as separate complete sentences. Since they are related to one another, they are treated as independent clauses, separated by a comma.

When separate independent clauses are joined by a conjunctive adverb such as *however, nevertheless, otherwise, therefore, besides, hence, indeed, instead, nonetheless, still, then,* or *thus,* a semicolon is used after the first clause.

The funds are inadequate; therefore, the project will close down.
Enrollments exceed all expectations; however, there is a teacher shortage.
He knew the tickets for the performance would be scarce; therefore, he arrived at the concert hall two hours early.

For more information on **conjunctive adverbs**, see page 48 and under commas above.

A semicolon is used before "i.e.", "e.g.", "that is", "for example", "etc.", when the next part of the sentence is a complete clause.

On the advice of his broker, he chose to invest in major industries; i.e., he invested in steel, automobiles, and oil.
She organizes her work well; for example, she puts correspondence in folders of different colors to indicate degrees of urgency.

Series

Long or possibly ambiguous items in a series, especially when those items already include commas, are separated by a semicolon.

In the next year, they plan to open stores in Sewickley, Pennsylvania; Belleville, Illinois; Breckenridge, Colorado; and Martinez, California.
Academically talented students were selected on the basis of grades; tests of vocabulary, memory, reading, inductive reasoning, math, and perceptual speed and accuracy; and teacher recommendations.

As commas must be used to separate cities and states, a semicolon is used to separate the city and state units from one another, as reflected in the first example.

In the second example, since the list following "grades" is particularly long, a semicolon is used to separate the list from the main clause.

Slash, *see* **Forward Slash above.**
Underlining, *see* **Italics above.**

Capitalization

Many of the rules of capitalization are discussed under Proper Nouns, on page 5. As noted, proper nouns—names of specific people, places, organizations, groups, events, etc.—are capitalized.

In addition, the proper adjectives derived from those proper nouns are also capitalized.

Canadian
Jeffersonian

Note: When proper nouns and adjectives have taken on a specialized meaning, they are often no longer capitalized.

My brother ordered a turkey sandwich with russian dressing.
The shop specializes in china and plaster of paris ornaments.

Normally, the proper adjectives "russian," and the proper nouns "china," and "paris" would be capitalized; however, in the above examples, because these words are being used in a particular, specialized sense in which the places to which they normally refer is secondary, the words are not capitalized.

Titles of Works and People

The important words in titles are capitalized. This includes the first and last words and all other words except articles, prepositions, and coordinating conjunctions, such as and, but, and or.

Gone with the Wind
With Malice toward None
The Universe Within
The Brain: A User's Manual

Titles of people are capitalized when they are used before a name or when they are used in place of a name to refer to the specific person who holds the title.

Queen Victoria reigned from 1837 to 1901. The Queen's husband, Prince Albert, died in 1861.
President Lincoln was assassinated in 1865. The President and his wife were attending a performance at Ford's Theater.

When the word refers to the office, and not the person who occupies that office, it is not capitalized.

Some of England's greatest novels were written while she was queen.
During the years he was president, the South seceded from the Union, and the Civil War began.

Kinship or family terms are capitalized when they are used before a name or alone in place of a name. They are not capitalized when they are preceded by modifiers.

I'm expecting Aunt Alice to drop by this weekend.
I forgot to call Mother on her birthday.

When kinship terms are preceded by a modifier, they are not capitalized.

I forgot to call my mother on her birthday.

Geography

Geographical features are capitalized when they are part of the official name.

The Sonoran Desert is in southern Arizona.
The Arizona desert is beautiful in the spring.

In the second example, "desert" is not part of the official name of the desert in Arizona and is therefore not capitalized.

In the plural, they are capitalized when they precede names, but not when they follow.

In recent years, Lakes Erie and Ontario have been cleaned up.
The Hudson and Mohawk rivers are both in New York State.

Points of the compass are capitalized only when they are used as the name of a section of the country, as in the third example below.

We've been driving east for over two hours.
He was born in southwestern Nebraska.
We visited the South last summer and the Southwest the year before.

PART TWO

Enhancing Vocabulary

5

Building Blocks of English

Introduction

This chapter of the *Random House Writer's Reference* is designed to help you both increase the range of your vocabulary and use words more accurately and concisely. Thousands of English words are built on Latin, Greek, and Old English prefixes, suffixes, and roots. The first three sections of this chapter focus on these building blocks of English. You can use the next sections to look up the histories and meanings of a variety of words. The following section lists words from specialized vocabularies and the last section provides a short discussion on short forms (abbreviations, acronyms) of words.

Prefixes

A prefix is a letter or group of letters placed at the beginning of a word. When a prefix is added to a word, it changes the meaning of that word, making a new word.

Common Prefixes

Below are common Latin, Greek, and Old English prefixes. The meanings of these prefixes, their variations, and examples of words that use these prefixes are also included. A list of all prefixes follows below.

Prefix	Language	Meaning	Variations	Examples
a-	Old English	on, to, at, by		ablaze, afoot
a-	Greek	not, without		atypical, asexual

Building Blocks of English

Prefix	Language	Meaning	Variations	Examples
			an-	anarchy
ad-	Latin	to, toward		adjoin, adverb
			a-	ascribe
			ac-	accede
			af-	affix
			ag-	aggregate
			at-	attempt
apo-	Greek	off, away		apology, apostrophe
be-	Old English	over, around		bespeak, besiege
bio-	Greek	life		biography
com-	Latin	with, together		commotion
			co-	cohabit, coworker
			col-	collaborate
			con-	concede, conduct
			cor-	correlate, correspond
de-	Latin	down		depress, deform
dis-	Latin	away, apart, opposite of		disagree, dishonest
			di-	divert
			dif-	diffuse
epi-	Greek	beside, upon		epigraph, epidermis
			ep-	epoch
ex-	Latin	out		exchange, excavate
			e-	elongate, evaporate
			ec-	eccentric
			ef-	effluent, effuse
in-	Latin	in, into		inscribe, inhabit

Prefix	Language	Meaning	Variations	Examples
			il-	illuminate
			im-	import, impart
			ir-	irradiate
in-	Latin	not		inflexible, indecent
			ig-	ignoble
			il-	illiterate, illegal
			im-	immodest, impatient
			ir-	irregular
mis-	Old English	wrong, badly		mistake, misspell
over-	Old English	beyond, above		overreach, overawe
para-	Greek	beside		paragraph, paraphrase
pre-	Latin	before		premature
pro-	Latin	forward		proclaim
re-	Latin	again, back		recover, return
syn-	Greek	together, with		synthesis, synonym
			syl-	syllable, syllogism
			sym-	symbiosis, symphony
un-	Old English	not		unwilling, unethical

List of Prefixes

a-[1] from Old English, used 1. before some nouns to make them into adverbs showing "place where": a- + shore: ashore (= on [or into] the shore). 2. before some verbs to make them into words showing a state or process: a- + sleep: asleep (= sleeping); a- + blaze: ablaze (= blazing).

a-[2] a variant spelling of an-. It comes from Latin and is used before some adjectives to mean "not"; a- + moral: amoral (= without morals); a- + tonal: atonal (= without tone).

ab- from Latin, used before some words and roots to mean "off; away": abnormal (= away from what is normal). Compare a-²

ad- from Latin, meaning "toward" and indicating direction or tendency: ad- + join: adjoin (= join toward, attack).

ambi- from Latin, meaning "both" and "around." These meanings are found in such words as: ambiguous, ambivalence, ambiance.

amphi- from Greek, meaning "both; on two sides." This meaning is found in such words as: amphibian, amphibious, amphitheater.

an- from Greek, used before roots or stems beginning with a vowel or the letter h, meaning "not; without; lacking": anaerobic (= without oxygen); anonymous (= without name). Compare a-²

ante- from Latin, used before roots, meaning 1. happening before: antebellum (= before the war). 2. located in front of: anteroom (= room located in front of another).

anti- from Greek, used before nouns and adjectives, meaning 1. "against, opposed to": anti-Semitic, antislavery. 2. "preventing, counteracting, or working against: anticoagulant, antifreeze. 3. "destroying or disabling": antiaircraft, antipersonnel. 4. "identical to in form or function, but lacking in some important ways": anticlimax, antihero, antiparticle. 5. "an antagonist or rival of": Antichrist, antipope. 6. "situated opposite": anticlerical. Also, before a vowel, ant-.

apo- from Greek, meaning "away, off, apart": apo- + strophe: apostrophe (= a turn away, digression).

aqua- from Latin, meaning "water." This meaning is found in such words as: aquaculture, aqualung, aquarium, aquatic, aqueduct, aqueous, aquifer.

auto- from Greek, meaning "self." This prefix is included in such words as: autocrat, autograph, autonomous, autonomy, autopsy. Also, especially before a vowel, aut-.

baro- from Greek, meaning "weight." This meaning is found in such words as: barograph, barometer, baroreceptor.

be- from Old English, used 1. to make verbs meaning "to make, become, treat as": be- + cloud: becloud (= make like a cloud, hard to see); be- + friend: befriend (= treat someone as a friend). 2. before adjectives and verbs ending in -ed to mean "covered all over; completely; all around": be- + decked: bedecked (= decked or covered all over); be- + jeweled: bejeweled (= covered with jewels).

bi- from Latin, meaning "twice, two." This prefix is included in such words as: biennial, bisect, bicentennial, bigamy, biped, binoculars, bilateral, bipartisan, biweekly. Usage. In some words, especially words referring to time periods, the prefix bi- has two meanings: "twice a + ~" and "every two + ~-s". Thus, biannual means both "twice a year" and "every two years." Check these words before you use them.

bio- from Greek, meaning "life." This meaning is found in such words as: biodegradable, biology, biosphere.

Building Blocks of English   161

centi- from Latin, used before roots to mean "hundredth" or "hundred": centiliter (= one-hundredth of a liter); centipede (= creature having one hundred feet).

chiro- from Greek, meaning "hand." This meaning is found in such words as: chirography, chiropodist, chiropractor, chiromancy.

circum- from Latin, meaning "round, around." This meaning is found in such words as circuit, circuitous, circumcise, circumference, circumnavigate, circumstance, circumvent, circumlocution, circus.

co- from Latin, meaning 1. "joint, jointly, together." This meaning is found in such words as: cochair, costar, coworker. 2. "auxiliary, helping." This meaning is found in such words as: copilot.

col-¹ var. of com- before the letter l: collateral.

col-² var. of colo- before a vowel: colectomy.

com- from Latin, meaning "with, together with." This meaning is found in such words as: combine, compare, commingle. For variants before other sounds, see co-, col-¹, con-, cor-.

con- a variant spelling of com-. It comes from Latin, meaning "together, with." This meaning is found in such words as: convene, condone, connection.

contra- from Latin, meaning "against, opposite, opposing." This meaning is found in such words as: contraband, contraception, contradict, contrary.

cor- another form of com- that is used before roots beginning with r: correlate.

counter- from Middle English, meaning "against, counter to, opposed to." This meaning is found in such words as: counterattack, counteroffer, counterclockwise.

de- from Latin, used to form verbs and some adjectives meaning 1. "motion or being carried down from, away, or off": deplane (= move down or off an airplane); "descend" (= move or go down); 2. "reversing or undoing the effects of an action": deflate (= reverse the flow of air out of something); "dehumanize" (= reverse the positive, humanizing effects of something); 3. "taking out or removal of a thing": decaffeinate (= take out the caffeine from something); "declaw" (= remove the claws of an animal); 4. "finishing or completeness of an action": defunct (= no longer of use, completely nonfunctioning); "despoil" (= completely spoil).

deci- from Latin, meaning "ten." This meaning now appears in the names of units of measurement that are one-tenth the size of the unit named by the second element of the compound: decibel (= one-tenth of a bel); deciliter (= one-tenth of a liter). See the root dec-.

dem- from Greek, meaning "people." This meaning is found in such words as: demagogue, democracy, demography.

demi- from French, meaning "half." This meaning is found in such words as: demigod, demitasse.

demo- like dem-, from Greek, meaning "people, population." This meaning is found in such words as: democracy, demography.

di- from Greek, meaning "two, double." This meaning is found in such words as: diptych, dioxide.

dia- from Greek, meaning "through, across, from point to point; completely."

These meanings are found in such words as: diachronic, diagnosis, dialogue, dialysis, diameter, diaphanous, diarrhea, diathermy.

dis- from Latin, meaning "apart." It now has the following meanings: 1. "opposite of": disagreement (= opposite of agreement). 2. "not": disapprove (= not to approve); dishonest (= not honest); disobey (= not obey). 3. "reverse; remove": disconnect (= to remove the connection of); discontinue (= to stop continuing); dissolve (= remove the solidness of; make liquid).

dys- from Greek, meaning "ill, bad." This meaning is found in such words as: dysentery, dyslexia, dyspepsia.

electro- from New Latin, meaning "electric" or "electricity": electro- + magnetic: electromagnetic (magnetism developed by an electric current)

em- a form of en- used before roots beginning with b, p, and sometimes m: embalm. Compare im-1.

en- ultimately from Latin, used before adjectives or nouns to form verbs meaning 1. "to cause (a person or thing) to be in (the place, condition, or state mentioned); to keep in or place in": en- + rich: enrich (= to cause to be rich); en- + tomb: entomb (= to cause to be in a tomb); 2. "to restrict on all sides, completely": en- + circle: encircle (= to restrict on all sides within a circle).

epi- from Greek, meaning 1. "on, upon, at" (epicenter); 2. "outer, exterior" (epidermis); 3. "accompanying, additional" (epiphenomenon).

eu- from Greek, meaning "good, well"; it now sometimes means "true, genuine." This meaning is found in such words as: eugenics, eulogize, eulogy, euphemism, euphoria, euthanasia.

Euro- contraction of "Europe," used with roots and means "Europe," "Western Europe," or "the European Community": Euro- + -centric: Eurocentric (= centered on Europe); Euro- + -crat: Eurocrat (= bureaucrat in the European Community). Also, esp. before a vowel, Eur-.

ex- from Latin, meaning 1. "out, out of, away, forth." It is found in such words as: exclude, exhale, exit, export, extract. 2. "former; formerly having been": ex-member (= former member).

exo- from Greek, meaning "outside, outer, external": exocentric. Also, before a vowel, ex-.

extra- from Latin, meaning "outside of; beyond": extra- + galactic: extragalactic (= outside the galaxy); extra- + sensory: extrasensory (= beyond the senses).

fore- from Old English, used before nouns, meaning 1. "before (in space, time, condition, etc.)": fore- + -cast: forecast (= prediction before weather comes); fore- + taste: foretaste (= a taste before the event takes place); fore- + warn: forewarn (= to warn ahead of time). 2. "front": fore- + head: forehead (= front of the head). 3. "preceding": fore- + father: forefather (= father that came before). 4. "superior": fore- + man: foreman (= superior to the other workers).

hemo- (or hema-) from Greek, meaning "blood." This meaning is found in such words as: hemoglobin, hemophilia, hemorrhage, hemorrhoid. Also, especially before a vowel, hem-.

hyper- from Greek, used 1. before nouns and adjectives meaning "excessive; overly; too much; unusual": hyper- + critical: hypercritical (= overly critical); hyper- + inflation: hyperinflation (= inflation that is unusual or too high). Compare super-. 2. in computer words to refer to information that is linked to data on the display, i.e., anything not rigidly accessed in a step-by-step mannerhyper- + text: hypertext (= text or information that the user can gain access to in the order he or she chooses).

hypo- from Greek, used before roots, meaning "under, below": hypo- + dermic: hypodermic (= under the skin); hypo- + thermia: hypothermia (= heat or temperature below what it should be). Also, especially before a vowel, hyp-.

il-[1] another form of in-[2] that is used before roots beginning with l; it means "not": il- + legible: illegible (= that cannot be easily read).

il-[2] another form of in-1 that is used before roots beginning with l; it means "in, into": il- + -luminate: (= light): illuminate (= shine on or into).

im-[1] another form of in-[2] that is used before roots beginning with p, b, and m; it means "not": im- + possible: impossible (= that is not possible).

im-[2] another form of in-[1] that is used before roots beginning with p, b, and m; it means "in, into": im- + -migrate: immigrate (= travel in or into).

in-[1] from Old English, used before verbs and nouns and means "in; into; on": in- + come: income (= money coming in); in- + corporate (= body): incorporate (= make into one body); in- + land: inland (= in the land).

in-[2] from Latin, used before adjectives, meaning "not": in- + accurate: inaccurate (= not accurate); in- + capable: incapable (= not capable); in- + direct: indirect (= not direct). For variants before other sounds, see im-, il-, ir-.

inter- from Latin, meaning "between, among": intercity (= between cities); interdepartmental (= between or among departments).

intra- from Latin, meaning "within": intraspecies (= within species). Compare intro-, inter-.

intro- from Latin, meaning "inside, within": intro- + duce (= lead): introduce (= bring inside or within to meet someone); intro- + version (= a turning): introversion (= a turning inside or within). Compare intra-.

ir-[1] another form of in-[1] that is used before roots beginning with r: ir- + radiate: irradiate.

ir-[2] another form of in-[2] that is used before roots beginning with r: ir- + reducible: irreducible.

iso- from Greek, meaning "equal." This meaning is found in such scientific and chemical words as: isochromatic.

kilo- from Greek, used before quantities, meaning "thousand": kilo- + liter: kilometer (= one thousand meters); kilo- + watt: kilowatt (= one thousand watts).

mal- from Latin, meaning "bad; wrongful; ill." This meaning is found in such words as: maladroit, malcontent, malfunction.

maxi- contraction of the word *maximum*, meaning "very large or long in comparison with others of its kind." This meaning is found in such words as: maxiskirt.

mega- from Greek, meaning 1. "extremely large, huge": megalith (= extremely large stone or rock); megastructure (= a huge structure). 2. "one million of the units of (the base root or word)": megahertz (= one million hertz); megaton (= one million tons). 3. "very large quantities or amounts": megabucks (= a great deal of money); megadose (= a large dose of medicine) 4. "things that are extraordinary examples of their kind": megahit (= a smash movie or stage hit); megatrend (= important, very popular trend).

meta- from Greek, meaning "after, along with, beyond, among, behind." These meanings are found in such words as: metabolism, metamorphosis, metaphor, metaphysics.

micro- from Latin, meaning 1. "small or very small in comparison with others of its kind": micro- + organism: microorganism (= very small living creature). 2. "restricted in scope": micro- + habitat: microhabitat; micro- + economics: microeconomics. 3. "containing or dealing with texts that require enlargement to be read": micro- + film: microfilm. 4. "one millionth": micro- + gram: microgram. Also, especially before a vowel, micr-.

mid- from Old English, meaning "being at or near the middle point of": midday; mid-Victorian; mid-twentieth century.

milli- from Latin, meaning 1. "one thousand": milli- + -pede (= foot): millipede (= a small creature with very many legs). 2. "in the metric system: equal to $\frac{1}{1000}$ of the unit mentioned": milli- + meter: millimeter (= $\frac{1}{1000}$ of a meter).

mini- contraction of the word *minimum*, meaning 1. "of a small or reduced size in comparison with others of its kind": mini- + car: minicar; mini- + gun: minigun. 2. "limited in scope, intensity, or duration": mini- + boom (= economic upturn): miniboom (= short-lived economic boom); mini- + course: minicourse (= short course of study). 3. "of clothing: short; not reaching the knee": mini- + dress: minidress; mini- + skirt: miniskirt. See min-, micro-.

mis- from Old English, used before nouns, verbs, and adjectives meaning 1. "mistaken; wrong; wrongly; incorrectly": mis- + trial::mistrial (= a trial conducted improperly); mis- + print: misprint (= something incorrectly printed); misfire: (= fail to fire properly). 2. "the opposite of": mis- + trust: mistrust (= the opposite of trust).

mono- from Greek, meaning "one, single, lone." This meaning is found in such words as: monarch, monastery, monochrome, monocle, monogamy, monogram, monograph, monolingual, monolith, monologue, mononucleosis, monopoly, monopterous, monorail, monosyllable, monotonous.

multi- from Latin, meaning "many, much, multiple, many times, more than one, composed of many like parts, in many respects": multi- + colored: multicolored (= having many colors); multi- + vitamin: multivitamin (= composed of many vitamins).

neo- from Greek, meaning "new." It has come to mean "new, recent, revived, changed": neo- + colonialism: neocolonialism (= colonialism that has been revived); neo- + -lithic: neolithic (= of a recent Stone Age). Also, especially before a vowel, ne-.

neuro- from Greek, meaning "nerve, nerves." Its meaning now includes "nervous system," and this meaning is found in such words as: neurology, neurosurgery.

non- from Latin, usually meaning "not," used 1. before adjectives and adverbs and means a simple negative or absence of something: non- + violent: nonviolent. 2. before a noun of action and means the failure of such action: non- + payment: nonpayment (= failure to pay). 3. before a noun to suggest that the thing mentioned is not true, real, or worthy of the name, as in nonbook, noncandidate, nonevent.

ob- from Latin, used before roots, meaning "toward, to, on, over, against: ob- + -jec: object.

octa- from Greek, meaning "eight": octa- + -gon: octagon (= eight-sided figure).

omni- from Latin, meaning "all": omni- + directional: omnidirectional (= in all directions).

ortho- from Greek, meaning "straight, upright, right, correct": ortho- + graph: orthography (= correct writing); ortho- + dontics: orthodontics (= dentistry dealing with straightening teeth); ortho- + pedic: orthopedic (= correction of improper bone structure from childhood).

out- from Old English, used 1. before verbs, meaning "going beyond, surpassing, or outdoing (the action of the verb)": out- + bid: outbid; out- + do: outdo; out- + last: outlast. 2. before nouns to form certain compounds meaning "outside; out": out- + cast: outcast; out- + come: outcome; out- + side: outside.

over- from Old English, meaning 1. the same as the adverb or adjective over, as in: overboard; overcoat; overhang; overlord; overthrow. 2. "over the limit; to excess; too much;" to overact (= to act too much); overcrowd (= to crowd too many people or things into); overaggressive (= too aggressive); overfull; overweight. 3. "outer," as when referring to an outer covering: overskirt (= a shirt worn over something, such as a gown).

pan- from Greek, meaning "all." This meaning is found in such words as: panorama, pantheism. It is also used in terms that imply or suggest the union of all branches of a group: Pan-American; Pan- + hellenic (Greek): Panhellenic (= all Greeks united in one group); Pan-Slavism (= all the people of Slavic background united).

para-[1] from Greek, meaning 1. "at or to one side of, beside, side by side." This meaning is found in such words as: parabola, paragraph. 2. "beyond, past, by": paradox. 3. "abnormal, defective": paranoia. 4. "before names of jobs or occupations: ancilliary, subsidiary, assisting." This meaning is found in such words as: paralegal, paraprofessional. Also, especially before a vowel, par-.

para-[2] taken from *parachute,* and used to form compounds that refer to persons or things that use parachutes or that are landed by parachute: paratrooper.

penta- from Greek, meaning "five": penta- + -gon: pentagon (= five-sided figure).

per- from Latin, used before roots, meaning "through, thoroughly, completely, very": per- + -vert: pervert (= a person completely turned away from the normal); per- + -fect: perfect (= thoroughly or completely done).

peri- from Greek, used before roots, meaning 1. "about, around": peri- + meter: perimeter (= distance around an area); peri- + scope: periscope (= instrument for looking around oneself). 2. "enclosing, surrounding": peri- + cardium: pericardium (= a sac surrounding the heart). 3. "near": peri- + helion: perihelion (= point of an orbit nearest to the sun).

petro-[1] from Greek, meaning "rock, stone": petro- + -ology: petrology (= the study of rocks or stone).

petro-[2] taken from *petroleum* and used to form compounds: petro- + chemistry: petrochemistry.

photo- from Greek, meaning "light": photo- + biology: photobiology; photo- + -synthesis: phosynthesis (= formation of carbohydrates in plants from exposure to light). Also means "photographic" or "photograph": photo- + copy: photocopy.

poly- from Greek, meaning "much, many": polyandry (= the custom of having many husbands); polyglot (= speaking many languages).

post- from Latin, meaning "after (in time), following (some event); behind, at the rear or end of": post- + industrial: postindustrial (= after the industrial age); post- + war: postwar (= after the war).

pre- from Latin, 1. meaning "before, in front of, prior to, in advance of, being more than, surpassing": pre- + -dict: predict (= say in advance of something); pre- + eminent: preeminent (= surpassing or being more than eminent); pre- + face:: preface (= something written in front of a book, etc.) 2. used before verbs to form new verbs that refer to an activity taking place before or instead of the usual occurrence of the same activity: pre- + board: preboard (= to board an airplane before the other passengers); pre- + cook: precook (= cook before regular cooking). 3. used in forming adjectives that refer to a period of time before the event, period, person, etc., mentioned in the root: pre- + school: preschool (= before the age of starting school); pre- + war: prewar (= before the war started).

pro-1 from Latin, 1. meaning "forward, forward movement or location; advancement": proceed; progress; prominent; promote; propose. 2. used before roots and words, meaning "bringing into existence": procreate; produce. 3. used before roots and words, meaning "in place of": pronoun. 4. used to form adjectives, meaning "favoring the group, interests, course of action, etc., named by the noun; calling for the interests named by the noun": pro- + choice: pro-choice (= in favor of allowing a choice to be made regarding abortions); pro- + war: prowar (= in favor of fighting a war).

pro-2 from Greek, meaning 1. "before, beforehand, in front of": prognosis; prophylactic; prothesis; proboscis. 2. "primitive or early form": progestationalprosimian.

proto- from Greek, meaning "first, foremost, earliest form of": proto- + lithic: prototypeprotoplasm. Also, especially before a vowel, prot-.

pseudo- from Greek, meaning 1. "false; pretended; unreal": pseudo- + intellectual: pseudointellectual (= a person pretending to be an intellectual). 2. "closely or deceptively resembling": pseudo- + carp: pseudocarp (= a fish closely resembling a carp); pseudo- + -pod: pseudopod (= a part of an animal that closely resembles a foot). Also, especially before a vowel, pseud-.

psycho- from Greek, meaning "soul; mind." This meaning is found in such words as: parapsychology, psychedelic, psychiatry, psychic, psychological, psychology, psychopath, psychosis, psychotic.

pyro- from Greek, meaning "fire, heat, high temperature": pyromaniac, pyrotechnics.

quasi- from Latin, meaning "as if, as though." It is used before adjectives and nouns and means "having some of the features but not all; resembling; almost the same as": quasi-scientific, quasiparticle, quasi-stellar.

radio- ultimately from Latin radius, meaning "beam, ray." It is used before roots and nouns and means "radiant energy": radiometer. It is also used to mean "radio waves": radiolocation, radiotelephone. Other meanings are: 1. "the giving off of rays as a result of the breakup of atomic nuclei": radioactivity, radiocarbon. 2. X rays: radiograph; radiotherapy.

re- from Latin, used 1. before roots and sometimes words to form verbs and nouns meaning or referring to action in a backward direction: re- + -cede: recede (= fall back); re- + -vert: revert (= turn back). 2. to form verbs or nouns showing action in answer to or intended to undo or reverse a situation: rebel, remove, respond, restore, revoke. 3. to form verbs or nouns showing action that is done over, often with the meaning that the outcome of the original action was in some way not enough or not long lasting, or that the performance of the new action brings back an earlier state of affairs: recapture, reoccur repossess resole (= put another sole on a shoe), retype.

retro- from Latin, meaning "back, backward": retro- + -gress: retrogress (= proceed backward); retro- + rocket: retrorocket.

self- from Old English, used 1. before nouns to refer to something that one does by oneself or to oneself: self-control (= control of oneself), self-government, self-help, self-portrait. 2. before adjectives and nouns to refer to an action that is done without assistance: self-adhesive, a self-loading gun, self-study.

semi- from Latin, meaning 1. "half": semiannual, semicircle. 2. "partially; partly; somewhat": semiautomatic, semidetached, semiformal. 3. "happening or occurring twice in (a certain length of time)": semiannual.

sex- from Latin, meaning "six": sexpartite (= having six parts or divisions).

socio- from Latin, used before roots and sometimes words, meaning "social; sociological; society": socio- + economic: socioeconomic; socio- + -metry: sociometry (= social statistics).

step- from Old English, used before words to name a member of a family related by the remarriage of a parent and not by blood: When my father married his second wife, she already had a son who became my stepbrother.

sub- from Latin, meaning 1. "under, below, beneath": subsoil, subway. 2. "just outside of, near": subalpine, subtropical. 3. "less than, not quite": subhuman, subteen. 4. "secondary, at a lower point in a hierarchy": subcommittee, subplot. Sometimes this prefix is spelled as su-, suc-, suf-, sug-, sum-, sup-, sur-, sus-.

super- from Latin, meaning 1. "above, beyond; above or over (another); situated or located over": superimpose, superstructure, superficial. 2. "an individual, thing, or property that surpasses customary or normal amounts or levels, as being larger, more powerful, or having something to a great degree or to too great a degree": superconductivity, superman, supercomputer, superhighway, superhuman, supercritical, supercool.

supra- from Latin, meaning "above, over; beyond the limits of": supraorbital, supranational. Compare super-.

sur- from French, meaning "over, above, in addition": surcharge, surname, surrender.

sym- another form of the prefix syn-. It appears before roots beginning with b, p, m: symbol, symphony, symmetry.

syn- from Greek, meaning "with; together." This meaning is found in such words as: synchronous, idiosyncrasy, photosynthesis, synagogue, synchronize, synonym, synthesis. See sym-.

tele- 1. from Greek, meaning "far." It is used before roots and sometimes words and means "reaching over a distance, carried out between two remote points, performed or operating through electronic transmissions": telegraph, telekinesis, teletypewriter. 2. tele- is also used to refer to something that appears or could appear on television: telegenic, telethon. Also, esp. before a vowel, tel-.

trans- from Latin, used 1. before verb roots that refer to movement or carrying from one place to another; it means "across; through": transfer, transmit, transplant. 2. to mean "complete change": transform, transmute. 3. before roots to form adjectives that mean "crossing, going beyond, on the other side of (the place or thing named)": transnational, trans-Siberian.

tri- from Latin, meaning "three": triatomic, trilateral.

ultra- from Latin, meaning 1. "located beyond, on the far side of": ultraviolet. 2. "carrying to the furthest degree possible, on the fringe of": ultraleft, ultramodern. 3. "extremely": ultralight. 4. "going beyond normal or customary bounds or limits": ultramicroscope, ultrasound, ultrastructure.

un-[1] from Old English, used freely to form adjectives and the adverbs and nouns formed from these adjectives. It means "not," and it brings negative or opposite force: unfair, unfairly, unfairness; unfelt; unseen; unfitting; unformed; unheard of; unrest; unemployment.

un-[2] from Old English, used 1. before verbs, meaning "a reversal of some action or state, or a removal, a taking away, or a release": unbend, uncork, unfasten. 2. before some verbs to intensify the meaning: unloose (= let loose with force).

under- from Old English, meaning 1. "a place or situation below or beneath": underbrush, undertow. 2. "lower in grade, rank or dignity": undersheriff, understudy. 3. before adjectives to mean "of lesser degree, extent, or amount": undersized. 4. "not showing enough; too little": underfed.

vice- from Latin, meaning "in place of, instead of." It is used before roots and sometimes words and means "deputy"; it is used especially in the titles of officials who serve in the absence of the official named by the base word: viceroy: vice- + roy ("king"); vice-chancellor; vice-chairman.

Suffixes

A suffix is a letter or group of letters placed at the end of a word to change its grammatical function, tense, or meaning. Suffixes can be used to create a verb from a noun or adjective or an adjective from a verb, for example. They can change a word's tense as well; "-ed" can make a present-tense verb into a past participle, for instance. They can even change a word's meaning; the suffix "-ette," for example, can make a word into its diminutive: "kitchen" becomes "kitchenette."

Common Suffixes

Just as recognizing a small number of prefixes can help you figure out many unfamiliar words, so knowing a few common suffixes can help you build a more powerful vocabulary. A list of the most common suffixes is below, followed by a list of all suffixes.

Suffix	Meaning	Variations	Examples
-able	capable of being		lovable, affordable
		-ible	reversible
-aceous	resembling or having		carbonaceous
-age	act or process of; quantity or measure		marriage, coverage; footage
-al	resembling or pertaining to		natural, accidental
-an	one that does or deals with		comedian, historian

Suffix	Meaning	Variations	Examples
-ate	to make marked by		alienate, regulate passionate, affectionate
-ation	the act or condition of		allegation, affirmation
-en	to make		weaken, moisten
-er	one that does or deals with		worker, teacher
		-ar	scholar
		-ier	furrier
		-or	bettor
-esque	in the manner of; like		Lincolnesque
-ferous	bearing or conveying		odoriferous
-ian	a person who is, does, or participates in		comedian
-ic	associated with		democratic
-ish	similar to; like a		foolish; babyish
-ism	the quality or practice of		absolutism, baptism
		-ition	recognition
		-tion	commotion
-itis	inflammation		tonsillitis
-less	without		guiltless, helpless
-ous	full of		perilous
		-ious	gracious, vicious

Suffix	Meaning	Variations	Examples
-ship	occupation or skill; condition of being		authorship, penmanship; friendship
-ty	the state of	-ity	modesty security

List of Suffixes

-ability ultimately from Latin, a combination of -able and -ity, used to form nouns from adjectives that end in -able: capable (adjective): capability (noun); reliable (adjective): reliability (noun).

-able ultimately from Latin, added to verbs to form adjectives meaning "capable of, fit for, tending to": teach + -able: teachable (= capable of being taught); photograph + -able: photographable = (fit for photographing). Compare -ible.

-aceous from Latin, meaning "having the nature of, made of." This meaning is found in such words as herbaceous, cretaceous.

-acious from Latin, used after some roots to form adjectives meaning "tending to; abounding in": tenacious (from ten- "hold on" + -acious) = tending to hold on; loquacious (from loq[u]- "talk" + -acious) = tending to talk. Compare -ous.

-acity from Middle English, used after some roots to form nouns with the meaning "tendency toward; abundance in": tenacity (from ten- "hold on" + -acity) = tendency toward holding on.

-age ultimately from Latin, used to form an unspecified mass or amount or abstract nouns 1. from other nouns, with meanings such as "collection" (coinage = a collection or group of coins) and "quantity or measure" (footage = quantity of feet in measurement). 2. from verbs, with meanings such as "process" (coverage = the act or process of covering), "the outcome of, the fact of" or "the physical effect or remains of" (spoilage = the result of spoiling; wreckage = the remains of wrecking), and "amount charged" (towage = charge for towing; postage = amount charged for posting, that is, sending through the mail).

-aholic originally taken from the word *alcoholic,* and now used to form new words with the general meaning "a person who is addicted to or strongly desires" the activity being shown by the initial part of the word. Thus, a chargeaholic is someone who uses a charge card a lot; a foodaholic is someone who always wants food. Compare -holic.

-al-[1] from Latin, added to nouns to form adjectives meaning "relating to, of the kind of, having the form or character of": autumn + -al: autumnal (= relating to the season autumn); nature + -al: natural (= having the character of nature).

-al-[2] from Latin, added to verbs to form nouns meaning "the act of": deny + -al: denial (= the act of denying); refuse + -al: refusal (= the act of refusing).

-ally form from -all + -ly, used to form adverbs from certain adjectives ending in -ic: terrific (adj.) + -ally: terrifically (adv.).

-an from Latin, meaning "of, pertaining to, having qualities of," 1. added to names of places or people to form adjectives and nouns meaning a. being connected with a place: Chicago + -an: Chicagoan; b. having membership in a group of: Episcopal + -(i)an: Episcopalian; 2. used to form adjectives meaning "of or like (someone); supporter or believer of": Christ + -(i)an: Christian; Freud + -(i)an: Freudian (= supporter of or believer in the theories of Sigmund Freud). 3. used to form nouns from words ending in -ic or -y meaning "one who works with": electric + -(i)an: electrician; comedy + -an: comedian.

-ance ultimately from Latin, used 1. after some adjectives ending in -ant to form nouns meaning "quality or state of": brilliant + -ance: brilliance. 2. after some verb roots to form nouns: appear + -ance: appearance; resemble + -ance: resemblance. See -ant, -ence.

-ant from Latin, used 1. after some verbs to form adjectives meaning "doing or performing (the action of the verb)": please + -ant: pleasant (= doing the pleasing). 2. after some verbs to form nouns meaning "one who does or performs (the action of the verb, often a formal action)": serve + -ant: servant (= one who serves); apply (+ ic) + -ant: applicant (= one who formally applies, as for a job). 3. after some verbs to form nouns meaning: "substance that does or performs (the action of the verb)": cool (verb = "to make cool") + -ant: coolant (= substance to keep engines cool). See -ent.

-ar from Latin, used 1. after some nouns (many of which have an l before the end) to form adjectives: circle + -ar: circular; single + -ar: singular. 2. after some verbs to form nouns meaning "one who does or performs an act of": beg + -ar: beggar; lie + -ar: liar.

-ard from French, used after some verbs and nouns to form nouns that refer to persons who regularly do an activity, or who are characterized in a certain way, as indicated by the stem: dullard (= one who is dull); drunkard (= one who is drunk).

-arian from Latin, used 1. after some nouns and adjectives that end in -ary to form personal nouns: library + -arian: librarian; seminary + -arian: seminarian; veterinary + -arian: veterinarian. 2. after some roots to form nouns meaning "a person who supports, calls for, or practices the principles of (the root noun)": authority + -arian: authoritarian (= one who believes in central authority); totality + -arian: totalitarian (= one who believes in total governmental rule).

-art variant form of -ard, found in such words as: braggart.

-ary from Latin, used 1. after some nouns to form adjectives meaning: "relating to, connected with": element + -ary: elementary; honor + -ary: honorary. 2. after some roots to form personal nouns, or nouns that refer to objects that hold or contain things: secretary; libr- (= root meaning "book") + -ary: library (= place for holding books); glossary (= place containing specialized words and their meanings). 3. after some nouns to form adjectives meaning "contributing to; for the purpose of": inflation + -ary: inflationary (= contributing to inflation); compliment + -ary: complimentary (= for the purpose of complimenting).

-ate 1. from Latin, used to form adjectives meaning "showing; full of": passion + -ate: passionate (= showing passion); consider + -ate: considerate (= showing the action of considering); literate. 2. used to form verbs meaning "cause to become (like); act as": regular + -ate: regulate (= make regular, act by rule); active + -ate: activate (= cause to become active); hyphenate; calibrate. 3. used to form nouns meaning a. "a group of people": elector + -ate: electorate (= group who elect). b. "an area ruled by": caliph (a kind of ruler) + -ate: caliphate (= area ruled by a caliph); protector + -ate: protectorate (= area ruled by a protecting nation). c. "the office, institution, or function of": consul + -ate: consulate; magistrate; potentate.

-ation from Latin, used after some verbs or adjectives (some of which end in -ate) to form nouns meaning "state or process of": starve + -ation: starvation (= condition of starving); separate + -ation: separation (= state of being separate).

-ative from Latin, used after some verbs (some of which end in -ate) and nouns to form adjectives: regulate + -ative: regulative (= with the power to regulate); norm (= rule) + -ative: normative (= having rules).

-ator from Latin, used after verbs ending in -ate to form nouns meaning "person or thing that does or performs (the action of the verb)": agitate + -ator: agitator (= person who agitates; machine that agitates); vibrate + -ator: vibrator (= thing that vibrates); narrator; generator; mediator; incubator.

-based from the word *base,* used 1. after nouns to form adjectives. 2. after nouns of place to form adjectives meaning "operating or working from": ground + -based: ground-based (= operating from the ground); New York + -based: New York–based (= working from New York). 3. after nouns to form adjectives meaning "making use of": computer + -based: computer-based (= making use of computers; as in "computer-based instruction"); logic + -based: logic-based (= making use of logic).

-burger taken from the word *hamburger,* and used after roots and some words to form nouns that mean "the food added to, or substituted for, a basic hamburger": cheese + -burger: cheeseburger (= a hamburger with cheese added on top); fish + -burger: fishburger (= fish substituted for the meat of a hamburger).

-cracy ultimately from Greek, meaning "power; rule; government," used after roots to form nouns meaning "rule; government": auto- + -cracy: autocracy = government by one ruler); theo- ("God") + -cracy: theocracy (= a country governed by the rule of God or a god). Compare -crat.

-crat ultimately from Greek, meaning "ruler; person having power," used after roots to form nouns meaning "ruler; member of a ruling body": auto- + -crat: autocrat (= a ruler governing alone). Compare -cracy.

-cy from French and Latin, used 1. to form nouns from adjectives that have stems that end in -t, -te, -tic, and especially -nt a. to form abstract nouns: democrat + -cy: democracy; accurate + -cy: accuracy; expedient + -cy: expediency; lunatic + -cy: lunacy. b. to form action nouns: vacant + -cy: vacancy; occupant + -cy: occupancy. 2. to form nouns meaning "rank or office of": captain + -cy: captaincy (= rank or office of a captain); magistra(te) + -cy: magistracy (= office of a magistrate).

-dom from Old English, used after some nouns and adjectives to form nouns meaning 1. "domain or area ruled": king + -dom: kingdom (= area a king rules). 2. "collection of persons": official + -dom: officialdom (= a collection of officials). 3. "rank": earl + -dom: earldom (= the rank or position of an earl). 4. "general condition": free + -dom: freedom (= general condition of being free).

-ed from Old English, 1. added to words with the following rules of form: a. for most regular verbs that end in a consonant, -ed is added directly afterwards: cross + -ed: crossed. When the verb ends in -y, the -y changes to -i and -ed is added: ready + -ed: readied. If the root ends in -e, an e is dropped: save + -ed: saved. b. The pronunciation of the suffix -ed depends on the sound that appears before it. After the sounds p, k, f, th, s, sh, and ch, the suffix is pronounced (t): cross + -ed: crossed (kr(tmst); after the sounds t, d, it is pronounced (id): edit + -ed: edited (ed'i tid); after all other sounds it is pronounced (d): budge + -ed: budged (bujd). 2. carries a number of different meanings. It is used a. to form the past tense and past participle of regular verbs: He crossed the river. He had crossed the river when we got there. b. to form an adjective indicating a condition or quality due to action of the verb: inflated balloons (= balloons that have been inflated). c. after nouns to form adjectives meaning "possessing, having, or characterized by (whatever the noun base is)": beard + -ed: bearded (= possessing or having a beard).

-ee from French, used 1. after verbs that take an object to form nouns meaning "the person who is the object of the action of the verb": address + -ee: addressee (= the person whom someone else addresses). 2. after verbs that do not take an object to form nouns meaning "the one doing or performing the act of the verb": escape + -ee: escapee (= one performing the act of escaping). 3. after other words to form nouns meaning "the one who is or does": absent + -ee: absentee (= one who is absent).

-eer from French, used to form nouns meaning "the person who produces, handles, or is associated with" the base word: engine + -eer: engineer (= person handling an engine).

-en from Old English, used 1. a. after some adjectives to form verbs meaning "to be or make": hard + -en: harden (= to be or make hard). b. after some nouns to form verbs meaning "to add to, cause to be, or have": length + -en: lengthen (= to add length to; make long). 2. after some nouns that are materials or sources of something to form adjectives that describe the source or material: gold + -en: golden (= like gold).

-ence from Latin, used 1. after some adjectives ending in -ent to form nouns meaning "quality or state of": abstin(ent) + -ence: abstinence. 2. after some verb roots to form nouns: depend + -ence: dependence. See -ance, -ent.

-ent from Latin, used 1. after some verbs to form adjectives meaning "doing or performing (the action of the verb)": differ + -ent: different. 2. after some verbs to form nouns meaning "one who does or performs (the action)": stud(y) + -ent: student (= one who studies). See -ant, -ence.

-er-[1] from Old English, used 1. after verbs to form nouns meaning "a person, animal, or thing that performs the action of the verb" or "the person, animal, or thing used in performing the action of the verb": bake + -er: baker (= a person who bakes); teach + -er: teacher (= a person who teaches); fertilize + -er: fertilizer (= a thing that is used to fertilize) 2. after nouns to form new nouns that refer to the occupation, work, or labor of the root noun: hat + -er: hatter (= one whose work is making hats); roof + -er: roofer (= one whose occupation is repairing roofs). 3. after nouns to form new nouns that refer to the place of origin, or the dwelling place, of the root noun: Iceland + -er: Icelander (= person who originally comes from Iceland); southern + -er: southerner (= a person who originally comes from, or lives in, the south). Compare -ier, -or.

-er-[2] from Middle English, regularly used to form the comparative form of short adjectives and adverbs: hard + -er: harder; small + -er: smaller; fast + -er: faster.

-ery (or -ry) from French, used 1. to form nouns that refer to a. things in a collection: green + -ery: greenery (= green plants as a group); machine + -ery: machinery (= a group or collection of machines) b. people in a collection: Jew + -ry: Jewry (= Jews as a group); peasant + -ry: peasantry (= peasants as a group) c. an occupation, activity, or condition: dentist + -ry: dentistry (= occupation of a dentist); rival + -ry: rivalry (= condition of being a rival); rob + -ery: robbery (= activity of robbing or being robbed). 2. to form nouns that refer to a place where the activity of the root is done: bake + -ery: bakery (= place where baking is done); wine + -ery: winery (= place where wine is made).

-ese ultimately from Latin, used 1. after nouns that refer to place names: a. to form adjectives to describe things made in or relating to the place: Japan + -ese: Japanese (= of or relating to Japan or its people); Vienna + -ese: Viennese (= of or relating to Vienna or its people) b. to form nouns with the meanings "the people living in (the place)" or "the language of (the place)": Vietnam + -ese: Vietnamese (= the people living in or the language spoken in Vietnam). 2. to form nouns that describe in an insulting or humorous way the language characteristic of or typical of the base word: Brooklyn + -ese: Brooklynese (= the language characteristic of Brooklyn); journal + -ese: journalese (= the language typical of journalists).

-esque from French, used after nouns and proper names to form adjectives meaning "resembling," "in the style or manner of," "suggesting the work of" the person or thing denoted by the base word: Kafka + -esque: Kafkaesque (= in the style or manner of Franz Kafka); Lincoln + -esque: Lincolnesque (= in the style of Abraham Lincoln); picture + -esque: picturesque (= resembling or suggesting a picture).

-ess from French, used to form a feminine noun: count + -ess: countess; god + -ess: goddess; lion + -ess: lioness. Usage. The use of words ending in ess declined sharply in the latter half of the twentieth century, but some are still current: actress (but some women prefer actor); adventuress; enchantress; governess (only in its child-care sense); heiress (largely in journalistic writing); hostess (but women who conduct radio and television programs are hosts); seamstress; seductress; temptress; and waitress.

-est from Old English, regularly used to form the superlative form of short adjectives and adverbs: fast + -est: fastest; soon + -est: soonest; warm + -est: warmest.

-ette from French, used 1. after nouns to form nouns that refer to a smaller version of the original noun or root: kitchen + -ette: kitchenette (= small kitchen); novel + -ette: novelette (= smaller novel). 2. after nouns to form nouns that refer specifically to a female: major + -ette: majorette (= female leader of a band, or baton twirler); usher + -ette: usherette (= female usher in a movie theater). 3. after nouns to form nouns that refer to a name that is an imitation product of the root: leather + -ette: leatherette (= imitation leather product). Usage. English nouns in which -ette signifies a feminine role or identity have been thought of as implying inferiority or unimportance and are now generally avoided. Only (drum) majorette is still widely used, usually indicating a young woman who twirls a baton with a marching band.

-ferous from the root -fer + the suffix -ous. This suffix is found in such words as: coniferous, pestiferous.

-fest from German, added to nouns to form nouns meaning "an assembly of people engaged in a common activity" named by the first element of the compound: gab + -fest: gabfest (= group of people gabbing or talking a lot); song + -fest: songfest (= assembly of people singing together).

-fold from Old English, used after words that refer to a number or quantity to form adjectives meaning "having the number of kinds or parts" or "multiplied the number of times": four + -fold: fourfold (= multiplied four times); many + -fold: manyfold (= having many parts or kinds).

-footed from the word *foot*, added to nouns to form adjectives meaning "having (the kind of, number of, etc.) a foot or feet indicated": a four-footed animal (= an animal having four feet).

-free from Old English, used after nouns to form adjectives meaning "not containing (the noun mentioned); without": sugar + -free: sugar-free (= not containing sugar); trouble + -free: trouble-free (= without trouble).

-ful from Old English, used 1. after nouns to form adjectives meaning "full of; characterized by": beauty + -ful: beautiful (= full of beauty); care + -ful: careful (= characterized by care). 2. after verbs to form adjectives meaning "tending to; able to": harm + -ful: harmful (= tending to harm); wake + -ful: wakeful (= tending to stay awake). 3. after nouns to form nouns meaning "as much as will fill": spoon + -ful: spoonful (= as much as will fill a spoon); cup + -ful: cupful (= as much as will fill a cup).

-fy ultimately from Latin, used 1. after roots to form verbs meaning "to make; cause to be; render": pure + -fy: purify (= to make pure); simple + -fy: simplify (= make simple); liquid + -fy: liquefy (= to make into a liquid). 2. to mean "cause to conform to": citify (= cause to conform to city ways). Compare -ify.

-gate derived from *Watergate*, originally the name of a hotel complex where officials of the Republican Party were caught trying to burglarize Democratic Party headquarters. Watergate came to be associated with "a political cover-up and scandal." The suffix is used after some nouns to form nouns that refer to scandals resulting from concealed crime in government or business: Iran-Contra + -gate: Iran-Contragate (= a scandal involving arms sales and purchases with Iran and the Nicaraguan Contras).

-gon from Greek, meaning "side; angle." This suffix is used after roots to form nouns that refer to plane figures having the number of sides mentioned: poly- (= many) + -gon: polygon (= a many-sided figure).

-gram from Greek, meaning "what is written." It is used after roots to form nouns that refer to something written or drawn, either by hand or machine: cardio- (= of or relating to the heart) + -gram: cardiogram (= a recording and diagram of a heartbeat, drawn by a machine). Compare -graph.

-hearted from Middle English, used after adjectives to form adjectives meaning "having the character or personality of (the adjective mentioned)": cold + -hearted: coldhearted (= having a cold heart; unkind or mean); light + -hearted: lighthearted (= feeling light and happy).

-holic another form of -aholic: choco(late) + -holic: chocoholic (= person addicted to chocolate).

-hood from Old English, used to form nouns meaning 1. "the state or condition of": likely + -hood: likelihood (= the state or condition of being likely); child + -hood: childhood (= the state or period of time of being a child). 2. "a body or group of persons of a particular character or class": priest + -hood: priesthood (= a body of priests).

-ian from Latin, used to form nouns and adjectives that have a connection to the root word: Orwell + -ian: Orwellian (= interested in, or relating to, the writing of George Orwell); Washington + -ian: Washingtonian (= a person who lives in Washington).

-iatrics from Greek, used after some roots to form nouns meaning "healing; the medical practice of": ger- (= elderly people) + -iatrics: geriatrics (= the healing of older people); ped- (= child) + -iatrics: pediatrics (= medical practice involving children).

-iatry from Greek, used after some roots to form nouns meaning "healing; the medical practice of": pod- (= foot) + -iatry: podiatry (= the healing of the foot); psych- (= the mind) + -iatry: psychiatry (= the medical practice dealing with the mind).

-ibility from Latin, used to form nouns from adjectives that end in -ible: reducible (adj.): reducibility (= the state or condition of being reducible, of being able to be reduced); flexible (adj.): flexibility (= the state or condition of being able to move smoothly). See -ability, -able, -ible.

-ible a variant form of -able, used after roots, mostly of verbs, to form adjectives meaning "capable of, fit for, tending to": cred- (= believe) + -ible: credible (= that can be believed); vis- (= see) + -ible: visible (= that can be seen); reduce + -ible: reducible (= that can be reduced). See -ability, -able, -ibility.

-ic from Middle English, used after nouns to form adjectives meaning "of or relating to": metal + -ic: metallic; poet + -ic: poetic. This suffix is also used after nouns to form adjectives meaning "having some characteristics of; in the style of": ballet + -ic: balletic; sophomore + -ic: sophomoric; Byron + -ic: Byronic (= in the style of the writer Byron).

-ical a combination of -ic and -al1, used after roots to form adjectives meaning "of or relating to": rhetor- + -ical: rhetorical. This suffix originally provided synonyms to adjectives that ended in -ic: poet + -ic: poetic; poet + -ical: poetical. But some of these pairs of words or formations are now different in meaning: econom- + -ic: economic (= of or relating to economics); econom- + -ical: economical (= being careful in spending money); histor- + -ic: historic (= having a long history; important); histor- + -ical: historical (= happening in the past).

-ician extracted from *physician, musician,* etc., used after nouns or roots to form nouns meaning "the person having the occupation or work of": beauty + -ician: beautician (= person who works in a beauty shop); mort- (= death) + -ician: mortician (= person working to prepare dead people for burial).

-ics from Latin, used after roots to form nouns meaning "a body of facts, knowledge, or principles." Such nouns usually correspond to adjectives ending in -ic or -ical: eth- (= custom; character) + -ics: ethics (= the principles of good character); phys- (= body) + -ics: physics (= the principles of bodies in motion and at rest).

-ier from French, used after nouns or roots to form nouns meaning "person or thing that does (the action of the word mentioned); person or thing in charge of (the word mentioned)": finance + -ier: financier (= person doing finance); cour- (= run) + -ier: courier (= messenger); hotel + -ier: hotelier (= person in charge of hotels). Compare -er-1.

-ify from French, used to form verbs meaning "cause to be in (a stated condition); to make or cause to become (a certain condition)": intense + -ify: intensify (= cause to be intense); speechify (= make speeches). See -fy.

-in extracted from *sit-in*, used after some verbs to form nouns that refer to organized protests through, using, or in support of the named activity: pray + -in: pray-in (= a protest in which participants engage in passive resistance and prayer).

-ine-[1] from Latin, used after some roots or nouns to form adjectives meaning "of, relating to, or characteristic of; of the nature of; made of": crystal + -ine: crystalline (= of, like, or made of crystal); equ- (= horse) + -ine: equine (= of or relating to horses).

-ine-[2] from French, used after some roots to form nouns that name chemical substances and elements: caffe- (= coffee) + -ine: caffeine (= a chemical substance found in coffee); chlor- + -ine: chlorine.

-ing-[1] 1. from Old English, used after verbs to form nouns that express the action of the verb or its result, product, material, etc.: build + -ing: building:

the art of building; a new building. 2. after roots (other than verb roots) to form nouns: off + -ing: offing.

-ing-[2] from Middle English, used after verbs to form the present participle of verbs: walk + -ing: walking: Is the baby walking yet? These participles are often used as adjectives: war + -ing: warring: warring factions. Some adjectives ending in -ing are formed by combining a prefix with a verb. Thus *outgoing* is formed from out- + the present participle form of the verb go (= going). Other examples: uplifting, outstanding, incoming.

-ion ultimately from Latin, used after some roots to form nouns that refer to action or condition: uni- (= one) + -ion: union (= condition of being one). Compare -tion.

-ious from Latin, a variant form of -ous, used after roots to form adjectives: hilar- (= cheerful) + -ious: hilarious (= very funny).

-ise chiefly British. See -ize.

-ish from Old English, used 1. after nouns or roots to form adjectives meaning a. relating to; in the same manner of; having the characteristics of: brute + -ish: brutish. b. of or relating to the people or language of: Brit- + -ish: British; Swede + -ish: Swedish. c. like; similar to: baby + -ish: babyish; mule + -ish: mulish; girl + -ish: girlish. d. addicted to; inclined or tending to: book + -ish: bookish (= tending to read books a great deal). e. near or about: fifty + -ish: fiftyish (= nearly fifty years old). 2. after adjectives to form adjectives meaning "somewhat, rather": old + -ish: oldish (= somewhat old); red + -ish: reddish (= somewhat red); sweet + -ish: sweetish.

-ism from Greek, used 1. after verb roots to form action nouns: baptize: bapt- + -ism: baptism. 2. to form nouns showing action or practice: adventure + -ism: adventurism (= the action or practice of taking risks in intervening in international affairs). 3. used to form nouns showing state or condition: alcoholism (= disease or condition in which alcohol is involved). 4. after roots to form nouns showing the names of principles or doctrines: Darwinism (= principles of Darwin's theory of evolution); despotism. 5. to form nouns showing an example of a use: witticism (= example of something witty); Africanism (= word from Africa or from an African language). Compare -ist, -ize.

-ist from French and Latin, forms nouns usually corresponding to verbs ending in -ize and nouns ending in -ism, and referring to a person who practices or is concerned with something: novel + -ist: novelist (= someone writing a novel); terrorist (= one who practices terrorism, one who terrorizes).

-ite from Latin, used after nouns and roots to form nouns meaning: 1. "a person associated with or living in a place; a person connected with a tribe, leader, set of beliefs, system, etc.": Manhattan + -ite: Manhattanite; Israel + -ite: Israelite; Labor + -ite: Laborite (= someone following the Labor Party). 2. "mineral or fossil; explosive; chemical compound or drug product": anthracite, cordite, dynamite, sulfite.

-itis ultimately from Greek, used 1. after roots that refer to an inflammation or disease affecting a certain part of the body: appendix + -itis: appendicitis; bronchi (= part of the lungs) + -itis: bronchitis. 2. to form nouns made up for a particular occasion to refer to something comparable in a funny way to a disease: The teenagers seem to be suffering from telephonitis (= excessive use of the telephone, as if using it were a disease).

-ive from French and Latin, used after roots or nouns to form adjectives meaning "having a tendency or connection with; like": act(ion) + -ive: active (= tending to be full of action or activity); sport + -ive: sportive (= to like sports).

-ize ultimately from Greek, used to form verbs meaning 1. "to make; cause to become": fossil + -ize: fossilize (= to make something into a fossil); sterile + -ize: sterilize (= to make something sterile). 2. "to convert into, give a specified character or form to; change to a state of": computer + -ize: computerize (= make an office use computers); dramat- + -ize: dramatize (= give the form of a drama to some other piece of work); American + -ize: Americanize (= convert to an American character). 3. "to subject to; cause to undergo or suffer from (an emotion or a process, sometimes named after its originator)": hospital + -ize: hospitalize (= cause to undergo treatment in a hospital); terror + -ize: terrorize (= cause to suffer terror); galvan- + -ize: galvanize (= to coat metal or stimulate electrically, as by the experiments of L. Galvani, Italian physicist. Also, chiefly British, -ise.

-less from Old English, used 1. after nouns to form adjectives meaning "without, not having (the thing or quality named by the noun)": care + -less: careless; shame + -less: shameless 2. after verbs to form adjectives meaning "that cannot be" plus the -ed/en form of the verb; or "that never" plus the -s form of the verb: tire + -less: tireless (= that never tires); count + -less: countless (= that cannot be counted).

-let from Middle English, used 1. after a noun to form a noun that is a smaller version of the original noun or root: book + -let: booklet (= a smaller book); pig + -let: piglet (= a smaller pig). 2. after a noun to form a noun that is a band, ornament, or article of clothing worn on the part of the body mentioned: ankle + -let: anklet (= piece of clothing like a sock worn on the ankle); wrist + -let: wristlet (= ornament like a bracelet worn on the wrist).

-like from Middle English, used after nouns to form adjectives meaning "of or resembling (the noun base)": child + -like: childlike; life + -like: lifelike.

-ling from Old English, used 1. to form a noun that indicates a feeling of distaste or disgust for the person or thing named: hire + -ling: hireling (= someone hired to do menial or distasteful tasks); under + -ling: underling. 2. to form a noun that is a smaller version or example of the base word: prince + -ling; duck + -ling: duckling.

-logy from Greek, meaning "word." It is used after roots to form nouns meaning "field of study, discipline; list of": astro- (= star) + -logy: astrology (= study of the influence of stars or events); bio- (= life) + -logy: biology (= study of living things).

-ly from Middle English, used 1. after adjectives to form adverbs: glad + -ly: gladly; gradual + -ly: gradually. 2. after nouns that refer to units of time, to form adjectives and adverbs meaning "at or for every (such unit of

Building Blocks of English

time)": hour + -ly: hourly (= at every hour); day + -ly: daily (= on or for every day). 3. after nouns to form adjectives meaning "like (the noun mentioned):" saint + -ly: saintly; coward + -ly: cowardly.

-man from Old English, used to form nouns meaning "person, or man, who is or does (something connected with the noun base)": mail + -man: mailman (= person who delivers mail).

-mania from Greek, used after roots to form nouns meaning "great or strong enthusiasm for (the element of the root)": biblio- (= book) + -mania: bibliomania (= excessive or strong interest or enthusiasm for books).

-ment from French and Latin, used 1. after verbs to form nouns that refer to the action of the verb: govern + -ment: government. 2. after verbs to form nouns that refer to a state or condition resulting from the action of a verb: refresh + -ment: refreshment. 3. after verbs to form nouns that refer to a product resulting from the action of a verb: frag- + -ment: fragment (= a piece resulting from the breaking off of something).

-ness from Old English, used after adjectives and verbs ending in -ing or -ed/-en to form nouns that refer to the quality or state of the adjective or verb: dark + -ness: darkness; prepared + -ness: preparedness (= a state of being prepared).

-o derived from Romance-language nouns ending in -o, used 1. as the final element in certain nouns that are shortened from longer nouns (and often made into slang words in the process): ammo (from "ammunition"); combo (from "combination"); promo (from "promotion"). 2. after certain adjectives and nouns to form nouns that have an unfavorable or insulting meaning: weird + -o: weirdo (= a very weird person); wine + -o: wino (= someone who drinks too much wine). 3. after certain nouns and adjectives to form informal nouns or adjectives; these are often used when speaking directly to another: kid + -o: kiddo (= a kid or person); neat + -o: neato (= an informal use of "neat"); right + -o: righto (= an informal use of "right").

-off from Old English, used to form nouns that name or refer to a competition or contest, especially between finalists or to break a tie: cook + -off: cook-off (= a cooking contest); runoff (= a deciding final contest).

-oid from Greek, used to form adjectives and nouns meaning "resembling, like," with the suggestion of an incomplete or imperfect similarity to the root element: human + -oid: humanoid (= resembling a human, but not quite the same).

-onym from Greek, meaning "word, name." This meaning is found in such words as: pseudonym, homonym.

-or from French, used to form nouns that are agents, or that do or perform a function: debtor, tailor, traitor, projector, repressor, sensor, tractor.

-ory-[1] 1. from Middle English, used after nouns and verbs that end in -e to form adjectives meaning "of or relating to (the noun or verb mentioned)": excrete + -ory: excretory (= of or relating to excreting); sense + -ory: sensory (= of or relating to the senses). 2. after certain roots to form adjectives meaning "providing or giving": satisfact- + -ory: satisfactory (= giving satisfaction).

-ory-[2] from Latin, used after roots to form nouns that refer to places or things that hold (the root), or places that are used for (the root): cremat- + -ory: crematory (= a place where bodies are cremated); observat(ion) + -ory: observatory (= place where observations of the heavens are made).

-ose-[1] from Latin, used after roots to form adjectives meaning "full of, abounding in, given to, or like (the root)": verb- (= word) + -ose: verbose (= full of words); bellic- (= war) + -ose: bellicose (= eager for fighting or war).

-ose-[2] extracted from *glucose,* used after roots to form nouns that name sugars, carbohydrates, and substances that are formed from proteins: fruct- + -ose: fructose (= a fruit sugar); lact- + -ose: lactose (= a milk sugar); prote- + ose: proteose (= a compound made from protein).

-ous from French, used 1. after roots to form adjectives meaning "possessing, full of (a given quality)": glory + -ous: glorious; wonder + ous: wondrous; covet + -ous: covetous; nerve + -ous: nervous. 2. after roots to form adjectives referring to the names of chemical elements: stannous chloride; SNC12.

-person from Latin, used to replace some paired, sex-specific suffixes such as -man and -woman or -er[1] and -ess: salesman/saleswoman are replaced by sales + -person: salesperson.

-phile from Greek, used 1. after roots and sometimes words to form nouns meaning "lover of, enthusiast for (a given object)": biblio- + -phile: bibliophile (= lover of books); Franco- + -phile: Francophile (= lover of France or French things). 2. after roots to form nouns meaning "a person sexually attracted to or overly interested in (a given object)": pedo- + -phile: pedophile (= someone with a sexual attraction for children).

-phobe from Greek, used after roots and sometimes words to form nouns that refer to persons who have a fear of something named by the root or preceding word: Anglo- + phobe: Anglophobe (= fear of English-speakers or of England).

-phobia from Greek, used after roots and sometimes words to form nouns with the meaning "dread of, unreasonable hatred toward (a given object)": agora- (= open space) + phobia: agoraphobia (= fear of open spaces); claustro- (= narrow spaces) + -phobia: claustrophobia (= hatred of small or narrow spaces).

-phobic from Greek, used after roots and words to form adjectives or nouns meaning "(a person) having a continuous, irrational fear or hatred toward" the object named in the root or preceding word: claustro- (= narrow spaces) + -phobic: claustrophobic (= [a person] having a fear or hatred of small or narrow spaces).

-proof ultimately from Latin, used to form adjectives meaning "resistant; not allowing through" the word mentioned: child + -proof: childproof (= resistant to a child's opening it); water + proof: waterproof (= not allowing water through).

-ry See -ery.

-s-[1] **(or -es)** from Old English, used after the root form of verbs and marks the third-person singular present indicative form, agreeing with a subject that is singular: He walks. She runs. The wind rushes through the trees.

-s-[2] **(or -es)** from Old English, used after nouns and marks the plural form: weeks; days; bushes; taxes; ladies; pianos; potatoes.

-ship from Old English, used to form nouns meaning 1. "state or condition of": friend + -ship: friendship; kin + -ship: kinship. 2. "the skill or ability of": statesman + -ship: statesmanship; apprentice + -ship: apprenticeship. 3. "the relation of": fellow + -ship: fellowship.

-sick from Old English, used to form adjectives meaning "sick or ill of or from (the noun of the root)": car + -sick: carsick (= sick from traveling in a car); air + -sick: airsick (= sick from flying in a plane).

-some-[1] from Old English, used to form adjectives meaning "like; tending to": burden + -some: burdensome (= like a burden); quarrel + -some: quarrelsome (= tending to quarrel).

-some-[2] from Old English, used to form nouns meaning "a collection (of the number mentioned) of objects": threesome (= a group of three).

-speak from Old English, used after the ends of words and sometimes roots to form compound nouns (often slang) that name the style or vocabulary of a certain field of work, interest, time period, etc., that is mentioned in the first word or root: ad(vertising) + -speak: adspeak (= the jargon of advertising); art + -speak: artspeak (= the language used in discussing art); future + -speak: futurespeak.

-ster from Old English, used at the ends of words to form nouns, often implying a bad or negative sense, and referring esp. to one's occupation, habit, or association: game + ster: gamester (= one greatly interested in games); trick + -ster: trickster (= one who uses or enjoys dishonest tricks).

-th ultimately from Greek, used after words that refer to numbers to form adjectives referring to the number mentioned: four + -th: fourth; tenth.

-tion from Latin, used after verbs to form nouns that refer to actions or states of the verb: relate + -tion: relation; sect- + -tion: section; abbreviate + -tion: abbreviation. Compare -ion.

-tious from Latin, used after roots to form adjectives, some of which are related to nouns: fiction: fictitious; ambition: ambitious; caution: cautious; rambunctious; propitious.

-tude from Latin, used after roots, especially adjectives, to form nouns that refer to abstract ideas: exact + -tude: exactitude; apt + -tude: aptitude; gratitude; altitude. In general, an "i" is added between consonants.

-ty from French, used after adjectives to form nouns that name or refer to a state or condition: able + -ty: ability; certain + -ty: certainty; chaste + -ty: chastity.

-ure from French, used after roots and verbs to form abstract nouns that refer to action, result, and instrument or use: press- + -ure: pressure; legislate + -ure: legislature; fract- + ure: fracture.

-**ville** from French, used 1. in place names, where it meant "city, town": Charlottesville. 2. after roots or words to form informal words, not all of them long-lasting, that characterize a condition, place, person, group, or situation: dulls + -ville (= a dull, boring situation); gloomsville.

-**ward** from Old English, used to form adjectives or adverbs meaning "in or toward a certain direction in space or time": backward. Also, -wards.

-**ways** from Middle English, used to form adjectives or adverbs meaning "in a certain direction, manner, or position": sideways.

-**wide** from Old English, used to form adjectives meaning "extending or applying throughout a certain, given space," as mentioned by the noun: community + -wide: communitywide (= applying to or throughout the community); countrywide; worldwide.

-**wise** from Old English, used 1. to form adjectives and adverbs meaning "in a particular manner, position, or direction": clockwise (= moving in a direction like the hands of a clock). 2. to form adverbs meaning "with reference to": Timewise we can finish the work, but qualitywise, I'm not so sure.

-**woman** from Middle English, used to form nouns meaning "involving a woman; a woman in the role of": chairwoman; spokeswoman.

-**worthy** from Old English, used to form adjectives meaning 1. "deserving of, fit for": news + -worthy: newsworthy (= fit for the news); trust + -worthy: trustworthy. 2. "capable of travel in or on": road + -worthy: roadworthy (= capable of traveling on the road); seaworthy.

-**y-**[1] from Old English, used to form adjectives meaning "having, showing, or similar to (the substance or action of the word or stem)": blood + -y: bloody; cloud + -y: cloudy; sexy; squeaky.

-**y-**[2] **(or -ie)** from Middle English, used 1.a. to form nouns that bring or add a meaning of dearness or familiarity to the noun or adjective root, such as proper names, names of pets, or in baby talk: Bill + -y: Billy; Susan + -ie: Susie; bird + -ie: birdie; sweetie. b. to form nouns that are informal, new, or intended to be new; sometimes these have slightly unpleasant meanings or associations: boondocks: boon- + -ies: boonies; group + -ie: groupiepreemie (= a premature baby); rookie. 2. after adjectives to form nouns, often with the meaning that the noun is an extreme (good or bad) example of the adjective or quality: bad + -ie: baddie; big + -ie: biggie; toughie; sharpie; sickie; whitey. Compare -o.

-**y-**[3] from Latin, used after verbs to form nouns of action and certain other abstract nouns: inquire + -y: inquiry; in + fame + -y: in-famy.

Roots

Aside from understanding the meanings of the various prefixes and suffixes, one of the quickest and most effective ways to improve your vocabulary is by learning to recognize the most common word, since any one of them can help you define a number of English words. Whenever you come upon an unfamiliar word, first check to see if it has a recognizable root. Even if you cannot define a word exactly, recognizing the root will still give you a general idea of the word's meaning. In this section, meanings of the most common Greek and Latin roots are provided. They are followed by definitions and examples of other commonly used roots.

Common Greek and Latin Roots

Root	Language	Meanings	Example
ag	Latin	act	agent
aster, astro	Greek	star	asterisk
cad, cas	Latin	fall	cadence
cap, cept	Latin	take, hold	receptacle
ced, cess	Latin	go	recessive
chrom	Greek	color	chromatic
chron, chrono	Greek	time	chronograph
cid, cis	Latin	kill, cut	incision
clud, clus	Latin	shut	seclusion
cosmo	Greek	world	cosmopolitan
cred	Latin	believe	credible
cur(r), curs	Latin	run	concur
dem	Greek	people	democracy
fer	Latin	bear	odoriferous
her, hes	Latin	cling	adhere
ject	Latin	throw	projection
leg, lect	Latin	read	legible
meter	Greek	measure	thermometer
onym	Greek	name, word	pseudonym
path	Greek	feeling	apathy
pel(l), puls	Latin	drive	repulse
phob	Greek	fear	claustrophobia
phon	Greek	sound	cacophony
pon, posit	Latin	put	postpone
port	Latin	carry	portable
psycho	Greek	mind	psychology
rupt	Latin	break	abrupt
scrib, script	Latin	write	inscription
sect	Latin	cut	dissect
sent, sens	Latin	feel	sensitive
sequ, secut	Latin	follow	sequel

Root	Language	Meanings	Example
soph	Greek	wisdom	sophistry
spect	Latin	look, prospect	outlook
sta, stat	Latin	stand	stable
tang, tact	Latin	touch	tactile, tangible
termin	Latin	end	terminate
tract	Latin	pull, draw	tractor
ven, vent	Latin	come	convene
vert, vers	Latin	turn	invert
vid, vis	Latin	see	provident
vinc, vict	Latin	conquer	invincible
volv, volut	Latin	roll, turn	evolve

List of Roots

-acr- from Latin, meaning "sharp." This meaning is found in such words as: acerbic, acrid, acrimonious, exacerbate.

-acro- from Greek, meaning "high." This meaning is found in such words as: acrobat, acronym, acrophobia.

-act- from Latin, meaning "to do; move." It is related to the root -ag-. This meaning is found in such words as: act, action, exact, transact.

-ag- from Latin and Greek, meaning "to move, go, do." This meaning is found in such words as: agent, agenda, agile, agitate.

-agon- from Greek, meaning "struggle, fight." This meaning is found in such words as: agony, antagonist, protagonist.

-agr- from Latin, meaning "farming; field." This meaning is found in such words as: agriculture, agronomy.

-alesc- from Latin, meaning "grow, develop." This meaning is found in such words as: adolescence, adolescent, coalesce.

-alg- from Greek, meaning "pain." This meaning is found in such words as: analgesic, neuralgia, nostalgia.

-ali- from Latin, meaning "other, different." This meaning is found in such words as: alias, alibi, alien, alienate.

-alte- from Latin, meaning "other, different." This meaning is found in such words as: alter, alternate, alternative, alternator, altruism, altruist.

-alti- from Latin, meaning "high; height." This meaning is found in such words as: altimeter, altitude, alto, exalt.

-am-[1] from Latin, meaning "love, like." This meaning is found in such words as: amiable, amorous, amour, paramour.

-am-[2] from Latin, meaning "take out; come out." This meaning is found in such words as: example, sample.

-ambl- from Latin, meaning "walk." This meaning is found in such words as: amble, ambulance, ambulate, perambulator, circumambulate.

-ampl- from Latin, meaning "enough; enlarge." This meaning is found in such words as: ample, amplify, amplitude.

Building Blocks of English 187

-andro- from Greek, meaning "male; man." This meaning is found in such words as: androgynous, android, polyandry.

-anima- from Latin, meaning "spirit, soul." This meaning is found in such words as: animate, animosity, animus, equanimity, inanimate.

-ann- from Latin, meaning "year." This meaning is found in such words as: annals, anniversary, annual, annuity, biannual, semiannual, superannuated.

-anthro- from Greek, meaning "man; human." This meaning is found in such words as: anthropocentric, anthropoid, anthropology, anthropomorphism, misanthrope. See also -andro-.

-apt- from Latin, meaning "fit, proper." This meaning is found in such words as: adapt, apt, aptitude, inept.

-arch- 1. from Greek, meaning "chief; leader, ruler." This meaning is found in such words as: archbishop, archdiocese, archpriest, monarch, matriarch, patriarch, anarchy, hierarchy, monarchy. 2. also used to form nouns that refer to persons who are the most important, most notable, or the most extreme examples of (the following noun): archenemy (= the most important enemy); archconservative (= the most extreme example of a conservative). 3. also appears with the meaning "first, earliest, original, oldest in time." This meaning is found in such words as: archaeology, archaism, archaic, archetype.

-arm- from Latin, meaning "weapon." This meaning is found in such words as: armada, armament, arms, disarmament.

-astro- (**or -aster-**) from Greek, meaning "star; heavenly body; outer space." These meanings are found in such words as: aster, asterisk, asteroid, astrology, astronomy, astronaut, disaster.

-athl- from Greek, meaning "contest, prize." This meaning is found in such words as: athlete, athletics, pentathlon.

-aud- from Latin, meaning "hear." This meaning is found in such words as: audible, audience, audio, audit, audition, auditorium.

-bat- from Latin, meaning "beat, fight." This meaning is found in such words as: battalion, batten, batter, battle, combat.

-bell- from Latin, meaning "war." This meaning is found in such words as: antebellum, bellicose, belligerence, belligerent.

-bene- from Latin, meaning "well." This meaning is found in such words as: benediction, benefactor, beneficial, benefit, benevolent, beneficent.

-biblio- from Greek, meaning "book." This meaning is found in such words as: bible, bibliography, bibliophile.

-botan- from Greek, meaning "plant, herb." This meaning is found in such words as: botanical, botany.

-brev- from Latin, meaning "short." This meaning is found in such words as: abbreviate, abridge, brevity, brief.

-cad- (**or -cas-**) from Latin, meaning "fall." This meaning is found in such words as: cadence, cadenza, decadent. See also -cide-2.

-cap- from Latin, meaning "take, hold." This meaning is found in such words as: capacious, captures, caption.

188   Building Blocks of English

-caut- from Latin, meaning "care; careful." This meaning is found in such words as: caution, cautious, caveat, precaution.

-cede- from Latin, meaning "go away from; withdraw; yield." This meaning is found in such words as: accede, antecedent, cede, concede, precede, precedent, recede, secede. See also -ceed-, -cess-.

-ceed- from Latin, meaning "go; move; yield." It is related to -cede-. This meaning is found in such words as: proceed, succeed.

-ceive- from Latin, meaning "get, receive." This meaning is found in such words as: conceive, deceive, misconceive, perceive, receive, transceiver.

-celer- from Latin, meaning "swift, quick." This meaning is found in such words as: accelerate, celerity, decelerate.

-cent- from Latin, meaning "one hundred." This meaning is found in such words as: cent, centavo, centigrade, centimeter, centennial, centipede, century, percent.

-cep- from Latin, meaning "get, receive, take." This meaning is found in such words as: accept, anticipate, perception, reception. See also -ceive-.

-cern- from Latin, meaning "separate; decide." These meanings are found in such words as: concern, discern.

-cert- from Latin, meaning "certain; sure; true." This meaning is found in such words as: ascertain, certain, certificate, certify, concert, disconcerted.

-cess- from Latin, meaning "move, yield." It is related to -cede-. This meaning is found in such words as: access, accessible, accessory, cession, process, procession, recess, recession, success, succession.

-chor- from Greek, meaning "sing; dance." This meaning is found in such words as: choir, choral, chord, chorus, choreograph, chorister.

-chrom- from Greek, meaning "color." This meaning is found in such words as: chromatic, chromosome, monochrome, polychromatic.

-chron- from Greek, meaning "time." This meaning is found in such words as: anachronism, chronic, chronicle, chronology, synchronize.

-cide-[1] from Latin, meaning "kill; cut down." This meaning is found in such words as: biocide, genocide, germicide, herbicide, homicide, insecticide, matricide, patricide, suicide.

-cide-[2] from Latin, meaning "fall; happen." It is related to -cad-. This meaning is found in such words as: accident, incident.

-cise- from Latin, meaning "cut (down)." It is related to -cide-2. This meaning is found in such words as: circumcise, decisive, incision, incisor, incisive, precise, scissors.

-claim- from Latin, meaning "call out; talk; shout." This meaning is found in such words as: acclaim, claim, clamor, exclaim, proclaim.

-clos- from Latin, meaning "close." This meaning is found in such words as: cloister, close, closet, disclose, enclose.

-clud- (or -clus-) from Latin, meaning "to close, shut." This meaning is found in such words as: include, seclude, inclusion, seclusion.

-cord- from Latin, meaning "heart." This meaning is found in such words as: accord, concord, concordance, cordial, discord.

-corp- from Latin, meaning "body." This meaning is found in such words as:

corpora, corporal, corporation, corps, corpse, corpus, corpuscle, incorporate.

-cosm- from Greek, meaning "world, universe; order, arrangement." This meaning is found in such words as: cosmetic, cosmic, cosmopolitan, cosmos, microcosm.

-cour- ultimately from Latin where it has the meaning "run; happen." It is related to -cur-. This meaning is found in such words as: concourse, courier, course, discourse, recourse.

-cred- from Latin, meaning "believe." This meaning is found in such words as: credence, credential, credible, credit, credo, credulous, creed, incredible.

-cres- from Latin, meaning "grow." This meaning is found in such words as: crescendo, crescent, decrease, increase.

-culp- from Latin, meaning "blame." This meaning is found in such words as: culpable, culprit, exculpate.

-cum- from Latin, meaning "with." It is used between two words to mean "with; combined with; along with": a garage-cum-workshop (= a garage that is combined with a workshop).

-cur- from Latin, meaning "run; happen." This meaning is found in such words as: concur, concurrent, currency, current, curriculum, cursive, cursor, cursory, occur, occurrence, recur, recurrence. See also -cour-.

-cura- from Latin, meaning "help; care." This meaning is found in such words as: accurate, curable, curate, curator, curative, cure, manicure, pedicure, secure, sinecure.

-cycle- from Greek, meaning "cycle; circle; wheel." This meaning is found in such words as: bicycle, cycle, cyclo, cyclone, cyclotron, recycle, tricycle.

-dece- from Latin, meaning "correct, proper." This meaning is found in such words as: decent, indecent.

-dent- from Latin, meaning "tooth." This meaning is found in such words as: dental, dentifrice, dentist, dentistry, denture.

-derm- from Greek, meaning "skin." This meaning is found in such words as: dermatitis, dermatology, dermis, epidermis, hypodermic, pachyderm, taxidermy.

-dict- from Latin, meaning "say, speak." This meaning is found in such words as: benediction, contradict, Dictaphone, dictate, dictator, diction, dictionary, dictum, edict, predict.

-doc- from Latin, meaning "to teach." This meaning is found in such words as: docile, doctor, doctrine, document.

-dox- from Greek, meaning "opinion, idea, belief." This meaning is found in such words as: doxology, orthodox.

-drom- from Greek, meaning "run; a course for running." This meaning is found in such words as: aerodrome, dromedary, hippodrome, palindrome, syndrome, velodrome.

-du- from Latin, meaning "two." This meaning is found in such words as: dual, duel, duet, duo, duplex, duplicity.

-duc- from Latin, meaning "to lead." This meaning is found in such words as:

abduct, abduction, adduce, aqueduct, conducive, conduct, deduce, deduct, ducal, duct, duke, educate, induce, induction, introduce, oviduct, produce, production, reduce, reduction, seduce, seduction, viaduct.

-dur- from Latin, meaning "hard; strong; lasting." These meanings are found in such words as: durable, duration, duress, during, endure.

-dyn- from Greek, meaning "power." This meaning is found in such words as: dynamic, dynamism, dynamite, dynamo, dynasty.

-equa- (or **-equi-**) from Latin, meaning "equal; the same." This meaning is found in such words as: equable, equal, equanimity, equilibrium, equity, equivocal, inequality, inequity, unequal.

-fac- from Latin, meaning "do; make." This meaning is found in such words as: benefactor, de facto, facsimile, fact, faction, faculty, manufacture. See also -fec-, -fic-.

-face- from Latin, meaning "form; face; make." It is related to -fac-. This meaning is found in such words as: deface, efface, facade, face, facet, facial, surface.

-fec- from Latin, meaning "do; make." It is related to the root -fac-. This meaning is found in such words as: affect, defecate, defect, effect, infect.

-fed- from Latin, meaning "group; league; trust." This meaning is found in such words as: confederate, federal, federalize, federation.

-fend- from Latin, meaning "strike." This meaning is found in such words as: defend, defense, defensive, fend, forfend, indefensible, offend, offense, offensive.

-fer- from Latin, meaning "carry." This meaning is found in such words as: confer, defer, differ, efferent, ferrous, ferry, infer, pestiferous, prefer, transfer.

-fess- from Latin, meaning "declare; acknowledge." This meaning is found in such words as: confess, confession, confessional, profess, profession, professional, professor.

-fic- from Latin, meaning "make, do." It is related to -fac- and -fec-. This meaning is found in such words as: beneficial, certificate, efficacy, fiction, honorific, horrific, pacific, prolific, simplification.

-fid- Latin, meaning "faith; trust." This meaning is found in such words as: confide, confidence, fidelity, fiduciary.

-fin- from Latin, meaning "end; complete; limit." This meaning is found in such words as: confine, define, definite, definition, final, finale, finance, fine, finish, finite.

-fix- from Latin, meaning "fastened; put; placed." This meaning is found in such words as: affix, fixation, infix, prefix, suffix.

-flat- from Latin, meaning "blow; wind." This meaning is found in such words as: conflate, deflate, flatulence, inflate.

-flect- from Latin, meaning "bend." It is related to -flex-. This meaning is found in such words as: deflect, inflect, genuflect, reflect.

-flex- from Latin, meaning "bend." It is related to -flect-. This meaning is found in such words as: circumflex, flex, flexible, reflex, reflexive.

-flor- from Latin, meaning "flower." This meaning is found in such words as:

efflorescence, flora, floral, florescence, florid, florist, flour, flourish, flower.
-**flu-** from Latin, meaning "flow." This meaning is found in such words as: affluence, affluent, confluence, effluence, effluent, flu, flue, fluctuate, fluent, fluid, flume, fluoride, flux, influence, influenza.
-**foli-** from Latin, meaning "leaf." This meaning is found in such words as: defoliate, foil, foliage, folio, portfolio.
-**form-** from Latin, meaning "form, shape." This meaning is found in such words as: conform, deform, formalize, format, formula, malformed, multiform, nonconformist, perform, platform, reform, transform, uniform.
-**fort-** from Latin, meaning "strong; strength." This meaning is found in such words as: comfort, discomfort, effort, fort, forte, fortify, fortitude, fortress, uncomfortable.
-**fortun-** from Latin, meaning "by chance; luck." This meaning is found in such words as: fortuitous, fortunate, fortune, misfortune, unfortunate.
-**frac-** Latin, meaning "break; broken." This meaning is found in such words as: fractious, fracture, fragile, fragment, frail, infraction, refraction.
-**frat-** from Latin, meaning "brother." This meaning is found in such words as: fraternal, fraternity, fratricide.
-**fug-** from Latin, meaning "flee; move; run." This meaning is found in such words as: centrifugal, centrifuge, fugitive, fugue, refuge, subterfuge.
-**funct-** from Latin, meaning "perform, execute; purpose, use." This meaning is found in such words as: defunct, disfunction, function, functional, malfunction, perfunctory.
-**fus-** from Latin, meaning "pour, cast; join; blend." This meaning is found in such words as: confuse, defuse, diffuse, effusive, fuse, fusion, infuse, profuse, suffuse, transfusion.

-**gam-** from Greek, meaning "marriage." This meaning is found in such words as: bigamy, bigamist, gamete, misogamist, polygamy.
-**gen-** from Greek and Latin, meaning "race; birth; born; produced." These meanings are found in such words as: antigen, carcinogen, congenital, degenerate, engender, erogenous, eugenics, gender, gene, generate, genus, homogenize.
-**geo-** from Greek, meaning "the earth; ground." This meaning is found in such words as: apogee, geography, geology, geopolitics, perigee.
-**gest-** from Latin, meaning "carry; bear." This meaning is found in such words as: congestion, digest, gestation, gesticulate, gesture, ingest, suggest.
-**glot-** from Greek, meaning "tongue." This meaning is found in such words as: diglossia, epiglottis, gloss, glossary, glossolalia, glottis, isogloss, polyglot.
-**gnos-** from Greek and Latin, meaning "knowledge." This meaning is found in such words as: agnostic, cognition, cognizant, diagnosis, diagnostic, incognito, precognition, prognosis, recognize.
-**grad-** from Latin, meaning "step; degree; rank." This meaning is found in such words as: biodegradable, centigrade, degrade, grad, gradation, gradient, gradual, graduate, retrograde, undergraduate, upgrade. See also -gress-.
-**graph-** from Greek, meaning "written down, printed, drawn." This meaning

is found in such words as: autograph, bibliography, biography, calligraphy, cartography, choreography, cinematography, cryptography, demographic, digraph, epigraph, ethnography, geography, graph, graphic, graphite, hagiography, holography, homograph, ideograph, lexicography, lithography, mimeograph, monograph, oceanography, orthography, paragraph, phonograph, photograph, pictograph, polygraph, pornography, seismograph, telegraph, typography. See also -gram.

-grat- from Latin, meaning "pleasing; thankful; favorable." This meaning is found in such words as: congratulate, grateful, gratify, gratis, gratitude, gratuitous, gratuity, ingrate, ingratiate, ingratitude.

-greg- from Latin, meaning "group; flock." This meaning is found in such words as: aggregate, congregate, desegregate, egregious, gregarious, segregate.

-gress- from Latin, meaning "step; move." It is related to -grad-. This meaning is found in such words as: aggression, congress, digress, egress, ingress, progress, regress, transgress.

-gyn- from Greek, meaning "wife; woman." This meaning is found in such words as: androgyny, gynecology, misogyny.

-hab- from Latin, meaning "live, reside." This meaning is found in such words as: cohabit, habitant, habitable, habitat, habitation, inhabit.

-habil- from Latin, meaning "handy; apt; able." These meanings are found in such words as: ability, able, habilitate, rehabilitate.

-hale- from Latin, meaning "breathe." This meaning is found in such words as: exhale, halitosis, inhale.

-hap- from Old Norse, meaning "luck; chance." This meaning is found in such words as: haphazard, hapless, happen, mishap, perhaps.

-helio- from Greek, meaning "sun." This meaning is found in such words as: aphelion, heliocentric, helium, perihelion.

-here- from Latin, meaning "cling, stick tight." It is related to -hes-. This meaning is found in such words as: adhere, adherent, cohere, coherence, coherent. See also -hes-.

-hes- Latin, meaning "cling, stick to." It is related to -here-. This meaning is found in such words as: adhesive, cohesive, hesitate.

-hetero- from Greek, meaning "the other of two; different." This meaning is found in such words as: heterogeneous, heterosexual.

-hexa- from Greek, meaning "six." This meaning is found in such words as: hexagon, hexameter.

-homo- from Greek, meaning "same, identical." This meaning is found in such words as: homogeneous, homogenize, homonym.

-horr- from Latin, meaning "shake, tremble." This meaning is found in such words as: abhor, abhorrent, horrendous, horrible, horrify, horror.

-hum- from Latin, meaning "ground." This meaning is found in such words as: exhume, humble, humiliate, humility, humus, posthumous.

-hydr- from Greek, meaning "water." This meaning is found in such words as: anhydrous, carbohydrate, dehydration, hydrant, hydrate, hydraulic, hydrocarbon, hydroelectric, hydrofoil, hydrogen, hydrophobia, hydroplane, hydroponics, hydrotherapy.

-jec- from Latin, meaning "throw; be near; place." This meaning is found in such words as: eject, adjacent, adjective, ejaculate, abject, dejection, conjecture, object, reject, inject, project, interject, trajectory, subject.

-jour- from French and ultimately from Latin, meaning "daily; of or relating to one day." This meaning is found in such words as: adjourn, journal, journey, sojourn.

-jud- from Latin, meaning "judge." It is related to -jur- and -jus-. This meaning is found in such words as: adjudge, adjudicate, injudicious, judge, judicial, misjudge, nonjudgmental, prejudgment, prejudice.

-junc- from Latin, meaning "join; connect." This meaning is found in such words as: adjoin, adjunct, conjunction, disjointed, disjunctive, enjoin, injunction, join(t), rejoinder, subjunctive.

-jur- from Latin, meaning "swear." It is related to the root -jus-, meaning "law; rule." This meaning is found in such words as: abjure, conjure, injure, juridical, jurisdiction, jury, perjure.

-jus- from Latin, meaning "law; rule; fair; just." It is related to the root -jur-. This meaning is found in such words as: adjust, just, justice, maladjusted, readjust, unjust.

-lab- from Latin, meaning "work." This meaning is found in such words as: belabor, collaborate, elaborate, labor, laborious.

-laps- from Latin, meaning "slip; slide; fall; make an error." This meaning is found in such words as: collapse, elapse, lapse, prolapse, relapse.

-lat-[1] from Latin, meaning "carried." This meaning is found in such words as: ablative, collate, correlate, dilatory, elated, oblate, prelate, prolate, relate, relative.

-lat-[2] from Latin, meaning "line; side." This meaning is found in such words as: bilateral, collateral, dilate, equilateral, lateral, latitude, unilateral, vasodilator.

-lax- from Latin, meaning "loose, slack." This meaning is found in such words as: lax, laxative, relax.

-lec- from Latin and Greek, meaning "gather; choose" and also "read." This meaning is found in such words as: collect, eclectic, eligible, elite, ineligible, election, lectern, lector, lecture, recollect, select. *See also -leg-*.

-leg- from Latin, meaning "law" and "to gather," also "to read." It is related to -lec-. These meanings are found in such words as: delegate, eclectic, illegal, illegible, intellect, intelligent, legacy, legal, legate, legend, legible, legion, legitimate, legislate, paralegal, privilege, relegate, sacrilege.

-lev- from Latin, meaning "lift; be light." This meaning is found in such words as: alleviate, cantilever, elevate, elevator, levee, lever, leverage, levitate, levity, levy, relevant, relieve.

-liber- from Latin, meaning "free." This meaning is found in such words as: deliver, liberal, liberate, libertine, liberty, livery.

-libr- from Latin, meaning "book." This meaning is found in such words as: libel, library, libretto.

-libra- from Latin, where it has the meaning "balance; weigh." This meaning is found in such words as: deliberate, equilibrium, librate.

-lig- from Latin, meaning "to tie; bind." This meaning is found in such words as: ligament, ligature, obligate, oblige, religion.

-lim- from Latin, meaning "line; boundary; edge; threshold." This meaning is found in such words as: eliminate, illimitable, limbic, limbo, liminal, limit, preliminary, sublime, subliminal. *See also* -lin-.

-lin- from Latin, meaning "string; line." This meaning is found in such words as: crinoline, colinear, curvilinear, delineate, line, lineage, lineal, lineament, linear, linen, lingerie, matrilinear, patrilineal, rectilinear. The meaning is also found in many compound words with line as the last part, such as baseline, guideline, hairline, pipeline, sideline, underline. *See also* -lim-.

-ling- from Latin, meaning "tongue." This meaning is found in such words as: bilingual, interlingual, language, lingo, linguine, linguistic, monolingual.

-lit- from Latin, meaning "letter; read; word." This meaning is found in such words as: alliteration, illiterate, letter, literacy, literal, literary, obliterate, transliteration.

-lith- from Greek, meaning "stone." This meaning is found in such words as: lithium, lithography, megalith, microlith, monolith, neolithic, paleolithic.

-loc- from Latin, meaning "location; place." This meaning is found in such words as: allocate, collocation, dislocate, echolocation, local, locale, locate, locative, locomotive, locus, relocate.

-log- from Greek, meaning "speak; word; speech." This meaning is found in such words as: analog, apology, chronology, decalogue, dialogue, doxology, epilogue, eulogy, ideology, homologous, illogical, logarithm, logic, logo, monologue, neologism, philology, syllogism, tautology, terminology.

-loq- (or **-loc-**) from Latin, meaning "speak; say." This meaning is found in such words as: circumlocution, elocution, eloquent, grandiloquent, interlocutor, locution, loquacious, magniloquent, soliloquy, ventriloquist.

-lu- (or **-lav-**) from Latin, meaning "wash." This meaning is found in such words as: dilute, lavatory, ablution.

-luc- from Latin, meaning "light." This meaning is found in such words as: elucidate, lucid, Lucite, lucubrate, pellucid, relucent, translucent.

-lud- (or **-lus-**) from Latin, meaning "to play." This meaning is found in such words as: allude, allusion, collusion, delude, elusive, illusion, illusory, interlude, ludicrous, prelude.

-lys- from Greek and Latin, meaning "to break down, loosen, dissolve." This meaning is found in such words as: analysis, catalyst, dialysis, electrolysis, electrolyte, hydrolysis, paralysis, paralytic, palsy, urinalysis.

-man-[1] from Latin, meaning "hand." This meaning is found in such words as: amanuensis, legerdemain, maintain, manacle, manage, manual, maneuver, manufacture, manure, manuscript.

-man-[2] from Latin, meaning "stay; to last or remain." This meaning is found in such words as: immanent, impermanent, permanent, remain.

-mand- from Latin, meaning "order." This meaning is found in such words as: command, countermand, demand, mandate, mandatory, remand.

-mater- from Latin, meaning "mother." This meaning is found in such words as: maternal, maternity, matriarch, matricide, matrimony, matrix, matron.

-mech- from Greek (but for some words comes through Latin), meaning "machine," and therefore "instrument or tool." This meaning is found in such

Building Blocks of English 195

words as: machination, machine, machinery, mechanic, mechanical, mechanize.

-medi- from Latin, meaning "middle." This meaning is found in such words as: immediate, intermediate, media, medial, median, mediate, mediator, medieval, mediocre, medium, multimedia.

-mem- from Latin, meaning "mind; memory." This meaning is found in such words as: commemorate, immemorial, memento, memo, memorandum, memoir, memorabilia, memorial, memory, remember, remembrance.

-men- from Latin, meaning "mind." This meaning is found in such words as: commentary, mental, mentality, mention, reminiscent.

-merc- from Latin, meaning "trade." This meaning is found in such words as: commerce, commercial, infomercial, mercantile, mercenary, merchant.

-merg- from Latin, meaning "plunge; dip; mix." This meaning is found in such words as: emerge, emergency, immerse, immersion, merge, merger, submerge.

-meter- from Greek, where it has the meaning "measure." This meaning is found in such words as: anemometer, barometer, centimeter, chronometer, diameter, geometry, kilometer, meter, metric, metronome, nanometer, odometer, parameter, pedometer, perimeter, symmetry.

-migr- from Latin, meaning "move to a new place; migrate." This meaning is found in such words as: emigrant, emigrate, immigrate, migrant, migrate, transmigration.

-min- from Latin, meaning "least; smallest." This meaning is found in such words as: diminish, diminution, diminutive, miniature, minimal, minimum, minor, minority, minuend, minus, minute.

-mir- from Latin, meaning "look at." This meaning is found in such words as: admirable, admire, admiration, miracle, miraculous, mirage, mirror.

-mis- from Latin, meaning "send." It is related to -mit-. This meaning is found in such words as: admission, commissar, commissary, commission, compromise, demise, dismiss, emissary, impermissible, intermission, missal, missile, mission, missionary, missive, omission, permission, permissive, promise, promissory, remiss, submission, surmise, transmission.

-misc- from Latin, meaning "mix." This meaning is found in such words as: miscegenation, miscellaneous, miscellany, miscible, promiscuous.

-miser- from Latin, meaning "wretched." This meaning is found in such words as: commiserate, miser, miserable, miserly, misery.

-mit- from Latin, meaning "send." It is related to -mis-. This meaning is found in such words as: admit, commit, committee, emit, intermittent, noncommittal, omit, permit, remit, remittance, submit, transmit.

-mne- from Greek, meaning "mind; remembering." This meaning is found in such words as: amnesia, amnesty, mnemonic.

-mob- from Latin, meaning "move." It is related to -mot- and -mov-. This meaning is found in such words as: automobile, mobile, mobility, mobilize.

-mod- from Latin, meaning "manner; kind; measured amount." This meaning is found in such words as: accommodate, commodious, immoderate, immodest, modal, mode, model, modern, modest, modicum, module, mood, outmoded, remodel.

-mon- from Latin, meaning "warn." This meaning is found in such words as: admonish, admonitory, admonition, monitor, monitory, monition, monster, monstrous, monument, premonition, summon.

-monstr- from Latin, meaning "show; display." This meaning is found in such words as: demonstrate, monstrance, muster, remonstrate.

-mor- from Latin, meaning "custom; proper." This meaning is found in such words as: amoral, demoralize, immoral, moral, morale, morality, mores.

-morph- from Greek, meaning "form; shape." This meaning is found in such words as: allomorph, amorphous, anthropomorphism, metamorphic, metamorphosis, morph, morpheme, morphine.

-mort- from Latin, meaning "death." This meaning is found in such words as: amortize, immortal, immortality, immortalize, morgue, mortal, mortality, mortgage.

-mot- from Latin, meaning "move." It is related to -mov-. This meaning is found in such words as: automotive, commotion, demote, emote, emotion, immotile, locomotive, motif, motion, motive, motivate, motor, promote, remote.

-mov- from Latin, meaning "move." It is related to -mot-. This meaning is found in such words as: movable, move, movement, removal, remove, unmoving.

-mut- from Latin, meaning "change." This meaning is found in such words as: commute, commutation, immutable, mutate, mutation, mutual, parimutuel, permutation, permute, transmute.

-nat- (or -nasc-) from Latin, meaning "born; birth." This meaning is found in such words as: cognate, denatured, innate, naive, nascent, natal, nativity, nation, national, native, nature, naturalize, supernatural.

-naut- from Greek, meaning "sailor." It has become generalized to mean "traveler." These meanings are found in such words as: aeronautic, astronaut, cosmonaut, nautical, nautilus.

-nav- from Latin, meaning "boat, ship." It is related to -naut-. This meaning is found in such words as: circumnavigate, naval, nave, navicular, navigable, navigate, navy.

-nec- (or -nex-) from Latin, meaning "tie; weave; bind together." This meaning is found in such words as: annex, connect, disconnect, interconnect, nexus, unconnected.

-neg- from Latin, meaning "deny; nothing." This meaning is found in such words as: abnegate, negate, negation, negative, neglect, negligee, negligence, negligible, renegade, renege.

-noc- (or -nox-) from Latin, meaning "harm; kill." This meaning is found in such words as: innocent, innocuous, nocuous, noxious, obnoxious.

-noct- from Latin, meaning "night." This meaning is found in such words as: equinoctial, noctambulism, nocturnal, nocturne.

-nom-[1] from Greek, meaning "custom; law; manage; control." This meaning is found in such words as: agronomy, anomalous, anomaly, anomie, astronomy, autonomic, autonomous, autonomy, economy, gastronome, gastronomy, taxonomy.

-nom-[2] from Latin and from Greek, meaning "name." This meaning is found in such words as: binomial, cognomen, denomination, ignominous, ignominy, monomial, nomen, nomenclature, misnomer, nominal, nominate, nominative, noun, onomastic, onomatopoeia, polynomial, pronominal.

-norm- from Latin, meaning "a carpenter's square; a rule or pattern." This meaning is found in such words as: abnormal, enormous, enormity, norm, normal, normalcy, normalize, paranormal, subnormal.

-nota- from Latin, meaning "note." This meaning is found in such words as: annotate, connotation, denote, notable, notary, notarize, notation, note, notorious, notoriety.

-nounce- from Latin, meaning "call; say." It is related to -nunc-. This meaning is found in such words as: announce, denounce, mispronounce, pronounce, renounce.

-nov- from Latin, meaning "new." This meaning is found in such words as: innovate, innovation, nova, novel, novella, novelette, novelist, novelty, novice, novitiate, renovate, renovation.

-null- from Latin, meaning "none; not one." This meaning is found in such words as: annul, null, nullify.

-num- from Latin, meaning "number." This meaning is found in such words as: enumerate, innumerable, number, numeral, numerator, numerous, outnumber, supernumerary.

-nunc- from Latin, meaning "call; say." It is related to -nounce-. This meaning is found in such words as: annunciation, denunciation, enunciate, mispronunciation, nuncio, renunciation.

-ocul- from Latin, meaning "eye." This meaning is found in such words as: binocular, monocle, ocular, oculist.

-oper- from Latin, meaning "work." This meaning is found in such words as: cooperate, inoperative, opera, operate, opus.

-opt- from Latin, meaning "choose; choice." This meaning is found in such words as: adopt, co-opt, opt, option, optional.

-opti- from Greek, meaning "light; sight." This meaning is found in such words as: autopsy, biopsy, myopia, myopic, ophthalmology, optic, optical, optician, optometrist, optometry, synoptic.

-ord- from Latin, meaning "order; fit." This meaning is found in such words as: coordinate, extraordinary, inordinate, insubordinate, ordain, order, ordinance, ordinal, ordinary, ordination, subordinate.

-orga- from Greek, meaning "tool; body organ; musical instrument." This meaning is found in such words as: disorganize, inorganic, microorganism, organ, organize, reorganize.

-ori- from Latin, meaning "rise; begin; appear." This meaning is found in such words as: aboriginal, aborigine, abort, abortion, disorient, orient, orientation, origin, original.

-pac- from Latin, meaning "peace." This meaning is found in such words as: pacific, pacify, pact.

-pact- from Latin, meaning "fasten." This meaning is found in such words as: compact, impact, impacted, subcompact.

-pand- from Latin, meaning "spread; get larger." This meaning is found in such words as: expand, expansion, expanse, expansive, spandrel.

-par- from Latin, meaning "equal; a piece." This meaning is found in such words as: apart, apartheid, bipartisan, comparable, compare, compartment, counterpart, depart, department, departure, disparage, impart, incomparable, pair, par, parenthesis, part, partial, participle, particle, particular, partisan, partition, party, repartee.

-pare-[1] from Latin, meaning "prepare." This meaning is found in such words as: apparatus, disparate, pare, prepare, preparation, rampart, repair, separate.

-pare-[2] from Latin, meaning "to bring forth; breed." This meaning is found in such words as: multiparous, parent, postpartum, parturition, vivaparous.

-pass-[1] from Latin, meaning "step; pace." This meaning is found in such words as: bypass, compass, encompass, impasse, pass, passable, passage, passageway, passport, surpass, trespass, underpass.

-pass-[2] from Latin, meaning "suffer; experience." It is related to -pat-. This meaning is found in such words as: compassion, compassionate, dispassionate, impassioned, impassive, passion, passive.

-pat- from Latin, meaning "suffer; experience." It is related to -pass-[2]. This meaning is found in such words as: compatible, impatience, impatient, incompatible, patience, patient, simpatico.

-path- from Greek, meaning "suffering; disease; feeling." This meaning is found in such words as: antipathy, apathetic, apathy, empathy, homeopathy, osteopath, pathetic, pathology, pathos, psychopath, sympathetic, sympathize, sympathy, telepathy.

-patr- from Latin, meaning "father." This meaning is found in such words as: compatriot, expatriate, paterfamilias, paternal, paternity, patriarch, patrician, patricide, patriot, patron, patroon, patronymic.

-ped-[1] from Latin, meaning "foot." This meaning is found in such words as: biped, centipede, expedient, expedite, expedition, impede, impediment, millipede, moped, pedal, pedicure, pedestal, pedestrian, pedometer, quadruped.

-ped-[2] from Greek, meaning "child." This meaning is found in such words as: encyclopedia, orthopedic, pedagogue, pedagogy, pederasty, pediatrics, pediatrician, pedophile.

-pel- from Latin, meaning "drive; push." It is related to the root -puls-. This meaning is found in such words as: compel, dispel, expel, impel, propel, propeller, repel, repellant.

-pen- from Latin and Greek, meaning "penalty; wrong," and hence "repent." These meanings are found in such words as: impenitent, penal, penalize, penitence, penology, repent, repentance, subpoena.

-pend- from Latin, meaning "hang; be suspended or weighed." This meaning is found in such words as: append, appendage, appendix, compendium, depend, expend, impending, independent, pending, pendant, pendulum, pendulous, spend, stipend, suspend.

-pet- from Latin, meaning "seek; strive for." This meaning is found in such words as: appetite, centripetal, compete, competition, competence, competent, impetigo, impetuous, impetus, perpetual, petition, petulant, repeat, repetition.

-phil- from Greek, meaning "love; loving." This meaning is found in such words as: hemophilia, necrophilia, philander, philanthropic, philanthropy, philharmonic, philodendron, philology, philosophy.

-phon- from Greek, meaning "sound; voice." This meaning is found in such words as: cacophony, euphony, homophone, microphone, megaphone, phoneme, phonetic, phonics, phonograph, phonology, polyphony, saxophone, stereophonic, symphony, telephone, xylophone.

-phys- from Greek, meaning "origin; form; nature; natural order." This meaning is found in such words as: geophysics, metaphysics, physic, physician, physics, physiognomy, physiology, physique.

-plac- from Latin, meaning "to please." This meaning is found in such words as: complacent, implacable, placate, placebo, placid.

-plaud- from Latin, meaning "clap; noise." It is related to the root -plod-. This meaning is found in such words as: applaud, plaudit, plausible.

-plen- from Latin, meaning "full." It is related to the root -plet-. This meaning is found in such words as: plenary, plenipotentiary, plenitude, plenteous, plenty, plenum, replenish.

-plet- from Latin and Greek, meaning "full." This meaning is found in such words as: complete, deplete, plethora, replete. See also -plen-.

-plex- from Latin, meaning "fold." It is related to the root -plic-. This meaning is found in such words as: complex, duplex, multiplex, perplex, Plexiglas, plexus.

-plic- from Latin, meaning "fold, bend." This meaning is found in such words as: accomplice, application, complicate, complicity, duplicate, duplicity, explicable, explicate, explicit, implicate, implicit, inexplicable, multiplication, replica, replicate, supplicant. See also -plex-.

-plod- from Latin, meaning "noise." This meaning is found in such words as: explode, implode. See also -plaud-.

-ploy- from French and ultimately from Latin, meaning "bend; fold; use; involve." It is related to -plic-. This meaning is found in such words as: deploy, employ, employee, employer, employment, ploy.

-pod- from Greek, meaning "foot." This meaning is found in such words as: antipode, arthropod, chiropodist, podiatrist, podiatry, podium, pseudopod, tripod.

-point- from French and ultimately from Latin, meaning "point, prick, pierce." It is related to the root -punct-. This meaning is found in such words as: appoint, disappoint, midpoint, pinpoint, point, pointless, viewpoint.

-poli- from Latin, meaning "polish, smooth." This meaning is found in such words as: impolite, polish, polite.

-polis- from Greek, meaning "city." This meaning is found in such words as: cosmopolitan, geopolitical, impolitic, megalopolis, metropolis, metropolitan, necropolis, police, policy, politicize, political, politico, politics, polity.

-pon- from Latin, meaning "put, place." It is related to the root -posit-. This meaning is found in such words as: component, deponent, exponent, opponent, postpone, proponent.

-**pop-** from Latin, meaning "people." This meaning is found in such words as: populace, popular, popularity, popularize, populate, populous.

-**port-** from Latin, meaning "carry; bring." This meaning is found in such words as: comport, comportment, deport, export, import, importance, important, opportune, opportunity, portable, portage, portfolio, porter, portmanteau, purport, rapport, report, support, transport, transportation.

-**posit-** from Latin, meaning "to put, place." It is related to the root -pon-. This meaning is found in such words as deposit, position, postpone.

-**pot-** from Latin, meaning "power; ability." This meaning is found in such words as: impotence, impotent, omnipotent, plenipotentiary, potent, potential, potency.

-**pound-** from French and ultimately from Latin, meaning "put; place." It is related to the root -pon-. This meaning is found in such words as: compound, expound, impound, propound.

-**preci-** from Latin, meaning "value; worth; price." This meaning is found in such words as: appreciate, depreciate, precious, price, semiprecious.

-**prehend-** from Latin, meaning "seize; grasp hold of; hold on to." This meaning is found in such words as: apprehend, comprehend, misapprehend, prehensile. See also -pris-.

-**press-** from Latin, meaning "squeeze; press (down)." This meaning is found in such words as: acupressure, compress, compression, decompress, decompression, depress, depression, express, impress, impressive, irrepressible, oppress, press, pressure, repress, suppress.

-**prim-** from Latin, meaning "first." This meaning is found in such words as: primacy, primary, primal, primeval, primate, prime, primitive, primo, primogeniture, primordial, prince, principal, principle, unprincipled.

-**pris-** from French and ultimately from Latin, meaning "grasp; take hold; seize." It is related to the root -prehend-. This meaning is found in such words as: apprise, comprise, enterprise, prison, prize, reprisal, reprise, surprise.

-**priv-** from Latin, meaning "separated; apart; restricted." This meaning is found in such words as: deprivation, deprive, privacy, private, privation, privatize, privilege, privy, underprivileged.

-**prob-** from Latin, meaning "prove." This meaning is found in such words as: approbation, improbable, opprobrious, opprobrium, probable, probability, probate, probation, probe, probity, reprobate. See also -prov-.

-**propr-** from Latin, meaning "one's own." This meaning is found in such words as: appropriate, expropriate, improper, impropriety, misappropriate, proper, property, proprietary, proprietor, propriety.

-**prov-** from French and ultimately from Latin, meaning "prove." It is related to the root -prob-. This meaning is found in such words as: approve, approval, disapprove, disprove, improve, proof, prove, proven.

-**prox-** from Latin, meaning "close; near." This meaning is found in such words as: approximate, approximation, proximity.

-**pter-** from Greek, meaning "wing; feather." This meaning is found in such words as: archaeopteryx, dipterous, helicopter, monopterous, pterodactyl.

-**pugn-** from Latin, meaning "fight; fist." This meaning is found in such words as: impugn, pugilism, pugnacious, repugnant.

Building Blocks of English

-**puls**- from Latin, meaning "push; drive." This meaning is found in such words as: compulsion, expulsion, impulse, impulsive, propulsion, pulsar, pulsation, pulse, repulse, repulsive. See also -pel-.
-**punct**- from Latin, meaning "point; prick; pierce." This meaning is found in such words as: acupuncture, compunction, expunge, punctilious, punctual, punctuality, punctuation, puncture, pungent. See also -point-.
-**pur**- from Latin, meaning "pure." This meaning is found in such words as: expurgate, impure, impurity, pure, purgative, purgatory, purge, purify, puritan, purity.
-**pute**- from Latin, meaning "to clean, prune; consider; think." This meaning is found in such words as: amputate, compute, computation, deputy, dispute, disreputable, impute, indisputable, putative, reputable, reputation.

-**quad**- from Latin, meaning "four, fourth." This meaning is found in such words as: quad, quadrangle, quadrant, quadriplegic, quadruped, quadruplet.
-**quer**- from Latin, meaning "seek; look for; ask." This meaning is found in such words as: conquer, query. See also -quir-, -ques-, -quis-.
-**ques**- from Latin, meaning "seek; look for; ask." This meaning is found in such words as: conquest, inquest, quest, question, request.
-**quie**- from Latin, meaning "quiet, still." This meaning is found in such words as: acquiesce, acquiescent, disquieting, quiescent, quiet, quietude.
-**quir**- from Latin, meaning "seek; look for." This meaning is found in such words as: acquire, inquire, inquiry, require, requirement. See also -quis-, -quer-.
-**quis**- from Latin, meaning "seek; look for." This meaning is found in such words as: acquisition, exquisite, inquisitive, inquisition, perquisite, prerequisite, requisite. See also -quir-.
-**quit**- from Latin, meaning "release; discharge; let go." This meaning is found in such words as: acquit, quit, quite, requite, unrequited.
-**quot**- from Latin, meaning "how many; divided." This meaning is found in such words as: quota, quotation, quote, quotidian, quotient.

-**rape**- from Latin, meaning "carry off by force." This meaning is found in such words as: enrapture, rape, rapid, rapine, rapt, rapture.
-**rase**- from Latin, meaning "rub; scrape." This meaning is found in such words as: abrasion, erase, raze, razor.
-**ratio**- from Latin, meaning "logic; reason; judgment." This meaning is found in such words as: irrational, overrated, rate, ratify, ratio, ration, rational.
-**real**- from Latin, meaning "in fact; in reality." This meaning is found in such words as: real, reality, realistic, realize, really, surreal.
-**rect**- from Latin, meaning "guide; rule; right; straight." This meaning is found in such words as: correct, direct, erect, indirect, insurrection, misdirect, resurrection, rectangle, rectify, rectitude, rector, rectum.
-**reg**- from Latin, meaning "rule; direct; control." This meaning is found in such words as: deregulate, interregnum, irregular, regal, regalia, regency, regular, regicide, regime, regimen, regiment, region, regional.
-**rend**- from Latin, meaning "give." This meaning is found in such words as: render, rendition, surrender.

-roga- from Latin, meaning "ask; demand." This meaning is found in such words as: abrogate, arrogant, derogatory, interrogate, prerogative, surrogate.

-rota- from Latin, meaning "round." This meaning is found in such words as: orotund, rotary, rotate, rotation, rotogravure, rotor, rotund, rotunda.

-rupt- from Latin, meaning "break." This meaning is found in such words as: abrupt, corrupt, disrupt, erupt, eruption, incorruptible, interrupt, rupture.

-salv- from Latin, meaning "save." This meaning is found in such words as: salvation, salvage, salver, salvo.

-san- from Latin, meaning "health." This meaning is found in such words as: insane, insanitary, sanatorium, sane, sanitary, sanitize.

-sanct- from Latin, meaning "holy." This meaning is found in such words as: sacrosanct, sanctify, sanction, sanctity, sanctuary.

-sat- from Latin, meaning "full, enough, sufficient." This meaning is found in such words as: dissatisfy, dissatisfaction, insatiable, sate, satiated, satire, satisfy, satisfaction, saturate, unsatisfied.

-scend- from Latin, meaning "climb." This meaning is found in such words as: ascend, condescend, descend, transcend, transcendent.

-schol- from Latin, meaning "school." This meaning is found in such words as: scholar, scholastic, school, unschooled.

-sci- from Latin, meaning "to know." This meaning is found in such words as: conscience, conscious, omniscient, omniscience, prescient, prescience, science, scientific.

-scope- from Greek, meaning "see." This meaning is found in such words as: fluoroscope, gyroscope, horoscope, microscope, microscopic, oscilloscope, periscope, radioscopy, spectroscope, stethoscope, telescope, telescopic.

-scrib- from Latin, meaning "write." This meaning is found in such words as: ascribe, circumscribe, conscribe, describe, indescribable, inscribe, prescribe, proscribe, scribble, scribe, subscribe, transcribe.

-script- from Latin, meaning "writing." This meaning is found in such words as: description, inscription, scripture.

-sect- from Latin, meaning "cut." This meaning is found in such words as: bisect, dissect, intersect, resection, section, sector, vivisection.

-semble- from Latin, meaning "seem; appear(ance)." This meaning is found in such words as: assemble, assembly, dissemble, ensemble, resemblance, resemble, semblance.

-sene- from Latin, meaning "old." This meaning is found in such words as: senate, senescence, senescent, senile, senior.

-sens- from Latin, meaning "sense; feel." This meaning is found in such words as: consensus, dissension, extrasensory, insensible, insensitive, nonsense, sensation, sensational, sense, senseless, sensitive, sensor, sensory, sensual, sensuous. See also -sent-.

-sent- from Latin, meaning "feel." It is related to the root -sens-. This meaning is found in such words as: assent, consent, dissent, presentiment, resent, resentful, resentment, scent, sentence, sentient, sentiment.

-seq- from Latin, meaning "follow." This meaning is found in such words as:

consequence, consequent, consequential, inconsequential, obsequious, sequel, sequence, sequential, subsequent.
-**serv-**[1] from Latin, meaning "slave." This meaning is found in such words as: deserve, disservice, servant, serve, service, servile, servitude, subservient.
-**serv-**[2] from Latin, meaning "save." This meaning is found in such words as: conserve, conservation, observe, observation, preserve, preservation, reserve, reservation, reservoir, unreserved.
-**sess-** from Latin, meaning "sit; stay." It is related to the root -sid-. This meaning is found in such words as: assess, assessor, dispossess, intersession, obsession, possession, repossession, session.
-**sid-** from Latin, meaning "sit; stay; live in a place." This meaning is found in such words as: assiduous, dissident, insidious, preside, president, presidium, presidio, reside, residual, residue, siege, subside, subsidiary, subsidy, subsidize. See also -sess-.
-**sign-** from Latin, meaning "sign; have meaning." This meaning is found in such words as: assign, assignation, consign, co-sign, design, designate, ensign, insignia, insignificant, resign, signal, signature, signet, significant, signify.
-**simil-** from Latin, meaning "alike, similar." This meaning is found in such words as: assimilate, assimilation, dissimilar, dissimulate, facsimile, similar, simile, simulcast, simulate, simultaneous, verisimilitude.
-**sist-** from Latin, meaning "remain; stand; stay." This meaning is found in such words as: assist, consist, desist, inconsistent, insist, irresistible, persist, resist, subsist, subsistence.
-**soc-** from Latin, meaning "partner; comrade." This meaning is found in such words as: associate, association, disassociate, disassociation, social, socialize, society, unsociable, and the prefix socio-.
-**sola-** from Latin, meaning "soothe." This meaning is found in such words as: console, consolation, disconsolate, inconsolable, solace.
-**sole-** from Latin, meaning "only; alone." This meaning is found in such words as: desolate, desolation, sole, soliloquy, solipsism, solitaire, solitary, solitude, solo.
-**solv-** from Latin, meaning "loosen; release; dissolve." This meaning is found in such words as: absolve, dissolve, insolvent, resolve, solve.
-**som-** from Greek, meaning "body." This meaning is found in such words as: chromosome, psychosomatic, ribosome, somatic.
-**son-** from Latin, meaning "sound." This meaning is found in such words as: consonant, dissonant, dissonance, resonant, resonance, resonate, resound, sonar, sonata, sonic, sonnet, sonogram, sound, supersonic, ultrasonic, unison.
-**soph-** from Greek, meaning "wise." This meaning is found in such words as: philosopher, philosophy, sophism, sophistry, sophisticated, sophomore, theosophical, theosophy, unsophisticated.
-**sort-** from Latin, meaning "kind; type; part." This meaning is found in such words as: assorted, consort, consortium, resort, sort.
-**spec-** from Latin, meaning "look at; examine." This meaning is found in such

words as: aspect, expect, inspect, inspector, inspection, introspection, irrespective, perspective, prospect, prospective, prospectus, respect, respectable, retrospect, special, specialty, specialize, species, specific, specify, specimen, specious, spectacle, spectacular, spectrum, speculate, suspect.

-sper- from Latin, meaning "hope; hope for; expect." This meaning is found in such words as: desperado, desperate, prosper, prosperity, prosperous.

-spir- from Latin, meaning "breathe; have a longing for." This meaning is found in such words as: aspire, conspire, expire, inspire, perspire, respiration, respiratory, respire, spiracle, spirit, transpire.

-spond- from Latin, meaning "pledge; promise." This meaning is found in such words as: correspond, correspondent, correspondence, despondent, respond, transponder.

-stab- from Latin, meaning "stand." This meaning is found in such words as: establish, instability, stabilize, stable, unstable.

-stan- from Latin, meaning "stand; remain." This meaning is found in such words as: constant, circumstance, distance, distant, happenstance, inconstant, inconstancy, insubstantial, stance, stanch, stanchion, stand, stanza, stanch, substance, substantial, substantive, transubstantiation.

-stat- from Latin (and in some cases from Greek), meaning "stand; remain." This meaning is found in such words as: hemostat, instate, interstate, misstate, overstate, photostat, prostate, reinstate, rheostat, state, static, station, statistics, stative, statute, status, statutory, thermostat, understate.

-stin- from Latin, meaning "separate; mark by pricking." This meaning is found in such words as: distinct, distinguish, indistinct, indistinguishable, instinct.

-stit- from Latin, meaning "remain; stand." This meaning is found in such words as: constitute, constitution, destitute, institute, prostitute, prostitution, reconstitute, restitution, substitute, superstition, unconstitutional.

-strain- from French and ultimately from Latin, meaning "stretch; tighten; bind." It is related to the root -strict-. This meaning is found in such words as: constrain, restrain, strain, strait, straiten, unrestrained.

-strat- from Latin, meaning "cover; throw over" and "level." These meanings are found in such words as: prostrate, strata, stratify, stratosphere, stratum, substrate.

-strict- from Latin, meaning "draw tight; bind; tighten." This meaning is found in such words as: constrict, district, redistrict, restrict, strict, stricture, vasoconstrictor.

-stroph- from Greek, meaning "turn; twist." This meaning is found in such words as: apostrophe, catastrophe, strophe.

-stru- from Latin, meaning "build, as by making layers; spread." This meaning is found in such words as: construct, construction, construe, destruct, destruction, indestructible, infrastructure, instruct, instruction, instrument, instrumentation, misconstrue, obstruct, reconstruct, structure.

-stud- from Latin, meaning "be busy with; devote oneself to." This meaning is found in such words as: student, studio, study, understudy.

-suade- from Latin, meaning "recommend; urge as being agreeable or sweet." This meaning is found in such words as: dissuade, persuade.

-sum- from Latin, meaning "take up; pick up." This meaning is found in such words as: assume, assumption, consume, consumption, presume, presumption, presumptuous, resume, resumé, resumption, subsume, sumptuous.

-tact- (or **-tang-**) from Latin, meaning "touch." This meaning is found in such words as: contact, intact, tact, tactile, tangent, tangible.

-tail- from French and ultimately from Latin, meaning "cut." This meaning is found in such words as: curtail, detail, entail, retail, tailor.

-tain- from French and ultimately from Latin, meaning "hold." It is related to the root -ten-. This meaning is found in such words as: abstain, attain, contain, detain, entertain, maintain, obtain, pertain, rein, retain, retinue, sustain.

-tech- from Greek, meaning "skill; ability." This meaning is found in such words as: polytechnic, pyrotechnic, tech, technical, technician, technique, technology.

-temp- from Latin, meaning "time." This meaning is found in such words as: contemporary, contretemps, extemporaneous, tempo, temporary, temporize.

-ten- from Latin, meaning "hold." This meaning is found in such words as: abstinence, content, continent, countenance, incontinent, impertinent, incontinence, lieutenant, pertinent, retentive, sustenance, tenable, tenacious, tenant, untenable. See also -tain-.

-tend- from Latin, meaning "stretch; stretch out; extend; proceed." This meaning is found in such words as: attend, contend, distend, extend, intend, portend, pretend, superintend, tend, tender, tendency, tendon.

-term- from Latin, meaning "end; boundary; limit." This meaning is found in such words as: determine, exterminate, indeterminate, interminable, predetermine, term, terminal, terminate, terminology, terminus.

-terr- from Latin, meaning "earth; land." This meaning is found in such words as: extraterrestrial, extraterritorial, subterranean, terrace, terrain, terrarium, terrestrial, terrier, territory.

-test- from Latin, meaning "witness." This meaning is found in such words as: attest, contest, detest, incontestable, intestate, pretest, protest, protestation, Protestant, test, testament, testate, testify, testimonial, testimony.

-theo- from Greek, meaning "god." This meaning is found in such words as: atheism, atheist, monotheism, pantheon, polytheism, theocracy, theology, theosophy.

-therm- from Greek, meaning "heat." This meaning is found in such words as: hypothermia, thermal, thermodynamics, thermometer, thermostat.

-thes- from Greek, meaning "put together; set down." This meaning is found in such words as: antithesis, epenthesis, hypothesis, parenthesis, photosynthesis, prosthesis, synthesis, synthetic, thesis.

-tom- from Greek, meaning "cut." This meaning is found in such words as: anatomy, appendectomy, atom, diatom, dichotomy, hysterectomy, lobotomy, mastectomy, tome, tomography, tonsilectomy, vasectomy.

-ton- from Greek, meaning "sound." This meaning is found in such words as: atonal, baritone, detonate, intonation, intone, monotone, monotonous, overtone, semitone, tonal, tone, tonic, undertone.

206   Building Blocks of English

-tort- from Latin, meaning "twist." This meaning is found in such words as: contort, distort, extort, retort, tort, torte, tortilla, tortuous, torture.

-tox- from Latin, meaning "poison." This meaning is found in such words as: antitoxin, detoxify, intoxicated, intoxication, toxic, toxin.

-trac- from Latin, meaning "pull." This meaning is found in such words as: abstract, attract, attraction, contract, contraction, detract, distract, extract, extractor, intractable, protracted, protractor, retract, subcontract, subtract, tract, tractable, traction, tractor.

-troph- from Greek, meaning "food, nourishment." This meaning is found in such words as: atrophy, isotrophy, phototrophic, trophic.

-trude- from Latin, meaning "thrust, push." This meaning is found in such words as: extrude, intrude, obtrude, protrude.

-turb- from Latin, meaning "stir up." This meaning is found in such words as: disturb, disturbance, imperturbable, masturbate, perturb, perturbation, turbid, turbine, turbo, turbulent.

-type- from Greek, meaning "impression." This meaning is found in such words as: archetype, atypical, prototype, stereotype, type, typical, typify, typography.

-ult- from Latin, meaning "beyond; farther." This meaning is found in such words as: antepenultimate, penultimate, ulterior, ultimatum, ultimate, and the prefix ultra-.

-uni- from Latin, meaning "one." This meaning is found in such words as: reunion, reunite, unicameral, unicorn, unicycle, uniform, unify, unilateral, union, unique, unisex, unit, unitary, unite, university.

-urb- from Latin, meaning "city." This meaning is found in such words as: conurbation, suburb, suburban, suburbanite, suburbia, urb, urban, urbane.

-vac- from Latin, meaning "empty." This meaning is found in such words as: evacuate, vacancy, vacant, vacate, vacation, vacuous, vacuum.

-vade- from Latin, meaning "go." This meaning is found in such words as: evade, invade, pervade.

-val- from Latin, meaning "value; worth; health; be strong." This meaning is found in such words as: devalue, equivalent, evaluate, prevalent, undervalue, value, valiant, valid, validate, valor.

-var- from Latin, meaning "change." This meaning is found in such words as: invariable, variable, variance, variant, variation, varied, variegate, variety, variform, various, vary.

-vec- from Latin, meaning "drive; convey." This meaning is found in such words as: convection, invective, vector.

-ven- from Latin, meaning "come." This meaning is found in such words as: advent, adventure, avenue, circumvent, contravene, convene, convention, convenience, convent, covenant, event, eventual, inconvenience, inconvenient, intervene, invent, invention, inventory, misadventure, prevent, provenance, revenue, souvenir, unconventional, uneventful, venture, venturesome, venue.

Building Blocks of English 207

-venge- from Latin, meaning "protect, avenge, punish." This meaning is found in such words as: avenge, revenge, vengeance.

-ver- from Latin, meaning "true; truth." This meaning is found in such words as: veracious, veracity, verily, verify, verisimilitude, veritably, verity.

-verb- from Latin, meaning "word." This meaning is found in such words as: adverb, adverbial, proverb, proverbial, verb, verbal, verbalize, verbatim, verbiage, verbose.

-verg- from Latin, meaning "turn; bend." This meaning is found in such words as: converge, diverge, verge. See also -vert-.

-vert- (or -vers-) from Latin, meaning "turn; change." This meaning is found in such words as: adversary, adverse, advertise, advertisement, aversion, avert, controversial, controversy, conversation, conversant, converse, conversion, convert, diverse, diversion, divert, extrovert, extroversion, inadvertent, incontrovertible, introvert, invert, inversion, irreversible, obverse, perverse, perversion, pervert, reversal, reverse, revert, subversive, subversion, subvert, transverse, traverse, universal, universe, versatile, verse, versed, version, versus, vertebra, vertebrate, vertex, vertical, vertiginous, vertigo.

-via- from Latin, meaning "way; route; a going." This meaning is found in such words as: deviant, devious, obviate, trivial, via, viaduct.

-vict- from Latin, meaning "conquer." It is related to the root -vinc-. This meaning is found in such words as: convict, evict, victor, victorious, victory.

-vide- from Latin, meaning "see." It is related to the root -vis-. This meaning is found in such words as: evidence, evident, provide, providence, providential, video, videodisc, videocassette, videotape.

-vinc- from Latin, meaning "conquer; defeat." This meaning is found in such words as: convince, evince, invincible, vincible. See also -vict-.

-vis- from Latin, meaning "see." This meaning is found in such words as: advice, advisable, advise, envisage, envision, inadvisable, invisible, provision, proviso, revise, revision, supervise, supervision, supervisor, television, visa, visage, vis-à-vis, visible, vision, visit, visor, vista, visual. See also -vide-.

-vit- from Latin, meaning "life; living." It is related to the root -viv-. This meaning is found in such words as: aqua vitae, curriculum vitae, revitalize, vita, vital, vitalize, vitamin.

-viv- from Latin, meaning "life; alive; lively." This meaning is found in such words as: convivial, revival, revive, survival, survive, survivor, viva, vivacious, vivid, viviparous, vivisection.

-voc- from Latin, meaning "call." This meaning is found in such words as: advocate, avocation, convocation, convoke, equivocal, evocative, evoke, invocation, invoke, irrevocable, provocation, provocative, provoke, revocation, revoke, unequivocal, unprovoked, vocabulary, vocal, vocation, vociferous.

-vol- from Latin, meaning "wish; will." This meaning is found in such words as: benevolent, involuntary, malevolent, volition, voluntary, volunteer.

-volv- (or -volut-) from Latin, meaning "turn, roll." This meaning is found in such words as: evolve, revolve, evolution, revolution.

208 Building Blocks of English

-vor- from Latin, meaning "eat." This meaning is found in such words as: carnivore, carnivorous, devour, herbivore, omnivore, omnivorous, voracious.
-vot- from Latin, meaning "vow." This meaning is found in such words as: devote, devotee, devout, vote.
-voy- from French and ultimately from Latin, meaning "way; send." This meaning is found in such words as: envoy, invoice, voyage.

ABBREVIATIONS USED

adj.	adjective	*colloq.*	colloquial	*interj.*	interjection	*pron.*	pronoun
adv.	adverb	*conj.*	conjunction	*l.c.*	lower case	*pt.*	past tense
art.	article	*def.*	definition	*n.*	noun	*sing.*	singular
aux.	auxiliary	*esp.*	especially	*pl.*	plural	*usu.*	usually
cap.	capital	*fem.*	feminine	*prep.*	preposition	*v.*	verb

PRONUNCIATION KEY

a	act, bat	ī	ice, bite	ou	out, loud	z	zeal, lazy, those
ā	able, cape	j	just, edge	p	page, stop	zh	vision, measure
â	air, dare	k	kept, make	r	read, cry	ə	occurs only in un-
ä	art, calm	l	low, all	s	see, miss		accented syllables
b	back, rub	m	my, him	sh	shoe, push		and indicates the
ch	chief, beach	n	now, on	t	ten, bit		sound of
d	do, bed	ng	sing, England	th	thin, path		a *in* alone
e	ebb, set	o	box, hot	th	that, other		e *in* system
ē	equal, bee	ō	over, no	u	up, love		i *in* easily
f	fit, puff	ô	order, bail	û	urge, burn		o *in* gallop
g	give, beg	oi	oil, joy	v	voice, live		u *in* circus
h	hit, hear	o͝o	book, put	w	west, away		
i	if, big	o͞o	ooze, rule	y	yes, young		

6

Word Histories

However helpful it is to learn how to figure out the meanings of words from their prefixes, suffixes, and roots, you may sometimes encounter an unusual or exotic word that resists the universal formulas. Some words can only be understood by puzzling through their histories. Often the most powerful words come to us through mythology or biblical stories, historical events or literary works, obscure languages or twisted etymologies. Words, like people, have a past, and as with people, some words have more interesting stories than others. Knowing a word's history can help you remember it and incorporate it into your daily speech. Familiarizing yourself with the history of a word can help you retain its meaning and make it part of the stock of words on which you draw in speech and writing. Many of the words below are derived from earlier terms that can provide a window on the past, as well as suggesting the ways in which the genius of the English language borrows and adapts words for its own purposes. If you understand the meaning and history of these words and use them properly, you will make your speech and writing more colorful, interesting, and effective.

aberration (ab′ə rā′shən) This word comes from the Latin verb aberrare (to wander away from). A person with a psychological *aberration* exhibits behavior that strays from the accepted path; hence the word means deviation from what is common, normal, or right.

abominate (əbom′ə nāt′) *Abominate* is from the Latin abominor (I pray that the event predicted by the omen may be averted). The Romans murmured the word to keep away the evil spirits whenever anyone said something unlucky. Today we use it to mean "to regard with intense aversion or loathing; abhor."

abracadabra (ab′rə kə dab′rə) This intriguing-sounding word was first used as a charm in the second century. The Romans believed that the word had the ability to cure toothaches and other illnesses. Patients seeking relief wrote the letters in the form of a triangle on a piece of parchment and wore it around their necks on a length of thread. Today *abracadabra* is used as a pretend conjuring word. It also means "meaningless talk, nonsense."

aegis (ē′jis) When Zeus emerged victorious from his rebellion against the Titans, he attributed his success in part to his shield, which bore at its center the head of one of the Gorgons. The shield was reputedly made of goatskin, and hence its name, aigis, was said to derive from the Greek *aig* (the stem of aix, or goat). Our present use of the word to mean "protection or sponsorship" evolved from the notion of eighteenth-century English writers who assumed that the egis of Zeus or Athena—or their Roman counterparts Jove and Minerva—protected all those who came under its influence. Today the preferred spelling of the word is *aegis*.

albatross (al′bə trôs′) Generations of students have enjoyed "The Rime of the Ancient Mariner" by Samuel Taylor Coleridge (1772–1834). One of the seminal works of the Romantic movement in England, this haunting, dreamlike poem tells the tale of a sailor forced by his shipmates to wear suspended from his neck the corpse of the albatross, or frigate bird, that he carelessly shot down with his crossbow. Since seamen traditionally regarded the bird as a lucky omen, they attributed the many disasters that befell the ship thereafter to the man who killed it. The poem is so famous and beloved that the word *albatross* has come to mean "a seemingly inescapable moral or emotional burden, as of guilt or responsibility; a burden that impedes action or progress."

aloof (ə lōōf′) This was originally a sailor's term, a loof, meaning "to the luff or windward direction," perhaps from the Dutch *te loef* (to windward). Etymologists believe that our use of the word to mean "at a distance, especially in feeling or interest," comes from the idea of keeping a ship's head to the wind, and thus clear of the lee shore toward which it might drift.

amazon (am′ə zon′) The word comes ultimately from the Greek, but the origin of the Greek word is uncertain. *Amazon* refers to a tall, powerful, aggressive woman. The Amazons of legend were female warriors who were allied with the Trojans against the Greeks.

ambrosia (am brō′zhə) Originally, *ambrosia* was the food of the Olympian gods (as nectar was their drink). The word comes from the Greek *a*, (not) and *brostos* (mortal), hence, eating ambrosia conferred immortality. Today the word means "an especially delicious food, with the implication that the concoction is savory enough to be fit for the gods." A popular dessert by this name contains shredded coconut, sliced fruits, and cream.

antimacassar (an′ti mə kas′ər) In the 1800s, macassar oil was imported from Indonesia to England as a popular remedy for baldness. Based on its reputation, men began to apply it liberally to their scalps, but the oil stained the backs of sofas and chairs where they rested their oily heads. Therefore, homemakers began to place pieces of fabric over sofa and chair backs, since these scraps could be washed more easily than stained upholstery. These fabric pieces came to be called *antimacassars*—against macassar oil. These little doilies are now regarded as collectible relics of the Victorian era because of their elaborate designs and fine handiwork—now a lost art.

apartheid (ə pärt′hāt, -hīt) *Apartheid*, the term for a policy of racial segregation and discrimination against nonwhites, entered English from Afrikaans, the language of South Africa's Dutch settlers, the Boers. They created the word from the Dutch word for apart and the suffix -heid, related to our suffix -hood. Thus, the word literally means apartness or separateness. It was first used in 1947, in a South African newspaper. Apartheid is no longer practiced in South Africa, but the term has passed into general use to describe extreme racism.

Arcadian (är kā′dē ən) The residents of landlocked Arcadia, in ancient Greece, did not venture to other lands. As a result, they maintained traditional ways and lived what others imagined to be a simpler life. Ancient classical poets made *Arcadia* a symbol for a land of pastoral happiness. In the sixteenth century, English poet Sir Philip Sidney imagined a bucolic land he called Arcadia. The word has retained this meaning, and today we consider residents of an Arcadian place to be rustic, simple, and innocent.

argosy (är′gə sē) In the Middle Ages, cities on the Mediterranean coast maintained large fleets to ship goods around the known world. Ragusa was a Sicilian city well known for its large ships, called ragusea. In English, the initial two letters became switched, creating argusea. From there it was a short step to *argosy,* "a large merchant ship, especially one with a rich cargo." Because of Ragusa's wealth, the word argosy also came to mean "an opulent supply or collection."

Bacchanalia (bä′kə näl′ē ə, -näl′yə) In Greek times, a Bacchanalia was a religious festival in honor of Bacchus, the god of wine and protector of the vineyards. Bacchus was also a god of vegetation and fertility, and his religious ceremonies ultimately degenerated into occasions for drunkenness, lewd behavior, and other excesses. Therefore, the word *bacchanalia* (or *bacchanal*) has come to mean "drunken revelry; orgy."

Balkanize (bôl′kə nīz′) After centuries of war, in 1912 the Balkan nations united to conquer the Turks and divide the spoils among themselves. The following year, however, the Balkan nations quarreled over how to divide their booty and began to fight among themselves. From this experience comes the verb *Balkanize,* "to divide a country or territory into small, quarrelsome, ineffectual states." The term has taken on new pungency since the breakup of the former Yugoslavia in the 1990s.

ballyhoo (bal′ē hōō′) The word *ballyhoo* is of uncertain origin. Some have connected it with the Irish town of Ballyhooy, known for the rowdy and often uncontrolled quarrels of its inhabitants. Today the word is an Americanism with a specific meaning: "a clamorous attempt to win customers or advance a cause; blatant advertising or publicity."

billingsgate (bil′ingz gāt′) In the 1500s, Belin's gate, a walled town within London, was primarily a fish market. The name was soon distorted to "billingsgate," and since many fishwives and seamen were known for their salty tongues, the word *billingsgate* came to mean "coarse or vulgar abusive language."

blarney (blär′nē) According to Irish legend, anyone who kisses a magical stone set twenty feet beneath the ground of a castle near the village of Blarney, in Ireland, will henceforth possess the gift of eloquence. One story claims the Blarney stone got its powers from the eloquence of the seventeenth-century Irish patriot Cormac McCarthy, whose soft speech won favorable terms from Elizabeth I after an Irish uprising. From this stone-kissing custom, *blarney* has come to mean "flattering or wheedling talk; cajolery."

blitzkrieg (blits′krēg′) The German word *Blitzkrieg*, literally a lightning war, describes the overwhelming Nazi attacks during World War II. In 1940, Germany pounded Poland into submission in two weeks; in six weeks, it crushed the French army. Although ultimately the Germans met defeat, their method of attack has found a place in our language, and *blitzkrieg* has come to denote an overwhelming, all-out attack that causes substantial, widespread damage.

bluestocking (blōō′stok′ing) A *bluestocking* is a woman with considerable scholarly, literary, or intellectual ability or interest. The word originated in connection with intellectual gatherings held in London about 1750 in the homes of women bored by the more frivolous pastimes of their age. Lavish evening dress was not required at these affairs; in fact, to put at ease visitors who could not afford expensive clothing, the women themselves dressed simply. One of the male guests went so far as to wear his everyday blue worsted stockings rather than the black silk ones usually worn at evening social gatherings. In response to their interests and dress, the English naval officer Admiral Edward Boscawen (1711–1761) is said to have sarcastically called these gatherings the Blue Stocking Society.

bohemian (bō hē′mē ən) In the early fifteenth century, a band of gypsies took up residence in Paris. Knowing that they had come from somewhere in central Europe, the French dubbed the gypsies in the belief that they were natives of Bohemia. Working from the stereotyped view of gypsies as free spirits, the French then applied the term *bohemian* to any person with artistic or intellectual aspirations, who lives an unconventional life.

bolshevik (bōl′shə vik) At a rally of Communist leaders in 1903, Lenin garnered a majority of the votes. He cleverly dubbed his supporters *Bolsheviks* (the majority). His move was effective propaganda. Even though his supporters actually comprised only a minority, the name stuck and came to be associated with a member of the Russian Communist party. The word is also used in a derogatory sense to denote "an extreme political radical; a revolutionary."

bootlegger (bōōt′leg′r) Originally, a *bootlegger* was a person who smuggled outlawed alcoholic liquor in the tops of his tall boots. The term was more common during the Prohibition era of the early twentieth century, but it is still used to mean someone who unlawfully makes, sells, or transports alcoholic beverages without registration or payment of taxes.

bowdlerize (bōd′lə rīz′, boud′-) In 1818, Scottish physician Dr. Thomas

Bowdler published a new edition of Shakespeare's works. The value of his edition, he stated, lay in the fact that he had edited it so all "words and expressions are omitted which cannot with propriety be read aloud to the family." Good intentions aside, he found himself being held up to ridicule. From his name is derived the word *bowdlerize,* meaning to expurgate a literary text in a prudish manner.

boycott (boi′kot) In an attempt to break the stranglehold of Ireland's absentee landlords, Charles Stewart Parnell advocated in 1880 that anyone who took over land from which a tenant had been evicted for nonpayment of rent should be punished "by isolating him from his kind as if he was a leper of old." The most famous application of Parnell's words occurred soon after on the estate of the earl of Erne. Unable to pay their rents, the earl's tenants suggested a lower scale, but the manager of the estate, Captain Charles Cunningham Boycott, would not accept the reduction. In retaliation, the tenants applied the measures proposed by Parnell, not only refusing to gather crops and run the estate, but also intercepting Boycott's mail and food, humiliating him in the street, and threatening his life. Their treatment of Boycott became so famous that within a few months the newspapers were using his name to identify any such nonviolent coercive practices. Today *boycott* means "to join together in abstaining from, or preventing dealings with, as a protest."

bromide (brō′mīd) *Bromides* are chemicals, several of which can be used as sedatives. In 1906, the American humorist Gelett Burgess first used the word to mean "a boring person, one who is likely to serve the same purpose as a sedative." The term was then extended to mean "a platitude, the kind of remark one could expect from a tiresome person."

bugbear (bug′bâr′) The word refers to a source of fears, often groundless. It comes from a Welsh legend about a goblin in the shape of a bear that ate up naughty children.

caprice (kə prēs′) *Caprice,* meaning "a sudden, unpredictable change of mind, a whim," doesn't remind us of hedgehogs, yet these animals probably played a role in this word's past. Caprice comes ultimately from the Italian word *capriccio* (fright, horror). The word is thought to be a compound of *capo* (head) and *riccio* (hedgehog), because when people are very frightened, their hair stands on end, like a hedgehog's spines.

carpetbagger (kär′pət bag′ər) After the Civil War, many unscrupulous Northern adventurers flocked to the South to become profiteers and to seize political power during the chaotic Reconstruction period. The epithet *carpetbagger* referred to the unstable future symbolized by the flimsy carpetbags in which they carried their possessions. We still use this vivid term to describe any person, especially a politician, who takes up residence in a new place for opportunistic reasons.

chagrin (shə grin′) The word *chagrin,* meaning a feeling of vexation due to disappointment, does not derive from *shagreen* (a piece of hard, abrasive leather used to polish metal), even though both words are spelled identically in French. French scholars connect *chagrin,* "vexation, grief," with an Old French verb, *chagreiner* (to turn melancholy or gloomy), which evolved in part from a Germanic word related to English grim.

charlatan (shär'lə tən) During the Renaissance, the village of Cerreto, in Umbria, Italy, was noted for its medical quacks, who became known as cerretanos, after the town's name. The combination of cerretano with *ciartatore* (an imitative word meaning chatterer), created the Italian term cialatano. When the word was transplanted to the shores of England, it remained nearly intact as *charlatan*, "a person who pretends to special knowledge or skill; fraud."

chauvinism (shō'və niz'əm) One of Napoléon's most dedicated soldiers, Nicolas Chauvin, was wounded seventeen times fighting for his emperor. After he retired from the army, he spoke so incessantly of the majestic glory of his leader and the greatness of France that he became a laughingstock. In 1831, his name was used for a character in a play who was an almost idolatrous worshiper of Napoléon. The word "chauvin" became associated with this type of extreme hero worship and exaggerated patriotism. Today, while we still use the term *chauvinism* to refer to zealous and belligerent nationalism, it also refers to extreme bias or partiality toward any group of which one is a member. In particular, chauvinism reflects a belief that one's own gender is superior to the other.

chimerical (kī' mer'i kəl, -mēr'-) The Chimera was a fire-breathing monster of classical myth that was represented as having a lion's head, a goat's body, and a serpent's tail. According to Greek myth, it was slain by the gallant warrior Bellerophon, who attacked it astride the winged horse Pegasus. Later the word meant any horrible or grotesque imaginary creature; then, a fancy or dream. Today we use *chimerical* to mean "unreal or imaginary; wildly fanciful or unrealistic."

cornucopia (kôr'nə kō'pēə , -nyə-) According to Greek mythology, to save the infant Zeus from being swallowed by his father Cronus, his mother, Rhea, hid her son in a cave and tricked Cronus into swallowing a stone wrapped in a cloth. The infant was then entrusted to the care of the nymph Amaltheia, who fed him goat's milk. One day she filled a goat's horn with fresh fruit and herbs. The horn was thereafter magically refilled, no matter how much the child ate. To the Greeks, this boundless source was the horn of Amaltheia; to the Romans, it was the cornu copiae, from *cornu* (horn) and *copia* (plenty). We know a *cornucopia* as a horn containing food or drink in endless supply or horn of plenty. It is often used as a symbol of abundance.

cynosure (sī'nə shŏŏr', sin'ə-) According to the myth, Zeus chose to honor the nymph who cared for him in his infancy by placing her in the sky as a constellation. One of her stars was so brilliant and stationary that all the other stars seemed to revolve around it. To the practical-minded ancient mariners, however, the bottom three stars of the constellation looked like a dog's tail. They named the entire constellation Cynosura (dog's tail). From its name we get our word *cynosure*, "something that attracts attention by its brilliance or interest." By the way, we now call the constellation

Ursa Minor, or Little Bear, and the bright star Polaris, better known as the Pole Star or North Star.

desultory (des′əl tôr′ē) Some Roman soldiers went into battle with two horses, so when one steed wearied, the soldier could vault onto the second horse striding along parallel to the first without losing any time. The same skill was employed by circus performers, especially charioteers, who could leap between two chariots riding abreast. Such a skilled horseman was called a *desultor* (a leaper). Perhaps because these equestrians stayed only briefly on their mounts, the word *desultory* acquired its present meaning: "lacking in consistency, constancy, or visible order."

diadem (dī′ə dem′) In his quest to create a vast, unified empire with Babylon as its capital, the Macedonian hero Alexander the Great adopted a number of Persian and Oriental customs. He began to wear a blue-edged white headband with two ends trailing to the shoulders, a Persian symbol of royalty. The Greeks called this headpiece a *diadema* (literally a binding over). The headpiece was adopted by other monarchs through the ages and further embellished with gold and gems, eventually evolving into a rich crown. Today a *diadem* is a crown or a headband worn as a symbol of royalty.

draconian (drā kō′nē ən, drə-) Draco (c. 621 b.c.) was a Greek politician who is most famous for his codification of Athenian customary law. Though little of his code is extant, later commentators on his work indicated that the death penalty was prescribed for the most trivial offenses. Therefore, his name has come down to us to refer to "punishment or rule that is unusually cruel or severe."

ebullient (i bul′yənt, i bo͞ol′-) This word derives from the Latin *ebullire* (to boil over). A person who is *ebullient* is overflowing with fervor, enthusiasm, or excitement.

El Dorado (el′də rā′dō, -rä′-) The word comes from Spanish legends of an incredibly wealthy city in South America, so rich that its streets were paved with gold. Many adventurers set off to find this elusive city; in 1595 Sir Walter Raleigh ventured into Guiana in a vain attempt to locate it. Among the Spaniards, the king of this fabulous land came to be called El Dorado (the Golden One). Today *El Dorado* is used generally to mean any fabulously wealthy place.

enclave (en′klāv, än′-) The word *enclave* refers to "a country or territory entirely or mostly surrounded by another country." More generally, it means "a group enclosed or isolated within a larger one." The word comes ultimately from Latin *inclavare* (to lock in).

epicure (ep′i kyo͝or′) Epicurus was a Greek philosopher who lived from 342 to 270 b.c. He believed that pleasure, attained mainly through pure and noble thoughts, constituted the highest happiness. After his death, his disciples spread his views. Their critics argued that Epicurus's theory was little more than an excuse for debauchery. From this argument we derive the present-day meaning of *epicure*, "a person with luxurious tastes or habits, especially in eating or drinking."

esoteric (esə′ ter′ik) From the Greek *esoterikos* (inner), the word was used to describe the secret doctrines taught by the philosopher Pythagoras to a select few of his disciples. Hence *esoteric* means "understood by or meant only for those who have special knowledge or interest: recondite."

eunuch (yoo′nək) A *eunuch* is a castrated man, especially formerly, one employed by Oriental rulers as a harem attendant. The word is based on the Greek eunouchos, from *eune* (bed) and *echein* (to keep), since a eunuch is perfectly suited for guarding a woman's bed. The word is used figuratively to refer to "a weak, powerless person."

expedite (ek′spə dīt′) The word *expedite* means "to speed up the progress of something." It comes from the Latin *expedire* (to set the feet free).

expunge (ik spunj′) To indicate that a soldier had retired from service, the ancient Romans wrote a series of dots or points beneath his name on the service lists. The Latin *expungere* thus meant both to prick through and to mark off on a list. Similarly, the English word *expunge* means "to strike or blot out; to erase."

Faustian (fou′stē ən) The story of Dr. Faustus, a medieval alchemist or magician who sold his soul to the devil in exchange for knowledge and power, has its roots in German legend. Its most famous interpretations are to be found in the works of the English dramatist Christopher Marlowe (c. 1558) and the German poet Goethe (1770 and 1831), but the theme has proved so enduring that it found a new popularity in the mid-twentieth-century Broadway musical *Damn Yankees*, about a ballplayer willing to trade his soul for a pennant win over the then-indomitable New York Yankees. A *Faustian* bargain, therefore, is one sacrificing spiritual values for power, knowledge, or material gain. The word may also mean "characterized by spiritual dissatisfaction or torment, or obsessed with a hunger for knowledge or mastery."

fiasco (fē as′kō) *Fiasco* is the Italian word for flask or bottle. How it came to mean "a complete and ignominious failure" is obscure. One theory suggests that Venetian glassblowers set aside fine glass with flaws to make into common bottles.

filibuster (fil′ə bus′tər) In the seventeenth century, English seamen who attacked Spanish ships and brought back wealth from New Spain were called buccaneers. In Holland, they were known as *vrijbuiters* (free robbers). In French, the word became first fribustier and then flibuster. In Spain, the term was filibustero. Then, when the nineteenth-century American soldier of fortune William Walker tried to capture Sonora, Mexico, the Mexicans promptly dubbed him a filibuster. Today the term refers to "the use of irregular or disruptive tactics, such as exceptionally long speeches, by a member of a legislative assembly." The current use of the word may have arisen through a comparison of a legislator's determination to block a bill with the tactics used by William Walker to evade the law.

galvanize (gal′və nīz′) In the mid-eighteenth century, Luigi Galvani, a professor of anatomy at the University of Bologna, concluded that the nerves are a source of electricity. Although Volta later proved his theory incorrect, Galvani's pioneering work inspired other scientists to produce electricity by chemical means. From the old-fashioned term *galvanism* (electricity), which honors Galvani, we have derived the word *galvanize* "to stimulate; startle into activity."

gamut (gam′ət) Guido of Arezzo, one of the greatest musicians of medieval times, is credited with being the first to use the lines of the staff and the spaces between them. He used the Greek letter gamma for the lowest tone in the scale. This note was called gamma ut. Contracted to *gamut*, it then designated the entire scale. The word quickly took on a figurative as well as a literal sense. Today *gamut* is defined as the entire scale or range, as in the phrase "to run the gamut."

gargantuan (gär gan′choo ən) The sixteenth-century French writer François Rabelais created a giant he named Gargantua after a legendary giant of the Middle Ages. To fuel his enormous bulk—Gargantua rode on a horse as large as six elephants—he had to consume prodigious amounts of food and drink. Today we use the word *gargantuan* to mean "gigantic, enormous."

garret (gar′ət) Originally, the French word *garite* (a watchtower from which a sentry could look out for approaching enemies). Among the linguistic innovations the Normans brought when they conquered England was the word garite. In England the word came to mean "a loft or attic," and its spelling was altered to *garret*.

gazette (gə zet′) In the beginning of the sixteenth century, Venetians circulated a small tin coin of little value they called a gazzetta, a diminutive of the word *gaza* (magpie). Soon after, the government began to print official bulletins with news of battles, elections, and so forth. Because the cost of the newspaper was one gazzetta, the leaflet itself eventually came to be called a gazzetta. By the end of the century, the term was used in England as well. The present spelling is the result of French influence. Today a *gazette* is "a newspaper or official government journal."

gerrymander (jer′ē man′dər, ger′-) In 1812, Massachusetts governor Elbridge Gerry conspired with party members to change the boundaries of voting districts to enhance their own political clout. Noticing that one such district resembled a salamander, a newspaper editor coined the term *gerrymander* to describe the practice of dividing a state, county, etc., into election districts to give one political party a majority while concentrating the voting strength of the other party into as few districts as possible.

Gorgon (gôr′gən) The name comes from the Greek myth of the three monstrous sisters who inhabited the region of Night. Together they were known as the Gorgons, and their individual names were Stheno, Euryale, and Medusa. Little has been written about the first two. Medusa was the most hideous and dangerous; her appearance, with her head of writhing serpents, was so ghastly that anyone who looked directly at her was turned to stone. Therefore, the current meaning of *gorgon* is "a mean or repulsive woman."

gossamer (gä′sə mər) In early times, November was a time of feasting and merrymaking in Germany. The time-honored meal was roast goose. So many geese were eaten that the month came to be called *Gänsemonat* (goose month). The term traveled to England but in the course of migration, it became associated with the period of unseasonably warm autumn weather we now call Indian summer. During the warm spell, large cobwebs are found draped in the grass or suspended in the air. These delicate, airy webs, which we call gossamer, are generally believed to have taken their name from goose summer, when their appearance was most noticeable. We now define *gossamer* as "something fine, filmy, or light." It also means "thin and light."

gregarious (gri gar′ē əs) The Latin term for a herd of animals is *grex*. Because a group of people banded together in military formation resembles a herd of animals, the word grex was applied to people as well as animals. The way the people grouped together was called gregarius, like a herd. The word has come down to us as *gregarious*, meaning "friendly or fond of the company of others."

guillotine (gil′ə tēn′, gē′-) After the outbreak of the French Revolution, Dr. Joseph Ignace Guillotin became a member of the National Assembly. During an early debate, he proposed that future executions in France be conducted by a humane beheading machine that he had seen in operation in another country. His suggestion was received favorably; in 1791, after Dr. Guillotin had retired from public service, the machine that bears his name was designed by Antoine Louis and built by a German named Schmidt. The guillotine was first used in 1792 to behead a thief. At that time, the device was called a Louisette after its designer; but the public began calling it after Dr. Guillotin, the man who had first advocated its use. The device proved very popular among the masses, so popular it seemed to demand more victims to satisfy their blood lust. During the subsequent Reign of Terror, more than 17,000 people were guillotined, including Robespierre, the author of the Terror.

halcyon (hal′sē ən) According to classical mythology, the demigod Halcyone threw herself into the sea when she saw the drowned body of her beloved mortal husband. After her tragic death, the gods changed Halcyone and her husband into birds, which they called *halcyons* (our present-day kingfishers). The Greeks believed the sea calmed as the birds built their nests and hatched their eggs upon its waves during the seven days before and after the winter solstice. This period came to be known as halcyon days. The adjective is now used to mean "calm, peaceful, prosperous, or joyful."

hector (hek′tər) Hector was a great Trojan hero, son of King Priam. As Homer recounts in the *Iliad*, Hector took advantage of his enemy Achilles's departure from the Greek camp to drive the Greeks back to their ships and slay Achilles's dearest friend, Patroclus. To the Romans, who regarded themselves as descendants of the Trojans, Hector was a symbol of courage. But in the seventeenth century, the name was applied to the gangs of bullies who terrorized anyone who ventured into the back streets of London. It is to their transgressions that we owe the present use of *hector*, "to harass or persecute."

Hegira (hi jī′rə, hejə′rə) Around the year 600, the prophet Muhammad (570?–632) began to preach the new faith of Islam. To escape persecution, he was forced to flee his home in Mecca. Eventually, his followers increased, and by his death in 632 he controlled Arabia. Within a century, the empire of Islam had spread throughout western Asia and northern Africa. The turning point, Muhammad's flight from Mecca, came to be called the *Hegira*, after the Arabic word for flight or emigration. The Hegira is the starting point on the Muslim calendar, and we now apply the word to any flight or journey to a desirable or congenial place.

helot (hel′ət, hē′lət) Around the eighth century b.c., the Spartans conquered and enslaved the people of the southern half of the Peloponnisos. They called these slaves *helots*, perhaps from the Greek word meaning to enslave. Today helot still means "serf or slave; bondsman." Fans of the 1941 movie *Meet John Doe* may recall that this is the favorite epithet of Gary Cooper's hobo sidekick, played by Walter Brennan, which he applies to anyone who threatens his freewheeling lifestyle.

helpmeet (help′mēt′) This synonym for helpmate, companion, wife, or husband is the result of a misunderstanding. The word comes from Genesis 2:18, "And the Lord God said, It is not good that the man should be alone; I will make him an help meet for him." In this passage, "meet" means proper or appropriate, but the two words came to be read as one, resulting in the word's current spelling.

herculean (hûr′ ky lē′ ən) Hercules, who was by far the most popular Greek hero, is often portrayed as a muscular he-man wearing a lion skin and bearing a huge club. As an infant, he strangled two serpents in his cradle. Later, he performed the prodigious twelve labors, slaying one monster after another and cleansing the Augean stables to gain immortality among the gods. Sophocles, Euripides, and Seneca all celebrated his exploits in their plays. We use the word *herculean* to mean "of enormous power, size, or courage," or to describe a task requiring extraordinary strength or exertion.

hermetic (hûr met′ik) The Greeks linked the Egyptian god Thoth with Hermes, calling him Hermes Trismegistus (Hermes Three-Times Greatest). He was accepted as the author of the books that made up the sum of Egyptian learning, called the Hermetic Books. Since these forty-two works largely concerned the occult sciences, *hermetic* came to mean "secret," and in a later usage, "made airtight by fusion or sealing."

hobnob (häb′näb′) Those who *hobnob* with their buddies associate on very friendly terms or drink together. The word comes from the Anglo-Saxon *haebbe* (to have) and *naebbe* (to have not). In the 1700s, hobnob meant to toast friends and host alternate rounds of drinks. Each person thus had the pleasure of treating, creating a sense of familiarity. Today this usage survives, even if those hobnobbing are teetotalers.

Hobson's choice (häb′sənz) Thomas Hobson (1544–1631) was a stable owner in Cambridge, England, who gave his name to this very useful, pithy phrase meaning "the choice of taking that which is offered or nothing at all; the lack of a real alternative." Hobson gave his customers only one choice of a mount: that of the horse nearest the stable door. In a charming 1954 film of this title directed by David Lean, Charles Laughton hams it up as a prosperous but dipsomaniacal bootmaker hoist by his own petard when he banishes his oldest spinster daughter after she marries his best cobbler. When Hobson (the bootmaker) refuses to deal fairly with their demands for more equitable treatment as the mainstays of the business, the young couple set up in a nearby shop of their own that steals away his former customers. In the end, Hobson's choice is unavoidable and nonnegotiable: he is forced to turn over his shop to the clever couple and retire from business.

horde (hôrd) Upon the death of Genghis Khan, his grandson Batu Khan led the Mongol invasion of Europe, cutting a merciless swath from Moscow to Hungary. At each post, Batu erected a sumptuous tent made of silk and leather. His followers called it the "sira ordu," the silken camp. In Czech and Polish the Turkic "ordu" was changed to "horda." The name came to be applied not only to Batu's tent but also to his entire Mongol army. Because of the terror they inspired across the land, "horde" eventually referred to any Tartar tribe. Today, it means any large crowd; swarm.

hoyden (hoid′ən) A *hoyden* is "a boisterous, ill-bred girl; a tomboy." The word is usually linked to the Dutch *heyden* (a rustic person or rude peasant, originally a heathen or pagan) and is related to the English word heathen. At first in English the word meant a rude, boorish man, but beginning in the 1600s it was applied to girls in the sense of a tomboy. How the change came about is uncertain.

iconoclast (ī kän′ə klast′) An *iconoclast* is "a person who attacks cherished beliefs or traditional institutions." It is from the Greek *eikon* (image) and *klastes* (breaker). Although the contemporary usage is figurative, the word was originally used in a literal sense to describe the great controversy within the Christian church in the eighth century over religious images. One camp held that all visual representations should be destroyed because they encouraged idol worship; the other, that such artworks simply inspired the viewers to feel more religious. By the mid-eighth century, untold numbers of relics and images had been destroyed. The issue was not settled for nearly a century, when the images were restored to the church in Constantinople.

imp (imp) In Old English, an *imp* was "a young plant or seedling." Eventually, the term came to be used figuratively to indicate "a descendant of a royal house, usually a male." Probably because of the behavior of such children, the word became synonymous with a young demon. Since the sixteenth century, the original meaning of imp as scion has been completely dropped, and the word is now used exclusively to mean "a little devil or demon, an evil spirit, or an urchin."

impeccable (im pek′ə bl) The word comes from the Latin *impeccabilis* (without sin). The religious meaning has been only slightly extended over the years. Today an *impeccable* reputation is "faultless, flawless, irreproachable."

inchoate (in kō′it, -āt) *Inchoate* comes from the Latin *inchoare* (to begin). Thus, an inchoate plan is not yet fully developed, or rudimentary.

incubus/succubus (in′kyə bəs, ing′-; suk′yə bəs) In the Middle Ages, women were thought to give birth to witches after being visited in their sleep by an *incubus,* or evil male spirit. The female version of this spirit, said to be the cause of nightmares, was a *succubus.* Because the evil spirit pressed upon the sleeper's body and soul, the term incubus also means something that oppresses like a nightmare.

insolent (in′sə lənt) The word comes from the Latin *insolentem* (not according to custom). Those who violate custom are likely to offend, so *insolent* evolved to imply that the person was also vain and conceited. From this meaning we derive our present usage: "contemptuously rude or impertinent in speech or behavior."

interloper (in′tər lō′pər) The word *interloper* was used in the late sixteenth century to describe Spanish traders who carved out for themselves a piece of the successful trade the British had established with the Russians. The word was formed on the analogy of landloper, meaning one who trespasses on another's land, from a Dutch word literally meaning land runner. Although the dispute over the Spanish intrusion was settled within a few years, the word remained in use to mean "a person who intrudes into some region or field of trade without a proper license; one who thrusts himself or herself into the affairs of others."

intransigent (in tran′sə jənt) When Amadeus, the son of Victor Emmanuel II of Italy, was forced to abdicate the throne of Spain in 1873, those favoring a republic attempted to establish a political party. This group was called in Spanish Los Intransigentes, from *in* (not) and *transigente* (compromising) because they could not come to terms with the other political parties. The term passed into English as *intransigent.* Today the word retains the same meaning: "uncompromising or inflexible."

jackanapes (jak′ə nāps′) Today the word is used to describe "an impertinent, presumptuous young man; a whippersnapper." Although its precise origin is uncertain, we know that the term was first used as an uncomplimentary nickname for William de la Pole, duke of Suffolk, who was murdered in 1450. His badge was an ape's clog and chain. In a poem of the time, Suffolk was called the Apeclogge, and later referred to as an ape called Jack Napes.

jeroboam (jer′ə bō′əm) We now use the term *jeroboam* to refer to "a wine bottle having a capacity of about three liters." Historically, Jeroboam was the first king of the Biblical kingdom of Israel, described in I Kings 11:28 as "a mighty man of valor," who, three verses later, "made Israel to sin." Some authorities trace the origin of today's usage to the king, reasoning that since an oversized bottle of wine can cause sin, it too is a jeroboam.

jingoism (jing′gō iz′əm) This word, meaning "belligerent patriotism and the advocacy of an aggressive foreign policy," has an obscure source. It was extrapolated from the phrase "by jingo" in a political song written by George Ward Hunt supporting the use of British forces in the Russo-Turkish War of 1877-1878 on the side of the Turks. Fortunately, cooler heads prevailed, but the term has been current ever since to describe such hotheaded, opportunistic aggression.

jitney (jit′nē) The origin of this term has long baffled etymologists. The word first appeared in American usage in the first decade of the twentieth century as a slang term for a nickel. It then became associated with the public motor vehicles whose fare was five cents. Some authorities have theorized that the term is a corruption of *jeton*, the French word for token. Today a *jitney* is a small passenger bus following a regular route at varying hours.

junket (jung′kət) At first, the word referred to a basket of woven reeds used for carrying fish; it is ultimately derived from Latin *juncus* (reed). Then the basket was used to prepare cheese, which in turn came to be called junket. Since the basket also suggested the food it could carry, junket later evolved to mean a great feast. Today we use the term in closely related meanings: "a sweet custard-like food or flavored milk curdled with rennet or a pleasure excursion."

juggernaut (jug′ər nôt′, -not′) Our modern word *juggernaut* comes from the Hindi name for a huge image of the god Vishnu, Jagannath, at Puri, a city in Orissa, India. Each summer, the massive statue is moved to a new location a little less than a mile away from the old one. Early tourists to India brought back strange stories of worshipers throwing themselves under the wheels of the wagon carrying the idol. Since any shedding of blood in the presence of the god is sacrilege, what these travelers probably witnessed was a weary pilgrim being accidentally crushed to death. Thus, thanks to exaggeration and ignorance, *juggernaut* came to mean "blind and relentless self-sacrifice," however, today it is chiefly used to mean any large, overpowering, or destructive force.

kaleidoscope (kə lī′də skōp′) Invented in 1816 by Scottish physicist Sir David Brewster, the *kaleidoscope* is a scientific toy constructed of a series of mirrors within a tube. When the tube is turned by hand, symmetrical, ever-changing patterns can be viewed through the eyepiece. Brewster named his toy from the Greek *kalos* (beautiful), *eidos* (form), and *skopos* (watcher). In general, we use the term to mean "a continually shifting pattern or scene" or the instrument (often a toy) that, by enabling light to pass through turning shards of colored glass, produces these shifting patterns.

knave (nāv) In Old English, the word *knave* (then spelled cnafa) referred to a male child, a boy. It was later applied to a boy or man employed as a servant. Many of these boys had to be wily to survive their hard lot; thus the word gradually evolved to mean "a rogue or rascal."

kowtow (kow′tou′) The Chinese people, who were largely isolated from the West until Portuguese traders established a post outside Canton, regarded their emperor as a representation of God on Earth. Those approaching the emperor had to fall to the ground and strike their heads against the floor as a sign of humility. This was called a *kowtow*, from the Chinese word that meant knock-head. As a verb, the English word follows the original meaning: "to touch the forehead to the ground while kneeling, as an act of worship"; but from this meaning we have derived a figurative use as well: "to act in an obsequious manner; show servile deference."

kudos (koo′dōz, kyoo′-) Although *kudos* has come down to us from the Greek intact in both form and meaning—"praise, glory"—in the process it has come to be regarded as a plural word, although it is singular. As a result, another new word has been formed, kudo. Although purists still prefer "kudos is" to "kudos are," only time will tell if the transformation to kudo/kudos becomes permanent.

labyrinth (lab′ə rinth′) According to the Greek myth, King Minos of Crete ordered Daedalus to build a prison for the Minotaur, a half-bull, half-human monster. Daedalus succeeded by creating a series of twisting passageways that kept the monster imprisoned. Today a *labyrinth* is "a devious arrangement of linear patterns forming a design; a maze."

lackey (lak′ē) After their invasion of Spain in 711, the Moors conquered nearly the entire country and established a glittering civilization. But it was not to last. By 1100, Christians had already wrested half of Spain from the Moors. Two hundred years later, the Moors retained only a small toehold; and a hundred years after that, they were driven out of Europe entirely. As the Moors suffered repeated defeats, their captured soldiers became servants to their Spanish conquerors. They were called *alacayo"* The initial "a" was later dropped, and the word was rendered in English as *lackey,* "a servile follower."

laconic (lə ko′nik) In Sparta, the capital of the ancient Greek region of Laconia, children were trained in endurance, cunning, modesty, and self-restraint. From the terse style of speech and writing of the Laconians we derive the English word *laconic.* Today the word retains this meaning: "expressing much in few words."

lacuna (lə kyoo′nə) *Lacuna,* "a gap or missing part; hiatus," comes from the identical Latin word, *lacuna* (a hollow). It first entered English to refer to a missing part in a manuscript. It is also the root of lagoon.

lampoon (lam poon′) *Lampoon,* "a sharp, often virulent satire," comes from the French word *lampon,* which is thought to come from *lampons* (let's drink), a common ending to seventeenth-century French satirical drinking songs. We also use the word as a verb meaning "to mock or ridicule."

lethargy (leth′ər jē) The Greeks believed in an afterlife. In their mythology, the dead crossed the river Lethe, which flowed through Hades, the underground realm. Anyone who drank its water forgot the past. The Greek word *lethargia* derives from *lethe* (forgetfulness), which is the root of our English word *lethargy* "drowsiness or sluggishness."

libertine (lib′ər tēn′) In ancient Rome, *libertinus* referred to a freed slave. Since those freed from slavery were unlikely to be strict observers of the laws that had enslaved them in the first place, *libertine* came to designate "a person who is morally or sexually unrestrained."

lilliputian (lil′ə pyoo′shən) *Gulliver's Travels,* the enduring masterpiece by Jonathan Swift (1667–1745), is a scathing satire on politics and society that purports to be an account of the voyages of a naive traveler named

Lemuel Gulliver to Brobdinag, a land of giants, and Lilliput, a country inhabited by people who measure around six inches tall. In honor of this Swiftian work, we use the word *lilliputian* to refer first of all to a person or thing that is extremely small but also one that is narrow; petty; trivial.

lyceum (lī sē′əm) The Lyceum was the shrine dedicated to Apollo by the Athenians. The name came from the Greek Lykeion, meaning Wolf Slayer, a nickname of Apollo. The shrine was a favorite haunt of the Athenian philosophers, especially Aristotle, who taught his disciples while walking along its paths. Thus, the word *lyceum* came to mean "an institute for popular education, providing discussions, lectures, concerts, and so forth." The term is most popular in New England, and it is often used as a proper name for theaters.

macadam (mə kad′əm) While experimenting with methods of improving road construction, John McAdam, a Scotsman, concluded that the prevailing practice of placing a base of large stones under a layer of small stones was unnecessary. As surveyor-general for the roads of Bristol, England, in the early nineteenth century, McAdam built roads using only six to ten inches of small crushed stones, thereby eliminating the cost of constructing the base. Not only were the results impressive, but the savings were so remarkable that his idea soon spread to other countries. McAdam's experiments led to our use of the term *macadam* for a road or pavement of compacted crushed stones, usually bound with asphalt or tar.

Machiavellian (mak′ē ə vel′ē ən) The Florentine political philosopher Nicolò Machiavelli (1469–1527) was a fervent supporter of a united Italy. Unfortunately, his methods for achieving his goals placed political expediency over morality. His masterpiece, *The Prince* (1513), advocated deception and hypocrisy on the grounds that the end justifies the means. The adjective *Machiavellian* means "unscrupulous, cunning, and deceptive in the pursuit of power."

macabre (mə kä′brə, -kä′bər) In modern usage, *macabre* means "gruesome and horrible; pertaining to death." Its history is uncertain. However, most etymologists believe that the word's use in the French phrase *Danse Macabre* (dance of Macabre), a translation of Medieval Latin "chorea Macchabeorum," connects the word with the Maccabees, the leaders of the Jewish rebellion against Syria about 165 b.c. whose death as martyrs is vividly described in the Book of Maccabees (a part of the Apocrypha).

maelstrom (māl′strəm) The word's figurative meaning, "a restless, disordered state of affairs," is derived from its literal one. Today's meaning comes from Maelstrom, the name of a strong tidal current off the coast of Norway. Because of its configuration, the current creates a powerful whirlpool. According to legend, the current was once so strong that it could sink any vessel that ventured near it.

martinet (mär′tən et′) In a move to improve his army, in 1660 Louis XIV hired Colonel Jean Martinet, a successful infantry leader, to devise a drill for France's soldiers. Martinet drilled his soldiers to such exacting standards that his name came to be applied to any officer intent on maintaining military discipline or precision. Thus, in English, a *martinet* is "a strict disciplinarian, especially a military one." Interestingly, in France, Martinet's name acquired no such negative connotation.

maudlin (môd′lən) This word, meaning "tearfully or weakly emotional," comes from the miracle plays of the Middle Ages. Although these plays depicted many of the Biblical miracles, the most popular theme was the life of Mary Magdalene. The English pronounced her name "maudlin," and since most of the scenes in which she appeared were tearful, this pronunciation of her name became associated with mawkish sentimentality.

meander (mē an′dər) In ancient times, the Menderes River in western Turkey was so remarkable for its twisting path that its Greek name, Maiandros, came to mean a winding course or route. In Latin this word was spelled *maeander*, hence English meander, used mainly as a verb and meaning "to proceed by a winding or indirect course."

mecca (me′ kə) The prophet Muhammad (570?–632), the founder and great lawgiver of Islam, was born to a wealthy family in the city of Mecca, in Saudi Arabia, long a center of pagan religious sects. At the age of forty, he was selected by Allah to be the Arabian prophet of true religion and the successor of Jesus Christ; many of his revelations were later collected in the Koran. The prophet's flight, or hegira, from Mecca under the threat of a murder plot in the year 622 is now considered the beginning of the Muslim era, the date from which the calendar is calculated. Muhammad spent the rest of his life in Medina, but he captured Mecca in a bloodless battle in 630 to complete his conquest of Arabia. Each of the 1.1 billion Muslims in the world is required to pray five times a day while facing Mecca, regarded as the holiest city of Islam. No non-Muslims are permitted to enter the city and every one of the faithful who is financially able is required to make the annual hajj, or pilgrimage, to Mecca at least once.

meerschaum (mēr′shəm, -shôm) Since it is white and soft and often found along seashores, ancient people believed this white claylike mineral was foam from the ocean turned into stone. As a result, in all languages it was called sea foam. It was of little use until German artisans began to carve it into pipes. Meerschaum absorbs nicotine from tobacco, and it acquires a deep honey color as it does so. Because the Germans were the first to find a use for it, the German name stuck: *meer* (sea), *schaum* (foam). In English *meerschaum* often means "a tobacco pipe with a bowl made of meerschaum (the mineral)."

mentor (men′tôr) In Homer's *Odyssey*, Mentor is Odysseus's friend and tutor to his son Telemachus. Today the word *mentor* means "trusted teacher or guide."

mercurial (mər kyoor′ē əl) Even schoolchildren are familiar with the character of the Mad Hatter from Lewis Carroll's account of *Alice's Adventures in Wonderland* and the concomitant phrase "as mad as a hatter," but few people are aware that the phrase had a basis in reality: many hatmakers indeed were known to go mad as a result of the use of mercury, a poisonous substance, in their work. The celebrated English physicist and mathematician Sir Isaac Newton (1642–1727) was also known to behave somewhat strangely at times following his scientific experiments with mercury. Today we use the word *mercurial* to mean "changeable; fickle; flighty; erratic or sometimes animated; lively."

mesmerize (mez′mə rīz′, mes′-) The Austrian doctor Friedrich Anton Mesmer first publicly demonstrated the technique of hypnotism in 1775. Today the term *mesmerize* is still used as a synonym for hypnotize, but it has broadened to also mean "spellbind or fascinate."

miscreant (mis′krē ənt) The word's source, the Old French *mes* (wrongly) and *creant* (believing), tells us that *miscreant* was originally used to describe a heretic. The word has evolved over the centuries, however, to refer to "a base, villainous, or depraved person."

mountebank (moun′tə bangk′) During the Middle Ages, Italians conducted their banking in the streets, setting up business on convenient benches. In fact, the Italian word *banc* has given us our word bank. People with less honest intentions realized that it would be relatively easy to cheat the people who assembled around these benches. To attract a crowd, these con men often worked with jugglers, clowns, rope dancers, or singers. Since they always worked around a bench, they were known as *montimbancos*. Although the word was Anglicized to *mountebank*, it still refers to "a huckster or charlatan who sells quack medicines from a platform in a public place, appealing to his audience by using tricks, storytelling, and so forth."

mugwump (mug′wump′) This word entered the English language in a most curious fashion. In the mid-1600s, the clergyman John Eliot, known as the Apostle to the Indians, translated the Bible into the Algonquian language. When he came to the thirty-sixth chapter of Genesis, he had no word for duke, so he used *mugquomp*, an Algonquian term for chief or great man. Historians of the language theorize that the term might already have been in circulation at that time, but they know for certain that by 1884 it was in fairly general use. In the presidential election that year, a group of Republicans threw their support to Grover Cleveland rather than to the party's nominee, James G. Blaine. The newspapers scorned the renegade Republicans as *mugwumps*, "those who thought themselves too good to vote for Blaine." The scorned Republicans got the last word when they adopted the same term to describe themselves, saying they were independent men proud to call themselves mugwumps, or great men. Today we use the term *mugwump* to describe "a person who takes an independent position or one who is neutral on a controversial issue."

nabob (nā′bob) The Mogul emperors, who ruled India from the sixteenth century until the middle of the nineteenth century, delegated authority to men who acted as governors of various parts of India. To the native Indians, such a ruler was known as a *nawwab* (deputy). The word was changed by the Europeans into *nabob*. The nabobs were supposed to tithe money to the central government, but some of the nabobs withheld the money, and thereby became enormously wealthy. From their fortunes came the European custom of using the word *nabob* to refer to "a person, especially a European, who had attained great wealth in India or another country of the East." The usage spread to England, and today we use the term to describe any very wealthy or powerful person.

namby-pamby (nam′bē pam′bē) The term *namby-pamby*, used to describe "anything weakly sentimental, pretentious, or affected," comes from Henry Carey's parody of Ambrose Philips's sentimental children's poems. Carey titled his parody "Namby Pamby," taking the namby from the diminutive of Ambrose and using the first letter of his surname, P, for the alliteration. Following a bitter quarrel with Philips, Alexander Pope seized upon Carey's parody in the second edition of his *Dunciad* in 1733. Through the popularity of Pope's poem, the term namby-pamby passed into general usage.

narcissism (när′sə siz′əm) The word *narcissism*, "inordinate fascination with oneself," comes from the Greek myth of Narcissus. According to one version of the legend, an exceptionally handsome young man fell in love with his own image reflected in a pool. When he tried to embrace his image, he drowned. According to another version, Narcissus fell in love with his identical twin sister. After her death, he sat and stared at his own reflection in the pool until he died from grief.

nemesis (nem′ə sis) Nemesis was the Greek goddess of vengeance, whose task it was to punish the proud and the insolent. Today a *nemesis* is "an agent or act of retribution or punishment, or something that a person cannot conquer or achieve."

nepenthe (ni pen′thē) According to Greek legend, when Paris kidnapped Helen and took her to Troy, he wanted her to forget her previous life. In Homer's version of the tale, Paris gave Helen a drug thought to cause loss of memory. The drug was called *nepenthes*. The word has come down to us with its meaning intact: "anything inducing a pleasurable sensation of forgetfulness."

nepotism (nep′ə tiz′əm) This word for patronage bestowed or favoritism shown on the basis of family relationships, as in business or politics, can be traced to the popes of the fifteenth and sixteenth centuries. To increase their power, these men surrounded themselves with people they knew would be loyal—members of their own family. Among the most popular candidates were the popes' own illegitimate sons, called nephews, from the Latin *nepos* (a descendant), as a mark of respect. Eventually the term *nepotism* came to mean "favoritism to all family members, not just nephews."

noisome (noi′səm) Although the words appear to have the same root, noisome bears no relation to the word noise. *Noisome* means "offensive or disgusting, as an odor," and comes from the Middle English word *noy* (harm). The root is related, however, to the word annoy, "to molest or bother."

nonplus (nän plus′, nän′plus′) The word *nonplus* means "to make utterly perplexed; to puzzle completely." The original Latin phrase was *non plus ultra* (no more beyond), allegedly inscribed on the Pillars of Hercules, beyond which no ship could safely sail.

nostrum (nos′trəm) The word *nostrum,* "a patent or quack medicine," became current around the time of the Great Plague in the mid-seventeenth century. Doctors were helpless to combat the disease, so charlatans and quacks flooded the market with their own secret—and useless—concoctions. To make their medicines seem more effective, they labeled them with the Latin word *nostrum* (our own), as in *nostrum remedium,* (our own remedy), which makes no claims at all for the remedy's effectiveness.

oscillate (os′ə lāt′) In ancient Rome, the grape growers hung little images with the face of Bacchus, the god of wine, on their vines. The Latin word for face is *os,* so a little face would be called an *oscillum*. Because the images swung in the wind, some students of language concluded that the Latin verb *oscillare* came from a description of this swinging face. Most scholars have declined to make this connection, saying only that our present word *oscillate,* "to swing to and fro," is derived from Latin *oscillare* (to swing), which in turn comes from *oscillum* (a swing).

ostracize (os′trə sīz′) The word ostracize comes originally from the Greek *ostrakon* (tile, potsherd, shell). It refers to the ancient Greek practice of banishing a man by writing his name on a shell or a bit of earthen tile. Anyone considered dangerous to the state was sent into exile for ten years. The judges cast their votes by writing on the shells or pottery shards and dropping them into an urn. The word *ostracize* retains the same sense: "to exclude, by general consent, from society."

paladin (pa′lə din) The original paladins were Charlemagne's twelve knights. According to legend, the famous paladin Roland was caught in an ambush and fought valiantly with his small band of followers to the last man. Because of his actions, *paladin* has come down to us as "any champion of noble causes."

palaver (pə la′vər, pə lä′vər) The word *palaver* derives ultimately from the Greek word *parabola* (comparison, literally a placing beside). From this came the English parable, a story that makes comparisons. In Latin the word came to mean speech, talk, word. Later, Portuguese traders carried the term to Africa in the form *palavra* and used it to refer to the long talks with native chiefs required by local custom. English traders picked up the word in the eighteenth century, spelling it as we do today. The word retains its last meaning, "a long parley, especially one with people indigenous to a region or profuse, idle talk."

pander (pan′dər) *Pander,* "to act as a go-between in amorous intrigues or to act as a pimp or procurer or to cater basely," comes from the medieval story of Troilus and Cressida. In his retelling, Chaucer describes how the love-stricken Troilus calls upon his friend Pandarus, kin to Cressida, to aid him in his quest for her love. Much of Chaucer's tale is devoted to the different means used by Pandarus to help Troilus win his love. Shakespeare later recycled the same legend. As the story gained in popularity the name Pandarus was changed in English to pandare and then to pander. The noun now has the negative connotation of "pimp or procurer for illicit sexual intercourse."

pariah (pə rī′ə) The term *pariah,* "an outcast," comes from the name of one of the lowest castes in India. Composed of agricultural laborers and household servants, it is not the lowest caste, but its members are still considered untouchable by the Brahmans. The British used the term pariah for anyone of low social standing. Pariah now is used to describe any outcast among his or her own people.

pecuniary (pi kyoo′nē er′ē) The Romans measured a man's worth by the number of animals he kept on his farm. They adapted the Latin word for a farm animal, *pecu,* to refer to individual wealth. But as people acquired new ways of measuring wealth, such as money and land, the Roman word evolved into pecunia, which referred most specifically to money. From this came the adjective *pecuniary,* "pertaining to or consisting of money."

pecksniffian (pek snif′ē ən) The often lovable, sometimes villainous, but always memorable eccentrics that populate the literary universe of Charles Dickens made him one of the most popular and enduring English novelists of the nineteenth century. Indeed we often speak of peculiar characters with notable quirks as being Dickensian. Everyone knows that a scrooge is a miser, thanks to the numerous versions of *A Christmas Carol* that are performed every year at Christmastime. Far fewer people are familiar with Seth Pecksniff, a minor character in *Martin Chuzzlewit* (1843), one of Dickens' lesser-known works. But he so thoroughly embodies the trait of hypocritically affecting benevolence or high moral principles that we can find no better word to describe such pious frauds than *pecksniffian.*

pedagogue (ped′ə gog′, -gô′) Wealthy Greek families kept a special slave to supervise their sons. The slave's responsibilities included accompanying the boys as they traveled to and from school and walked in the public streets. To describe a slave's chores, the Greeks coined the term *paidagogos* (a leader of boys). Occasionally, when the slave was an educated man captured in warfare and sold into slavery, the slave also tutored his charges. From the Greek word we derived the English *pedagogue,* "teacher or educator."

phantasmagoria (fan taz′mə gôr′ēə) In the early years of the nineteenth century, an inventor named Philipstal created a wondrous device for producing optical illusions. By projecting colored slides onto a thin silk screen, Philipstal made his spectral images appear to move. Today, of course, we take such motion-picture illusions for granted, but in the age of the magic lantern, such visions were marvelous indeed. Philipstal named his invention *phantasmagoria,* which we now apply to "a shifting series of phantasms or deceptive appearances, as in a dream."

pharisaical (far′ əsā′əkəl) The Pharisees were one of the two great Jewish sects of the Old Testament; their opponents were known as Sadducees. The Pharisees placed great emphasis on the strict observance of religious law, rites, and ceremonies. By the time of Jesus, many of the common people had become alienated from the Pharisees, who, according to the Gospels, "preach but do not practice." The word *pharisaical* reflects this New Testament view of the Pharisees and now means "practicing external ceremonies without regard to the spirit; hypocritical."

philistine (fi′lə stēn′,-stĭn′) The Philistines were a non-Semitic people who settled in ancient Palestine after their migration from the Aegean area in the twelfth century b.c. As rivals of the Israelites for many centuries, they have long suffered from an undeserved bad reputation: there is no real historical proof to indicate that they were as rough and uncivilized as the modern word *philistin* suggests. The word is used to refer to "a person who is lacking in or smugly indifferent to culture and aesthetic refinement; one who is contentedly commonplace in ideas and tastes."

phoenix (fē′niks) According to legend, the phoenix was a fabulous Arabian bird that ignited itself on a pyre of flames after its allotted life span of 500 years; a new phoenix then arose from its ashes. Thus, the symbol of the phoenix has often been used to designate the cycle of death and resurrection. We use the word to describe "a person or thing that has been restored after suffering calamity or apparent annihilation."

Pollyanna (pol′ē anə′) Pollyanna, the child heroine created by the U.S. writer Eleanor Porter (1868–1920), was immortalized on the silver screen in 1960 by the young Hayley Mills. An orphan who comes to live with her strict, dour, but very rich and influential aunt, the high-spirited girl gradually wins over the unhappy townspeople and even her mean old aunt with her ingenuous charm and cheerful outlook. Since many adult readers tend to find the story somewhat treacly, a *Pollyanna* now means "an excessively or blindly optimistic person."

pompadour (pom′pə dôr′, -do͞or′) Sheltered by a wealthy family and educated as though she were their own daughter, at twenty the exquisite Jeanne Antoinette Poisson Le Normant d'Étioles married her protector's nephew and began her reign over the world of Parisian fashion. Soon after, King Louis XV took her as his mistress, established her at the court of Versailles, and gave her the estate of Pompadour. The Marquise de Pompadour created a large and high-swept hairstyle memorialized by her name. The upswept style is still known by her name whether it is used to describe a man's or a woman's hairdo.

pooh-bah (po͞o′bä′) The *Mikado* (1885) is probably the most popular light opera written by the collaborative team of Gilbert and Sullivan. Ostensibly the story of the thwarted love of Nanki-Poo for the beauteous Yum-Yum, set at the imperial court of Japan, it is actually an incisive satire on the society of the Victorian era. The absurd character of the overbearing high official known as Pooh-Bah has given us this generic term meaning "a person who holds several positions at once or—more pungently—any pompous, self-important person."

precipitate (pri sip′ə tāt′) The word *precipitate* is based on the Latin root *caput* (head). In fact, the word was first used to apply to those who had been executed or killed themselves by being hurled or jumping headlong from a precipice or high place. Later, the word came to mean "to rush headlong." From this has come today's meaning, "to hasten the occurrence of; to bring about prematurely."

precocious (pri kō′shəs) To the Romans, the Latin word *praecox*, the source of English precocious, was a culinary term meaning precooked. In time, however, its meaning was extended to acting prematurely. It is this later meaning of *precocious* that we use today: "unusually advanced in development, especially mental development."

pretext (prē′tekst) *Pretext* comes from the Latin word *praetexta*, meaning an ornament, such as the purple markings on a toga denoting rank. In addition to its literal sense, however, the word carried the connotation of something to cloak one's true identity. We have retained only the word's figurative meaning, "something that is put forward to conceal a true purpose or object, an ostensible reason."

prevaricate (pri var′ə kāt′) Today *prevaricate* means "to speak falsely or misleadingly with deliberate intent; to lie." It has its origin in a physical act. The Latin verb *praevaricare* means "to spread apart." The plowman who prevaricated, then, made crooked ridges, deviating from straight furrows in the field.

procrustean (prō krus′tē ən) According to one version of the Greek myth, Procrustes was a bandit who made his living waylaying unsuspecting travelers. He tied everyone who fell into his grasp to an iron bed. If they were longer than the bed, he cut short their legs to make their bodies fit; if they were shorter, he stretched their bodies until they fit tightly. Hence, *procrustean* means "tending to produce conformity through violent or arbitrary means."

profane (prə fān′, prō-) Only fully initiated men were allowed to participate in Greek and Roman religious rites; those not admitted were called profane, from *pro* (outside) and *fanum* (temple). When the word came into English, it was applied to persons or things not part of Christianity. Probably in reference to the contempt of nonbelievers, *profane* now means "characterized by irreverence for God or sacred things."

proletariat (prō′lə târ′ē ət) Proletariat derives from the Latin *proletarius* (a Roman freeman who lacked property and money). The word came from *proles* (offspring, children). Although the freemen had the vote, many wealthy Romans despised them, saying they were useful only to have children. They called them *proletarii* (producers of children). Karl Marx picked up the word in the mid-nineteenth century as a label for the lower-class working people of his age. *Proletariat* retains the same meaning today: "members of the working class, especially those who do not possess capital and must sell their labor to survive."

Promethean (prə mē′thē ən) According to Greek myth, as punishment for stealing fire from the gods and giving it to mortal humans, Prometheus was bound to the side of a mountain, where he was attacked daily by a fierce bird that feasted upon his liver. At night his wounds healed; the next day he was attacked anew. Because of his extraordinary boldness in stealing the divine fire, the word *Promethean* has come to mean "creative, boldly original."

protean (prō′tē ən) According to Greek legend, Proteus was a sea god who possessed the power to change his shape at will. He also had the ability to foretell the future, but those wishing to avail themselves of his power first had to steal up on him at noon when he checked his herds of sea calves, catch him, and bind him securely. Thus bound, Proteus would change shape furiously, but the petitioner who could keep him restrained until he returned to his original shape would receive the answer to his question—if he still remembered what he wanted to know. From Proteus, then, we get the word *protean* "readily assuming different forms or characters; variable."

pundit (pun′dit) Today we use the word *pundit* to mean "an expert or authority"; but in the nineteenth century, the word was usually applied to a learned person in India. It comes from the Hindi word *pandit* (learned man), a Brahman with profound knowledge of Sanskrit, Hindu law, and so forth.

pygmy (pig′mē) The ancient Greeks were entranced by stories of a tribe of dwarfs in the Upper Nile who were so small that they could be swallowed by cranes. To describe these tiny people, the Greeks used the word *pygmaios*, which also referred to the distance on a person's arm from the elbow to the knuckles. The word became the English *pygmy*, "a tiny person or thing; a person or thing of small importance."

Pyrrhic victory (pir′ik) Pyrrhus (c. 318–272 b.c.) was a Greek warrior-king whose incessant warfare against the Romans as well as fellow Greeks ultimately brought ruin on his own kingdom. He defeated the Romans at Aesculum in 279, but his losses were so heavy that he was later said by the Greek historian and biographer Plutarch to have declared, "One more such victory and I am undone." Thus a *Pyrrhic victory* is a victory or attainment achieved at too great a cost to be worthwhile.

quack (kwak) Noticing how the raucous shouts of the charlatans selling useless concoctions sounded like the strident quacks of ducks, the sixteenth-century Dutch called these charlatans *quacksalvers*—literally, ducks quacking over their salves. The term quickly spread through Europe. The English shortened it to *quack*, and used it to describe "any fraudulent or ignorant pretender to medical skills," the meaning we retain today.

quintessence (kwin te′səns) The word comes from the medieval Latin term *quinta essentia* (the fifth essence). This fifth primary element was thought to be ether, supposedly the constituent matter of the heavenly bodies. The other four elements were thought to be air, fire, earth, and water. Medieval alchemists tried to isolate ether through distillation. These experiments gave us the contemporary meaning of *quintessence*: "the pure and concentrated essence of a substance; the most perfect embodiment of something."

quisling (kwiz′ling) This term refers to "a traitor, a person who betrays his or her own country by aiding an enemy and often serving later in a puppet government." It is directly derived from the name of Vidkun Quisling (1887–1945), a Norwegian army officer turned fascist who collaborated with the Nazis early in World War II.

quixotic (kwik sot′ik) The word *quixotic*, meaning "extravagantly chivalrous or romantic," is based on the character of Don Quixote, the chivalrous knight in Cervantes' 1605 masterpiece *Don Quixote de la Mancha*. The impractical, visionary knight was ludicrously blind to the false nature of his dreams.

quorum (kwôr′ əm) The word *quorum* was first used as part of a Latin phrase meaning "to select people for official court business." Ultimately, it came to mean "the number of members of a group or organization required to be present to transact business; legally, usually a majority."

Rabelaisian (rabə lā′zē ən, -zhən) A classic old New Yorker cartoon shows two laughing men in Renaissance dress, one of whom is saying, "Ho ho ho! Monsieur Rabelais, there is just no word to describe that earthy humor of yours!" The joke is that there is one and only one such word, and that word is *Rabelaisian*. The masterpiece of François Rabelais, *Gargantua and Pantagruel*, contains serious discussions of education, politics, and philosophy, but it is most remarkable for its broad, ribald, often scatological humor—a humor unique in world literature for its daring and immodest hilarity that has given birth to the word *Rabelaisian*, meaning "coarsely humorous."

rake (rāk) *Rake*, meaning "a dissolute person, especially a man," was originally *rakehell*. In the sixteenth century, this colorful term was used to describe a person so dissipated that he would rake hell to find his pleasures. Rakehell is now considered a somewhat archaic term to describe such roués; *rake* is the more common word.

recalcitrant (ri kal′sə trənt) The word was formed from the Latin prefix *re-* (back) and *calcitrare* (to kick). Thus, a *recalcitrant* person is "one who kicks back, resisting authority or control."

requiem (rek′wē əm) A *requiem* is a mass celebrated for the repose of the souls of the dead. It comes from the opening line of the Roman Catholic mass for the dead: "Requiem aeternam dona ers, Domine," meaning "Give them eternal rest, Lord." It can refer more loosely to any memorial for the dead, or a tribute, as in the title of the film *Requiem for a Heavyweight*, about a washed-up prizefighter.

rhubarb (roo′bärb) In conventional usage, the word refers to "a long-stalked plant, used in tart conserves and pie fillings"; it is also a slang term for "quarrel or squabble." The ancient Greeks gave the plant its name. Since it grew in an area outside of Greece, they called it *rha barbaron*. *Rha* was the name of the plant and *barbaro* meant foreign.

rialto (rē al′tō) In the late sixteenth century, the Venetians erected a bridge across the Grand Canal. Since the bridge spanned deep waters, it was called the Rialto (deep stream). The bridge led to the creation of a busy shopping area in the center of the city. From this shopping center we derive our present meaning of *rialto*, "an exchange or mart." The word is also used to refer to a theater district, especially Broadway, in New York City.

rigmarole (ri′gəmə rōl′) In fourteenth-century England, a register of names was called a rageman. Later it became a ragman, then ragman roll. As it changed, the term evolved to refer to a series of unconnected statements. By the 1700s, the word had become *rigmarole*, with its present meaning, "an elaborate or complicated procedure."

rostrum (ros′trəm) Today a *rostrum* is "any platform, stage, or the like for public speaking." The word comes from the victory in 338 b.c. of the Romans over the pirates of Antium (Anzio), off the Italian coast. The victorious consul took back to Rome the prows of the six ships he had captured. These were attached to the lecterns used by Roman speakers. They came to be called *rostra* (beaks). We use the singular, *rostrum*.

sarcophagus (sär kä′fə gəs) Although the majority of ancient Greeks favored burial or cremation, some obtained limestone coffins that could dissolve a body in little over a month. The coffin was called a *sarcophagus*, from the Greek *sarx* (flesh) and *phagos* (eating). Today we use the term to refer to "a stone coffin, especially one bearing sculpture, an inscription, etc., often displayed as a monument."

sardonic (sär don′ik) The ancient Greeks described a plant on the island of Sardinia whose flesh, if eaten, caused the victim's face to become grotesquely convulsed, as if in scornful laughter. The Greek name for Sardinia was Sardos; therefore, *sardonios* came to refer to any mocking laughter. The English word eventually became *sardonic*, "characterized by bitter irony or scornful derision."

scapegoat (skāp′gōt′) The term *scapegoat*, "a person made to bear the blame for others or to suffer in their place," comes from the sixteenth chapter of Leviticus, which describes how the high priest Aaron was directed to select two goats. One goat was to be burned as an offering to the Lord; the other, an "escape goat" for atonement, was to be presented alive to the Lord and sent away into the wilderness to carry away the sins of the people. The word scape was a shortening of escape.

shibboleth (shi′bə lith, -leth′) In the twelfth chapter of Judges, Jephthah and his men gained a victory over the warriors of Ephraim. After the battle, Jephthah gave his guards the password *shibboleth* to distinguish friends from foes; he picked the word because the Ephraimites could not pronounce the "sh" sound. His choice was shrewd, and many of his enemies were captured and killed. Thus, *shibboleth* has come to mean "a peculiarity of pronunciation, usage, or behavior that distinguishes a particular class or set of persons." It also can mean "slogan; catchword."

shrew (shroo) In Old English, the word *shrew* described a small, fierce rodent. The word was later applied to a person with a violent temper and tenacious personality similar to the rodent's. Although *shrew* has retained this meaning, it is usually applied only to a woman.

silhouette (sil′oo et′) At the urging of his mistress, Madame de Pompadour, the French king Louis XV appointed Etienne de Silhouette as his finance minister. His mission was to enact strict economic measures to rescue the government from near-bankruptcy. At the same time, there was a revival of the practice of tracing profiles created by shadows. Since they replaced more costly paintings, these outlines came to be derided as "les Silhouettes"—another of his money-saving measures. Although Silhouette lasted in office less than a year, he achieved a sort of immortality when his name became permanently associated with "a two-dimensional representation of the outline of an object, as a person's profile, generally filled in with black."

simony (sī'mə nē, si'-) Simon the sorcerer offered to pay the Apostle Peter to teach him the wondrous cures he had seen Peter perform, not understanding that his feats were miracles rather than magic tricks. From Simon's name comes the term *simony*, "the sin of buying or selling ecclesiastical preferments."

sinecure (sī'nə kyŏŏr', sin'i-) *Sinecure*, a word meaning "an office or position requiring little or no work, especially one yielding profitable returns," originally began as a church term, from the Latin *beneficium sine cura* (a benefice without care). It referred to the practice of rewarding a church rector by giving him a parish for which he had no actual responsibilities. The real work was carried on by a vicar, but his absent superior received the higher recompense. Although the church practice was abolished in the mid-nineteenth century, the term is often used today in a political context.

siren (sī'rən) The Sirens of Greek legend were three sea nymphs with the head of a woman and the body of a bird who inhabited an island surrounded by rocky shoals and lured passing mariners to their death with their enchanting songs. Jason and the Argonauts were saved from them by the lyre-playing of Orpheus, which was even sweeter than the Sirens' song. Odysseus, who could not resist the temptation of listening to them, instructed his shipmates to tie him to the mast and plug up their own ears to avoid a shipwreck. Today a *siren* is "a seductively beautiful or charming woman, especially one who beguiles men; an enchantress."

Sisyphean (si' səfē'ən) In Greek mythology, Sisyphus was the founder and king of Corinth who was condemned to Tartarus for his disrespect to Zeus. There he performed the eternal task of rolling a heavy stone to the top of a steep hill, where it inevitably slipped away from him and rolled back down again. His punishment has given us the term *Sisyphean*, meaning "futile or hopeless, especially in relation to an impossible task." In a 1942 essay, the existentialist writer Albert Camus (1913–1960) popularized the myth as a metaphor for modern life.

solecism (sä' ləsi zəm, sō'l-) To the ancient Greeks, the people of the colony of Soloi spoke inexcusably poor Greek. The Greeks were perhaps most offended by the Solois' errors in grammar and usage. They called such barbarous speech *soloikismos* (the language of Soloi). Through Latin, the word became *solecism*, "a substandard or ungrammatical usage, a breach of good manners or etiquette."

solomonic (sälə mä'nik) Solomon, the tenth-century b.c. Hebrew king who was the son and successor of David, was renowned for his wisdom. Probably most famous was his decision in the case of the two women who claimed to be the mother of the same infant. When Solomon announced his decision to resolve the bitter dispute by severing the child in two and awarding one half to each of the disputants, one woman enthusiastically agreed to comply with his judgment while the other offered to give up the child rather than seeing it murdered before her eyes. Solomon handed over the child to the second woman, whom he deemed to be its true mother. Thus, we say that a *solomonic* decision or person is one that is "wise or reasonable in character; sagacious."

sophistry (sof′ ə strē) In the fifth century b.c., the Sophists were peripatetic Greek teachers paid to instruct the sons of the upper class who sought political and legal careers in pragmatic rhetorical skills. They sought knowledge primarily as a source of intellectual amusement, power, and social prominence. Thus, they were noted more for their ingenuity and speciousness in argumentation than for their desire to discover the truth or establish moral principles. Some of them even boasted that they could "make the worst appear the better reason." Gorgias, one of the leading lights of the Sophist school, argued that nothing exists and nothing is knowable, since reality is entirely relative to the subjective experience of the individual. Not surprisingly, Socrates, who would accept no payment for his teaching, regarded their influence as pernicious. The current meaning of *sophistry*, therefore, is "a subtle, tricky, superficially plausible but generally fallacious method of reasoning; a false argument or fallacy."

spartan (spär′tən) Sparta was the rival city-state of ancient Greece that ultimately destroyed the high civilization of Athens in the petty squabbles of the Peloponnesian War (431–404 b.c.). Both empires were equally ruthless, but the Spartans were renowned for their superior military discipline, which began in early childhood. A famous story tells of the proud stoicism of a boy who allowed a fox smuggled into school under his clothing to slowly disembowel him rather than cry out and admit his transgression. So extreme was their emphasis on the virtues of self-denial and toughness that the word *spartan* came to be synonymous with "a person who is sternly disciplined and rigorously simple, frugal, or austere."

spoonerism (spoo′nə ri′zəm) The English clergyman W. A. Spooner (1844–1930) was notorious for his habit of transposing the initial letters or other sounds of words, as in "a blushing crow" for "a crushing blow." Since the good reverend was not unique in his affliction, we use the word *spoonerism* to describe "an unintentional transposition of sounds."

stoic (stō′ik) The Stoics were philosophers of ancient Greece who believed in self-restraint. Their name comes from Greek *stoa* (porch), where they habitually walked. The word *stoic* describes a person who is "impassive, calm, and austere."

Svengali (sven gä′lē) In one of his most memorable film roles, the great matinee idol John Barrymore steals the show as the evil hypnotist Svengali, a mad genius whose intense, piercing gaze is irresistible to the innocent artist's model Trilby, the heroine of the novel published in 1894 by George Du Maurier. Under his tutelage, Trilby is transformed into a great singer. Barrymore appears as a ghoulish, bearded creature dressed in disheveled clothing like a sort of dissolute monk. The 1931 film, of course, was called *Svengali*, not (like the original novel) *Trilby*. His is the image we summon up when we think of a *Svengali*, "a person who completely dominates another, usually with evil or selfish motives."

sybarite (si′bə rīt′) The ancient Greek colony of Sybaris in southern Italy was known for its luxurious lifestyle. The residents were so famous for their opulent ways that the word *sybarite* came to be used for "any person devoted to luxury and pleasure."

sycophant (sik′ə fənt, -fant′) The word *sycophant* now means "a self-seeking, servile flatterer." Originally, it was used to refer to an informer or slanderer. Curiously, it comes from Greek *sykon* (fig) and *-phantes* (one who shows); thus, a fig-shower. One explanation for this odd coinage is that in ancient Greece a sycophant was an informer against merchants engaged in the unlawful exportation of figs.

sylph (silf) A German alchemist of the 1700s coined the term *Sylphis* to describe the spirits of the air. He envisioned them as looking like humans but able to move more swiftly and gracefully. Over the years, the word evolved to mean "a slender, graceful girl or woman."

tantalize (tan′tə līz′) For his transgressions against the Greek god Zeus, Tantalus was condemned to Tartarus, where he stood in a pool with his chin level with the water, eternally parched with thirst. When he bowed his head to drink, the water ebbed away. Above his head were trees laden with juicy fruits, but when he tried to seize them, the wind swept them out of his reach. From this hellish dilemma, we derive the word *tantalize*, "to torment with the sight of something desired but out of reach; tease by arousing expectations."

tartar (tär′tər) The fierce Genghis Khan and his successors led an army of bloodthirsty warriors, including the Ta-ta Mongols, in a series of conquests throughout Asia and into Europe. Their name, *Tartar* or *Tatar*, became closely associated with brutal massacres. Today the word *tartar* refers to "a savage, ill-tempered, or intractable person."

tariff (tar′if) *Tariff*, "an official schedule of duties or customs imposed by a government on imports and exports," comes from the Arabic term for inventory, *tarif*. Perhaps because this story is so unexciting, a false etymology claims that the word instead comes from the name of a Moorish town near the straits of Gibraltar formerly used as a base for daring pirate raids. Colorful, but not true. The word is also used more loosely to mean "cost or price of admission."

tartuffe (tär tōof′, -toof′) The French actor and playwright Molière (1622–1673) is famed for his farces and comedies of manners, which ridicule human foibles and excesses in the person of a main character that epitomizes such vices as hypocrisy, misanthropy, affected intellectualism, and social snobbery. The title character of *Le Tartuffe*, first performed in 1664, is the source for this word meaning "a hypocritical pretender to piety; a religious hypocrite."

tawdry (tô′drē) In the seventh century, an Englishwoman named Etheldreda fled her husband to establish an abbey. When the Venerable Bede recounted her story in the early eighth century, he claimed that her death had been caused by a tumor in her throat, which she believed was a punishment for her early vanity of wearing jewelry about her neck. Her abbey eventually became the Cathedral of Ely; her name, Audrey. In her honor, the cathedral town held an annual fair where "trifling objects" were hawked. One theory as to the development of the word *tawdry* relates to the hawkers' cry, "Saint Audrey's lace!" This became "Sin t'Audrey lace" and then "tawdry lace." By association with these cheap trinkets, the word *tawdry* has come to mean "gaudy, showy, or cheap."

termagant (tûr′mə gənt) The word *termagant*, meaning "a violent, turbulent, or brawling woman," comes from a mythical deity that many Europeans of the Middle Ages believed was worshiped by the Muslims. It often appeared in morality plays as a violent, overbearing personage in a long robe. In modern usage, *termagant* is applied only to women.

thespian (thes′pē ən) A Greek poet named Thespis, who flourished circa 534 b.c., enlarged the traditional celebrations at the festival of Dionysus by writing verses to be chanted alternately by individuals and the chorus. This opportunity to be a solo performer was a first. From the poet's name we derive the word *thespian*, "an actor or actress."

toady (tō′dē) In the seventeenth century, people believed that toads were poisonous, and anyone who mistakenly ate a toad's leg instead of a frog's leg would die. Rather than swear off frogs' legs, people sought a cure for the fatal food poisoning. Charlatans would sometimes hire an accomplice who would pretend to eat a toad, at which point his employer would whip out his instant remedy and "save" his helper's life. For his duties, the helper came to be called a "toad-eater." Since anyone who would consume anything as disgusting as a toad must be completely under his master's thumb, "toad-eater" or *toady* became the term for "an obsequious sycophant; a fawning flatterer."

treacle (trē′kəl) Originally, treacle was an ointment used by the ancient Romans and Greeks against the bite of wild animals. But in the eighteenth and nineteenth centuries, competing quack medicine hawkers added sweetening to make their bitter potions more palatable. After a while, the sweetening agent itself, usually molasses, came to be called *treacle*. We retain this meaning and have extended it to refer figuratively to "contrived or unrestrained sentimentality" as well.

Tweedledum and Tweedledee (twēd′əl dum′ and twēd′əl dē′) The chubby schoolboy characters of Tweedledum and Tweedledee, famous for their recitation in Lewis Carroll's *Through the Looking Glass* of "The Walrus and the Carpenter," actually have an earlier historical counterpart. This humorous coinage, devised in imitation of the sounds of their musical compositions, was apparently first applied to Italian composer Giovanni Bononcini (1670–1747) and his German-born rival Georg Friedrich Handel (1685–1759). Whichever reference you prefer, the term *Tweedledum and Tweedledee* still means "two persons nominally different but practically the same; a nearly identical pair."

utopia (yoo tō′pē ə) Sir Thomas More (1478–1535) was one of the great humanists of the Renaissance era in England. More held important government offices under Henry VIII, but as a devout Roman Catholic, he refused to accept the Act of Supremacy, which made the king the head of the English Church. He was imprisoned in the Tower of London and ultimately beheaded under a charge of treason. His *Utopia* (1516) is an account of an ideal state founded entirely on reason. More derived the title of his masterpiece from the Greek for "not a place." The popularity of this specific work has transformed the word *utopia* into a generic term meaning "any ideal place or state; a visionary system of social or political perfection."

vie (vī) The word *vie*, "to strive in competition or rivalry with another, to contend for superiority," was originally a shortened version of *envien*, a sixteenth-century gaming term meaning to raise the stake. The contraction, *vie*, came to mean "to contend, compete."

wiseacre (wīz′ā′kər) Although the word acre in wiseacre makes it appear that the term refers to a unit of measurement, *wiseacre* is actually used contemptuously to mean "a wise guy or a smart aleck." The term comes from the Dutch *wijssegger* (soothsayer). Since soothsayers were considered learned, it was logical to call them wise, which is what *wij* means. The word acre is a mispronunciation of the Dutch *segger* (sayer). There is a famous story in which the word was used in its present sense. In response to the bragging of a wealthy landowner, the English playwright Ben Jonson is said to have replied, "What care we for your dirt and clods? Where you have an acre of land, I have ten acres of wit." The chastened landowner is reported to have muttered: "He's Mr. Wiseacre."

wormwood (wûrm′wo͝od′) *Wormwood* is the active narcotic ingredient of absinthe, a bitter green liqueur now banned in most Western countries. Originally, however, the herb was used as a folk remedy for worms in the body. Because of the herb's bitter qualities, we also use it figuratively to mean "something bitter, grievous, or extremely unpleasant."

yahoo (yä′hoo) This word for "a coarse, uncouth person" was coined by Jonathan Swift in his 1726 novel *Gulliver's Travels*. In Swift's satire, the Yahoos were a race of humanoid brutes ruled by the Houyhnhnms, civilized horses.

Borrowed Words

The roots of English are Anglo-Saxon, but the English language has been influenced by so many other languages over the centuries that we can hardly say we speak a purely Germanic language. Around one-fifth of our vocabulary stems from those Germanic roots, and these basic words comprise the vast majority of the ones we use to communicate with each other every day. It is estimated that around three-fifths of our vocabulary derives from French, Latin, and Greek; the remaining one-fifth has been borrowed from languages all around the globe. In this section, the meanings of a variety of useful borrowed words are discussed. They are grouped according to their base language: French, German, Greek, Italian, Japanese, Latin, Spanish, and Yiddish.

French

Nearly half of our French borrowings came into English before the fifteenth century; thereafter, the adaptations tended to be of a more literary nature.

agent provocateur (ā′jənt prə vok′ ətûr′, toor′) outside agitator.
arriviste (ar′ē vēst′) a person who has recently acquired wealth or status; upstart.
au courant (ō′ koo rän′) up-to-date; fully aware; cognizant.
au fait (ō fe′) well-versed; expert; experienced.
avant-garde (ä vänt′gärd′, vant′-, av′änt-, ä′vänt-) the advance group in any field, especially in the visual, literary, or musical arts, whose works are unorthodox and experimental.
beau monde (bō′ mond′, -môd′) the fashionable world; high society.

Borrowed Words

bête noire (bāt′ nwär′) pet peeve; annoyance.
bonhomie (bon′ əmē′, bō′n-) good nature; geniality.
bon mot (bôn mō′) clever turn of phrase; witticism.
bon vivant (bon′vē vänt′, bô′vē vən′) a person who lives luxuriously and enjoys good food and drink.
cachet (ka shā′) superior status; prestige; a distinguishing feature.
canaille (kə nī′, -nāl′) the common people; rabble.
carte blanche (kärt′ blänch′, blänsh′) full authority or access; unconditional authority.
causerie (kō′zə rē′) informal conversation; chat.
cause célèbre (kōz sə leb′) any controversy that attracts great public attention.
chic (shēk) attractive and fashionable in style; stylish.
comme il faut (kô mēl fō′) as it should be; proper; appropriate.
connoisseur (kon′ ə sûr′, -so͞or′) a person who is especially competent to pass critical judgments in art or in matters of taste.
contretemps (kon′trə tän′) mishap; inconvenience.
coterie (kō′tə rē) a group of close associates; exclusive group or clique.
coup d'état (ko͞o′ dā tä′) a sudden and decisive action in politics, especially one effecting a change of government, illegally or by force.
coup de grâce (ko͞o′ də gräs′) final blow; a finishing or decisive stroke.
cul-de-sac (kul′də sak′) a street, lane, etc., closed at one end; blind alley.

déclassé (dā′kla sā′, -klä-) reduced to or having low status.
decolletage (dā′kolə täzh′) the neckline of a dress cut low in the front or back and often across the shoulders.
demimonde (dem′ ē mond′) a group that has lost status or lacks respectability.
denouement (dā′no͞o män′) resolution or outcome, especially of a story.
de rigueur (də ri gûr′, -rē) strictly according to the rules; required.
dernier cri (dern′yā krē′) the last word; the ultimate; latest fashion.
detritus (di trī′təs) debris; rubbish.
de trop (də trō′) too much or too many; unwanted; in the way.
divertissement (di vûr′tis mənt; dē ver tēs -män′) a diversion or entertainment.
doyen (doi en′; dwa yan′) the senior member of a group or profession; a leader or ultimate authority in a field.

echelon (esh′ə lon′) a level of authority, rank, or command.
éclat (ā klä′) flair, dash; brilliance; showy or elaborate display; acclaim or acclamation.
élan (ā län′, ā län′) vivacity; verve.
éminence grise (ā mē näns grēz′) a person who exercises power unofficially and surreptitiously.
enfant terrible (än fän te rē′bl) irresponsible person; unconventional or shocking person; incorrigible child.
engagé (än ga zhā′) politically committed; involved in a cause.

Borrowed Words 243

en masse (än mas′) as a group.
ennui (än wē′) boredom; a sense of weariness and discontent.
en passant (än′ pa sän′, än′) in passing; by the way.
envoy (en′voi, än′-) a diplomatic agent; an accredited messenger or representative.
esprit de corps (e sprē′ də kô′) a sense of union and of common interests and responsibilities, as developed among a group of persons associated together.

fait accompli (fe tə kôn plē′) accomplished act; done deal.
fracas (frā′kəs, frak′əs) noisy disturbance; disorderly fight.

gaffe (gaf) blunder; faux pas.
gaucherie (gō′shə rē′) awkwardness; vulgarity.
Grand Guignol (grän gē nyô′) a drama emphasizing horror or sensationalism.

habitué (hə bich′o͞o ā′) a frequent visitor to a place; regular client; devotee.
hauteur (hō tûr′, ō tûr′) snobbishness; aloofness; superior air; haughtiness; arrogance.

idée fixe (ē′dā fēks′) a fixed idea; obsession.
ingénue (an′zhə no͞o′, aN′-) a naive or innocent young woman.

joie de vivre (zhwä′də vēv′, vē′vr) a delight in being alive.

laissez-faire (les′ā fâr′) the theory that government should intervene as little as possible in economic affairs.
lèse majesty (lēz′ ma′jə stē) an attack on a ruler or established authority; an affront to dignity.

maladroit (mal′ ə droit′) lacking in adroitness; awkward.
mêlée (mā′lā, mā lāú′) a confused, general hand-to-hand fight.
mélange (mā länzh′, -länj′) mixture; medley.
métier (mā′tyā, mā tyā′) vocation or calling; forte.
milieu (mil yo͞o′, mēl-) an environment; medium.

motif (mō tēf′) a recurring theme; a repeated element of design.
mot juste (mō zhyst′) precise word; pithy phrase.
mystique (mi stēk′) an aura of mystery; a framework of beliefs lending enhanced value or meaning to a person or thing.

nom de guerre (nom′ də gâr′) an assumed name; pseudonym; stage name; alias.
nouveau riche (no͞o′vō rēsh′) a newly rich person, especially one who is ostentatious or uncultivated.

parvenu (pär′və no͞o′, -nyo͞o′) newcomer; upstart.

penchant (pen′chənt) a strong inclination, taste, or liking for something.
pied-à-terre (pē ā′də târ′) a part-time or temporary residence.
pièce de rèésistance (pyes də rā zē stäns′) showpiece; principal object or event.
poseur (pô zûr′) a person who attempts to impress others by assuming or affecting a manner, degree of elegance, etc.
précis (prā sē′, prā′sē) a short, concise summary.
protégé (prō′tə zhā′, prō′tə zhā′) a person under the patronage or care of someone influential who can further his or her career.

raconteur (rak′on tûr′, -tōōr′) a person who is skilled in relating anecdotes.
rapport (ra pôr′, rə-) a harmonious or sympathetic relationship or connection.
rapprochement (rap′rōsh mäN′) an establishment or renewal of friendly relations.
recherché (rə shâr′shā) esoteric or obscure; select or rare; mannered or affected.
rendezvous (rän′də vōō′, -dā-) an agreement between two or more people to meet at a certain time and place.
repartee (rep′ər tē′, -tā′, -är-) witty conversation; a quick reply.
riposte (ri pōst′) a quick, sharp retort; retaliation.
risqué (ri skā′) racy, indelicate, or suggestive.

saboteur (sab′ə tûr′) a person who deliberately destroys property, obstructs services, or undermines a cause.
sang-froid (sän frwä′) self-possession; composure; calmness or equanimity.
savoir-faire (sav′wär fâr′) know-how; tact; social polish.
soigné (swèän yā′) well-groomed; carefully or elegantly done.
succès d'estime (sүk se des tēm′) critical success; success achieved by merit rather than popularity.

tête-à-tête (tāt′ ə tāt′, tet′ ə tet′) intimate, private conversation.
tour de force (tōōr′də fôs′) an exceptional achievement using the full skill, ingenuity, and resources of a person, country, or group.

vis-à-vis (vē′zə vē′) face to face; opposite; in relation to.
volte-face (volt fäs′, vōltə-) reversal; turnabout; about-face.

German

English is often described as a Germanic language, but it diverged from the language that is the ancestor of Modern German and dates from about fifteen hundred years ago. Most English words that come from German are relatively recent borrowings. German borrowings are especially common in intellectual fields, including science, philosophy, and psychology.

angst (angkst) a feeling of dread, anxiety, or anguish.

doppelgänger (dop′əl gang′ər) phantom double; a ghostly counterpart of a living person; alter ego; dead ringer.

echt (ekht) real; authentic; genuine.

ersatz (er′zäts, -säts) fake; synthetic; artificial.

festschrift (fest′shrift′) a volume of scholarly articles contributed by many authors to commemorate a senior scholar or teacher.

gemütlichkeit (gə myt′likh kīt′) comfortable friendliness; cordiality; congeniality.

gestalt (gə shtält′) a form having properties that cannot be derived by the summation of its component parts.

götterdämmerung (got′ər dam′ ə rōōng′) total destruction or downfall, as in a great final battle.

kaput (kä poot′, -pōōt′) finished; ruined; broken.

kitsch (kich) something of tawdry design, appearance, or content created to appeal to people having popular or undiscriminating taste.

lebensraum (lā′bəns roum′) additional space needed to function.

leitmotif (līt′mō tēf′) a recurring theme; a motif in a dramatic work that is associated with a particular person, idea, or situation.

lumpenproletariat (lum′pən prō′li târ′ē ət) a crude and uneducated underclass comprising unskilled laborers, vagrants, and criminals.

poltergeist (pōl′tər gīst′) a ghost that makes loud knocking or rapping noises.

realpolitik (rā äl′pō′ lē tēk′) political realism; specifically, a policy based on power rather than ideals.

schadenfreude (shäd′ən froi′də) pleasure felt at another's misfortune.

Sturm und Drang (shtoo˘rm′ ōōnt dräng′) turmoil; tumult; upheaval; extreme emotionalism.

übermensch (ōō′bər mensh′) superman; an ideal superior being.

verboten (fər bōt′ən, vər-) forbidden; prohibited.

wanderlust (won′dər lust′) a strong desire to travel.

weltanschauung (vel′tän shou′ōōng) world view; a comprehensive conception of the universe and humanity's relation to it.

weltschmerz (velt′shmerts′) sorrow that one feels is one's necessary portion in life; sentimental pessimism.

wunderkind (vōōn′dər kind′, wun′-) prodigy; gifted child; a person who succeeds at an early age.

zeitgeist (tsīt'gīst', zīt'-) the spirit of the time; the general trend of thought and feeling that is characteristic of the era.

Greek

We have seen the influence of Ancient Greece on the English language in some earlier chapters, but there are a number of other terms that are so pungent and precise that they survive in our vocabulary to this day. In many cases, Greek terms embody abstract concepts that are otherwise hard to describe in English.

acedia (ə sē'dē ə) listlessness, sloth; indifference; apathy.
alpha and **omega** (al'fə; ō mä'gə, ō mē'gə) the beginning and the end; the basic or essential elements.
anathema (ə nath'əmə) detested or loathed thing or person; curse.
anomie (an'ə mē') a sense of dislocation; alienation; despair.

catharsis (kə thär'sis) a purging of emotion or release of emotional tensions.
charisma (kə riz'mə) personal magnetism; the capacity to lead or inspire others.

despot (des'pət, -pot) absolute ruler; tyrant or oppressor.
diatribe (dī' ə trīb') a bitter denunciation; abusive criticism.

enigma (i nig'mə) puzzle, riddle; a person or thing of a confusing and contradictory nature.
ephemera (i fem'ərə) short-lived or transitory things.
epiphany (i pif' ənē) revelation; sudden, intuitive insight into reality.
epitome (i pit' əmē) embodiment; a person or thing that is typical of a whole class.
ethos (ē'thos, ē'thōs) the fundamental character or spirit of a culture; distinguishing character or disposition of a group.
euphoria (yōō fôr'ēa) elation; strong feeling of happiness, confidence, or well-being.
exegesis (ek'si jē'sis) a critical explanation or interpretation, especially of a text.

halcyon (hal'sē ən) happy, joyful, or carefree; prosperous; calm, peaceful, or tranquil.
hedonist (hēd'ən ist) a person who is devoted to self-gratification as a way of life; pleasure-seeker.
hoi polloi (hoi' pə loi') the common people; the masses.
hubris (hyoo'bris, hoo'-) excessive pride or self-confidence; arrogance.

iota (ī ōt'ə) a very small quantity; jot; whit.

metamorphosis (met′ə môr′ fə sis) transformation; profound or complete change.
miasma (mī az′mə) noxious fumes; poisonous effluvia; a dangerous, foreboding, or deathlike influence or atmosphere.
myriad (mir′ē əd) of an indefinitely great number; innumerable.
omphalos (om′fə läs) navel; central point.
panacea (panə′ sē′ə) cure-all; a solution for all difficulties.
pantheon (pan′thē on′) the realm of the heroes or idols of any group; illustrious leaders.
paradigm (par′ə dīm′) an example serving as a model; pattern.
pathos (pā′thos, -thōs) pity; compassion; suffering.
pedagogue (pedə′ gog′, -gôg′) a teacher; a person who is pedantic, dogmatic, and formal.
plethora (pleth′ərə) overabundance; excess; a great number.
protagonist (prō tag′ə nist) an actor who plays the main role; the chief proponent or leader of a movement or cause.
psyche (sī′kē) the human soul, spirit, or mind.

stasis (stā′sis) equilibrium or inactivity; stagnation.
stigma (stig′mə) a stain or reproach on one's reputation; a mark or defect of a disease.

trauma (trou′mə, trô′-) wound or shock; a wrenching or distressing experience.
troglodyte (trog′lə dīt′) cave dweller or Neanderthal; brutal or degraded person; reactionary.

Italian

Many of the Italian words that survive intact in the Englich vocabulary are musical, artistic, and architectural terms that reflect the Italian emphasis on refinement and good living. In addition, many terms that appear to be French are barely disguised versions of the original Italian (*caricature, burlesque, carnival, buffoon, facade*).

alfresco (al fres′kō) out-of-doors; in the open air.

bravura (brə vyo͞or′ə, -vo͞or′) a florid, brilliant style; a display of daring.

chiaroscuro (kē är′ə skyo͞or′ō, -sko͞or′ō) the distribution of light and dark areas, as in a picture.

cognoscenti (kän′yə shen′tē, käg′nə-) those in the know; intellectuals; well-informed persons.

crescendo (krə shen′dō, -sen′dō) a steady increase in force or loudness; a climactic point or peak.

dilettante (dil′ə tänt′, dil′i tän′tā) dabbler; amateur; devotee.

diva (dē′və) an exalted female singer; any goddess-like woman.

dolce far niente (dōl′chä fär nyen′tā) sweet inactivity.

focaccia (fō kä′chēə) a round, flat Italian bread, sprinkled with oil and herbs before baking.

imbroglio (im brōl′yō) a confused state of affairs; a complicated or difficult situation; bitter misunderstanding.

impresario (im′prə sär′ ē ō′) a person who organizes public entertainment; an entrepreneur, promoter, or director.

inamorata (in am′ə rä′tə, in′amə-) a female sweetheart or lover.

incognito (in′kog nē′tō) with one's identity hidden or unknown; in disguise.

la dolce vita (lä dōl′chä vē′tä) the good life.

manifesto (man′ə fes′tō) a public declaration of intentions, opinions, or objectives, as issued by an organization.

panache (pə nash′, -näsh′) a grand or flamboyant manner; flair; verve; stylishness.

pentimento (pen′tə men′tō) the reappearance of an earlier stage, as in a painting.

prima donna (prē′mə don′ə) the principal singer in an opera company; any vain, temperamental person who expects privileged treatment.

punctilio (pungk til′ē ō′) strict or exact observance of formalities; fine point or detail of conduct or procedure.

sotto voce (sot′ō vō′chē) in a soft, low voice, so as not to be overheard.

staccato (stə kä′tō) abruptly disconnected; disjointed; herky-jerky.

tempo (tem′pō) rate of speed; rhythm or pattern.

vendetta (ven det′ə) a prolonged or bitter feud or rivalry; the pursuit of vengeance.

virtuoso (vûr′choo ō′sō) highly skilled performer; a person who has special knowledge or skill in a field; highly cultivated person.

Japanese

The first European contact with Japan was made by Portuguese sailors in the sixteenth century, but it was not until the middle of the nineteenth century that the United States forced the opening of trade with the West. Many of our more recent borrowings from the Japanese are business terms; others are artistic or religious. The growing popularity of the martial arts has given us still other new words and concepts.

aikido (ī kē′dō) a form of self-defense using wrist, joint, and elbow grips to immobilize or throw one's opponent.

bushido (boo′shē dō′) the code of honor of the samurai, stressing loyalty and obedience.

dojo (dō′jō) a school or practice hall where martial arts are taught.

futon (foo′ton) a thick, quiltlike mattress placed on the floor for sleeping and folded up for seating or storage.

geisha (gā′shə, gē′-) a young woman trained as a gracious companion for men; hostess.

haiku (hī koo′) a short, pithy verse in three lines of five, seven, and five syllables.
hara-kiri (har′i kēr′ē, har′ē-) ritual suicide by disembowelment; any self-destructive act.

judo (joo′dō) a martial art based on jujitsu that bans dangerous blows or throws, stressing the athletic or sport element.
jujitsu (joo jit′soo) a method of self-defense that uses the strength and weight of one's opponent to disable him or her.

kabuki (kə boo′kē) a popular entertainment characterized by stylized acting, elaborate costumes, and exaggerated makeup.
kamikaze (kä′mi kä′zē) person on a suicide mission; a wild or reckless act.
karate (kə rä′tē) self-defense using fast, hard blows with the hands, elbows, knees, or feet.
karaoke (kar′ē ō′kē) an act of singing along to a music video, especially one that has had the original vocals electronically eliminated.
keiretsu (kā ret′soo) a loose coalition of business groups.
koan (kō′än) a nonsensical proposition or paradoxical question presented to a student of Zen as an object of meditation; unsolvable riddle.

ninja (nin′jə) a mercenary trained in martial arts and stealth.

noh (nō) classical lyric drama characterized by chants, the wearing of wooden masks, and highly stylized movements drawn from religious rites.

origami (ô′i gä′mē) the art of folding paper into representational forms.

roshi (rō′shē) a Zen master; a teacher in a monastery.

samurai (sam′ooˇ rī′) a noble warrior; warrior class.

satori (sə tôr′ē) enlightenment; ultimate insight into the nature of reality.

Shinto (shin′tō) the traditional Japanese system of nature and ancestor worship.

shogun (shō′gən, -gun) a military commander; war lord.

shoji (shō′jē) a room divider or sliding screen made of translucent paper.

sumo (soo′mō) a form of wrestling aimed at forcing one's opponent out of the ring or causing him to touch the ground with any body part other than the soles of the feet.

tanka (täng′kə) traditional verse form having five-line stanzas with alternate lines of five and seven syllables.

tatami (tä tä′mē) a woven straw mat used as a floor covering.

tsunami (tsoo nä′mē) a huge sea wave produced by an undersea earthquake or volcanic eruption.

tycoon (tī koon′) a businessperson of great wealth or power; magnate.

yakuza (yä′koo zä′) a member of a crime syndicate; racketeer; gangster.

zaibatsu (zī bät′ soo) a great industrial or financial conglomerate.

Zen (zen) a sect of Buddhism that emphasizes enlightenment through meditation.

Latin

The Latin influence on the English language comes primarily through the Romance languages, particularly French and to a lesser degree Italian, as well as through the borrowings associated with the renewed interest in classical sources during the Renaissance. Note how many Latin legal terms have been carried over into English.

ad hoc (ad hok′, hōk′) for a specific or particular purpose.
antebellum (an′tē bel′əm) prewar.

Borrowed Words   251

caveat (kav′ē ät′) a warning or caution; admonition.
decorum (di kô′əm) dignity; proper behavior, manners, or appearance.
de facto (dē fak′tō, dā) in fact; in reality; actually existing.
de profundis (dā prō foon′dis) out of the depths of sorrow or despair.
dementia (di men′shēa) madness; insanity; severely impaired mental function.
desideratum (di sid′ə rā′təm, -rä′-) something wanted or needed.
dolor (dō′lər) sorrow; grief.

ex cathedra (eks′ kə thē′drə) from the seat of authority; by virtue of one's office.
exemplar (ig zem′plər, -plär) model or pattern; example or instance; original or archetype.
exigent (ek′si jənt) urgent; pressing.
ex nihilo (eks nī′hi lō′, nē′-) out of nothing.
ex post facto (eks′ pōst′ fak′tō) after the fact; subsequently; retroactively.

factotum (fak tō′təm) assistant or aide; deputy.

imprimatur (im′pri mä′toor) sanction; approval.
in toto (in tō′tō) in all; completely, entirely; wholly.

literati (lit′ ə rä′tē) intellectuals or scholars; highly educated persons.

mea culpa (mā′ə kul′pə) my fault; an admission of guilt.
modus operandi (mō′dəs op′ə ran′dē, -dī) way of operating; method of working.

non compos mentis (non′ kom′pəs men′tis) of unsound mind; mentally incompetent.
nonsequitur (non sek′wi tər) something that does not follow from the preceding series; illogical conclusion.

odium (ō′dē əm) intense hatred or dislike; reproach or discredit.

pro forma (prō fôr′mə) done perfunctorily; done as a formality.
prolix (prō liks′, prō′liks) wordy; talkative; tediously long.

quidnunc (kwid′nungk′) busybody; a person eager to know the latest gossip.
quid pro quo (kwid′ prō kwō′) equal exchange; substitute; something given or taken in return for something else.

rara avis (râr′ə ā′vis) a rare person or thing; anything unusual; rarity.

sanctum sanctorum (sangk′təm sangk tôr′əm) sacred place; the holiest of places.
sine qua non (sin′ā kwä nōn′) an indispensable condition; prerequisite.
status quo (stā′təs kwō, stat′əs) conditions as they are now; the existing state.
sub rosa (sub rō′zə) confidentially; secretly; privately; undercover.

sui generis (soo′ē jen′ər is) of its own kind; unique; one of a kind; unparalleled.

terra incognita (ter′ə in kog′ni tə) unknown territory; an unexplored region; uncharted ground.

viva voce (vī′və vō′sē) aloud, orally; by word of mouth.
vox populi (voks′ pop′y lī′) popular opinion; the voice of the people.

Spanish

Spanish has had a less pervasive influence on the English language than some other European sources, but American English has borrowed a substantial number of useful words from the Spanish culture of the Southwest. For example, a number of unique American terms are actually mispronunciations of the original Spanish words: *vamoose, mustang, calaboose, lariat, buckaroo,* and *hoosegow* are all coinages from the West and Southwest that evoke the bygone world of the American cowboy.

aficionado (ə fish′yə nä′dō) fan; enthusiast; ardent devotee.

bodega (bō dä′gə) small grocery store; wineshop.
bonanza (bə nan′zə) stroke of luck; sudden source of wealth; spectacular windfall.
bravado (brə vä′dō) swaggering display of courage.

campesino (kam′pə sē′nō) a farmer or peasant.
caudillo (kou dē′lyō, -dē′yō) a head of state, especially a military dictator.
compañero (kom′pən yâr′ō) companion; partner; bosom buddy.

desperado (des′pə rä′dō) a bold, reckless criminal; outlaw.
duenna (doo en′ə, dyoo-) chaperone; an older woman who serves as an escort for young ladies.

embarcadero (em bär′kə dâr′ō) a pier, wharf, or jetty.
embargo (em bär′gō) a government order restricting commerce; any restraint or prohibition.

fiesta (fē es′tə) a festival or feast; any joyous or merry celebration.

garrote (gə rät′, -rät′) to strangle or throttle.
guerrilla (gə ril′ə) a member of a small, independent band of soldiers that harass the enemy by surprise raids, sabotage, etc.

incommunicado (in′kə myōō′ni kä′dō) in solitary confinement; without any means of communicating with others.

junta (hoon′tə, jun′tə) a small group ruling a country, especially after a revolutionary seizure of power.

lagniappe (lan yap′, lan′yap) bonus; gratuity or tip.

machismo (mä chēz′mō) an exaggerated sense of masculinity; boastful or swaggering virility.

peccadillo (pek′ə dil′ō) a minor offense; venial sin.
peon (pē′ən, pē′on) a farm worker or unskilled laborer; a person of low social status who does menial work; drudge.
presidio (pri sid′ē ō′) fort or garrison; military post.

ramada (rə mä′də) an open shelter with a thatched roof.

siesta (sē es′tə) a midafternoon rest; nap.

vigilante (vij′ə lan′tē) an unauthorized volunteer who takes the law into his or her own hands; a self-appointed avenger of injustice.

Yiddish

Yiddish, the language spoken by the Jews of Eastern Europe, derives from the German of the Middle Ages, with the addition of many Hebrew and Aramaic words. But Yiddish has absorbed many words and expressions from the native cultures of the countries where the Jews have settled. Since Hebrew is the traditional means of expression of learned Jews, Yiddish tends to be a folksy, colorful language that expresses the day-to-day concerns of the common people.

chutzpah (khoo͝t′spə, ho͝ot′-) gall; nerve; brashness.

golem (gō′ləm) robot; lifelike creature.
gonif (gon′əf) a thief, swindler, crook, or rascal.

haimish (hā′mish) homey; cozy.

klutz (kluts) clumsy or awkward person.
kvell (kvel) be delighted; take pleasure.
kvetch (kvech) complain, whine, nag; crotchety person.

macher (mä′khər) wheeler-dealer; big shot.
maven (mā′vən) expert; connoisseur.
megillah (mə gil′ə) tediously long story; rigmarole; complicated matter.
mensch (mensh) admirable person; decent human being.
meshuga (m shoog′ə) crazy; mad; nutty.

nebbish (neb′ish) nobody; loser; hapless person.
nosh (nosh) snack; nibble.
nudge (nooj) nag; annoy or pester; a pest or annoying person.

8 Specialized Vocabularies

Even after you have acquired a more powerful general vocabulary, you may still encounter terms that are unfamiliar to you because they are part of the special vocabulary of a discipline you have not studied. Many of these fields are central to modern life. Computer literacy, for example, is a necessity for people in virtually all trades and professions, and everyone is bound to have some dealings with the legal profession at some time.

Here is a brief selection of current and basic terminology drawn from 11 important spheres of American life: business, computers and technology, entertainment, fashion, food, law, politics, publishing, religion, science, and sports. These terms provide an introduction and orientation to the current status of each of these professions.

Business

aggregate supply/demand the total amount of goods and services produced in an economy during a specified period of time.
agreement a document setting forth an arrangement accepted by all parties.
AMEX American Stock Exchange: the second-largest stock exchange in the United States, located in New York City.
amortization the scheduled periodic repayment of a debt or loan at a rate sufficient to meet current interest and to extinguish the debt at the point of maturity; interest is usually charged only on the unpaid balance of the loan, though generally all payments are equal.
APR annual percentage rate: the annual rate of interest, or the total interest to be paid in a year divided by the balance due.

arbitrage the simultaneous purchase and sale of the same security or of equivalent securities for the purpose of profiting from differences in market prices (as between New York and Paris).

bean counter (slang) a person who makes judgments based primarily on numerical calculations.
bear a person who believes that stock prices will decline.
bear market a stock market characterized by a general decline in prices.
benchmark a variable (e.g., brand awareness) that is measured before and after an advertising campaign to help determine the campaign's effectiveness in influencing the target audience to buy the product.
black market the place where the illicit buying and selling of goods in violation of legal price controls occurs.
bull a person who believes that stock prices will rise.
bull market a stock market characterized by generally rising prices.

capital long-term assets (including office space, manufacturing equipment, etc.) in which a corporation has invested for the production of goods or services.
capital gains income from the sale of assets, such as bonds or real estate.
casual day a day (usually Friday) on which office workers are permitted to dress in sportswear. Also **dress-down day.**
CD certificate of deposit: a deposit account in a bank or savings-and-loan association, usually for a minimum of $1,000 and with a maturity of 30 days to several years, from which money usually cannot be withdrawn without loss of interest or other penalty and that earns interest at a rate established by law for accounts of less than $100,000 or at a rate that may be negotiable for larger accounts.
comp time (slang) compensatory time off from work, granted to an employee in lieu of overtime pay.
COBRA Consolidated Omnibus Budget Reconciliation Act: a federal law guaranteeing the right to continue participation in an employee health plan after coverage has been terminated due to layoff, divorce, etc.
consumer price index also called cost-of-living index: an index issued periodically by the Bureau of Labor Statistics that expresses the cost of goods and services purchased by typical wage earners as a percentage of the cost of the same goods and services in some base period.
contrarian a person who rejects the majority opinion, especially an investor who buys when others are selling and vice versa.

dead-cat bounce (slang) a temporary recovery in stock prices after a steep decline, often resulting from the purchase of securities that have been sold short.
dividend a distribution of a corporation's earnings to its shareholders.
Dow Jones Industrial Average an index of the relative price of securities based on the average daily prices of common stocks issued by selected

companies in the fields of industry and transportation and by selected public utilities.

downsize to reduce a labor force in size or number; to cut back the number of employees or lay off.

drive time the rush hour, when commuters listen to car radios: perceived as a time for generating advertising revenue.

emerging market a market in a less-developed country whose economy is just beginning to grow.

equity an interest in the net assets of a corporation.

escrow a bond, deed, sum of money, or article of property left in the care of a third party to be held until specified conditions are fulfilled.

EEC European Economic Community: an economic alliance established in 1958 by Belgium, France, Italy, Luxembourg, the Netherlands, and West Germany (since then it has been joined by Denmark, Greece, Ireland, Portugal, and Spain) to adopt common import duties and expedite trade among member nations. Current (2003) EU member nations are Austria, Belgium, Denmark, Finland, France, Germany, Greece, Ireland, Italy, Luxembourg, the Netherlands, Portugal, Spain, Sweden, and the United Kingdom.

FDIC Federal Deposit Insurance Corporation: a federal agency that insures deposits up to a maximum amount in all banks that belong to the Federal Reserve.

flex dollars money given by an employer to an employee that the employee can apply to various benefits.

futures contract agreements that promise the buying and selling of commodities or securities for delivery at a later date, often a year or more in the future.

golden parachute an employment agreement guaranteeing an executive substantial compensation in the event of dismissal.

gross the total of all earnings without deductions.

hedge fund an investment company that uses high-risk speculative methods to obtain large profits.

hedging to protect oneself against a possible loss (in an investment, in financial position, etc.) by diversifying one's investments, buying or selling commodity futures, and so forth.

impact to have an influence or effect (on). The word is used in many business and financial contexts: to impact sales; to impact profits; to impact the bottom line.

incentivize to give incentives to provide a reward (often monetary) to encourage a particular action, e.g., the government can incentivize the private sector to create jobs by providing companies with certain tax benefits.

index a quantity whose variation from one day to the next or over a period of time measures the change in relative value of prices or some other phenomenon.

IPO initial public offering: a company's first stock offering to the public.

junk bond slang term for a high-risk bond rated BB or lower. It offers a high return but is considered to have dubious backing; sometimes offered to shareholders in lieu of cash in takeover bids.

large cap referring to a stock with a market capitalization of $1 billion or more.

liquid an asset that can be quickly converted to cash (e.g., a marketable security, current accounts receivable).

margin the amount of an investor's equity in an investment made in part with money borrowed from a broker.

money market fund a mutual fund that invests in short-term corporate and government securities, including bonds, stocks, Treasury bills, and commercial paper, permitting small investors access to high-interest securities that would otherwise require an investment of more than $10,000.

mutual fund an investment company that invests its pooled funds in a diversified list of securities.

net a value reduced by all applicable deductions (i.e., net income is total or gross income reduced by the expenses incurred in the generation or earning of that income).

NAV net-asset value: the price of a share in a mutual fund, equal to the total value of the fund's securities divided by the number of shares outstanding.

option the right to buy or sell a security at a specified price within a specified period of time.

outsourcing the purchase of goods or contracting of services to an outside company.

OTC over-the-counter market: stock issued by a company that has insufficient earnings or shares outstanding to be listed by a stock exchange, or by a bank or insurance company, and which is traded between brokers acting either as principals or as agents for customers.

per capita the output by or for each person; the value of a nation's output divided by its population: a commonly used measure of a country's standard of living.

pit the physical area of a commodities market where traders conduct their business.

portfolio a collection of securities and other investments (e.g., real estate, precious metals, collectibles) held by or managed for a company or individual.

P/E price/earnings ratio: the price of a share of stock divided by earnings per share for a 12-month period (i.e., a stock selling for $10 a share and earning $1 per share has a price/earnings ratio of 10).

Specialized Vocabularies

price point the price for which something is sold on the retail market, emphasizing competitive prices for the same item.
proactive serving to prepare for, intervene in, or control an expected occurrence or situation. The word has been criticized for overuse and stigmatized as jargon.
proxy a written authorization for one person to act for another, as at a meeting of stockholders.

rally a sudden reversal of a downward trend in the prices of all stocks or in the price of a particular stock.
REIT real estate investment trust: a mutual fund that invests in real estate and must distribute at least 90 percent of its income as dividends.
risk the possibility or probability of an unfavorable occurrence.
road warrior (slang) a person who travels extensively on business.

securities stocks and bonds.
short selling borrowing shares from a broker and selling them, then buying back the same shares at a lower price.
small-cap referring to a stock with a market capitalization of less than $500 million and considered to have more growth potential.
SKU stockkeeping unit: a retailer-defined coding system used to distinguish individual items within a retailer's accounting and warehousing systems.
strike price the price at which an employee's stock option may be exercised, usually the market price at the time the option was granted.
superstore a very large store that stocks a great variety of merchandise.
synergy the action or interaction of two separate enterprises that when combined produce superior results, as in the case of a corporate merger.

tick a symbolic notation (e.g., asterisk, checkmark, number) used by an auditor to indicate a footnote that provides information regarding the amount thus indicated.

underwriter an investment firm that acquires new issues of stocks and bonds from a corporation and sells them to individual investors, thus assuming all the risks of ownership unless the arrangement is on a best-effort basis, in which case the underwriter acts merely as a broker.
UGMA Uniform Gifts to Minors Act: a law that provides a means to transfer securities or money to a minor without establishing a formal trust, the assets being managed by a custodian and the monies transferred being taxed at a lower rate.

Computers and Technology

alpha test an early test of new or updated computer software conducted by the developers of the program prior to beta testing by potential users.

Specialized Vocabularies

ASCII American Standard Code for Information Interchange: a standardized code in which characters are represented for computer storage and transmission by the numbers 0 through 127. See also **Unicode.**

applet a small application program that can be called up for use while working in another application. A typical example would be an on-screen calculator that you can use while working in a word processor.

application a specific kind of task, such as database management or word processing, that can be done using a particular program that is often referred to as an *application* or *application* program.

backup a copy or duplicate version, especially of a data file or program, retained for use in the event that the original becomes unusable or unavailable.

bay an open compartment in the console housing a computer's CPU in which a disk drive, tape drive, etc., may be installed. See also **drive bay.**

beta test a test of new or updated computer software or hardware conducted at select user sites just prior to release of the product. Experienced beta testers try to push a new program to its limits, to see what kinds of behavior will make it break. This helps the programmers to eliminate bugs.

boot to start (a computer) by loading the operating system.

browser an application program that allows the user to examine encoded documents in a form suitable for display, especially such a program for use on the World Wide Web.

bug a defect, error, or imperfection, as in computer software.

byte a group of adjacent bits, usually eight, processed by a computer as a unit.

cache (pronounced like *cash*, not *catch*) a piece of computer hardware or a section of RAM dedicated to selectively storing and speeding access to frequently used program commands or data.

CPU central processing unit: the key component of a computer. It houses the essential electronic circuitry that allows the computer to interpret and execute program instructions.

chat to engage in dialogue by exchanging electronic messages, usually in real time.

click to depress and release a mouse button rapidly, as to select an icon. Some functions in a program require a single click, some a double click.

CD-ROM a compact disc on which a large amount of digitized data can be stored.

compression reduction of the size of computer data by efficient storage. Compressed data can be stored in fewer bits than uncompressed data, and therefore takes up less space. This is useful not only for saving space on a hard disk, for example, but also for communicating data through a modem more rapidly.

cookie a message containing information about a user, sent by a Web server to a browser and sent back to the server each time the browser requests a Web page.

copy protection a method of preventing users of a computer program from making unauthorized copies, usually through hidden instructions contained in the program code.

crash (of a computer) to suffer a major failure because of a malfunction of hardware or software. A crash is usually not the user's fault.

cursor a movable, sometimes blinking symbol used to indicate where data (as text, commands, etc.) may be input on a computer screen.

cyber- a combining form representing *computer:* cybertalk; cyberart.

cyberspace the realm of electronic communication, as exemplified by the Internet.

database a collection of ordered, related data in electronic form that can be accessed and manipulated by specialized computer software. Commonly, database information is organized by records, which are in turn divided into fields.

desktop publishing the design and production of publications by means of specialized software enabling a personal computer to generate typeset-quality text and graphics. The kinds of publications that can be produced by means of desktop publishing now range from something as small as a business card to large books.

digital of or using data in the form of numerical digits and therefore readable by a computer.

DVD digital versatile disk: an optical disc that can store a very large amount of digital data, as text or images.

documentation instructional materials for computer software or hardware. Some materials still come in print, in books, or in brochures, but increasingly, documentation is available primarily on line, as through a program's Help files.

dot-com a company doing business mostly or solely on the Internet.

dot pitch a measure of the distance between each pixel on a computer screen. A lower number indicates a sharper image.

download to transfer (software or data) from a computer or network to a smaller computer or a peripheral device.

drive bay a compartment in the console that houses a computer's CPU in which a storage device, like a disk drive or tape drive, may be installed. Internal bays hold mass storage devices, like hard disks, while external or open bays house devices that give the user access to removable disks, tape, compact discs, etc.

export to save (documents, data, etc.) in a format usable by another application program.

fax modem a modem that can fax electronic data, as documents or pictures, directly from a computer. Many fax modems can also receive faxes in electronic form, which can then be printed out.

field a unit of information, as a person's name, that combines with related fields, as an official title, an address, or a company name, to form one complete record in a computerized database.

file a collection of related computer data or program records stored by name, as on a disk.

FTP File Transfer Protocol: a software protocol for exchanging information between computers over a network. Files are commonly downloaded from the Internet using FTP.

flame (slang) (esp. on a computer network) 1. an act or instance of angry criticism or disparagement. 2. to behave in an offensive manner; rant. 3. to insult or criticize angrily.

floppy disk a thin, portable, flexible plastic disk coated with magnetic material, for storing computer data and programs. Currently, the 3½-inch disk, housed in a square rigid envelope, is the common size used with personal computers.

folder a place on a disk for holding multiple files. Using folders, information can be organized in a hierarchical structure, with folders contained within other folders. The designation folder is used in environments with a graphical user interface, or **GUI**. The equivalent term in operating systems like DOS and Unix, known as command-line systems, and in early versions of Windows, was *directory*.

font a set of characters that have a given shape or design. The characters in a scalable font can be enlarged or reduced. A given font is a combination of the typeface, size, pitch, weight, and spacing.

freeware computer software distributed without charge. Compare **shareware**.

FAQ frequently asked questions: a document or Help file, in a question-and-answer format, that introduces newcomers to a technical topic, as in a **newsgroup**.

gigabyte a measure of data-storage capacity equal to a little over 1 billion (109) bytes, or 1,024 megabytes. Hard disk drives with a capacity of several gigabytes are no longer uncommon.

GUI graphical user interface: a software interface designed to standardize and simplify the use of computer programs, as by using a mouse to manipulate text and images on a display screen featuring icons, windows, and menus.

hacker a computer enthusiast who is especially proficient and who may or may not attempt to gain unauthorized access to computer systems.

hard copy computer output printed on paper; printout.

hard disk a rigid disk coated with magnetic material. Hard disks are used for storing programs and relatively large amounts of data. Such storage is permanent, in that a disk's contents remain on the disk when the computer is shut off and can be accessed again when the computer is turned on.

hardware all the physical devices included in a computer system, including the CPU, keyboard, monitor, internal and external disk drives, and separate peripherals like a printer or scanner.

HDTV high-definition television: a television system having a high number of scanning lines per frame, producing a sharper image and greater picture detail.

hypertext data electronic text, graphics, or sound, linked to one another in paths determined by the creator of the material. hypertext is usually stored with the links overtly marked, so a computer user can move nonsequentially through a link from one object or document to another.

HTML Hypertext Markup Language: a set of standards, a variety of SGML, used to tag the elements of a hypertext document; the standard for documents on the World Wide Web.

icon a small graphic image on a computer screen representing a disk drive, a file, or a software command, as a picture of a wastebasket to which a file one wishes to delete can be dragged with a mouse, or a picture of a printer that can be selected and clicked on to print a file.

inkjet printer a computer printer that prints text or graphics by spraying jets of ink onto paper to form a high-quality image approaching that of a laser printer.

install to put in place or connect for service or use; to install software on a computer; to install a scanner in one's computer system.

interface computer hardware or software designed to communicate information between hardware devices, between software programs, between devices and programs, or between a computer and a user.

Internet a large computer network linking smaller computer networks worldwide.

laptop a portable personal computer that is small, light, and thin enough to rest on the lap while in use. The screen is usually on the inside of the hinged top cover, becoming visible when one opens the computer. Most laptops can be operated either through an electrical connection or with batteries.

laser printer a high-speed, high-resolution computer printer that uses a laser to form dot-matrix patterns and an electrostatic process to print one page at a time.

macro a single instruction, for use in a computer program, that represents a sequence of instructions or keystrokes.

megabyte a measure of data-storage capacity equal to approximately 1 million bytes.

memory the capacity of a computer to store information, especially internally in RAM, while electrical power is on. Do not confuse memory with storage.

menu a list, displayed on a computer screen, from which one can choose options or commands.

modem an electronic device that allows the transmission of data to or from a computer via telephone or other communication lines.

monitor a component part of a computer system that includes a display screen for viewing computer data.

multimedia the combined use of several media, such as sound, text, graphics, animation, and video, in computer applications. Multimedia is featured, for example, in games and in reference works on CD-ROMs.

newsgroup a discussion group maintained on a computer network, usually focused on a specific topic.
notebook a small, lightweight laptop computer.

OCR optical character recognition: the reading of printed or typed text by electronic means, as by using a scanner and OCR software. In this process, the text is converted to digital data, which can then be manipulated and edited on the computer by using an application program, such as a word processor, spreadsheet, or database.

peripheral an external hardware device connected to a computer's CPU. Examples are printers, keyboards, and scanners.
pixel the smallest element of an image that can be individually processed in a video display system.
printout computer output produced by a printer; hard copy.

RAM random access memory: volatile computer memory that can store information while the electrical power is on. The information disappears when the computer is shut off. The amount of RAM a computer has is determined by the number and capacity of the RAM chips in the computer.
record a group of related fields treated as a unit in a database.
resolution the degree of sharpness of a computer-generated image, as on a display screen or printout. Resolution is measured by the number of pixels across and down on a screen and by the number of dots per linear inch on hard copy.

shareware computer software distributed without initial charge but for which the user is encouraged to pay a nominal registration fee after trying the program. Such fees cover support for continued use and often entitle the user to inexpensive updates.
software programs for directing the operation of a computer or for processing electronic data. Software is, roughly, divided into utility programs and application programs.
spreadsheet a large electronic ledger sheet that can be used for financial planning. Electronic spreadsheets provide calculations that enable the user to change estimated figures and see immediately what effect that change will have on the rest of the calculations in the spreadsheet.
SGML Standard Generalized Markup Language: a set of standards enabling a user to create an appropriate scheme for tagging the elements of an electronic document.
storage the capacity of a device, such as a hard disk or a CD-ROM, to hold programs or data permanently. In the case of hard disks, a user can remove such programs or data deliberately. Do not confuse storage with memory.

surge protector a device to protect computer circuitry from electrical spikes and surges by diverting the excess voltage through an alternate pathway.

typeface a design for a set of characters, especially numbers and letters, devised to provide the group of symbols with the unified look of a particular font. Popular typefaces often found on computer systems include Courier, Times Roman, and Helvetica, but the number of available typefaces has reached the thousands.

Unicode a standard for coding alphanumeric characters using sixteen bits for each character. Unlike ASCII, which uses eight-bit characters, Unicode can represent 65,000 unique characters. This allows a user of software that is Unicode-compatible to access the characters of most European and Asian languages.

URL Uniform Resource Locator: a protocol for specifying addresses on the Internet.

utility program a system program used to simplify standard computer operations, such as sorting, copying, or deleting files.

virtual temporarily simulated by software. You can have virtual memory on a hard disk or virtual storage in RAM. Virtual reality simulates a real-world environment.

Web site a connected group of pages on the World Wide Web regarded as a single entity, usually maintained by one person or organization, and devoted to one single topic or several closely related topics.

WYSIWYG What You See Is What You Get: of, pertaining to, or being a screen display that shows text as it will appear when printed, as by using display-screen versions of the printer's typefaces.

word processing the production and storage of documents using computers, electronic printers, and text-editing software.

World Wide Web a system of extensively linked hypertext documents; a branch of the Internet.

Entertainment

cliff-hanger a melodramatic adventure serial in which each installment ends in suspense.

demographic the statistical data of a human population, as those showing age, income, etc.

docudrama a fictionalized television drama depicting actual events.

gig a single professional engagement, as of jazz or rock.

marquee a projecting structure over the entrance of a theater that lists the event (movie, play, etc.) taking place.

miniseries a television film broadcast in consecutive parts over a span of days or weeks.

pilot a television program serving to introduce a possible new series.
premiere the first showing of a movie or play.
prime-time the hours, generally between 7 and 11 P.M., considered to have the largest television audience.
prequel a sequel to a film, play, etc., that prefigures the original.

ratings a percentage indicating the number of listeners to or viewers of a radio or television broadcast.

sitcom situation comedy.

Fashion

asymmetrical-cut referring to necklines or hemlines that are not symmetrical.
atelier a workshop or studio of a high-fashion designer.

backpack a pack or knapsack carried on one's back to keep the hands free; first popularized by campers and students, later made in leather and adopted by fashionable women in lieu of a handbag.
ballerina flats low-heeled women's shoes modeled on the soft exercise slippers worn by dancers.
bandage dress a dress of spandex that totally conforms to the wearer's body; originated by Hervé Léger.
bell-bottoms trousers with wide, flaring legs, modeled on sailor's pants.
bias-cut referring to fabric cut on the bias to drape gracefully on the body.
blouson a full-cut shirt or jacket tied at the waist for a balloon effect.
boat shoes rubber-soled moccasins worn to provide a firm grip on a boat's deck.
bodysuit a short, one-piece garment for women with a snap closure at the crotch, designed to eliminate bunching at the waist and create a smooth line under a skirt or pants; adapted from a dancer's leotard.
bomber jacket a short jacket with a fitted or elasticized waist, often made of leather and lined with fleece; originally worn by pilots.
bustier a women's tight-fitting, sleeveless, strapless top worn as a blouse and usually exposing décolletage; modeled on the corset.
button-down (as a collar) having buttonholes at the ends with which it can be buttoned to the front of the garment.

Specialized Vocabularies 267

caftan a full, long robe with loose sleeves, worn for lounging; based on similar Middle Eastern garments.
camisole a women's waist-length top with skinny shoulder straps, usually worn under a sheer bodice.
cargo pants loose-cut trousers with a number of deep pockets on the legs to accommodate extra baggage; originally a military style.
cat suit a one-piece garment for women with long sleeves and leggings, often made of polyester to cling tightly to the wearer.
Chanel bag a women's handbag of quilted leather suspended from the shoulder on a gold chain.
Chanel suit a women's suit, usually with a skirt and a cropped jacket having a round neck, several buttons, and often a braid trim.
chesterfield a single- or double-breasted overcoat with a velvet collar, often made of herringbone wool.
cornrows narrow braids of hair plaited tightly against the scalp.
corset a close-fitting, stiffened undergarment worn to shape and support the torso.
couturier a designer of fashionable, custom-made clothes for women.
cowboy boots chunky-heeled boots with a pointed toe and highly decorative stitching and embossing.
cowl-neck sweater a sweater with a neckline made of softly draped fabric.
crop top a casual pullover sport shirt cut short to expose the midriff.
cross-trainers athletic shoes designed to be used for more than one sport.

dreadlocks a hairstyle of many long, ropelike braids.
driving shoes soft, semiflexible leather or suede loafers with a rubber sole designed to grip the pedals of a car.
duffel coat a hooded overcoat of sturdy wool, usually fastened with toggle buttons.

embroidery the art of ornamental needlework.
epaulet an ornamental shoulder piece, especially on a uniform.
espadrilles flat shoes with a cloth upper, a rope sole, and sometimes lacing around the ankles.

fashionista an influential person in the fashion world; a devotee of fashion.
fashion police a jocular imaginary force invoked as criticism of a person who is badly or unstylishly dressed.
fashion victim a person whose attempts to follow the dictates of fashion have backfired ludicrously; one whose obsession with fashion is excessive.
faux fur artificial fleece dyed and styled to resemble animal fur.
fedora a soft felt hat with a curved brim.
fisherman's sweater an elaborately designed, solid-color, hand-knit and cable-stitched sweater of heavy wool; originally made by the wives of sailors in the Aran Islands of Ireland.
French cuffs generous fold-over shirt cuffs that require cufflinks or studs.

fun fur a fur jacket or coat dyed and cut in an outré style to be worn as sportswear.

gangsta a style derived from the inner-city ghetto emphasizing baggy clothing, designer sportswear, cutting-edge athletic shoes, and sometimes gold jewelry. Also *hip-hop.*

Gore-Tex a breathable, water-repellent fabric laminate originally used for outdoor sportswear, often produced in bright colors.

gothic a style marked by bizarre or outré makeup (for men as well as women), dress, and hairstyle in a Romantic vein reminiscent of classic horror films. Also *Goth.*

grunge a style marked by dirty, unkempt, often torn, secondhand clothing.

hair extensions false hair woven into a person's natural hair to give the illusion of greater length and fullness.

haute couture high fashion; the most fashionable, exclusive, and expensive designer clothing, made to measure of luxurious fabrics after extensive fittings.

high tops sneakers with fabric extending to the ankles.

jellies transparent polyurethane shoes with a cross-strap and very low heels.

Kelly bag a squarish or slightly trapezoidal women's handbag first made by Hermès for Princess Grace of Monaco.

kente a colorful striped fabric of Ghanaian origin often worn as a symbol of African-American pride.

khakis loose-fitting trousers made of a stout beige fabric, worn as casual sportswear.

leggings tight-fitting elasticized pants for women; modeled on dancer's tights.

little black dress a basic, unadorned black dress popularized by Coco Chanel in the early twentieth century for its flexibility and utility as a wardrobe mainstay, especially as a cocktail dress.

maxi coat a full-length overcoat extending to the ankles.

microfiber an extremely fine polyester fiber used in clothing.

motorcycle jacket a short leather jacket resembling a bomber jacket but usually embellished with zippers, buckles, studs, etc.

palazzo pants women's wide-legged trousers cut to resemble a long skirt.

pantsuit a softened version for women of the classic menswear suit, having a jacket with lapels and tailored trousers.

pareo a length of fabric tied at the side to drape over the hips, usually worn over a matching bathing suit. Also *sarong.*

parka a hooded, straight-cut jacket made of materials that provide warmth against very cold temperatures; often a down- or polyester-filled nylon shell, sometimes quilted for extra warmth.

Specialized Vocabularies 269

pea jacket a heavy, double-breasted, short wool jacket; originally worn by seamen. Also *pea coat.*
pedal pushers casual slacks reaching to mid-calf. Also *capri pants; clam diggers.*
platforms shoes with a thick insert of leather, cork, plastic, or other sturdy material between the upper and the sole.
polo coat a tailored overcoat of camel hair or a similar fabric, single- or double-breasted and often belted or half-belted.
power suit a tailored women's suit with jacket and skirt designed in imitation of a man's business suit and usually including shoulder pads; popular among businesswomen of the 1980s.

racer back a tank top with the back cut out to expose the shoulder blades; modeled on similar designs in bathing suits designed to cut friction in speed-swimming contests.
ready-to-wear ready-made clothing. Also *prêt-à-porter; off-the-peg; off-the-rack.*
Rugby shirt a full-cut, usually broad-striped cotton pullover with a contrasting white turnover collar and three-button placket; modeled on shirts worn by English rugby or soccer players.

sash a long band worn over one shoulder or around the waist.
sheath a close-fitting, simple, unbelted dress with a straight drape, usually sleeveless with a plain neckline.
shell a short, sleeveless, usually round-necked blouse for women, often worn under a jacket.
ski pants snug-fitting pants of a stretch fabric, usually having straps for the feet to keep the pants from bunching at the boot line.
skort a women's garment for the lower body that resembles a skirt but has separate openings for the legs.
slides backless women's shoes of varying heights. Also *mules.*
slingbacks open-backed women's shoes with a strap to secure the heel.
slip dress a loose-fitting unadorned dress with skinny straps, modeled on women's undergarments of the earlier twentieth century.
spandex a polyurethane fabric with elastic properties.
stilettos very high, narrow heels that taper to a point, used on women's shoes. Also *spike heels.*
supermodel a prominent fashion model who commands the highest fees and is sometimes recognized by first name only.
sweater set a short-sleeved, round-necked sweater for women accompanied by a matching cardigan. Also *twin set.*

tank top a low-cut, sleeveless pullover with shoulder straps, often made of a lightweight knit.
thigh-cut referring to bathing suits cut high on the thigh to expose the hip.
thigh-highs stockings that come to mid-thigh, often worn under a short skirt so the stocking tops are visible.
thong a skimpy garment for the lower body that exposes the buttocks, usu-

ally having a strip of fabric passing between the legs and attached to a waistband.

tunic a woman's straight upper garment, usually extending to the hips.

vintage referring to clothing that evokes the style of an earlier era in fashion and is often purchased at resale shops.

weave false hair woven into the natural hair.

wedgies women's shoes with a heel formed by a roughly triangular or wedge-like piece that extends from the front or middle to the back of the sole.

wrap dress a patterned polyester or cotton knit dress that ties on the side to drape naturally over the wearer's body; originated by Diane von Furstenberg in the 1970s and revived in the 1990s.

Food

baste to pour liquid over cooking meat at intervals.
bisque a thick cream soup, especially of pureed shellfish or vegetables.
bouquet garni a mix of herbs, often tied up in a piece of cheesecloth before being added to a pot containing a dish (often stew) to be cooked.
braise to cook in fat and then simmer in a small amount of liquid.

chutney a sweet-and-sour relish of Indian origin.
compote fruit stewed in a syrup.
consommé a clear soup made from rich stock.
crudites raw vegetables cut up and served with a dip.

dice to cut into small cubes.

fold to blend an ingredient into a mixture by turning one part over another.

julienne (of vegetables) cut into thin strips.

macerate to soften or separate into parts by steeping in a liquid.
marinate to steep (food) in a marinade.
mince to cut or chop into small pieces.

poach to cook (eggs, fish, etc.) in a hot liquid just below the boiling point.
puree a thick liquid prepared from cooked food passed through a sieve or broken down in a blender.

reduce to lower the amount of a liquid by simmering over heat.

sauté to fry in a small amount of fat.

soufflé a light, puffed baked dish made fluffy with stiffly beaten egg whites.
stock the broth from boiled meat, fish, or poultry.

Law

abet to encourage, instigate, or support some criminal activity. Used almost exclusively in the phrase *aid and abet*.
abscond to leave a jurisdiction in order to avoid arrest, service of a summons, or other imposition of justice.
abuse mistreatment of someone, such as physical abuse, psychological abuse, or sexual abuse. Abusive actions subject to legal intervention include (but are not limited to) child abuse and spousal abuse.
accessory a person who assists a criminal in committing a crime without being present when the crime is committed. An accessory is considered as culpable as someone who actually commits the crime.
adjourn to suspend or postpone a legal proceeding, either temporarily or indefinitely.
adjudication the hearing and disposition of a case in a proper court or agency. Adjudication includes a decision, as by a judge or jury, and, when appropriate, sentencing.
affidavit a formal written statement swearing to the truth of the facts stated and signed before a notary public. Dishonesty in an affidavit is either **false swearing** or perjury.
amicus curiae, pl. **amici curiae** (literally, *"friend of the court"*) someone who, although not a party to the litigation, volunteers or is invited by the court to submit views on the issues in the case.
amnesty a general pardon for offenses against a government.
arraignment the proceeding in which a criminal defendant is brought before the court, formally advised of charges, and required to enter a plea.
attachment the seizing or freezing of property by court order, either to resolve a dispute over ownership or to make the property available to satisfy a judgment against the owner.

bind to constrain or obligate, as by oath or law.
brief a memorandum of points of fact or of law for use in conducting a case.

certiorari a writ issuing from a superior court calling up the record of a proceeding in an inferior court for review. Also called **writ of certiorari**.
charge 1. a judge's instruction to the jury on a particular point of law. 2. a formal allegation that a person has violated a criminal law. 3. to make or deliver a charge.
class-action suit a legal proceeding brought by one or more persons representing the interests of a larger group.
code a systematically arranged collection of existing laws.

conflict of interest the circumstance of a public officeholder, business executive, or the like, whose personal interests might benefit from his or her official actions or influence, especially when those personal interests conflict with his or her duty.

contract an agreement between two or more parties for one to do or not do something specified in exchange for something done or promised by the other(s).

counterclaim a claim made to offset another claim, especially one made by the defendant against the plaintiff in a legal action.

cross-examination an examination, usually by a lawyer, of a witness for the opposing side, especially for the purpose of discrediting the witness's testimony.

deposition written testimony under oath.

discover to gain sight or knowledge of for the first time.

due process fair administration of the law in accordance with established procedures and with due regard for the fundamental rights and liberties of people in a free society.

escheat the reverting of property to the state when there are no persons that can be found who are legally qualified to inherit or to claim.

exclusionary rule a rule that forbids the introduction of illegally obtained evidence in a criminal trial.

executor a person named in a will to carry out its provisions.

extradition the surrender of a suspect by one state, nation, or authority to another.

false swearing the crime of making a false statement, as under oath knowing that the statement is not true. False swearing is not considered as serious a crime as perjury.

garnishment the attachment of money or property so they can be used to satisfy a debt.

grand jury a group of citizens assembled to hear evidence presented by a prosecutor against a particular person for a particular crime. A grand jury is convened to determine whether or not there is sufficient evidence to issue an indictment. The standards for indictment are considerably less than those for conviction at trial.

gravamen the fundamental part of an accusation; the essence of a complaint or charge.

habeas corpus a writ requiring a person to be brought before a court to determine whether the person has been detained legally.

hearsay evidence testimony based on what a witness has heard from another person rather than on direct personal knowledge or experience.

hostile witness a witness called by one side in a case who is known to be friendly to the other side or who turns out to be evasive in answering questions.

impeachment the institution of formal misconduct charges against a government official as a basis for removal from office.
indictment to charge with a crime or accuse of wrongdoing.
in flagrante delicto in the very act of committing the offense: *They were caught in flagrante delicto.*

judicial district a geographic division established for the purpose of organizing a court system.
jurisdiction the geographic area throughout which the authority of a court, legislative body, law-enforcement agency, or other governmental unit extends.

kangaroo court a mock court convened to reach a predetermined verdict of guilty, such as one set up by vigilantes.

litigant a party to a lawsuit.
litigation the process of making something the subject of a lawsuit; contesting an issue in a judicial proceeding.
litigator a lawyer who specializes in litigation.

malfeasance the performance by a public official of an act that is legally unjustified, harmful, or contrary to law.
mandamus a writ from a superior court to an inferior court, commanding that a specified thing be done; usually issued only in rare cases, to remedy an injustice.
monopoly the intentional acquisition or retention of exclusive control of a commodity or service in a particular market, especially so as to exclude competition and make possible the manipulation of prices.
motion a formal proposal, especially one made to a deliberative assembly such as a court.

nolo contendere (in a criminal case) a defendant's pleading that does not admit guilt but subjects him or her to punishment as though a guilty plea had been entered. Unlike a guilty plea, however, a plea of nolo contendere cannot be used as proof of guilt in a subsequent civil proceeding.

perjury the willful giving of false testimony under oath or affirmation, in a judicial or administrative proceeding, upon a point material to a legal inquiry. Compare **false swearing.**
plaintiff the person who starts a lawsuit by serving or filing a complaint.
plea a criminal defendant's formal response to charges. The defendant may plead *guilty, not guilty,* or *nolo contendere.*
plea bargain a practice in which a criminal defendant pleads guilty to a lesser charge rather than risk conviction for a graver crime.

precedent an act, decision, or case that may serve as an example, guide, or justification for subsequent ones.
prima facie (of a case, evidence, or proof) sufficient to support a contending party's claim and to warrant a verdict in favor of that party regarding that issue.
pro bono (of legal services) performed without fee, for the sake of the public good.
remand to send back, especially to return to custody, as to await further proceedings.
replevin an action for the recovery of tangible personal property wrongfully taken or detained by another.

special prosecutor an outside person appointed to investigate and, if warranted, prosecute a case in which the prosecutor who would normally handle the case has a conflict of interest.
statute of limitations a formal enactment defining the period of time after an event within which legal action arising from that event may be taken.
subornation of perjury the crime of inducing another person to commit perjury.
subpoena a writ to summon witnesses or evidence before a court.
surrogate court (in some states) a court having jurisdiction over the probate of wills, the administration of estates, etc.

tort a wrongful act resulting in injury, for which the injured party is entitled to compensation.

venue the county or judicial district where the courts have jurisdiction to consider a case.
voir dire an examination of a proposed witness or juror to determine if there are possible sources of bias that would militate against his or her objectivity in serving on a jury; an oath administered to a prospective witness or juror by which he or she is sworn to speak the truth so the examiner can ascertain his or her competence.

writ a court order by which a court commands a certain official or body to carry out a certain action.

Politics

Beltway the Washington, D.C., area; the U.S. government (used with *inside* or *outside*).
bipartisan representing, characterized by, or including members from two parties or factions.
bork to systematically attack (a candidate or the like), especially in the media.

cabinet a council advising a sovereign or a chief executive.
curve the forefront of any issue: *ahead of the curve; behind the curve.*

dark horse a little-known competitor or candidate who wins unexpectedly.
delegate a person designated to act for or represent another or others. Also a member of the lower house of the legislatures of Virginia, West Virginia, or Maryland.
détente a relaxing of tension, especially between nations.
dirty tricks unethical or illegal activities directed against a political opponent.
dove a person who advocates peace or a conciliatory military position.

filibuster the use of obstructive tactics, as exceptionally long speeches, to prevent or delay the adoption of a legislative measure.
full-court press an all-out effort.

-gate used to indicate political scandals, especially those resulting from a cover-up: *Watergate; Iran-Contra gate*
geopolitics the study of the influence of physical geography on the politics, national power, or foreign policy of a state.
goo-goo an idealistic supporter of political reform.
grass roots ordinary citizens, as contrasted with the leadership or elite.
gridlock a complete stoppage of normal activity: *legislative gridlock.*

hawk a person who advocates war or a belligerent military position.
Hill the United States Congress; Capitol Hill.
hot-button arousing passionate emotions: *hot-button issues.*

landslide an overwhelming victory, especially in an election.
left wing the liberal element in a political party or other group.
lobby a group of persons who try to influence legislators to vote in favor of a special interest.

nonproliferation the practice of curbing the creation and distribution of nuclear weapons.

policy wonk a person obsessively devoted to the most intricate details of policy.
populism a political philosophy or movement that promotes the interests of the common people.
pork barrel a government bill, policy, or appropriation that supplies funds for local improvements, designed to ingratiate legislators with their constituents.
progressive advocating reform, especially in political and social matters.

radical favoring drastic political, economic, or social reforms.
referendum the practice of referring legislative measures to the vote of the electorate for approval or rejection.

right wing the conservative element in a political party or organization.

smoking gun indisputable evidence or proof, as of a crime or misdeed.

sound bite a brief, striking remark taken from a speech for use in a news story.

spin a particular viewpoint or bias, as on a news issue; (as a verb) to put a spin on: *The press secretary spun the debate to make it look like his candidate won.*

spin doctor an expert in presenting information in the best possible light.

straw vote an unofficial vote taken to determine the general trend of opinion.

Teflon impervious to blame or criticism: *the Teflon president.*

wedge issue an issue that divides an otherwise united group or political party.

Publishing

advance payment made to an author before the publication of his or her text.

appendix supplementary material at the end of a text.

bind/bindery to secure a book within a cover/the place where books are secured in covers.

copy edit to edit the grammar and style of a text prior to publication.

copyright the exclusive right to use a literary, musical, or artistic work, protected by law for a specified period of time.

e-book reader portable electronic device used to download and read books or magazines that are in digital form.

edit to supervise the preparation of a publication.

epigraph an apt quotation at the beginning of a book or chapter.

epilogue a concluding part added to a literary work.

font a complete set of type of one style.

freelancer a copy editor, proofreader, indexer, etc. who sells his or her services without working on a regular basis for any single employer.

genre a class or category of artistic endeavor having a particular form, content, or technique.

house a publishing company where publishers, editors, designers, etc., prepare manuscripts for publication.

jacket the protective outer covering of a book (also a *dust jacket*).

manuscript a handwritten, typewritten, or computer-produced text.

permission(s) formal consent to reprint previously published material.

proofread to read printers' proofs, copy, etc., to detect and mark errors to be corrected.

public domain the legal status of material never or no longer protected by a copyright or patent.

publisher one who determines the text (printed or otherwise reproduced textual or graphic material) to be issued for sale. Often the head of a publishing company.

query to question.

release permission to publish, use, or sell something.

royalty an agreed portion of the income from a work paid to its author or composer.

serial text that is printed in installments at regular intervals.

sidebar a short feature alongside and highlighting a longer story.

Religion

acolyte an altar attendant in public worship; altar person.

agnostic a person who holds that the existence of the ultimate cause, as God, is unknown and unknowable.

animism the belief that natural objects and phenomena possess souls.

anti-Semite a person hostile toward Jews.

apocalypse a prophetic revelation, especially of a cataclysm in which good triumphs over evil.

Apocrypha a group of books not found in Jewish or Protestant versions of the Old Testament but included in the Septuagint and the Vulgate. Also, writings of doubtful authorship or authenticity.

Armageddon the place where the final battle between good and evil will be fought.

ascetic a person who practices self-denial, especially for religious reasons.

avatar an incarnation of a Hindu god.

baptism a ceremonial immersion in water, or application of water, as an initiatory sacrament of the Christian church.

blasphemy impious utterance or action concerning God or sacred things.

born again recommitted to faith through an intensely religious experience: a born-again Christian.

Brahma the chief member of the Hindu trinity, along with Vishnu and Siva.

Brahman a Hindu from the highest caste, often associated with the priesthood.

Buddha Indian religious leader: founder of *Buddhism*.

canon the works of an author accepted as authentic.
canonization to declare officially as a saint.
catechism summary of the principles of a Christian religion, in the form of questions and answers.
Confucianism the system of ethics, education, and statesmanship taught by Confucius.
creed an authoritative statement of the chief articles of Christian belief.
cult a religion considered to be false or extremist and that attracts a small number of devotees.
curate a cleric assisting a rector or vicar.

deacon a member of the clergy ranking just below a priest.
deism belief in the existence of a God on the evidence of reason and nature, with rejection of supernatural revelation.
demon an evil spirit; fiend.
diocese/archdiocese a district under the jurisdiction of a bishop/archbishop.
dogma a system of principles or tenets, as of a church.

ecumenical pertaining to, promoting, or fostering Christian unity throughout the world.
Epiphany a Christian festival, observed on January 6, commemorating the manifestation of Christ to the gentiles in the persons of the Magi.

fast to eat not at all, only sparingly, or of certain kinds of food.
Freemason a member of a secret fraternal association for mutual assistance and the promotion of brotherly love.
freethinker a person who forms opinions on the basis of reason alone, especially in religious matters.
free will the notion that human conduct expresses personal choice and is not determined by physical or divine forces.

gentile a person who is not Jewish, especially a Christian.
Gospel any of the first four books of the New Testament.
guru (in Hinduism) one's personal religious or spiritual instructor.

heresy a belief or opinion that is opposed to or differs from official church doctrine.
humanism any system of thought in which human interests, values, and dignity predominate.

incarnation to give a bodily form to, as in the Christian belief that Christ is God incarnate.

jihad a holy war undertaken as a sacred duty by Muslims.

karma (in Hinduism and Buddhism) action seen as bringing upon oneself inevitable results, either in this life or in a reincarnation.
Koran the sacred text of Islam.
Krishna an avatar of Vishnu and one of the most popular of Hindu deities.

Lent (in the Christian religion) a season of fasting and penitence, lasting the 40 weekdays from Ash Wednesday to Easter.
liturgy a form of public worship; ritual.

Mason See **Freemason**.
Messiah the promised and expected deliverer of the Jews; for Christians, Jesus Christ.
miracle an extraordinary occurrence that is ascribed to a divine or supernatural cause, especially to God.
mysticism the doctrine of an immediate spiritual intuition of truths or of a direct, intimate union of the soul with God through contemplation or spiritual ecstasy.

naturalism a theory that denies supernatural causes, often asserting that scientific explanations can account for phenomena.
New Age pertaining to a movement espousing a range of beliefs and practices traditionally viewed as occult or supernatural.
nirvana in Buddhism: release from the cycle of reincarnations as a result of the extinction of individual passion, hatred, and delusion.
numerology the study of numbers, as one's year of birth, to determine their supernatural meaning.

orthodox conforming to the approved form of any doctrine, philosophy, etc.

pantheism any religious belief or philosophical doctrine that identifies God with the universe.
Pentecost Christian holy day commemorating the Holy Spirit's appearance to the Apostles.
predestination the foreordination by God of whatever comes to pass, especially the salvation and damnation of souls.
purgatory (especially in the Roman Catholic belief) a place or state following death in which penitent souls are purified and thereby made ready for heaven.

Qur'an see **Koran**.

Reformation the sixteenth-century movement that resulted in the establishment of the Protestant churches.
reincarnation rebirth of the soul in a new body.

Sabbath an ordained day of rest and religious observance; Saturday among Jews and Sunday among many Christians.

Scripture the sacred writings of the Old or New Testament or both together.

shamanism especially among certain tribal peoples: a person who uses magic to cure illness, foretell the future, and control spiritual forces.

Shinto the native religion of Japan, primarily a system of nature and ancestor worship.

Siva "the Destroyer," the third member of the Hindu Trinity, along with Brahma and Vishnu.

stigmata marks resembling the wounds of the crucified body of Christ.

Talmud a collection of ancient Jewish law and tradition.

Taoism Chinese philosophical tradition advocating a life of simplicity and noninterference with the course of natural events.

tithe the tenth part of goods or income paid to support a church.

Torah a parchment scroll containing the Pentateuch, used in a synagogue.

Unitarian a member of a Christian denomination that gives each congregation complete control over its affairs.

Vishnu the second member of the Hindu trinity, along with Brahma and Siva.

voodoo a polytheistic religion deriving principally from African cult worship.

Yahweh a name of God transliterated by scholars from the Tetragrammation.

Zen a Buddhist movement that emphasizes enlightenment by means of meditation and direct, intuitive insights.

Zoroastrianism an Iranian religion founded by Zoroaster (circa 600 b.c.).

Science

antigravity a hypothesized force that behaves in ways opposite to gravity and repels matter.

antimatter matter composed only of antiparticles, which have attributes that are the reverse of those of matter. The basic difference between matter and antimatter is in the electric charge (negative vs. positive); for each particle of matter, there is a particle of antimatter.

antiparticle a particle whose properties, as mass, spin, or electric charge, have the same magnitude as, but the opposite algebraic sign of, a specific elementary particle. Where one is positive, the other is negative.

astronomy the science that deals with the universe beyond the earth's atmosphere, including the other planets in Earth's solar system, the stars, galaxies other than our own, and various other phenomena, such as **quarks** and **black holes**.

atom the basic component of an element, consisting of a nucleus containing combinations of neutrons and protons and one or more electrons bound to the nucleus by electrical attraction.

atomic weight the average weight of an atom of an element.

baryon a combination of three quarks that form the protons and neutrons of atomic nuclei.

big bang theory a theory that holds that our universe had its origins in an explosive cataclysm. Before that, the entire substance of the universe existed in a dense, compact kind of "cosmic soup"; since then, it has been expanding.

black hole a hypothetical massive object in space, formed by the collapse of a star at the end of its life, whose gravitational field is so intense that no electromagnetic radiation can escape, not even light.

convection the transfer of heat by the movement of the heated parts of a liquid or gas.

cosmology the branch of astronomy that deals with the general structure and evolution of the universe.

coulomb the basic unit of quantity of electricity, equal to the quantity of electric charge transferred in one second across a conductor.

cyclotron an accelerator in which particles are propelled in spiral paths by the use of a constant magnetic field. It is used to initiate nuclear transformations.

dark matter a hypothetical form of matter, probably making up more than 90 percent of the mass of the universe, that is invisible to electromagnetic radiation and therefore undetectable. It is thought to account for the gravitational forces that are observable in the universe.

ecosystem a system formed by the interaction of a community of organisms with its environment.

electric charge one of the basic properties of the elementary particles of matter giving rise to all electric and magnetic forces and interactions. The two kinds of charge are given negative and positive algebraic signs.

element one of a class of substances that cannot be separated into simpler substances by chemical means.

galaxy a large system of stars, such as our own Milky Way, held together by mutual gravitation and isolated from similar systems by vast regions of space.

global warming an increase in the earth's average atmospheric temperature that causes changes in climate.

gluon an unobserved massless particle that is believed to transmit the strong force between quarks, binding them together into **baryons** and **mesons.**

gravity the force of attraction by which terrestrial bodies tend to fall toward the center of the earth. It is also the similar attractive effect, considered as extending throughout space, of matter on other matter and on light.

inertia the property of matter by which it retains its state of rest or its velocity along a straight line so long as it is not acted upon by an external force.

light-year the distance traversed by light in one year, about 5.88 trillion miles (9.46 trillion kilometers).

mass the quantity of matter in a body as determined from its weight or measured by its motion.

MACHOs Massive Astrophysical Compact Halo Objects: brown dwarfs (small, cold stars), planets, or other objects hypothesized as constituting part of the dark matter in the halo of the Milky Way.

matter the substance or substances of which any physical object consists or is composed. Matter is made up of atoms; it has mass and can be measured.

meson a strongly interacting, unstable subatomic particle, other than a baryon, made up of two quarks and usually found in cosmic rays.

Milky Way the spiral galaxy containing our solar system. With the naked eye it is observed as a faint luminous band stretching across the heavens, composed of at least 100 billion stars, including the sun, most of which are too distant to be seen individually.

neutrino any of three uncharged elementary particles or antiparticles having virtually no mass.

neutron an elementary particle present in all atomic nuclei except hydrogen, having no electric charge, and having mass slightly greater than that of a proton.

neutron star hypothetically, an extremely dense, compact star composed primarily of neutrons, especially the collapsed core of a supernova.

nova a star that suddenly becomes thousands of times brighter and then gradually fades to its original intensity.

nuclear fission the splitting of the nucleus of an atom into nuclei of lighter atoms, accompanied by the release of great amounts of energy.

nuclear fusion a thermonuclear reaction in which nuclei of light atoms are fused, joining to form nuclei of heavier atoms, and releasing large amounts of energy.

nucleus the positively charged mass within an atom, composed of neutrons and protons, and possessing most of the mass but occupying only a small fraction of the volume of the atom.

particle 1. one of the extremely small constituents of matter, as an atom or nucleus. 2. an elementary particle, quark, or gluon.

periodic table a table illustrating the periodic system, in which the chemical elements, formerly arranged in the order of their atomic weights and now according to their atomic numbers, are shown in related groups.

pH the symbol used to describe the acidity or alkalinity of a chemical solution on a scale of 0 (more acidic) to 14 (more alkaline).

physics the science that deals with matter, energy, motion, and force.

planet 1. any of the nine large heavenly bodies revolving about our sun and shining by reflected light. In the order of their proximity to the sun, they are Mercury, Venus, Earth, Mars, Jupiter, Saturn, Uranus, Neptune, and Pluto. 2. a similar body revolving about a star other than our sun.
property an essential or distinctive attribute or quality of a thing.
proton a positively charged elementary particle that is a fundamental constituent of all atomic nuclei. It is the lightest and most stable baryon, having an electric charge equal in magnitude to that of the electron.
pulsar one of several hundred known celestial objects, generally believed to be rapidly rotating neutron stars, that emit pulses of radiation, especially radio waves, with a high degree of regularity.

quark any of the hypothetical particles that, together with their antiparticles, are believed to constitute all the elementary particles classed as baryons and mesons; they are distinguished by their flavors, designated as up (u), down (d), strange (s), charm (c), bottom or beauty (b), and top or truth (t), and their colors, red, green, and blue.

radio astronomy the branch of astronomy that uses extraterrestrial radiation in radio wavelengths for the study of the universe, rather than using visible light.

SETI Search for Extraterrestrial Intelligence: any of several research projects designed to explore the universe for signs of patterned signals that would indicate the presence of intelligent life in outer space.
solar system a sun together with all the planets and other bodies that revolve around it.
space-time the four-dimensional continuum, a combination of space and time, having three spatial coordinates and one temporal coordinate, in which all physical quantities may be located. The implication is that space and time are one thing, not separate.
spin the intrinsic angular momentum characterizing each kind of elementary particle, which exists even when the particle is at rest.
steady-state theory a theory in which the universe is assumed to have average properties that are constant in space and time so new matter must be continuously and spontaneously created to maintain average densities as the universe expands. This theory is now largely discredited in its original form. See **big bang theory.**
supernova the explosion of a star, possibly caused by gravitational collapse, during which the star's luminosity increases by as much as twenty magnitudes and most of the star's mass is blown away at very high velocity, sometimes leaving behind an extremely dense core.

theory of everything a theory, sought by scientists, that would show that the weak, strong, electromagnetic, and gravitational forces of the universe are components of a single force. This theory would unify all the forces of nature.

universe the totality of known or supposed objects and phenomena throughout space; the cosmos; macrocosm. Originally thought to include only our solar system, then expanded to admit our Milky Way galaxy, the concept of the universe now encompasses everything known or not yet known in space.

Sports

all-star game a sport contest consisting entirely of the top athletes of a sport.
assist a play helping a teammate to score or put out an opponent.

backhand (in tennis, squash, etc.) a stroke made with the back of the hand facing the direction of movement.
beach volleyball competitive volleyball played outdoors on sand.
bull pen a place where relief pitchers warm up during a baseball game.
bungee jumping jumping from a high surface to which one is attached by elasticized cords, so the body bounces back instead of hitting the ground.

center (in basketball, football, etc.) a player who plays primarily in the center of the field or court.
coin toss in football, the tossing of a coin to decide which team will kick first and which team will receive.
commissioner an official chosen by an athletic association to exercise broad authority.

draft the selection of persons for an athletic team.

extreme sports sports that are viewed as being very dangerous, such as **bungee jumping** or **sky surfing**.

face-off the act of putting the hockey puck into play by dropping it between two opposing players.
field goal a three-point goal made by place-kicking a football above the opponent's crossbar; a goal in basketball made while the ball is in play.
forehand of or being a stroke, as in tennis, made with the palm of the hand facing the direction of movement.
foul a violation of the rules of a sport or game; indicating the limits of a baseball field, i.e., foul lines;
full-court press a defensive strategy in basketball in which the defensive team pressures the offensive team the entire length of the court.

goal a place into which players of various games try to propel a ball or puck to score.

Hacky Sack a small leather beanbag juggled with the feet as a game.

Hail Mary a long football pass thrown in desperation, with a low chance of being caught.

high five a gesture of greeting or congratulation where one person slaps the open palm of another as it is held at head level.

in-line skate a roller skate having typically four hard-rubber wheels in a line resembling the blade of an ice skate.

in-your-face (in basketball) confrontational; provocative.

Jet Ski a small jet-propelled boat ridden like a motorcycle.

MVP most valuable player.

off side illegally beyond a prescribed area or in advance of the ball or puck during play.

pass to transfer (a ball or puck) to a teammate.

period one of the intervals of time into which a sports contest is divided.

play-off an extra game, inning, etc., played to settle a tie; a series of games played to decide a championship.

Rollerblade a brand of in-line skates.
rookie a first-year professional athlete.
roster the list of players on a team.

sideline either of the two lines defining the side boundaries of an athletic field or court.

sky surfing jumping from a plane with a parachute while wearing a board resembling a snowboard, so that one can "skate" on the air currents.

snowboard a board for gliding on the snow, resembling a wide ski, that one rides in an upright, standing position resembling the motion of surfing.

southpaw a left-handed person, especially a left-handed baseball pitcher.

trash-talking the use of aggressive, boastful, or insulting language, often employing slang.

triathlon an athletic contest consisting of swimming, running, and cycling.

Zamboni a machine for smoothing the ice at a rink.

9

Short Forms: Abbreviations and Acronyms

Some language experts regard the modern predilection for abbreviations, acronyms, and shortened forms as a kind of barbarism, but this trend reflects the pressures of modern life, as we attempt to compress long utterances into more compact expressive forms. Abbreviations are also a natural outgrowth of the underlying preference of English speakers for monosyllabic forms of expression. Here is an overview of shortened forms in English, along with some notes on their formation and use.

An **abbreviation** is a shortened or contracted form created from the initial or first few letters, or any group of letters, of a word or series of words. The series of words in the full form can be a title, name, or set phrase. Examples: *E* (for East); *Dr.* (for Doctor); *lb.* (for Latin "libra," pound); *etc.* (for et cetera).

An **initialism** is a shortened form created from the initial letters of a series of words, with each letter pronounced separately. Examples: *FDR* (for Franklin Delano Roosevelt); *CIA* (for Central Intelligence Agency).

An **acronym** is a pronounceable word created from the initial or first few letters of a series of words. Sometimes a vowel is inserted in the acronym to aid pronunciation. Very often the full or expanded form of an acronym is not widely known; few people know what the letters in laser stand for. The acronym may be a word that already exists in the language, such as *CARE* and *SHAPE*. Examples: *NASA* (for National Aeronautics and Space Administration); *scuba* (for self-contained underwater breathing apparatus).

A **hybrid** is a shortened form that cannot be neatly classified as an abbreviation, initialism, or acronym. One type of hybrid can be pronounced as the word it spells or as a series of letters, as *AWOL*.

Another type of hybrid is an initialism that is pronounced as a word, as *NAFTA*. There are also shortened forms composed of a short form and a word, as *D-day* and *CAT scan*. Sometimes a shortened form can be considered both an abbreviation and a word, as *math* (for mathematics) and *prof* (for professor).

A **symbol** is a letter, figure, or other conventional mark, or a combination of letters, used to designate an object, quality, process, etc. Symbols are used in specialized fields, such as physics and music. Examples: *Au* (for gold, the chemical element); *X* (for ten, the Roman numeral).

Formation and Use

Short forms are commonly encountered in newspapers, magazines, advertising, and daily conversation. In addition to the forms in general, everyday use, each specialized field has its own set of technical short forms.

Abbreviations, acronyms, and symbols are created for several reasons. They are easy to pronounce or remember, and they save time in speaking and writing. Many are catchy, such as *GUI* (Graphical User Interface) and *WYSIWYG* (What You See Is What You Get), or useful in advertising slogans and newspaper headlines. Some serve as euphemisms, such as *B.O.* for body odor.

A full form may have several different short forms in common use. Not all are equally correct, acceptable, or widespread. For example, *acct.* is more common than *acc.* as an abbreviation for *account*.

Many short forms are informal or slang, as *P.D.Q.* (for pretty damn quick) and *OK*. Others are formal or fully standard in the language. In fact, some short forms are used instead of their corresponding full forms. We commonly speak of VCRs, TVs, and HMOs, but rarely of videocassette recorders, televisions, and health maintenance organizations.

Although short forms are acceptable and widely used, some are not immediately recognizable. They may be derived from foreign words or phrases, such as *no.* from Latin *numero*. Some short forms stand for more than one full form and are therefore ambiguous. These forms should be defined the first time they are mentioned, and the short form can be used thereafter. Example: The Central Intelligence Agency (CIA) was established in 1947. The CIA is a federal agency that conducts intelligence activities outside the United States.

For abbreviations and initialisms, the trend is to leave out the periods, especially in scientific and technical notation and in capitalized forms, such as *F* (for Fahrenheit) and *RNA* (for ribonucleic acid). However, some short forms always take periods to avoid confusion, as *B.A.* (for Bachelor of Arts), *art.* (for article), *D.C.* (District of Columbia), and *no.* (for number).

The great majority of abbreviations are written with capital letters regardless of whether the constituent words are usually capitalized, as *LCD* (for liquid-crystal display). Acronyms are usually capitalized, as *NATO* (for North Atlantic Treaty Organization), but common ones often appear in lowercase, as *radar*. Short forms standing for proper nouns or important words in names or titles are usually capitalized, as *UFT* (for United Federation of Teachers) and *Span.* (for Spanish). Short forms standing for common nouns, adjectives, or adverbs are usually lowercased, as *spec.* (for special). Units of weight and measure, such as *kg* and *hr*, are written in lowercase. Symbols for chemical elements have only the first letter capitalized, as *Fe* (for iron).

The plural of a short form is often the same as the singular; in fact, there is a trend toward abolishing all pluralized forms. Short forms may be pluralized by adding "s" or "es," as *lbs.* (pounds), *nos.* (numbers), *HMOs* (health maintenance organizations), and *PCs* (personal computers). Sometimes apostrophes are used in plural forms, as *pj's*. There is a small group of abbreviations that form the plural by doubling a consonant, as *mss* (manuscripts), *ll* (lines), and *pp.* (pages).

Short forms can function as more than one part of speech. For example, *OK* is used as a noun, interjection, verb, adjective, and adverb. In these cases, the form is inflected in a predictable manner: *OK'ed* (or *OK'd*), *OK'ing*.

Part Three

Academic and Business Writing

10 The Stages of Writing

A research paper or essay could be the longest writing assignment you have ever done, and might even be the longest piece of writing you will ever do. Such a project may seem daunting at the outset, but even the largest animals can be tamed. With a combination of intuition and planning, you can manage a wide range of writing tasks with less difficulty than you might imagine. Here are some basic suggestions for each stage of your writing process.

1. **Clarify your task:** What are the key terms of the given topic (or if no specific topic is given, then what are the parameters of the assignment)? Your job here is to take these terms and make them compelling to you. You might try brainstorming first: just give yourself a few minutes of unstructured note-taking on anything that comes to mind as you read through the assignment. Are there words or ideas that you don't understand? Is there an explicit set of questions for you to answer? Your intuition is key here: you might find that certain questions are implied by the assigned topic.
2. **Come up with a research plan:** What are the central questions to be answered at the outset (the *who, what, when, where, why* questions)? Ask yourself what facts or secondary materials you will need to answer your questions. You may find it helpful to reread any relevant materials provided in class or in assigned readings and highlight key points that touch on your topic. Your goal now should be to define your research agenda: what do you hope to explore, prove (or disprove), or achieve in your paper?
3. **Research your topic creatively:** When you read through your brainstorming notes and your research questions/agenda, what keywords emerge that might be used to search for secondary sources? There are numerous print and online resources that can

help you locate the secondary sources best suited to your needs. Consult with a reference librarian for help in locating the best databases or search indexes. In your initial research, you may want to keep a log of the relevant contents (chapter headings or section titles) and bibliographic details of sources both read and unread. You may need to come back to a source that did not seem useful at first, so having those details could be helpful later. You could number each source in a master list and then keep your notes on each work on separate pages marked with the same number. Many people find it helpful to use index cards with a similar numbering system.

4. **Write a thoughtful outline:** Once your first round of research and note-taking is completed, you may find it helpful to list or cluster your key ideas. Looking at your ideas schematically may suggest avenues of argumentation and/or further avenues of research. As you review your list or cluster, ask yourself what form your paper might take: Will it develop thematically or chronologically? Will you examine one genre of materials and then another? Here you may wish to redefine the questions that you aim to answer or respond to in your work. Try to write the first two or three sentences of your paper. This exercise should force you to define the central argument of your paper. As you refine these ideas, you should begin to find a structure that best fits your argument. Once you have decided on a general structure for your paper, you can then frame your overall thesis and the general topical headings for each section (or each paragraph, of a shorter paper). Your outline will serve as a blueprint for your first draft—it is not a binding contract, but rather a guide to writing and shaping your paper.

5. **Remember why they call it a "rough draft":** Do not feel that your writing and your argumentation need to be fully polished at this point. You may even choose to write the body of your paper first, leaving the introduction for later. Some people find this a less intimidating way of beginning a term paper. In any case, you should keep your outline handy as you begin to formulate your specific arguments and their supporting interpretations or evidence. Be sure that each paragraph has a clear purpose, and that it develops an idea clearly introduced in its opening. Just as your introduction prepares your reader for the paper's thesis (or central argument), your topic sentence should clearly establish the main point of the paragraph. After completing your rough draft of the body of your paper, you may wish to rework (or draft) your introduction before beginning to write the conclusion. Your con-

clusion should build on, rather than simply restate, the ideas introduced and discussed in your paper. Think about the following questions: What is important about your thesis? With what impression do you want to leave your reader? Alternatively (or additionally), you could discuss some possible implications or interpretations of your argument. Your aim is to leave your reader with greater insight into the strengths and the potential of your ideas. You may not discover how to achieve this until your second or third draft. Allow as much time as possible for short breaks between the writing and revising of your drafts. You will edit and revise your own work much more effectively if you take the time to refresh your mind (and your eyes!).

6. **Be intellectually honest:** In your studies and your work, you will generate and develop many of your own ideas. In many cases, your work will also build on the ideas or words of others. You have an ethical responsibility to tell your readers which ideas and words are your own, and which are borrowed or cited from other sources. *Plagiarism* is defined as "the use or borrowing of another's words and/or ideas without proper acknowledgment." Word-for-word plagiarism is much easier to identify and avoid than paraphrased or conceptual plagiarism, but both kinds are equally serious forms of intellectual dishonesty. It is not necessary to cite the sources of generally-documented facts (e.g., the names of the U.S. presidents in sequential order, the official languages of Nigeria), nor for general observations or generic descriptions of places or objects (e.g., New York City is densely populated, Volkswagen makes automobiles). But many situations are not as easily defined as the above cases: nevertheless, it is always worth erring on the side of modesty, so it is better to give another source rather than to give yourself undue credit when determining the source of an idea or statement.

7. **Take the time to proofread and revise:** Once the hard work is done, you have the chance to polish your transitions, sharpen that introduction, and check carefully for any typos or grammatical errors. One helpful tactic: try writing a phrase or two to summarize each paragraph of your paper (beginning with the introduction). When you have completed that task, set it beside your original outline. Do they match? Note the sections where they diverge: are there any issues or ideas from your outline that might enhance those sections? Any positive departures from your outline? Could those departures benefit from changes to earlier sections? How well does your conclusion incorporate such departures? Does the conclusion end with grace or with exhaustion?

Give yourself the time to revise your conclusion with energy: you don't want to collapse in the final leg of your run. Proofreading tip: read your text backwards. It seems tedious, but is a highly effective way of catching misspellings, repeated words, and even some grammatical errors.

11

Academic Writing

Sample Research Paper (APA and MLA)

There are numerous formatting guidelines for academic writing. The two most commonly used are those published by the American Psychological Association (APA) and those of the Modern Language Association (MLA). The APA format generally applies to papers in the sciences and social sciences, and is often referred to as the "author-date" format, while the MLA guidelines embrace the humanities disciplines. Both APA and MLA require one-inch margins on all edges of the page and double-spacing throughout the paper. Both also require that the pages of the paper should be numbered in the upper right-hand corner using Arabic numerals. Their guidelines for citation of sources (both in-text and final), however, differ significantly from each other.

The sample research paper that follows demonstrates in-text citations in each format, as well as final References (APA) and Works Cited (MLA) lists. The first half of the paper, including the title page, conforms to the APA guidelines, while the second half follows the MLA formatting.

According to the APA guidelines, a short title should be provided throughout the paper (including on the title page, which would be numbered Page 1). This title (two to three words) should be one inch from the top of the page and flush right. Some guidelines for paper writing may demand that the title page not be numbered, in which case you would begin numbering consecutively on the following page (the abstract page in APA format), counting the title page as Page 1. Thus, the first numbered page would be Page 2. Page numbers should appear flush right, one half inch from the top.

The second half of this sample paper is formatted according to MLA guidelines. According to the MLA guidelines for pagination, no short title should appear in the header. MLA guidelines call for the incorporation of the title into the first page of your paper, unless otherwise requested.

Chanel:
An Enduring Style
Model Student, State College

Abstract

Coco Chanel's influence goes well beyond the realm of fashion. Through a combination of determined effort and good fortune, she worked her way up a steep social and economic slope to run a highly influential and successful business. Her ability to reinvent herself and to adapt her designs to the demands of a changing society enabled her to play a pivotal role in transforming women's lives across generations.

Chanel: An Enduring Style

How significant can "style" be? Can fashion have a meaningful impact on people's lives? Accounts of the life and work of Coco Chanel suggest that it can. In 1914, the French public saw the start of an extraordinary business. The opening of the House of Chanel presented a celebrity and a business that have lasted through two world wars and into a new century. The designer was so exceptional that mention of her name conjures a legendary style and look, and possibly even a lifestyle. Working in Paris at a time when art, music, and design were all cross-pollinating and flourishing in the city, Chanel found the perfect climate for her artistic creativity. This creativity was matched with a resourcefulness that enabled her to take advantage of her circumstances, however confining or fortunate they may have been. However, her creativity was not the only key to her success. Her knack and penchant for self-mythologization make her seem very much in sync with present-day popular culture, yet they might have derived instead from nineteenth-century social values. Chanel's childhood experiences of deprivation and of class prejudices may have been the catalysts of that drive and talent.

Coco Chanel spent her childhood far from the privileged metropolitan environment in which she spent the majority of her adult years. She was born Gabrielle Chanel in 1883 (she always claimed 1893) in Brive, a small town in the Auvergne province of France. She mythologized her childhood so effectively that biographers continue to differ on the dates and circumstances of her early life. Marcel Haedrich claims that when she was twelve, her mother died and her father placed her and her sisters in an orphanage (Haedrich, 1972). Other biographies date her mother's death to 1889, when she was six. There is general agreement that she spent most of her childhood in poverty and with the social stigma of rumored illegitimacy (Madsen, 1990). After her mother's death, she and her sisters had the added burdens of abandonment by her father and neglect by their caretakers (Haedrich, 1972). French provincial society was extremely socially rigid, and the humiliations and hardships endured by Chanel stoked her desire to escape the confinement of poverty and to become financially independent (Haedrich, 1972). At the age of eighteen, she was forced to leave the orphanage and she entered a convent boarding school in Moulins, where she spent two years as a scholarship student and novitiate. She left the boarding school after two years and moved in with her aunts to work as a seamstress in Moulins (Charles-Roux, 1979).

Her capacity for self-reinvention revealed itself in her forays as a professional singer and dancer, as an iconoclastic socialite, and finally as a milliner and clothier. She began dating a horse breeder and rider named Etienne Balsan, and eventually moved into his chateau at Royallieu with him, befriending his official mistress, Emilienne d'Alençon. Chanel soon replaced d'Alençon as official mistress, but remained close friends with her. She quickly befriended the wealthy aristocrats and riders who frequented the racetrack with Etienne. Chanel enjoyed going to the racetrack, and she soon became and accomplished rider herself. It was at the racetrack that Chanel dressed in the sports clothes that would be adopted by many women: a straw boater hat, white collar, necktie, and pin (Charles-Roux, 1979).

Another outgrowth of her time at the racetrack was Chanel's adoption of menswear. While women of fashion were wearing uncomfortable corsets, Chanel was wearing oversized coats, sweaters, and straight skirts cut simply. Her reason for dressing with such simplicity, according to Charles-Roux, was that she did not want to be identified as a "kept woman" (Charles-Roux, 1979, p. 78). In the course of defining herself against the women of her milieu, Chanel was developing what Charles-Roux claims was the "fundamental principle of her art: elements of male attire adapted to feminine use" (Charles-Roux, 1979, p. 78). Such androgyny in women's clothing anticipated many future fashion trends.

Well before beginning her design career, Chanel inspired many others to imitate her style. Her personal style marked her out as unique, and intrigued the men and women that she encountered. As striking as Chanel's contemporaries may have found her clothing, they were most outspokenly impressed by her hats. Many of these friends were actresses, among them a very famous one named Gabrielle Dorziat. Dorziat, among others, had Chanel create some hats for her. Chanel's talents as a designer and seamstress were put to further use by Etienne and his friends, who would have her make costumes for the plays they produced to amuse themselves. These efforts foreshadowed her later role as costume designer for the theatrical productions of Sergei Diaghilev's Ballets Russes and for the director Jean Cocteau.

By the spring of 1910, Chanel's ambitions grew beyond Royallieu and the Auvergne, and she suggested to Balsan that she should open a shop in Paris. Balsan did not take the request seriously, but Arthur "Boy" Capel, a champion polo player and friend of Etienne's who was dining with them, supported her idea. Etienne, to satisfy Chanel, set up a shop for her in his "bachelor's chambers" on the ground floor of 160 Boulevard Malesherbes. Boy Capel lived nearby and called on Chanel frequently. Later that year, Chanel went to live with Capel, and began making hats upstairs at 21 rue Cambon, just down the street from the place that would later become synonymous with the legendary House of Chanel. Her hats continued to grace the heads of noted actresses and aristocratic friends of Balsan and Capel. After her designs appeared to great acclaim in the Theatre de Vaudeville production of a play titled *Bel Ami,* Chanel opened a boutique in Deauville, just ten months prior to the outbreak of World War I. When war began in August 1914, Capel advised Chanel to remain in Deauville and keep her shop open. This was good advice, for women needed clothes in which they could be active, and Chanel's designs allowed for greater movement than the prevailing fashions. While the then-established designer Paul Poiret is credited with freeing women from corsets, his designs involved complicated draping and details such as feathers and bows (Galante, 1972). Chanel's corset-free, unfussy designs quickly became the new prevailing fashion (Charles-Roux, 1979).

By 1917, Chanel was an independent, successful businesswoman. Her relationship with Capel changed, however, when he married an ambulance driver that year. Chanel remained friends with him, and even designed clothes for his new wife, but she had lost a great love in her life. She spent much of this time at the sea and touring Europe with friends. On one of these tours, she met and befriended Misia Sert, who would prove a critical influence on her work. Like Chanel, Sert was a free spirit and a close friend of many of the great artists and writers of her time. Her relationships with Renoir (he painted a celebrated portrait of her), Toulouse-Lautrec, Stravinsky, and Debussy are well documented, and she moved even closer to the center of these artistic circles when Misia married the painter José Maria Sert y Badia. She introduced Chanel to many of these artists, among them the writer and director Jean Cocteau, for whom Chanel remained a close friend and collaborator for more than a decade. In 1923, Chanel designed the costumes for his adaptation of *Antigone*, which had its sets designed by Pablo Picasso.

During the 1920s, Chanel's designs became synonymous with "the whole notion of modernity," as her style embodied the clean-lined, fast-paced aesthetic of modern life (Charles-Roux, 1979, p. 209). This decade also saw the launching of her first perfume: Chanel No. 5 (in 1925), and of the design that would become the staple of every urban woman's wardrobe: the "little black dress", which appeared in a 1926 edition of *Vogue*. Chanel's success led her to move into 31 rue Cambon, in an area of Paris long associated with haute couture. The House of Chanel remained there, and Chanel lived in the apartment above it for the rest of her life (except for ten years spent in quasi-exile in Switzerland)

At this point, Chanel had become an international figure, both inspired by and inspiring the designs of the art deco period. Her multiuse clothes were well suited to a life in motion, which appealed to an increasingly mobile populace. American and English media assigned their most celebrated photographers to follow Chanel fashions, and soon she had an even broader market for her products. She was hired in 1931 to design clothing for several Hollywood-based productions of the movie producer Samuel Goldwyn. Photographers such as Edward Steichen and Cecil Beaton, who shot for the American and British *Vogue* magazines respectively, were not the only ones tracking Chanel. Iribe, an artist who got his start drawing caricatures for the newspaper *Le Temoin*, had Chanel pose for him, and grew to be one of her closest friends (and, it is alleged, a live-in lover). He later drew Chanel in the guise of Marianne, the iconic figure for France. Iribe died while vacationing with Chanel on the Riviera ("Chanel: The Final Phase," 2003)

By this time, France was hard-hit by economic depression, which deeply affected the fashion business as well. In 1933, ten thousand workers in the fashion trade were unemployed, and haute couture had dropped from its place as the second highest export in 1925, to the twenty-seventh highest in 1933 (Ewing, 1974). However, Chanel's business was not harmed, since her "... intuitive grasp of the needs of the time served her well" (Ewing, 1974). Instead, she had come to represent a different, more approachable sort of haute couture. In her own words: "Fashion does not exist unless it goes down into the streets. The fashion that remains in the salons has no more significance than a costume ball" (as qtd. Charles-Roux, 1979, p. 237).

During the late 1920s and early 1930s, Chanel was also carrying on a love affair with the duke of Westminster, which further influenced her work. The duke exposed her to British country life and to yachting, which inspired in her a love of traditional fabrics such as Scottish tweeds and sailing clothes. Her tweed suits, sailor-type blouses, pleated skirts, and cardigans are often linked to these influences, although she continued to mix these outfits with "sumptuous" jewelry, which supposedly shocked the British with whom she socialized (Charles-Roux, 1979, p. 225).

Chanel's use of jewelry was another example of her impact on modern design. Chanel began mixing her real gems with false ones, eventually introducing a collection of costume jewelry designed for people who could not afford or did not want to buy jewelry made of expensive metals and precious stones. Iribe designed some pieces for her, and she sold the jewelry in her rue Cambon shop. However, her costume jewelry line was merely a diversion from her real passion, which was for clothing and costume design.

With the help of Misia Sert, Chanel continued to meet and collaborate with many artists. One of Sert's friends was the author-choreographer Sergei Diaghilev, whom Chanel helped financially after his disastrous production of *Sleeping Beauty* forced him to leave London in debt. In 1924, Chanel helped him again by designing the costumes for *Le Train Bleu,* a ballet with sets designed by Cubist sculptor Henri Laurens. The curtain was painted by Pablo Picasso. She also worked with film director Jean Renoir (son of painter Auguste Renoir) on the costume designs for his 1939 film *La Règle de Jeu.* Chanel was not the only designer to collaborate with artists at this time. Indeed, other designers such as Poiret and Balenciaga worked very closely with artists as well. Chanel's collaborations with Diaghilev and with Jean Cocteau earned them much acclaim (Charles-Roux, 1979). During the 1930s, her work for the stage competed with, but also fed into, her work at Chanel.

After two monumental collaborations with Cocteau (*Oedipus Rex* in 1934 and *The Holy Grail* in 1937), Chanel again concentrated on designing clothes, as the House of Chanel faced intense competition from designer Elsa Schiaparelli. Schiaparelli's own career got a boost from *Vogue* magazine, when it named her sweater as Sweater of the Year for 1927 (Charles-Roux, 1979). The competition proved healthy for Chanel, for the business had its most successful year (up to that time) in 1938. By 1939, the House of Chanel occupied five houses on rue Cambon. Sadly, it was about to face hard times.

World War II rendered haute couture a very low priority. Chanel closed her salon immediately after war was declared. She received much criticism from the press and from her colleagues for this action, and she removed herself entirely from public life by retiring to her flat above the store on rue Cambon. During the German occupation of Paris, Chanel was allowed to remain in her apartment. She allowed no visitors, except for one German officer named Baron von Dincklage, nicknamed Spatz, who was allegedly a close associate of Joachim Von Ribbentrop, the German Foreign Minister later hanged at Nuremburg (Haedrich 147). After the Liberation, Chanel was asked many questions about Spatz by both French and

English officials, all of which she refused to answer. This chapter of Chanel's life holds many unanswered and troubling questions about her complicity with the occupation. The speculation about her affair and her apparently comfortable, if reclusive life, might have been a factor in her leaving France for Switzerland in 1944, and the cold public reception her 1954 comeback received. However, no conclusive evidence has ever emerged of any privileges extended to her or of her knowing complicity with the Nazis. Nevertheless, her move to Switzerland has been called an "exile of sorts" for her affair with the Nazi officer ("Women's History: Coco Chanel", par. 7).

Despite closing her store, Chanel continued to sell her perfume. Yet, as Marcel Haedrich reports it, she began to regret an unwise agreement made in 1924 (158). Two businessmen named Pierre and Paul Wertheimer suggested that, together with Chanel, they incorporate as Parfums Chanel to sell perfumes in France and worldwide. Chanel agreed and signed over to Parfums Chanel the rights to all the brands that she had marketed under the name Chanel, as well as the chemical formulas and the manufacturing processes. She received two hundred shares worth five hundred francs each, exempt from all obligations and representing ten percent of the capital (Haedrich 158). She would also have a ten percent share of all branches set up abroad. Chanel claimed that she was being cheated, and eventually sought legal help in 1939 to be released from her agreement. She discovered that the brothers had sold the old corporation to a new one, Chanel Incorporated, established in the United States, and had cut her share. Further, the brothers established tie-in contracts that forced merchants wanting to sell Chanel products into buying Bourjois (their own company) products as well (Haedrich 160). Her efforts to exact legal revenge on the businessmen drained her financially, and ultimately forced her to settle out of court with them. At this point, however, the deal that they struck with her was more than fair, allowing her to recoup her losses and gain income on past and future sales (Haedrich 158). Despite this demonstration of strength in her business dealings and the short-term financial gain, Chanel's reputation had taken a beating, ostensibly from her retirement and her association with von Dincklage (Charles-Roux 227).

Nevertheless, Chanel remained undaunted, and by 1954 was determined to make her comeback. On February 5, she showed her first collection since before the war. While she had been in retirement, however, a new designer had made a splash with a look antithetical to the Chanel Style. In 1947, Christian Dior emerged with the New Look, a full-skirted, fitted-waist, ankle-length style. It must have seemed to hearken back to corsets and hobble skirts for fans of Chanel's modern look. With this New Look in vogue, it was hard for the fashion world to readily accept the Chanel style again, perhaps the primary reason that her opening met with scorn from the French press and public. Nevertheless, she gained new fans in the United States with her elegant yet practical ready-to-wear designs. Americans could buy knockoffs or cheap imitations of her designs. Chanel knew that she could not prevent this from happening, and even went so far as to encourage it. She regained her footing on both continents, so to speak, by introducing a shoe and handbag collection. In 1956, she introduced another item that became a Chanel Classic, the two-tone sling-back pump, which furthered her French and international sales (Gold 83).

Her comeback was hard-fought and tenuous, which may have contributed to her increasingly secretive manner and her anxieties about her competitors and even about potential betrayals by her associates. Marcel Haedrich corroborates the fulfillment of those fears through his first-hand account of being shown hidden workrooms in the store in the late 1960s: ". . . Coco led me through the hole made in the wall to show me . . . a workroom filled with little tables for sewing machines . . . [and] an office for the 'foreman' hired to take her place in order to supply mini-skirted Chanels to anyone who wanted them" (Haedrich 213). Chanel forced the workrooms to close, and became even more explicitly determined to retain control over her designs. During her final years, she spoke frequently of her last collection, claiming that it would be a synthesis of all that she had done, and asserting that ". . . the collection is fundamental, because it is the future" (Haedrich 243). Into her eighty-seventh year, she could be found in her atelier late into the night: unstitching and pinning, smoothing and refitting the clothes onto the models themselves in preparation for the forthcoming collection (Charles-Roux 238). She died on January 10, 1971.

Chanel's design triumphs and influences carried well beyond her death, for her name was linked to both a "style" and a "length", and continues to evoke an image of comfortable elegance. Her obituary in *Time* magazine claimed that "[. . .] the French couturiere had long since established herself as the 20th century's single most important arbiter of fashion" ("Chanel No. 1", par. 1). The designers chosen to carry on the Chanel clothing line, particularly Karl Lagerfeld from 1982 on, retained many elements of the Chanel style, while adding their own flair (Donovan 116). Likewise, the appointment of fashion editor Frances Stein as artistic director of the Chanel Accessories Collection (mainly jewelry) marked something close to a fulfillment of Chanel's intention: she herself had offered Stein a job as her press attaché in the mid-1960s. Stein seems to understand Chanel's vision and was able to articulate it well: "Clothes and accessories should live [. . .] the key to modern dressing is a wardrobe that is movable. [. . .] With a few pieces, you can turn less into more . . ." (Weir 125). Chanel's theory, as interpreted above by Stein, is embodied in her suits. Chanel herself showed how a simple, well-tailored skirt, blouse, and jacket could be radically changed by the addition of a pin or a necklace. For contemporary women, such simple transformations could stretch tight schedules and budgets much farther.

Chanel was said to have "glamorized poverty," when in fact she inspired a style that could be adopted by women with very little disposable income and women of unlimited means. She consistently demonstrated a talent for turning something disparaged or seemingly commonplace into a desirable and elegant item or look. From her initial adoption of menswear and a cropped haircut (said to have been inspired by her accidental singeing of her hair), to her use of jersey fabric for dresses rather than for underwear or athletic uniforms, Chanel responded to her widely varying circumstances with tremendous creativity. She is famous for a number of pithy quotes, cited by many (notably by Charles-Roux in a section of his book called "The Maxims of Chanel"), which capture her approach to life as well as to fashion. Fashion (and life), according to Chanel, demands a sense of humor and of luxury as well as a practicality. As she argues: "An elegant woman should be able to do her marketing without making housewives laugh," while at the same time, she observes that: " 'Good taste' ruins certain real values of the spirit: taste itself, for instance" (quoted in Charles-Roux 237). Her sense of the ridiculous and frivolous side of fashion did not prevent her from responding to the enjoyment of luxury and the desire for beauty. Her designs embraced this desire while simultaneously aiming for practicality.

It is this versatility mixed with elegance that has given the Chanel style immortality. Chanel herself said: "A style does not go out of style as long as it adapts itself to its period. When there is an incompatibility between the style and a certain state of mind, it is never the style that triumphs" (quoted in Haedrich 251). She knew that her style was lasting, and that she was a pioneer in her field. She even lived to know that Katherine Hepburn would play her in a Broadway musical, *Coco*, based on her life. But what she was only dimly aware of was that her styles and her spirit would be admired and adopted by many women long after her death.

References [APA Format]

Charles-Roux, Edmonde. (1979). *Chanel and Her World*. London: The Vendome Press.

"Chanel No. 1." (1971, January 25). *Time*. Retrieved February 16, 2003, from http://www.time.com/time/time100/artists/profile/chanel_re_lated.html.

"Chanel: The Final Phase." (2003). *BA Education*. Retrieved February 17, 2003, from http://www.ba-education.demon.co.uk/for/fashion/chanel3.html.

Donovan, Carrie. (1982, December 12). "Reshaping the Classics at the House of Chanel." *New York Times* Magazine. 116.

Duka, John. (1984, March 27). "In Style." *New York Times*.

Ewing, Elizabeth. (1974). *History of Twentieth Century Fashion*. New York: Chas. Scribner's Sons.

Galante, Pierre. (1973). *Mademoiselle Chanel*. Transl. by Eileen Geist and Jessie Wood. Chicago, Illinois: Henry Regency Company.

Gold, Anna Lee. (1975). *Seventy-Five Years of Fashion*. New York: Fairchild Publications, Inc.

Haedrich, Marcel. (1972). *Coco Chanel: Her Life, Her Secrets*. Transl. by Charles Lam. Boston: Little, Brown and Company.

Hyde, Nina. (1984, March 28). "Style Plus." *Washington Post*. B3.

Madsen, Axel. (1990). *Chanel: A Woman of Her Own*. New York: Henry Holt.

Weir, June. (1982, November 7). "Carrying On: Fashion Profile." *New York Times* Magazine. 92.

Works Cited [MLA Format]

Charles-Roux, Edmonde. *Chanel and Her World*. London: The Vendome Press, 1979.

"Chanel No. 1." *Time* 25 Jan. 1971. Time Online. 16 Feb. 2003 <http://www.time.com/time/time100/artists/profile/chanel_related.html>.

"Chanel: The Final Phase." BA Education. 2003. 17 Feb. 2003. <http://www.ba-education.demon.co.uk/for/fashion/chanel3.html>

Donovan, Carrie. "Reshaping the Classics at the House of Chanel." *New York Times Magazine* 12 Dec. 1982: 116.

Duka, John. "In Style." *New York Times* 27 Mar. 1984.

Ewing, Elizabeth. *History of Twentieth Century Fashion*. New York: Chas. Scribner's Sons, 1974.

Galante, Pierre. *Mademoiselle Chanel*. Transl. by Eileen Geist and Jessie Wood. Chicago, Illinois: Henry Regency Company, 1973.

Gold, Anna Lee. *Seventy-Five Years of Fashion*. New York: Fairchild Publications, Inc, 1975.

Haedrich, Marcel. *Coco Chanel: Her Life, Her Secrets*. Transl. by Charles Lam. Boston: Little, Brown and Company, 1972.

Hyde, Nina. "Style Plus." *Washington Post* 28 Mar. 1984: B3.

Madsen, Axel. *Chanel: A Woman of Her Own*. New York: Henry Holt, 1990.

Weir, June. "Carrying On: Fashion Profile." *New York Times* Magazine 7 Nov. 1982: 92.

Reference Lists

Type of Document	Author-Page System (MLA) Works Cited	Author-Date (APA) References
Journal article	Stewart, Donald C. "What Is an English Major, and What Should It Be?" *College Composition and Communication* 40 (1989): 188–202.	Roediger, H. L. (1990). Implicit memory: A commentary. *Bulletin of the Psychonomic Society, 28,* 373–380.

Type of Document	Author-Page System (MLA) Works Cited	Author-Date (APA) References
Journal article two authors	Brownell, Hiram H., and Heather H. Potter. "Inference Deficits in Right-Brain Damaged Patients." *Brain and Language* 27 (1986): 310–21.	Tulving, E., & Schacter, D. L. (1990). Priming and human memory systems. *Science, 247,* 301–305.
Journal article more than two authors	Mascia-Lees, Frances E., Pat Sharpe, and Colleen B. Cohen. "Double Liminality and the Black Woman Writer." *American Behavioral Scientist* 31 (1987): 101–14.	Barringer, H. R., Takeuchi, D. T., & Xenos, P. C. (1990). Education, occupational prestige and income of Asian Americans: Evidence from the 1980 Census. *Sociology of Education, 63,* 27–43.
Book	Hammond, Nicholas G. *The Genius of Alexander the Great.* Chapel Hill: U of North Carolina P, 1997.	Rossi, P. H. (1989). *Down and out in America: The origins of homelessness.* Chicago: University of Chicago Press.
Book revised edition	Eagleton, Terry. *Literary Theory: An Introduction.* 2nd ed. Minneapolis: U of Minnesota P, 1996.	Kail, R. (1990). *Memory development in children* (3rd ed.). New York: Freeman.
Book corporate author	College Board. *College-bound Seniors: 1989 SAT Profile.* New York: College Entrance Examination Board, 1989.	American Psychiatric Association. (1987). *Diagnostic and statistical manual of mental disorders* (3rd ed., rev.). Washington, DC: Author.
Book no author	*Guidelines for the Workload of the College English Teacher.* Urbana: National Council of Teachers of English, 1987.	*Standards for educational and psychological tests.* (1985). Washington, DC: American Psychological Association.
Edited book	Kerckhove, Derrick de, and Charles J. Lumsden, eds. *The Alphabet and the Brain: The Lateralization of Writing.* Berlin: Springer-Verlag, 1988.	Campbell, J. P., Campbell, R. J., & Associates. (Eds.). (1988). *Productivity in organizations.* San Francisco, CA: Jossey-Bass.
Selection from edited book	Glover, David. "The Stuff That Dreams Are Made Of: Masculinity, Femininity, and the Thriller." *Gender, Genre and Narrative Pleasure.* Ed. Derek Longhurst. London: Unwin Hyman, 1989. 67–83.	Wilson, S. F. (1990). Community support and integration: New directions for outcome research. In S. Rose (Ed.), *Case management: An overview and assessment.* White Plains, NY: Longman.

Type of Document	Author-Page System (MLA) Works Cited	Author-Date (APA) References
Translated book	Mann, Thomas. *Buddenbrooks: The Decline of a Family.* Trans. John E. Woods. New York: Knopf, 1993.	Michotte, A. E. (1963). *The perception of causality* (T. R. Miles & E. Miles, Trans.). London: Methuen. (Original work published 1946)
Republished book	Hurston, Zora Neale. *Their Eyes Were Watching God.* 1937. Urbana: U of Illinois P, 1978.	Ebbinghaus, H. (1964). *Memory: A contribution to experimental psychology.* New York: Dover. (Original work published 1885; translated 1913)
Magazine article	Miller, Mark Crispen. "Massa, Come Home." *New Republic* 16 Sept. 1981: 29–32.	Gibbs, N. (1989, April 24). How America has run out of time. *Time,* pp. 58–67.
Newspaper article	"Literacy on the Job." *USA Today* 27 Dec. 1988: 6B.	Freudenheim, M. (1987, December 29). Rehabilitation in head injuries in business and health. *New York Times,* p. D2.
Review	Kidd, John. "The Scandal of *Ulysses.*" Rev. of *Ulysses: The Corrected Text,* by Hans Walter Gabler. *New York Review of Books* 30 June 1988: 32–39.	Falk, J. S. (1990). [Review of *Narratives from the crib*]. *Language, 66,* 558–562.
Report available from ERIC	Baurer, Barbara A. *A Study of the Reliabilities and Cost Efficiencies of Three Methods of Assessment for Writing Ability.* ERIC, 1981. ED 216 357.	Hill, C., & Larsen, E. (1984). *What reading tests call for and what children do.* Washington, DC: National Institute of Education. (ERIC Document Reproduction Service No. ED 238 904)
University report	Flower, Linda. The Role of Task Representation in Reading to Write. Technical Report No. 6. Berkeley: Center for the Study of Writing at U of California, Berkeley and Carnegie Mellon U, 1987.	Elman, J., & Zipser, D. (1987). *Learning the hidden structure of speech* (Report No. 8701). Institute for Cognitive Science, University of California, San Diego.
Dissertation	Hubert, Henry Allan. "The Development of English Studies in Nineteenth-Century Anglo-Canadian Colleges." Diss. U of British Columbia, 1988.	Thompson, I., (1988). *Social perception in negotiation.* Unpublished doctoral dissertation, Northwestern University, Evanston, IL.

Type of Document	Author-Page System (MLA) Works Cited	Author-Date (APA) References
Conference paper	Moffett, James. "Censorship and Spiritual Education." The Right to Literacy Conference. Columbus, Ohio, September 1988.	Hogan, R., Raskin, R., & Fazzini, D. (1988, October). *The dark side of charisma*. Paper presented at the Conference on Psychological Measures and Leadership, San Antonio, TX.

Preparing and Marking Up a Manuscript

1. Manuscripts being submitted for publication should be printed or typed on standard-size paper—8½ by 11 inches.
2. If the paper is being submitted for publication and will be edited and set into type, everything should be double-spaced—including block quotations, footnotes, and references—since it is difficult to edit material that has less than a full line of space between lines of text. Many instructors also prefer that papers be double-spaced.
3. Covers may be attractive for certain purposes, but most editors and instructors find that they make manuscripts more difficult to handle efficiently.
4. Pages must be numbered, preferably in the upper right-hand corner and far enough from the edge so the numbers are not accidentally left off when the manuscript is photocopied. Every manuscript should be copied or saved to a hard drive as a safeguard against loss of the original.
5. Word processing makes available several features that are not available on the conventional typewriter—italics, boldface, various typefaces, and different possibilities for spacing. If a manuscript or paper is being prepared for its final readership, then it makes sense to use these capabilities to make it as attractive and readable as possible. On the other hand, if the manuscript will be edited and set into type, it will be easier to deal with if a single typeface is used.
6. Always ask your instructor or publisher about the specific guidelines they expect you to follow. Knowing the required format in advance can save you a great deal of time.

Preparing and Marking Up a Manuscript 313

7. Always proofread your work carefully before submitting it. A manuscript that has mistakes in spelling and grammar will not be taken seriously by an editor and may be rejected by an instructor.

Proofreader's Marks

Mark in margin	Indication in text	Meaning of instruction
a/ʌ	Peter left town in hurry.	Insert at carets (∧)
⁁ or ɤ	Joan sent me the the book.	Delete
◡	ma ke	Close up; no space
⁁̃	I haven't seen them in years.	Delete and close up
stet	They phoned both Al and Jack.	Let it stand; disregard indicated deletion or change
¶	up the river. Two years	Start new paragraph
no ¶ or run in	many unnecessary additives. The most dangerous one	No new paragraph
tr	Put the book on the table. Put the table on the book.	Transpose
tr up or tr ↑	to Eva Barr, who was traveling abroad. Ms. Barr, an actress,	Transpose to place indicated above
tr down or tr ↓	in the clutch. The final score was 6-5. He pitched the last two innings.	Transpose to place indicated below
sp	He owes me 6 dollars.	Spell out
fig	There were eighteen members present.	Set in figures
#	It was a smallvillage.	Insert one letter space
# #	too late.After the dance	Insert two letter spaces

Preparing and Marking Up a Manuscript

Mark in margin	Indication in text	Meaning of instruction
hr #	jero^bam	Insert hair space (very thin space)
line #	Oscar Picks — # This year's Academy Awards nomination.	Insert line space
eq #	Ron ✓ got rid ✓ of the dog.	Equalize spacing between words
=	thre^e days late_r	Align horizontally
‖	the earth's surface, bounded by lines parallel to the equator	Align vertically
run over	enhance production⌡ 2. It will	Start new line
☐	☐ Rose asked the price.	Insert one em space
☐☐	☐☐ The Use of the Comma	Insert two em spaces
⌐	⌐ What's his last name?	Move left
⌐	April 2, 1945 ⌐	Move right
⌐⌐	⌐ Please go now. ⌐	Move up
⌐⌐	⌐ Well, that's that! ⌐	Move down
⌐ ⌐	⌐ ATOMIC ENERGY ⌐	Center (heading, title, etc.)
fl	⌐ 2. Three (3) skirts	Flush left
fr	Total: $89.50 ⌐	Flush right
sent/?	He˄the copy.	Insert missing word?
(ok?) or (?)	by Francis Gray. (She) wrote	Query or verify; is this correct?
(out: see copy)	the discovery of but near the hull ˄	Something missing
⊙	Anna teaches music˄	Insert period
ˆ,	We expect Eileen˄Tom, and Ken.	Insert comma
ˆ;	I came; I saw˄I conquered.	Insert semicolon
(:)	Ben got up at 6˄30 a.m.	Insert colon

Preparing and Marking Up a Manuscript 315

Mark in margin	Indication in text	Meaning of instruction
=	Douglas got a two‿thirds majority.	Insert hyphen
$\frac{1}{m}$	Mike then left‿very reluctantly.	Insert em dash
$\frac{1}{n}$	See pages 96‿124.	Insert en dash
ˀ	Don't mark the authorˇs copy. Don't mark the authors‿copy.	Insert apostrophe
!	Watch out‿	Insert exclamation point
?	Did she write to you‿	Insert question mark
ʿʿ/ʾʾ	‿Ode on a Grecian Urn,‿ by Keats	Insert quotation marks
ʿ/ʾ	She said, "Read ‿The Raven‿ tonight."	Insert single quotation marks
(/) or ⁅/⁆	The Nile is 3473 miles ‿5592 km‿ long.	Insert parentheses
[/] or ⁅/⁆	"He ‿Dickson‿ finished first."	Insert brackets
ital	I've seen <u>Casablanca</u> six times.	Set in *italics*
rom	⟨Gregory drove to Winnipeg.⟩	Set in roman
bf	See the definition of peace.⌇	Set in **boldface**
lf	She repaired ⟨the⟩ motor easily.	Set in lightface
Cap or u/c	the italian role in Nato	Set in CAPITAL letter(s)
sc	He lived about 350 B.C.	Set in SMALL CAPITAL letter(s)
lc or l/c	Of Mice ⁄And Men	Set in lowercase
u+lc or c+lc or uc+lc	STOP! STOP!	Set in uppercase and lowercase
⌄2	H₂O	Set as subscript
²⸝	A² + B2⸝	Set as superscript
×	They drove to ⓂMiami	Broken (damaged) type
wf	Turn ⓇRight	Wrong font

12 Business Writing

The following text is an example of an executive summary, commonly used in business to make a concise statement and provide reasons to support it.

Sample Executive Summary

Your opening paragraph should provide a brief description of the issue, project, law, company, product, or policy being profiled in the summary.

Example
Site Comparison for Maple Arts Center.
Costs/Benefits of House Resolution 1242; Development Potential for 22 North Shore Drive

The subsequent paragraph (or heading for list) should state the conclusion reached or the recommendation advocated by the summary writer (or group he or she represents). For instance: whether costs outweigh benefits, what development potential exists for property, what marketing/investment strategy is recommended. . . .

Example
After exploring four prospective sites for the center, the panel would pursue one of the following two possibilities: 1233 Second Street or 98876 Washington Avenue. The Second Street site is the most attractive site for many reasons, but it may go to another buyer.

The next section (which might be in paragraphs or in numbered or bullet points) should summarize the key supporting points, reasons, consequences, benefits, and/or attributes of the subject of the summary. You need to present these points as succinctly as possible, while still making as clear and strong a case for your recommendation or conclusion as possible.

Example 1
  Benefits/Costs of 1233 Second Street site:

  1. [First Reason] *Price of Second Street Property within proposed range (Washington Avenue price is higher, but still within range). See attached asking prices/property descriptions.*
  2. [Second Reason] *Ample space for on-site parking and greater accessibility to public transportation (Washington Avenue has latter, but no space for on-site parking). Proposed designs for both sites are attached.*
  3. [Third Reason] *Permission for late-night concerts and public events easily obtainable for Second Street location (also feasible, but riskier, for Washington Avenue).*
  4. [Fourth Reason] *Neighborhood needs and would welcome new cultural center (same holds for Washington Avenue, but with potentially greater resistance to noise/late-night events).*

Example 2
- First Reason
- Second Reason
- Third Reason
- Fourth Reason

The next section (which also could be in paragraphs or in numbered or bullet points) should present the potential counterarguments, problems, or hesitations regarding your conclusion or recommendation. If there are measures being taken to address these issues, the section should close with a summary of those measures.

Example
  Two additional sites (Plank Street and West Court) were ruled out because of zoning difficulties and unmanageable cost factors. The Second Street site has another interested buyer, but the seller believes that buyer will back out. Washington

Avenue seller is willing to accept the lower offer discussed at last meeting. We have a six-week window for the Washington Avenue property, during which we can press ahead with Second Street. We will be reconvening with neighborhood committees and City Zoning Office representatives on Wednesday, May 6.

The final paragraph or sentence should state expectations of next steps, follow-up, and/or further information or action needed.

Example
We have enclosed the proposed designs and zoning plans for both sites, with data on comparative public outreach and potential community relations. Our recommendation is that the review panel and board reconvene on Monday June 7 for site selection meeting. The later meeting date would allow for confirmation of availability of Second Street site.

Sample Cover Letter

February 8, 2003

Ms. XXX, Program Manager
GTT Corporation
19111 Wilshire Blvd.
Los Angeles, CA 90045

Dear Ms. XXX:
The opening sentence should state the purpose of the letter.

Example
I am applying for the position of Internet Marketing Assistant recently advertised in ZY *Chronicle.*

The next paragraph should describe the applicant's current and/or future availability and educational preparation for the position.

Example
I will graduate this June with a B.A. in communications and psychology from Alma Mater.

Relevant employment objectives are described in the next paragraph.

Example
My objective of combining work in the new media field with a marketing career makes this position particularly attractive to me. I am confident that my education and background have well prepared me for the demands and the responsibilities of working in this field.

The letter's next section should describe how the applicant's educational and employment background tie into the demands of the desired position.

Example
My studies in communications were enhanced by work experience as a marketing researcher for a small business in Los Angeles and an international manufacturing corporation in New York. Through my work with both companies, I gained valuable insight into the challenges facing both small and large businesses. I directed the latter corporation's expansion from direct mail to Internet sales, acquiring language and computer proficiencies well-suited to the international and technological needs of your company. Extracurricular involvement in campus theater productions and student counseling has further developed my communication skills.

Close the letter with information on enclosures and contacting.

Example
Enclosed is my résumé. Please feel free to contact me for any further information you may need. I look forward to speaking with you.

Sincerely,
Signature of Excellent Candidate
Your Mailing Address
Your Phone Number
Your e-mail address

Sample Business Memo

To: Julia J. Sacramento, Development Manager [all recipients and their job titles]
From: John Mason, Audience Services [your name]
Date: February 10, 2003
Subject: Benefit ticket prices [topic/issue in brief]

Open the memo with a statement of the context of the issue or the subject of the memo with your action taken or recommendation for future action to resolve or respond to it.

Example
Regarding our recent discussion of ticket prices for the June 15th benefit, the tiered solution that you suggested would work best. [Explain justification for action or recommendation] *However, I suggest that we increase the price for those invited to the cast party to $500 for the following reasons:* [list reasons or recommendations in bullet-point or as below]

Example
1) *Our venue for the party has a maximum capacity of 100 people.*
2) *We can guarantee a core group of donors to fill that venue (see enclosed list of donors).*
3) *We can allow for greater outreach at the lower price bracket while fulfilling the campaign goals (outreach survey enclosed).*

Close with reference to any potential follow-up, either on your part or by the reader.

I would be happy to discuss my suggestion with you in our Friday meeting.

Attach any details or supporting documentation referred to in your memo (see number 3).

Online Resources for Writers

Many universities have public Web sites (with partially restricted resources) on all types of writing. Below are several of the most accessible and helpful, but you can conduct your own Google search for other Web sites more suited to your specific needs.

Research Aids

Search engines such as Google (**www.google.com**), Yahoo (**www.yahoo.com**), or Alta Vista (**www.altavista.com**) will search and retrieve Web sites containing keywords (or subject words) in their titles and/or in their content.

The Librarians' Index to the Internet (www.lii.org) is another searchable database of Web sites scanned and accepted (but not necessarily endorsed) by a group of university librarians.

Other online and CD-ROM databases are available through most university and public libraries. The UC-Berkely library offers an excellent online tutorial on how to use the Internet in research: **www.lib.berkeley.edu/TeachingLib/Guides/Internet/Findinfo.html**.

Sites with advice and models for both academic and business writing include:

www.owl.english.purdue.edu
www.emory.edu/English/WC/writing.html
www.academicinfo.net
www.powa.org
www.engl.iastate.edu/owl/
www.indiana.edu/~wts/wts/resources.html, **a collation of various sites and articles on writing.**
www.resourcehelp.com/qserwrit.htm, a site with a guide to writing, frequently asked questions about writing, and advice for writers of all genres.
www.writerswrite.com, with information on books, publishing, and writing.

Ready-Reference Guide

The World

Nations of the World

Nation	Population (2000)	Area (sq. mi.)	Area (sq. km)	Capital
Afghanistan	26,813,057	252,000	652,680	Kabul
Albania	3,510,484	10,632	27,536	Tirana
Algeria	31,736,053	919,352	2,381,121	Algiers
Andorra	67,627	174	451	Andorra la Vella
Angola	10,366,031	481,226	1,246,375	Luanda
Antigua and Barbuda	66,970	170	440	Saint John's
Argentina	37,384,816	1,084,120	2,807,870	Buenos Aires
Armenia	3,336,100	11,490	29,759	Yerevan
Australia	19,357,594	2,974,581	7,704,164	Canberra
Austria	8,150,835	32,381	83,866	Vienna
Azerbaijan	7,771,092	33,430	86,583	Baku
Bahamas	297,852	5,353	13,864	Nassau
Bahrain	645,361	266	688	Manama
Bangladesh	131,269,860	54,501	141,157	Dhaka
Barbados	275,330	166	429	Bridgetown
Belarus	10,350,194	80,154	207,598	Minsk
Belgium	10,258,762	11,800	30,562	Brussels
Belize	256,062	8,866	22,962	Belmopan
Benin	6,590,782	44,290	114,711	Porto Novo
Bhutan	2,049,412	19,300	49,987	Thimphu
Bolivia	8,300,463	404,388	1,047,364	La Paz
Bosnia and Herzegovina	3,922,205	19,741	51,129	Sarajevo
Botswana	1,586,119	275,000	712,250	Gaborone
Brazil	174,468,575	3,286,170	8,511,180	Brasilia
Brunei	343,653	2,226	5,765	Bandar Seri Begawa

Nation	Population (2000)	Area (sq. mi.)	Area (sq. km)	Capital
Bulgaria	7,707,495	42,800	110,852	Sofia
Burkina Faso	12,272,289	106,111	274,827	Ouagadougou
Burundi	6,223,897	10,747	27,834	Bujumbura
Cambodia	12,491,501	69,866	180,952	Phnom Penh
Cameroon	15,803,220	179,558	465,055	Yaoundé
Canada	31,592,805	3,690,410	9,558,161	Ottawa
Cape Verde	405,163	1,557	4,032	Praia
Central African Republic	3,576,884	238,000	616,420	Bangui
Chad	6,707,078	501,000	1,297,590	N'Djamena
Chile	15,328,467	286,396	741,765	Santiago
China	1,273,111,290	3,691,502	9,560,990	Beijing
Colombia	40,349,388	439,828	1,139,154	Bogotá
Comoros	596,202	719	1,862	Moroni
Congo, Democratic Republic of	53,624,718	905,063	2,344,113	Kinshasa
Congo Republic	2,894,336	132,000	341,880	Brazzaville
Costa Rica	3,773,057	19,238	49,826	San José
Croatia	4,334,142	21,835	56,552	Zagreb
Cuba	11,184,023	44,200	114,478	Havana
Cyprus	762,887	3,572	9,251	Nicosia
Czech Republic	10,264,212	30,449	78,862	Prague
Denmark	5,352,815	16,576	42,931	Copenhagen
Djibouti	460,700	8,960	23,206	Djibouti
Dominica	70,766	290	751	Roseau
Dominican Republic	8,581,477	19,129	49,544	Santo Domingo
Ecuador	13,183,978	109,483	283,560	Quito
Egypt	69,536,644	386,198	1,000,252	Cairo
El Salvador	6,237,662	13,176	34,125	San Salvador
Equatorial Guinea	486,060	10,824	28,034	Malabo
Eritrea	4,298,269	47,076	121,926	Asmara
Estonia	1,423,316	17,413	45,099	Tallinn
Ethiopia	65,891,874	424,724	1,100,035	Addis Ababa
Fiji	844,330	7,078	18,332	Suva
Finland	5,175,783	130,119	337,008	Helsinki
France	59,551,227	212,736	550,986	Paris
Gabon	1,221,175	102,290	264,931	Libreville
Gambia	1,441,205	4,003	10,367	Banjul
Georgia	4,989,285	26,872	69,598	Tbilisi
Germany	83,029,536	137,852	357,036	Berlin
Ghana	19,894,014	91,843	237,873	Accra
Greece	10,623,835	50,147	129,880	Athens

Appendix

Nation	Population (2000)	Area (sq. mi.)	Area (sq. km)	Capital
Grenada	89,227	133	344	St. George's
Guatemala	12,974,361	42,042	108,888	Guatemala City
Guinea	7,613,870	96,900	250,971	Conakry
Guinea-Bissau	1,315,822	13,948	36,125	Bissau
Guyana	697,181	82,978	214,913	Georgetown
Haiti	6,964,549	10,714	27,749	Port-au-Prince
Honduras	6,406,052	43,277	112,087	Tegucigalpa
Hungary	10,106,017	35,926	93,048	Budapest
Iceland	277,906	39,709	102,846	Reykjavik
India	1,029,991,145	1246,880	3,229,419	New Delhi
Indonesia	228,437,870	741,100	1,919,449	Jakarta
Iran	66,128,965	635,000	1,644,650	Tehran
Iraq	23,331,985	172,000	445,480	Baghdad
Ireland	3,840,838	27,136	70,282	Dublin
Israel	5,938,093	7,984	20,678	Jerusalem
Italy	57,679,825	116,294	301,201	Rome
Jamaica	2,665,636	4,413	11,429	Kingston
Japan	126,771,662	141,529	366,560	Tokyo
Jordan	5,153,378	37,264	96,513	Amman
Kazakhstan	16,731,303	1,049,155	2,717,311	Akmola
Kenya	30,765,916	223,478	578,808	Nairobi
Kiribati	94,149	340	881	Tarawa
Korea, North	21,968,228	50,000	12,950	Pyongyang
South Korea	47,904,370	38,232	99,020	Seoul
Kuwait	2,041,961	8,000	20,720	Kuwait City
Kyrgyzstan	4,753,003	76,460	198,031	Bishkek
Laos	5,635,967	91,500	236,985	Vientiane
Latvia	2,385,231	25,395	65,773	Riga
Lebanon	3,627,774	3,927	10,170	Beirut
Lesotho	2,117,062	11,716	30,344	Maseru
Liberia	3,225,837	43,000	111,370	Monrovia
Libya	5,240,599	679,400	1,759,646	Tripoli
Liechtenstein	32,528	65	168	Vaduz
Lithuania	3,610,535	25,174	65,200	Vilnius
Luxembourg	442,972	999	2,587	Luxembourg
Macedonia	2,046,209	9,928	25,713	Skopje
Madagascar	15,982,563	226,657	587,041	Antananarivo
Malawi	10,548,250	49,177	127,368	Lilongwe
Malaysia	22,229,040	127,317	329,751	Kuala Lumpur
Maldives	310,764	115	297	Malé
Mali	11,008,518	478,841	1,240,198	Bamako
Malta	394,583	122	315	Valletta
Marshall Islands	70,822	70	181	Majuro
Mauritania	2,747,312	398,000	1,030,820	Nouakchott
Mauritius	1,189,825	788	2,040	Port Louis

Appendix 327

Nation	Population (2000)	Area (sq. mi.)	Area (sq. km)	Capital
Mexico	101,879,171	756,198	1,966,322	Mexico City
Micronesia	134,597	271	701	Kolonia
Moldova	4,431,570	13,100	33,929	Kishinev
Monaco	31,842	½	1.29	Monaco
Mongolia	2,654,999	600,000	1,554,000	Ulan Bator
Morocco	30,645,305	172,104	445,749	Rabat
Mozambique	19,371,057	297,731	771,123	Maputo
Myanmar (Burma)	41,734,853	261,789	678,033	Yangon
Namibia	1,797,677	317,500	822,317	Windhoek
Nauru	12,088	8	21	Yaren District
Nepal	25,284,463	54,000	139,860	Katmandu
Netherlands	15,981,472	16,163	41,862	Amsterdam
New Zealand	3,864,129	103,416	267,847	Wellington
Nicaragua	4,918,393	57,143	148,000	Managua
Niger	10,355,156	458,976	1,188,747	Niamey
Nigeria	126,635,626	356,669	923,772	Abuja
Norway	4,503,440	124,555	322,597	Oslo
Oman	2,622,198	82,800	214,452	Muscat
Pakistan	144,616,639	310,403	803,943	Islamabad
Palua	19,092	177	458	Koror
Panama	2,845,647	28,575	74,009	Panama City
Papua New Guinea	5,049,055	178,260	461,693	Port Moresby
Paraguay	5,734,139	157,047	406,751	Asunción
Peru	27,483,864	496,222	1,285,214	Lima
Philippines	82,841,518	114,830	297,409	Manila
Poland	38,633,912	121,000	313,390	Warsaw
Portugal	10,086,253	35,414	91,722	Lisbon
Qatar	769,152	8,500	22,015	Doha
Romania	22,364,022	91,654	237,383	Bucharest
Russia	145,470,197	6,593,000	17,075,870	Moscow
Rwanda	7,312,756	10,169	26,337	Kigali
St. Kitts-Nevis	38,756	104	269	Basseterre
St. Lucia	158,178	238	616	Castries
St. Vincent and the Grenadines	119,092	150	388	Kingstown
Samoa	179,058	1,133	2,934	Apia
San Marino	27,336	24	62	San Marino
São Tomé and Principe	165,034	387	1,002	São Tomé
Saudi Arabia	22,757,092	830,000	2,149,700	Riyadh
Senegal	10,284,929	76,084	197,057	Dakar
Seychelles	79,715	175	453	Victoria
Sierra Leone	5,426,618	27,925	72,325	Freetown

Appendix

Nation	Population (2000)	Area (sq. mi.)	Area (sq. km)	Capital
Singapore	4,300,419	240	621	Singapore
Slovakia	5,414,937	18,932	49,033	Bratislava
Slovenia	1,930,132	7,819	20,251	Ljubljana
Solomon Islands	480,442	11,458	29,676	Honiara
Somalia	7,488,773	246,198	637,652	Mogadishu
South Africa	43,586,097	472,000	1,222,480	Pretoria, Cape Town, Bloemfontain
Spain	40,037,995	194,988	505,018	Madrid
Sri Lanka	19,408,635	25,332	65,609	Colombo
Sudan	36,080,373	967,500	2,505,825	Khartoum
Suriname	433,998	63,251	163,820	Paramaribo
Swaziland	1,104,343	6,704	17,363	Mbabane
Sweden	8,875,053	173,394	449,090	Stockholm
Switzerland	7,283,274	15,944	41,294	Bern
Syria	16,728,808	71,227	184,477	Damascus
Taiwan	22,370,461	12,400	32,116	Taipei
Tajikistan	6,578,681	55,240	143,071	Dushanbe
Tanzania	36,232,074	363,950	942,630	Dodoma
Thailand	61,797,751	198,242	513,446	Bangkok
Togo	5,153,086	21,830	56,539	Lomé
Trinidad and Tobago	1,169,682	1,980	5,128	Port-of-Spain
Tunisia	9,705,102	48,330	125,174	Tunis
Turkey	66,493,970	300,948	779,455	Ankara
Turkmenistan	4,603,244	188,417	488,000	Ashgabat
Tuvalu	10,991	10	26	Funafuti Atoll
Uganda	23,985,712	91,343	236,578	Kampala
Ukraine	48,760,474	233,090	603,703	Kiev
United Arab Emirates	2,407,460	32,300	83,657	Abu Dhabi
United Kingdom	59,647,790	94,242	244,086	London
United States	278,058,881	3,615,122	9,363,165	Washington, D.C.
Uruguay	3,360,105	172,172	445,925	Montevideo
Uzbekistan	25,155,064	172,741	447,399	Tashkent
Vanuatu	192,910	5,700	14,763	Vila
Vatican City	870	108.8 acres	44 hectares	
Venezuela	23,916,810	352,143	912,050	Caracas
Vietnam	79,939,014	126,104	326,609	Hanoi
Yemen	18,078,036	207,000	536,130	Sanaa
Yugoslavia	10,677,290	39,449	102,172	Belgrade
Zambia	9,770,199	290,585	752,615	Lusaka
Zimbabwe	11,365,366	150,804	390,582	Harare

Continents

Name	Area (sq. mi.)	Area (sq. km)	Population (2000)
Asia	17,000,000	44,030,000	3,688,000,000
Africa	11,700,000	30,303,000	805,000,000
North America	9,400,000	24,346,000	481,000,000
South America	6,900,000	17,871,000	347,000,000
Antarctica	5,100,000	13,209,000	—
Europe	4,063,000	10,523,170	729,000,000
Australia	2,966,000	7,681,940	31,000,000

Great Oceans and Seas of the World

Ocean or Sea	Area (sq. mi.)	Area (sq. km)	Location
Pacific Ocean	70,000,000	181,300,000	Bounded by N and S America, Asia, and Australia
Atlantic Ocean	31,530,000	81,663,000	Bounded by N and S America, Europe, and Africa
Indian Ocean	28,357,000	73,444,630	S of Asia, E of Africa, and W of Australia
Arctic Ocean	5,540,000	14,350,000	N of North America, Asia, and the Arctic Circle
Mediterranean Sea	1,145,000	2,965,550	Between Europe, Africa, and Asia
South China Sea	895,000	2,318,050	Part of N Pacific, off coast of SE Asia
Bering Sea	878,000	2,274,000	Part of N Pacific, between N America and N Asia
Caribbean Sea	750,000	1,943,000	Between Central America, West Indies, and S America
Gulf of Mexico	700,000	1,813,000	Arm of N Atlantic, off SE coast of North America
Sea of Okhotsk	582,000	1,507,380	Arm of N Pacific, off E coast of Asia

Appendix

Ocean or Sea	Area (sq. mi.)	Area (sq. km)	Location
East China Sea	480,000	1,243,200	Part of N Pacific, off E coast of Asia
Yellow Sea	480,000	1,243,200	Part of N Pacific, off E coast of Asia
Sea of Japan	405,000	1,048,950	Arm of N Pacific, between Asia mainland and Japanese Isles
Hudson Bay	400,000	1,036,000	N America
Andaman Sea	300,000	777,000	Part of Bay of Bengal (Indian Ocean), off S coast of Asia
North Sea	201,000	520,600	Arm of N Atlantic, off coast of NW Europe
Red Sea	170,000	440,300	Arm of Indian Ocean, between N Africa and Arabian Peninsula
Black Sea	164,000	424,760	SE Europe-SW Asia
Baltic Sea	160,000	414,000	N Europe
Persian Gulf	92,200	238,800	Between Iran and Arabian Peninsula
Gulf of St. Lawrence	92,000	238,280	Arm of N Atlantic, between mainland of SE Canada and Newfoundland
Gulf of California	62,600	162,100	Arm of N Pacific, between W coast of Mexico and peninsula of Lower California

Notable Mountain Peaks

Name	Country or Region	Altitude (feet)	Altitude (meters)
Mt. Everest	Nepal-Tibet	29,028	8,848
K2	Kashmir	28,250	8,611
Kanchenjunga	Nepal-Sikkim	28,146	8,579
Makalu	Nepal-Tibet	27,790	8,470
Dhaulagiri	Nepal	26,826	8,180
Nanga Parbat	Kashmir	26,660	8,125
Annapurna	Nepal	26,503	8,078

Name	Country or Region	Altitude (feet)	Altitude (meters)
Gasherbrum	Kashmir	26,470	8,068
Gosainthan	Tibet	26,291	8,013
Nanda Devi	India	25,661	7,820
Tirich Mir	Pakistan	25,230	7,690
Muztagh Ata	China	24,757	7,546
Ismail Semani Peak	Tajikistan	24,590	7,495
Pobeda Peak	Kyrgyzstan-China	24,406	7,439
Lenin Peak	Kyrgyzstan-Tajikistan	23,382	7,127
Aconcagua	Argentina	22,834	6,960
Huascarán	Peru	22,205	6,768
Illimani	Bolivia	21,188	6,458
Chimborazo	Ecuador	20,702	6,310
Mt. McKinley	United States (Alaska)	20,320	6,194
Mt. Logan	Canada (Yukon)	19,850	6,050
Cotopaxi	Ecuador	19,498	5,943
Kilimanjaro	Tanzania	19,321	5,889
El Misti	Peru	19,200	5,880
Demavend	Iran	18,606	5,671
Orizaba (Citlaltepetl)	Mexico	18,546	5,653
Mt. Elbrus	Russian Federation	18,465	5,628
Popocatépetl	Mexico	17,887	5,450
Ixtacc'huatl	Mexico	17,342	5,286
Mt. Kenya	Kenya	17,040	5,194
Ararat	Turkey	16,945	5,165
Mt. Ngaliema (Mt. Stanley)	Zaire-Uganda	16,790	5,119
Mont Blanc	France	15,781	4,810
Mt. Wilhelm	Papua New Guinea	15,400	4,694
Monte Rosa	Italy-Switzerland	15,217	4,638
Mt. Kirkpatrick	Antarctica	14,855	4,528
Weisshorn	Switzerland	14,804	4,512
Matterhorn	Switzerland	14,780	4,505
Mt. Whitney	United States (California)	14,495	4,418
Mt. Elbert	United States (Colorado)	14,431	4,399
Mt. Rainier	United States (Washington)	14,408	4,392
Longs Peak	United States (Colorado)	14,255	4,345

332   Appendix

Name	Country or Region	Altitude (feet)	Altitude (meters)
Mt. Shasta	United States (California)	14,161	4,315
Pikes Peak	United States (Colorado)	14,108	4,300
Mauna Kea	United States (Hawaii)	13,784	4,201
Grand Teton	United States (Wyoming)	13,766	4,196
Mauna Loa	United States (Hawaii)	13,680	4,170
Jungfrau	Switzerland	13,668	4,166
Mt. Victoria	Papua New Guinea	13,240	4,036
Mt. Erebus	Antarctica	13,202	4,024
Eiger	Switzerland	13,025	3,970
Mt. Robson	Canada (B.C.)	12,972	3,954
Mt. Fuji	Japan	12,395	3,778
Mt. Cook	New Zealand	12,349	3,764
Mt. Hood	United States (Oregon)	11,253	3,430
Mt. Etna	Italy	10,758	3,280
Lassen Peak	United States (California)	10,465	3,190
Haleakala	United States (Hawaii)	10,032	3,058
Mt. Olympus	Greece	9,730	2,966
Mt. Kosciusko	Australia	7,316	2,230

World Time Differences

Amsterdam	6:00 p.m.
Athens	7:00 p.m.
Bangkok	Midnight
Berlin	6:00 p.m.
Bombay	10:30 p.m.
Brussels	6:00 p.m.
Buenos Aires	2:00 p.m.
Cape Town	7:00 p.m.
Dublin	5:00 p.m.
Havana	Noon
Istanbul	7:00 p.m.
Lima	Noon

Appendix 333

London	5:00 p.m.
Los Angeles	9:00 a.m.
Madrid	6:00 p.m.
Manila	1:00 a.m.*
Mexico City	6:00 p.m.
Montreal	Noon
Moscow	8:00 p.m.
New York City	Noon
Paris	6:00 p.m.
Prague	6:00 p.m.
Rio de Janeiro	2:00 p.m.
Rome	6:00 p.m.
Shanghai	1:00 a.m.*
Stockholm	6:00 p.m.
Sydney (N.S.W.)	3:00 a.m.*
Tokyo	2:00 a.m.*
Vienna	6:00 p.m.
Warsaw	6:00 p.m.
Zurich	6:00 p.m.

U.S. Time Differences

Atlanta	Noon	Los Angeles	9:00 a.m.
Baltimore	Noon	Memphis	11:00 a.m.
Boston	Noon	Miami	Noon
Buffalo	Noon	Milwaukee	11:00 a.m.
Chicago	11:00 a.m.	Minneapolis	11:00 a.m.
Cincinnati	Noon	Nashville	11:00 a.m.
Cleveland	Noon	New York	Noon
Columbus	Noon	New Orleans	11:00 a.m.
Dallas	11:00 a.m.	Omaha	11:00 a.m.
Denver	10:00 a.m.	Philadelphia	Noon
Des Moines	11:00 a.m.	Phoenix	10:00 a.m.
Detroit	Noon	Pittsburgh	Noon
El Paso	10:00 a.m.	Salt Lake City	10:00 a.m.
Honolulu	7:00 a.m.	San Diego	9:00 a.m.
Houston	11:00 a.m.	San Francisco	9:00 a.m.
Indianapolis	Noon	Seattle	9:00 a.m.
Juneau	8:00 a.m.	St. Louis	11:00 a.m.
Kansas City	11:00 a.m.	Washington, D.C.	Noon

*the next day

Appendix

Facts About the United States

State	Population (2000)	Area (sq. mi.)	Capital
Alabama	4,447,100	51,609	Montgomery
Alaska	626,932	586,400	Juneau
Arizona	5,130,632	113,909	Phoenix
Arkansas	2,673,400	53,103	Little Rock
California	33,871,648	158,693	Sacramento
Colorado	4,301,261	104,247	Denver
Connecticut	3,405,565	5,009	Hartford
Delaware	783,600	2,057	Dover
Florida	15,982,378	58,560	Tallahassee
Georgia	8,186,453	58,876	Atlanta
Hawaii	1,211,537	6,424	Honolulu
Idaho	1,293,953	83,557	Boise
Illinois	12,419,293	56,400	Springfield
Indiana	6,080,485	36,291	Indianapolis
Iowa	2,926,324	56,290	Des Moines
Kansas	2,688,418	82,276	Topeka
Kentucky	4,041,769	40,395	Frankfort
Louisiana	4,468,976	48,522	Baton Rouge
Maine	1,274,923	33,215	Augusta
Maryland	5,296,486	10,577	Annapolis
Massachusetts	6,349,0976	8,257	Boston
Michigan	9,938,444	58,216	Lansing
Minnesota	4,919,479	84,068	St. Paul
Mississippi	2,844,658	47,716	Jackson
Missouri	5,595,211	69,674	Jefferson City
Montana	902,195	147,138	Helena
Nebraska	1,711,263	77,237	Lincoln
Nevada	1,998,257	110,540	Carson City
New Hampshire	1,235,780	9,304	Concord
New Jersey	8,414,350	7,836	Trenton
New Mexico	1,819,046	121,666	Santa Fe
New York	18,976,457	49,576	Albany
North Carolina	8,049,313	52,586	Raleigh
North Dakota	642,200	70,665	Bismarck
Ohio	11,353,140	41,222	Columbus
Oklahoma	3,450,654	69,919	Oklahoma City
Oregon	3,421,399	96,981	Salem
Pennsylvania	12,281,054	45,333	Harrisburg
Rhode Island	1,048,319	1,214	Providence

State	Population (2000)	Area (sq. mi.)	Capital
South Carolina	4,012,012	31,055	Columbia
South Dakota	754,844	77,047	Pierre
Tennessee	5,689,283	42,246	Nashville
Texas	20,851,820	267,339	Austin
Utah	2,233,169	84,916	Salt Lake City
Vermont	608,827	9,609	Montpelier
Virginia	7,078,515	40,815	Richmond
Washington	5,894,121	68,192	Olympia
West Virginia	1,808,344	24,181	Charleston
Wisconsin	5,363,375	56,154	Madison
Wyoming	493,782	97,914	Cheyenne
Washington, D.C.	572,059	63	—
Total U.S.	278,058,881		

Major U.S. Cities

Rank	City	State	Population
1	New York City	New York	8,008,278
2	Los Angeles	California	3,694,742
3	Chicago	Illinois	2,896,047
4	Houston	Texas	1,953,633
5	Philadelphia	Pennsylvania	1,517,550
6	Phoenix	Arizona	1,321,190
7	San Diego	California	1,223,416
8	Dallas	Texas	1,188,589
9	San Antonio	Texas	1,151,268
10	Detroit	Michigan	951,270
11	San Jose	California	895,005
12	Indianapolis	Indiana	781,870
13	San Francisco	California	776,733
14	Jacksonville	Florida	735,617
15	Columbus	Ohio	711,548
16	Austin	Texas	656,562
18	Baltimore	Maryland	651,154
17	Memphis	Tennessee	650,100
19	Milwaukee	Wisconsin	596,974
20	Boston	Massachusetts	589,141
21	Washington	District of Columbia	572,059
22	El Paso	Texas	563,657
23	Seattle	Washington	563,372
24	Charlotte	North Carolina	558,549

Rank	City	State	Population
25	Denver	Colorado	554,636
26	Nashville-Davidson	Tennessee	545,534
27	Fort Worth	Texas	539,167
28	Portland	Oregon	529,148
29	Oklahoma City	Oklahoma	506,129
30	Tucson	Arizona	487,285
31	New Orleans	Louisiana	484,674
32	Las Vegas	Nevada	479,644
33	Cleveland	Ohio	477,459
34	Long Beach	California	461,522
35	Albuquerque	New Mexico	448,607
36	Kansas City	Missouri	441,545
37	Fresno	California	428,806
38	Virginia Beach	Virginia	425,257
39	Atlanta	Georgia	416,267
40	Sacramento	California	407,018
41	Oakland	California	399,484
42	Mesa	Arizona	397,763
43	Tulsa	Oklahoma	393,120
44	Omaha	Nebraska	390,159
45	Minneapolis	Minnesota	382,618
46	Honolulu	Hawaii	371,657
47	Miami	Florida	362,470
48	Colorado Springs	Colorado	360,979
49	Wichita	Kansas	351,028
50	St. Louis	Missouri	348,189
51	Santa Ana	California	337,977
52	Pittsburgh	Pennsylvania	334,563
53	Arlington	Texas	332,969
54	Cincinnati	Ohio	331,285
55	Anaheim	California	328,071
56	Toledo	Ohio	313,782
57	Tampa	Florida	303,463
58	Buffalo	New York	292,648
59	St. Paul	Minnesota	287,151
60	Raleigh	North Carolina	281,915
61	Corpus Christi	Texas	277,492
62	Aurora	Colorado	275,922
63	Newark	New Jersey	272,537
64	Lexington-Fayette	Kentucky	260,512
65	Anchorage	Alaska	260,283
66	Louisville	Kentucky	256,231

Rank	City	State	Population
67	Riverside	California	255,175
68	St. Petersburg	Florida	248,408
69	Stockton	California	243,771
70	Bakersfield	California	243,072
71	Birmingham	Alabama	242,820
72	Jersey City	New Jersey	240,055
73	Norfolk	Virginia	234,403
74	Baton Rouge	Louisiana	228,518
75	Hialeah	Florida	226,419
76	Lincoln	Nebraska	225,640
77	Greensboro	North Carolina	224,035
78	Plano	Texas	222,008
79	Rochester	New York	219,773
80	Glendale	Arizona	218,815
81	Akron	Ohio	217,074
82	Garland	Texas	215,794
83	Fort Wayne	Indiana	210,415
84	Madison	Wisconsin	208,126
85	Fremont	California	203,413
86	Scottsdale	Arizona	202,736
87	Montgomery	Alabama	201,587
88	Shreveport	Louisiana	200,114
89	Lubbock	Texas	199,572
90	Chesapeake	Virginia	199,184
91	Des Moines	Iowa	198,709
92	Grand Rapids	Michigan	197,800
93	Richmond	Virginia	197,790
94	Yonkers	New York	196,086
95	Spokane	Washington	195,629
96	Glendale	California	194,973
97	Tacoma	Washington	193,556
98	Modesto	California	188,856
99	Chandler	Arizona	176,652
100	Henderson	Nevada	175,750

*Source: U.S. Census Bureau

Distances Between U.S. Cities

	Atlanta	Chicago	Dallas	Denver	Los Angeles	New York	St. Louis	Seattle
Atlanta,	—	710	820	1,430	2,190	850	570	2,630
Boston,	1,110	1,000	1,750	2,000	3,020	210	1,210	3,020
Chicago,	710	—	920	1,020	2,050	810	290	2,050
Cincinnati,		Not covered						
Cleveland,	730	350	1,190	1,360	2,380	470	580	2,390
Dallas,	738	920	—	780	1,400	1,560	660	2,130
Denver,	1,430	1,020	780	—	1,030	1,790	860	1,340
Detroit,	730	280	1,160	1,280	2,290	650	530	2,330
El Paso,	1,440	1,460	620	690	820	2,150	1,180	1,170
Kansas City,	820	540	510	620	1,580	1,230	260	1,860
Los Angeles,	2,190	2,050	1,400	1,030	—	2,790	1,840	1,130
Miami,	660	1,400	1,340	2,110	2,720	1,330	1,230	3,300
Minneapolis,	1,120	410	950	920	1,860	1,230	630	1,650
New Orleans,	480	920	520	1,280	1,860	1,340	700	2,690
New York,	850	810	1,560	1,790	2,790	—	980	2,840
Omaha,	1,010	480	660	540	1,570	1,250	440	1,690
Philadelphia,	750	790	1,440	1,740	2,700	110	900	2,820
Pittsburgh,	680	480	1,210	1,430	2,430	380	610	2,520
St. Louis,	570	290	660	860	1,840	980	—	2,140
San Francisco,	2,480	2,170	1,750	1,260	390	2,930	2,120	810
Seattle	2,630	2,050	2,130	1,340	1,130	2,040	2,140	—
Washington, D.C.,	620	780	1,310	1,620	2,650	240	860	2,720

Major American Holidays

Holiday	Date
New Year's Day	January 1
Martin Luther King Day	Third Monday in January
President's Day	Third Monday in February
Memorial Day	Last Monday in May
Independence Day	July 4
Labor Day	First Monday in September
Columbus Day	October 12
Veterans Day	November 11
Election Day	Tuesday after first Monday in November
Thanksgiving Day	Fourth Thursday in November
Christmas Day	December 25

Presidents of the United States

Name (and party)	State of birth	Born	Term	Died
George Washington (F)	Va.	1732	1789–1797	1799
John Adams (F)	Mass.	1735	1797–1801	1826
Thomas Jefferson (D-R)	Va.	1743	1801–1809	1826
James Madison (D-R)	Va.	1751	1809–1817	1836
James Monroe (D-R)	Va.	1758	1817–1825	1831
John Quincy Adams (D-R)	Mass.	1767	1825–1829	1848
Andrew Jackson (D)	S.C.	1767	1829–1837	1845
Martin Van Buren (D)	N.Y.	1782	1837–1841	1862
William Henry Harrison (W)	Va.	1773	1841–1841	1841
John Tyler (W)	Va.	1790	1841–1845	1862
James Knox Polk (D)	N.C.	1795	1845–1849	1849
Zachary Taylor (W)	Va.	1784	1849–1850	1850
Millard Fillmore (W)	N.Y.	1800	1850–1853	1874
Franklin Pierce (D)	N.H.	1804	1853–1857	1869
James Buchanan (D)	Pa.	1791	1857–1861	1868
Abraham Lincoln (R)	Ky.	1809	1861–1865	1865
Andrew Johnson (R)	N.C.	1808	1865–1869	1875
Ulysses S. Grant (R)	Ohio	1822	1869–1877	1885
Rutherford Birchard Hayes (R)	Ohio	1822	1877–1881	1893
James Abram Garfield (R)	Ohio	1831	1881–1881	1881
Chester Alan Arthur (R)	Vt.	1830	1881–1885	1886
Grover Cleveland (D)	N.J.	1837	1885–1889	1908
Benjamin Harrison (R)	Ohio	1833	1889–1893	1901
Grover Cleveland (D)	N.J.	1837	1893–1897	1908
William McKinley (R)	Ohio	1843	1897–1901	1901
Theodore Roosevelt (R)	N.Y.	1858	1901–1909	1919
William Howard Taft (R)	Ohio	1857	1909–1913	1930
Woodrow Wilson (D)	Va.	1856	1913–1921	1924
Warren Gamaliel Harding (R)	Ohio	1865	1921–1923	1923
Calvin Coolidge (R)	Vt.	1872	1923–1929	1933
Herbert Clark Hoover (R)	Iowa	1874	1929–1933	1964
Franklin Delano Roosevelt (D)	N.Y.	1882	1933–1945	1945
Harry S. Truman (D)	Mo.	1884	1945–1953	1972

F-Federalist; D-Democrat; R-Republican; W-Whig

Appendix

Name (and party)	State of birth	Born	Term	Died
Dwight D. Eisenhower (R)	Tex.	1890	1953–1961	1969
John Fitzgerald Kennedy (D)	Mass.	1917	1961–1963	1963
Lyndon Baines Johnson (D)	Tex.	1908	1963–1969	1973
Richard Milhous Nixon (R)	Cal.	1913	1969–1974	1994
Gerald R. Ford (R)	Neb.	1913	1974–1977	
James Earl Carter, Jr. (D)	Ga.	1924	1977–1981	
Ronald Wilson Reagan (R)	Ill.	1911	1981–1989	
George H. W. Bush (R)	Mass.	1924	1989–1993	
William J. Clinton (D)	Ark.	1946	1993–2000	
George W. Bush (R)	Conn.	1946	2001–	

Space

Planets of the Solar System

	Distance from Sun in Miles	Mean Diameter in Miles	Number of Satellites
Mercury	36,000,000	3,000	1
Venus	67,000,000	7,600	1
Earth	93,000,000	7,900	1
Mars	141,000,000	4,200	2
Jupiter	489,000,000	87,000	58
Saturn	886,000,000	72,000	30
Uranus	1,782,000,000	31,000	21
Neptune	2,793,000,000	33,000	11
Pluto	3,670,000,000	1,900	1

First-Magnitude Stars (In Order of Brightness)

	Distance in Light-Years*
Sirius	8.6
Vega	26
Capella	43
Arcturus	40
Rigel	540

*Light-year = 5,880,000,000,000 miles

	Distance in Light-Years*
Procyon	10.4
Altair	16
Betelgeuse	190
Aldebaren	57
Spica	360
Pollux	32
Antares	125
Fomalhaut	24
Deneb	650
Regulus	56

Forms of Address

The forms of address shown below cover most of the commonly encountered problems in letter writing or correspondence. Although there are many alternative forms, the ones given here are generally preferred in conventional usage. *Salutation*, below, refers to the opening of a letter, e.g., Dear John Doe:

As a complimentary ending to a letter, use "Sincerely yours," but, when particular formality is preferred, use "Very truly yours."

Government (U.S)

Title	Address	Salutation
President	The President The White House Washington, D.C. 20500	Dear Mr. or Madam President:
Vice President	The Vice President United States Senate Washington, D.C. 20510	Dear Mr. or Madam Vice President:
Cabinet Member	The Honorable (full name) Secretary of (name of Dep't) Washington, D.C. (zip code of Dep't)	Dear Mr. or Madam Secretary:
Attorney General	The Honorable (full name) Attorney General Washington, D.C. 20530	Dear Mr. or Madam Attorney General:

Title	Address	Salutation
Senator	The Honorable (full name) United States Senate Washington, D.C. 20510	Dear Senator (last name):
Representative	The Honorable (full name) House of Representatives Washington, D.C. 20515	Dear Mr. or Madam (last name):
Chief Justice	The Chief Justice of the United States The Supreme Court of the United States Washington, D.C. 20543	Dear Mr. or Madam Chief Justice:
Associate Justice	Mr. or Madam The Supreme Court of the United States Washington, D.C. 20543	Dear Mr. or Madam Associate Justice (last name):
Judge of a Federal Court	The Honorable (full name) Judge of the (name of court; if a district court, give district) (Local address of court)	Dear Judge (last name):

Religious Leaders

Title	Address	Salutation
Minister, Pastor, Rector	The Reverend (full name) (Title), (name of church) (Local address)	Dear (Mr., Ms., Miss, or Mrs.) (surname)
Rabbi	Rabbi (full name) (local address)	Dear Rabbi (surname):
Catholic Cardinal	His Eminence (first name) Cardinal (last name)	**Formal:** Your Eminence: **Informal:** Dear

Title	Address	Salutation
Catholic Archbishop	The Most Reverend (full name) Archbishop of (province) (surname):	**Formal:** Your Excellency: **Informal:** Dear Archbishop (Local address)
Catholic Bishop	The Most Reverend (full name) Bishop of (province) (Local address)	**Formal:** Your Excellency: **Informal:** Dear Bishop (surname):
Catholic Monsignor	The Reverend Monsignor (full name)	**Formal:** Reverend Sir or Madam: **Informal:** Dear Monsignor (surname):
Catholic Priest	The Reverend (full name), (initials of order, if any) (Local address)	**Formal:** Reverend Sir: **Informal:** Dear Father (surname):
Catholic Sister	Sister (full name) (name of organization) (Local address)	Dear Sister (full name):
Catholic Brother	Brother (full name) (Name of organization) (Local address)	Dear Brother (given name):
Protestant Episcopal Bishop	The Right Reverend (full name) Bishop of (name) (Local address)	**Formal:** Right Reverend Sir or Madam: **Informal:** Dear Bishop (surname):
Protestant Episcopal Dean	The Very Reverend (full name) Dean of (church) (Local address)	**Formal:** Very Reverend Sir or Madam: **Informal:** Dear Dean (surname):
Methodist Bishop	The Reverend (full name) (Local address)	**Formal:** Reverend Sir or Madam: **Informal:** Dear Bishop (surname):
Mormon Bishop	Bishop (full name) Church of Jesus Christ of Latter-day Saints (Local address)	**Formal:** Sir: **Informal:** Dear Bishop (surname):

Miscellaneous

Title	Address	Salutation
President of a university or college	(Dr., Mr., Ms., Miss, or Mrs.) (full name) President, (Name of institution) (Local address)	Dear (Dr., Mr., Ms., Miss, or Mrs.) (surname):
Dean of a college or school	Dean (full name) School of (name) (Name of institution) (Local address)	Dear Dean (surname):
Professor	Professor (full name) Department of (name) (Name of institution) (Local address)	Dear Professor (surname):

Alphabetical List of the Elements

Name	Symbol	Atomic No.	Atomic Mass*	Name	Symbol	Atomic No.	Atomic Mass*
Actinium	Ac	89	(227)	Neodymium	Nd	60	144.24
Aluminum	Al	13	26.98154	Neon	Ne	10	20.18
Americium	Am	95	(243)	Neptunium	Np	93	(237)
Antimony	Sb	51	121.75	Nickel	Ni	28	58.71
Argon	Ar	18	39.948	Niobium	Nb	41	92.9064
Arsenic	As	33	74.9216	Nitrogen	N	7	14.0067
Astatine	At	85	(210)	Nobelium	No	102	(256)
Barium	Ba	56	137.34	Osmium	Os	76	190.2
Berkelium	Bk	97	(247)	Oxygen	O	8	15.999
Beryllium	Be	4	9.01218	Palladium	Pd	46	106.4
Bismuth	Bi	83	208.9808	Phosphorus	P	15	30.97376
Bohrium	Bh	107	(264)	Platinum	Pt	78	195.09
Boron	B	5	10.81	Plutonium	Pu	94	(242)
Bromine	Br	35	79.904	Polonium	Po	84	(210)
Cadmium	Cd	48	112.41	Potassium	K	19	39.098
Calcium	Ca	20	40.08	Praseodymium	Pr	59	140.907
Californium	Cf	98	(249)	Promethium	Pm	61	(147)
Carbon	C	6	12.011	Protactinium	Pa	91	(231)

*Approx. values for radioactive elements given in parentheses.

Name	Symbol	Atomic No.	Atomic Mass*	Name	Symbol	Atomic No.	Atomic Mass*
Cerium	Ce	58	140.12	Radium	Ra	88	(226)
Cesium	Cs	55	132.9054	Radon	Rn	86	(222)
Chlorine	Cl	17	35.453	Rhenium	Re	75	186.2
Chromium	Cr	24	51.996	Rhodium	Rh	45	102.9055
Cobalt	Co	27	58.9332	Rubidium	Rb	37	85.468
Copper	Cu	29	63.546	Ruthenium	Ru	44	101.07
Curium	Cm	96	(247)	Rutherfordium	Rf	104	(261)
Dubnium	Db	105	(262)	Samarium	Sm	62	150.4
Dysprosium	Dy	66	162.50	Scandium	Sc	21	44.9559
Einsteinium	Es	99	(254)	Seaborgium	Sg	106	(266)
Erbium	Er	68	167.26	Silicon	Si	14	28.086
Selenium	Se	34	78.96	Silver	Ag	47	107.87
Europium	Eu	63	151.96	Sodium	Na	11	22.9898
Fermium	Fm	100	(253)	Strontium	Sr	38	87.62
Fluorine	F	9	18.99840	Sulfur	S	16	32.06
Francium	Fr	87	(223)	Tantalum	Ta	73	180.948
Gadolinium	Gd	64	157.25	Technetium	Tc	43	(99)
Gallium	Ga	31	69.72	Tellurium	Te	52	127.60
Germanium	Ge	32	72.59	Terbium	Tb	65	158.9254
Gold	Au	79	196.967	Thallium	T1	81	204.32
Hafnium	Hf	72	178.49	Thorium	Th	90	232.0381
Hassium	Hs	108	(296)	Thulium	Tm	69	168.9342
Helium	He	2	4.00260	Tin	Sn	50	118.69
Holmium	Ho	67	164.9304	Titanium	Ti	22	47.9
Hydrogen	H	1	1.0079	Tungsten	W	74	183.85
Indium	In	49	114.82	Unnilhexium	Unh	106	(263)
Iodine	I	53	126.9045	Unnilpentium	Unp	105	(260)
Iridium	Ir	77	192.2	Unnilquadium	Unq	104	(257)
Iron	Fe	26	55.847	Unnilseptium	Uns	107	(262)
Krypton	Kr	36	83.80	Uranium	U	92	238.03
Lanthanum	La	57	138.91	Vanadium	V	23	50.941
Lawrencium	Lr	103	(257)	Xenon	Xe	54	131.30
Lead	Pb	82	207.2	Ytterbium	Yb	70	173.04
Lithium	Li	3	6.94	Yttrium	Y	39	88.9059
Luletium	Lu	71	174.97	Zinc	Zn	30	65.38
Magnesium	Mg	12	24.305	Zirconium	Zr	40	91.22
Manganese	Mn	25	54.9380	Mendelevium	Md	101	(256)
Mercury	Hg	50	200.59	Molybdenum	Mo	42	95.94

Weights and Measures

Weight/Measurement	Equivalents
Troy Weight	24 grains = 1 pennyweight
	20 pennyweights = 1 ounce
	12 ounces = 1 pound

Weight/Measurement   *Equivalents*

Avoirdupois Weight
27 11/32 grains = 1 dram
16 drams = 1 ounce
16 ounces = 1 pound
100 pounds = 1 short cwt (hundredweight)
20 short cwt = 1 short ton

Apothecaries' Weight
20 grains = 1 scruple
3 scruples = 1 dram
8 drams = 1 ounce
12 ounces = 1 pound

Linear Measure
12 inches = 1 foot
3 feet = 1 yard
5½ yards = 1 rod
40 rods = 1 furlong
8 furlongs (5,280 feet) = 1 statute mile

Mariners' Measure
6 feet = 1 fathom
1,000 fathoms = 1 nautical mile (approx.)
3 nautical miles = 1 league

Apothecaries' Fluid Measure
60 minims = 1 fluid dram
8 fluid drams = 1 fluid ounce
16 fluid ounces = 1 pint
2 pints = 1 quart
4 quarts = 1 gallon

Square Measure
144 square inches = 1 square foot
9 square feet = 1 square yard
30¼ square yards = 1 square rod
160 square rods = 1 acre
640 acres = 1 square mile

Cubic Measure
1,728 cubic inches = 1 cubic foot
27 cubic feet = 1 cubic yard

Surveyors' Measure
7.92 inches = 1 link
100 links = 1 chain

Liquid Measure
4 gills = 1 pint
2 pints = 1 quart
4 quarts = 1 gallon

Weight/Measurement	Equivalents
	31½ gallons = 1 barrel
	2 barrels = 1 hogshead
Dry Measure	2 pints = 1 quart
	8 quarts = 1 peck
	4 pecks = 1 bushel
Wood Measure	16 cubic feet = 1 cord foot
	8 cord feet = 1 cord
Angular and Circular Measure	60 seconds = 1 minute
	60 minutes = 1 degree
	90 degrees = 1 right angle
	180 degrees = 1 straight angle
	360 degrees = 1 circle

Metric System

The metric system is a decimal system of weights and measures, adopted first in France, but now widespread throughout the world. It is universally used in science, mandatory for use for all purposes in a large number of countries, and permitted for use in most (as in the United States and Great Britain).

The basic units are the *meter* (39.37 inches) for length, and the *gram* (.035 ounces) for mass or weight. Derived units are the *liter* (0.908 U.S. dry quart, or 1.0567 U.S. liquid quart) for capacity, being the volume of 1,000 grams of water under specified conditions, the *are* (119.6 square yards) for area, being the area of a square 10 meters on a side, and the stere (35.315 cubic feet) for volume, being the volume of a cube 1 meter on a side, the term stere being, however, usually restricted to measuring firewood.

Names for units larger and smaller than the above are formed from the above names by the use of the following prefixes:

Kilo = 1,000   deka = 10   centi = 0.01
Hecto = 100   deci = 0.1   milli = 0.001

To these can be added mega = 1,000,000, myria = 10,000, and micro = 0.000001. Not all the possible units are in common use. In many countries names of old units are applied to roughly similar metric units.

Weight/Measurement	Equivalents
Linear Measure	10 millimeters = 1 centimeter
	10 centimeters = 1 decimeter
	10 decimeters = 1 meter
	10 meters = 1 dekameter
	10 dekameters = 1 hectometer
	10 hectometers = 1 kilometer
Square Measure	100 sq. millimeters = 1 sq. centimeter
	100 sq. centimeters = 1 sq. decimeter
	100 sq. decimeters = 1 sq. meter
	100 sq. meters = 1 sq. dekameter
	100 sq. dekameters = 1 sq. hectometer
	100 sq. hectometers = 1 sq. kilometer
Cubic Measure	1,000 cu. millimeters = 1 cu. centimeter
	1,000 cu. centimeters = 1 cu. decimeter
	1,000 cu. decimeters = 1 cu. meter
Liquid Measure	10 milliliters = 1 centiliter
	10 centiliters = 1 deciliter
	10 deciliters = 1 liter
	10 liters = 1 dekaliter
	10 dekaliters = 1 hectoliter
	10 hectoliters = 1 kiloliter
Weights	10 milligrams = 1 centigram
	10 centigrams = 1 decigram
	10 decimgrams = 1 gram
	10 grams = 1 dekagram
	10 dekagrams = 1 hectogram
	10 hectograms = 1 kilogram
	100 kilograms = 1 quintal
	10 quintals = 1 ton

Signs and Symbols

Astrology

Signs of the Zodiac

Symbol	Name
♈	Aries, the Ram
♉	Taurus, the Bull
♊	Gemini, the Twins
♋	Cancer, the Crab
♌	Leo, the Lion
♍	Virgo, the Virgin
♎	Libra, the Scales
♏	Scorpio, the Scorpion
♐	Sagittarius, the Archer
♑	Capricorn, the Goat
♒	Aquarius, the Water Bearer
♓	Pisces, the Fishes

Astronomy

Astronomical Bodies

Symbol	Name(s)
☉	1. the sun. 2. Sunday.
☽ ●	1. the moon. 2. Monday.
●●	new moon.
☽) ☽ ●	the moon, first quarter.
○⊕	full moon.
☾ ☾ ☾ ●	the moon, last quarter.
☿	1. Mercury. 2. Wednesday.
♀	1. Venus. 2. Friday.
⊕ ♁ ⊖	Earth.
♂	1. Mars. 2. Tuesday.
♃	1. Jupiter. 2. Thursday.
♄	1. Saturn. 2. Saturday.
♅ ♆	Uranus.
♆	Neptune.
♇	Pluto.
✶✷	star.
☄	comet.

Biology

Symbol	Description
♂	male; a male organism, organ, or cell; a staminate flower or plant.
♀	female; a female organism, organ, or cell; a pistillate flower or plant.
□	a male.
○	a female.
×	crossed with; denoting a sexual hybrid.

Business

Symbol	Description
@	at; as in: eggs @ 99¢ per dozen or an e-mail address; as in: johndoe@server.com.
a/c	account.
B/E	bill of exchange.
B/L	bill of lading.
B/P	bills payable.
B/R	bills receivable.
B/S	bill of sale.
c&f.	cost and freight.
c/o	care of.
L/C	letter of credit.
O/S	out of stock.
P&L	profit and loss.
w/	with.
w/o	without.
#	1. (before a figure or figures) number; numbered; as in: #40 thread. 2. (after a figure or figures) pound(s); as in: 20#.

Monetary

Symbol	Description
$	1. dollar(s), in the United States, Canada, Liberia, etc. 2. peso(s), in Colombia, Mexico, etc. 3. cruzeiro(s), in Brazil. 4. escudo, in Portugal
¢	cent(s), in the United States, Canada, etc.
€	Euro
£	pound(s), in United Kingdom, Ireland, etc.

Symbol	Description
p	*new penny (new pence), in United Kingdom, Ireland, etc.*
/s.	*(formerly) shilling(s), in United Kingdom, Ireland, etc.*
d.	*(formerly) penny (pence), in United Kingdom, Ireland, etc.*
¥	*yen (pl. yen) in Japan.*

Miscellaneous

Symbol	Description
&	*the ampersand, meaning and.*
&c.	*et cetera; and others; and so forth; and so on.*
′	*foot; feet; as in: 6′ = six feet.*
″ ×	*inch; inches; as in: 6′2″ = six feet, two inches. 1. by: used in stating dimensions; as in: 2″ × 4″ × 1″; a 2″ × 4′ board. 2. a sign (the cross) made in place of a signature by a person who cannot write.*
†	*1. dagger. 2. died.*
‡	*double dagger.*
©	*copyright; copyrighted.*
®	*registered; registered trademark.*
*	*1. asterisk. 2. born.*
/	*slash; diagonal.*
¶	*paragraph mark.*
§	*section mark.*
"	*ditto; indicating the same as the aforesaid: used in lists, etc.*
...	*ellipses: used to show the omission of words, letters, etc.*
˜	*tilde.*
ˆ	*circumflex.*
¸	*cedilla; as in:ç.*
´	*acute accent.*
`	*grave accent.*
¨	*1. dieresis. 2. umlaut.*
¯	*macron.*
˘	*breve.*
℞	*take (L recipe).*
°	*degree(s) of temperature; as in: 99°F, 36°C.*

Index

Abbreviations, 144, 287–289
Academic writing, 297–315
  manuscript preparation in, 312–313
  proofreader's marks, 313–315
  references in, 309–312
  sample research paper, 297–309
  stages of, 293–296
Acronyms, 144, 287–289
Action verbs, 19–20
Active voice, 77–79
Adjective clauses, 51–52
Adjectives, 36–40
  adverbs versus, 42, 43
  commas to separate, 133
  compound, 141
  parallel structure for, 71
Adverb clauses, 52
Adverbs, 40–43
  conjunctive adverbs, 48–49
  prepositions and, 45
Agreement
  of collective nouns, 5–6
  of relative pronouns, 17–18
  of subject and verb, 55–58
American Psychological Association (APA) style, 297–298
  reference lists in, 309–312
  references in, 308

Antecedents, for pronouns, 9–10
Apostrophes, 128
Appositives, 37–38, 135–136, 137–138
Articles, definite and indefinite, 39
Auxiliary verbs, 22

Borrowed words, see Foreign words
Brackets, 128–129
Business memos, 321
Business vocabulary, 255–259
Business writing, 317–321

Capitalization, 151–153
  of short forms, 289
Case, of personal pronouns, 11–15
Clauses, 49, 51–53 commas to separate, 134–136
  semicolons to separate, 149–150
Collective nouns, 5–6, 82–83
Colons, 130–131
Commas, 132–137
Comparative degree, of adverbs, 43
Comparatives and superlatives, 40

Comparison
  adjectives of, 39
  adverbs of, 42–43
Complements, 58–60
Complex sentences, 62
Compound adjectives, 37, 141
Compound-complex sentences, 62
Compound nouns, 6–8
Compound personal pronouns, 15–16
Compound sentences, 61, 134
Computer vocabulary, 259–265
Conditional sentences, 76–77
Conjunctions, 45–49
Conjunctive adverbs, 48–49, 133
Correlative conjunctions, 46–47
Cover letters, 319–320

Dangling modifiers, 67–68
Dashes, 137–138
  hyphens versus, 140
Declarative sentences, 63
Definite articles, 39
Demonstrative pronouns, 19
Dependent clauses, 51–53
Determiners (noun markers), 38–39
Direct objects, 59
Direct quotations, 146–147
Division of words, 105
  hyphens for, 141–142
Drafts, 294–295

Ellipses, 138–139
Elliptical clauses, 53

Emphasis
  exclamation points for, 139–140
  italics for, 142
  quotation marks for, 147–148
Entertainment vocabulary, 265–266
Ergatives, 21
Exclamation points, 139
Exclamatory sentences, 63
Executive summaries, 317–319

Fashion vocabulary, 266–270
Food vocabulary, 270–271
Foreign words, 241–254
  French, 241–244
  German, 244–246
  Greek, 246–247
  Italian, 247–248
  italics for, 143
  Japanese, 249–250
  Latin, 250–252
  prefixes from, 157–169
  roots from, 185–208
  in short forms, 286
  Spanish, 252–253
  Yiddish, 253–254
Forward slashes (solidus; virgule), 140
Fragments, of sentences, 64–65
French words, 241–244
Future perfect tense, 29
Future tense, 28

Geographic names, 152–153
German words, 244–246
Gerunds, 14–15, 35–36

Greek
  prefixes from, 157–169
  roots from, 185–208
  words borrowed from, 246–247

Hybrids (short forms), 287–288
Hyphens, 140–142
  in compound nouns, 6
  dashes versus, 137
  rules for word division, 105

Idioms, 32
Imperative mood, 31–32, 73–74
Imperative sentences, 63
Indefinite articles, 39
Indefinite relative pronouns, 17–18
Independent clauses, 51, 149–150
Indicative mood, 31, 73–74
Indirect objects, 59
Indirect quotations, 146–147
Infinitives, 33–35
Initialisms, 287
Interjections, 49
Interrogative pronouns, 18–19
Interrogative sentences, 63
Intransitive action verbs, 20
Inverted sentences, 58
Irregular adjectives, 40
Irregular adverbs, 43
Irregular verbs, 23–25
Italian words, 247–248
Italics, 142–143

Japanese words, 149–250
Jargon, *see* Specialized vocabularies

Latin
  prefixes from, 157–169
  roots from, 185–208
  words borrowed from, 250–252
Law vocabulary, 271–274
Linking verbs, 21–22

Manuscript preparation, 312–313
  proofreader's marks, 313–315
Mass nouns, 6
Memos, 321
Misplaced modifiers, 66–67
Misspelled words, 105–112
Modern Language Association (MLA) style, 297–298
  reference lists in, 309–312
  works cited in, 309
Modifiers, 66–68
Mood of verbs, 31–32
  shifts in, 73–74

Nominative (subjective) case, 11–12
Nonrestrictive appositives, 135–136
Nonrestrictive clauses, 135
Noun clauses, 52–53
Noun phrases, 50–51
Nouns, 4–8
  as adjectives, 36
  parallel structure for, 72

plurals, 7–8
possessives, 6–7
types of, 5–6
usage of, 79–83
Number
  agreement of, in sentences, 55–58
  for collective nouns, 82–83
  shifts in, 81–82
Object complements, 59
Objective case, 12–14
Objects, of prepositions, 44–45
Offensive language, 138
Old English, 157–169
Outlines, 294

Parallel structure, 70–73
Parentheses, 129, 144–145
Participles, 35
Parts of speech, 3–49
  adjectives, 36–40
  adverbs, 40–43
  conjunctions, 45–49
  interjections, 49
  nouns, 4–8
  prepositions, 44–45
  pronouns, 8–19
  verbs, 19–36
  see also individual parts of speech, such as Nouns
Passive voice, 77–79
Past perfect tense, 29
Past tense, 27–28
Perfect infinitives, 33
Perfect tenses, 28–29
Periods, 143–144
  in short forms, 289

Person
  for collective nouns, 82–83
  shifts in, 79–81
Personal pronouns, 10–16
Perspective, shifts in, 81
Phrasal verbs, 33
Phrases, 49–51
  commas to separate, 134–137
  prepositional, 44–45
  transitional, 48–49
Plagiarism, 295
Plurals, 7–8
  agreement of, 55–58
  apostrophes for, 128
  of short forms, 289
Political vocabulary, 274–276
Positive degree, of adverbs, 42
Possession, apostrophes for, 128
Possessive case, 14–15
Possessives, 6–7
Predicate nominatives (subject complements), 60
Predicates, 58–60 Prefixes, 157–159
  list of, 159–169
Prepositional phrases, 44–45, 50
Prepositions, 44–45
  subordinating conjunctions versus, 48
Present infinitives, 34
Present perfect tense, 29
Present tense, 26–27
Progressive forms of verbs, 30–31

Pronouns, 8-19
  as adjectives, 36-37
  antecedents of, 9-10
  demonstrative, 19
  interrogative, 18-19
  personal, 10-16
  relative, 16-18
  usage of, 79-83
Proofreader's marks, 313-315
Proofreading, 295-296
Proper adjectives, 37, 141, 150
Proper nouns, 5, 142, 151
Publishing vocabulary, 276-277
Punctuation marks, 127-141

Question marks, 146
Questions
  interrogative pronouns in, 18-19
  interrogative sentences, 63
Quotation marks, 146-149
Quotations
  brackets in, 128-129
  ellipses in, 138-139

Reference lists, 309-312
References
  in APA format, 308
  in MLA format, 309
Regular verbs, 23
Relative pronouns, 16-18
Religious vocabulary, 277-280
Restrictive clauses, 134-135
Revisions, 295-296
Roots, of words, 184-185
  list of, 185-208
Run-on sentences, 65-66

Scientific vocabulary, 280-284

Semicolons, 149-151
Sentences, 49, 54-68
  conditional, 76-77 errors in, 63-68
  forms of, 60-62
  functions of, 62-63
  parallel structure in, 70-73
  predicates and complements in, 58-60
  punctuation marks for, 127-151
  subjects of, 54-58
Sentences fragments, 64-65
Series, items in
  commas to separate, 137
  parallel structure for, 72-73
  semicolons to separate, 150-151
Shifts
  in mood of verbs, 73-74
  in number, 81-82
  in person, 79-81
  in perspective, 81
  in tense of verbs, 74-77
  in tone and style, 69-70
  in voice, 79
Short forms (abbreviations and acronyms), 144, 287-289
Simple sentences, 61
Simple tenses, 26-28
Slashes (solidus; virgule), 140
Spanish words, 252-253
Specialized vocabularies, 255-285
  business, 255-259
  computers and technology, 259-265
  entertainment, 265-266

fashion, 266–270
food, 270–271
law, 271–274
politics, 274–276
publishing, 276–277
religion, 277–280
science, 280–284
sports, 284–285
Speech
  dashes in, 138
  ellipses in, 139
Spell checkers, 112
Spelling
  of frequently confused words, 112–126
  of frequently misspelled words, 105–112
  rules of, 103–105
  word division, rules of, 105
Split infinitives, 35
Sports vocabulary, 284–285
Squinting modifiers, 68
Stages of writing, 293–296
Style, 69–73
  parallel structure, 70–73
  shifts in tone and, 69–70
Subject complements (predicate nominatives), 60
Subjective (nominative) case, 11–12
Subjects, of sentences, 54–58
  active and passive voices for, 77–79
Subjunctive mood, 32, 73–74
Subordinating conjunctions, 47–48
Suffixes, 169–171
  list of, 171–184
Superlative degree, of adverbs, 43

Superlatives, 40
Syllables, 105
Symbols, 288

Technology vocabulary, 259–265
Tenses, 25–29
  of irregular verbs, 23–25
  shifts in, 74–77
Titles (of people), 151–152
Titles (of works)
  capitalization of, 150
  colons in, 131
  italics in, 142–143
  quotation marks for, 149
Tone, shifts in, 69–70
Transitional phrases, 48–49
Transitive action verbs, 20, 77

Underlining, 142–143
Usage glossary, 83–102

Verbals, 33
Verb phrases, 50
Verbs, 19–36
  active and passive voices of, 77–79
  gerunds and, 14–15
  infinitives, 33–35
  mood of, 31–32
  parallel structure for, 71–72
  participles, 35
  phrasal, 33
  progressive forms of, 30–31
  regular and irregular, 23–25
  shifts in mood of, 73–74
  shifts in tense of, 74–77
  shifts in voice of, 79
  tenses of, 25–29

Verbs (*cont.*)
  types of, 19–22
  verbals, 33
Voice, active and passive, 77–79

Word division, 105
  hyphens for, 141–142
Words
  from foreign languages, 241–254
  frequently confused, 112–126
  frequently misspelled, 105–112
  histories of, 209–239
  hyphens to divide, 141–142
  italics for, 142–143
  prefixes for, 157–169
  roots of, 184–208
  rules for dividing, 105
  spelling rules for, 103–105
  suffixes for, 169–184
  see also Foreign words
Writing
  business writing, 317–321
  proofreader's marks, 313–315
  stages of, 293–296
  see also Academic writing

Yiddish words, 253–254